ISBN 978-1-332-28962-2
PIBN 10309672

1 MONTH OF FREE READING

at

www.ForgottenBooks.com

By purchasing this book you are eligible for one month membership to ForgottenBooks.com, giving you unlimited access to our entire collection of over 700,000 titles via our web site and mobile apps.

To claim your free month visit:

www.forgottenbooks.com/free309672

HAVERFORD COLLEGE STUDIES

Published by the Faculty of

HAVERFORD COLLEGE.

No. 9   *Price $1.*

CONTENTS.

To obtain copies of this publication address the Secretary of Haverford College, Haverford College P. O., Pa.

BY

J. RENDEL HARRIS.

CHAPTER I.

ON THE LATIN TEXT OF THE CODEX SANGALLENSIS OF THE GOSPELS.

In my recent dissertation on the great Cambridge bilingual, the Codex Bezae, I have sought to recover the Latin of that famous text from the neglect or contempt into which it has fallen, and to shew to the critical students of the New Testament that this text is of all texts the most important for the recovery of the rude and primitive rendering of the Gospels and the Acts which was current in the early part of the second century. The method which I have adopted is fertile in valuable results beyond what my most sanguine ideas could have hoped. As soon as it is seen that the Latin is rarely, if ever, an accommodation to its conjugate Greek, while on the other hand the Greek is almost always accommodated to the Latin, a new light breaks upon the perplexing question of the genesis of the Western readings in the New Testament: and we are able to shew that the leading versions of the text go back into a common origin, which we designate as the Great Western Bilingual; a recension which was freely coloured both in Latin and in Greek by the opinions prevailing in the second century, and whose primitive structure was barbarous in speech, being sometimes pleonastic in its renderings and sometimes hideously literal, bristling with vulgarisms of a decidedly African type, and also with some forms of speech for which not even the barbarous African dialect can fairly be held accountable. It is a matter of the highest importance to collect from the primitive Latin and associated texts the surviving forms of this venerable version. Every old Latin text will help us somewhat to the recovery of the lost forms, or to the verification of forms deduced by critical analysis of the various texts and translations: in the present discussion we propose the question as to what light is thrown on the study of the primitive Latin of the Gospels by the text of the Codex Sangallensis, known in the critical apparatus by the sign Δ, or more exactly by the two signs Δ and δ according as we are quoting the Greek or the Latin of the bilingual.

The prospect of obtaining any results from such an examination is not a very hopeful one : we are, in fact, warned by Dr Hort that the Latin of the leading bilinguals is of no use for the study of the Greek text, inasmuch as it has been accommodated to the Greek ; that it is only sporadically of any use as a testimony to the Old Latin, viz. in those cases where the Latin differs from the Greek ; and lastly in the special case which we are going to discuss, the Latin text is simply that of the Vulgate. We repeat, for verification of these statements, some sentences from Dr Hort's *Introduction to the New Testament.*

pp. 82, 83. "The Gospels alone are extant in a series of tolerably complete Old Latin MSS. For most of the other books we have, strictly speaking, nothing but fragments and those covering only a small proportion of verses. The delusive habit of quoting as Old Latin the Latin texts of bilingual MSS. has obscured the real poverty of evidence. These MSS. are in Acts *Cod. Bezae* (D*d* as in the Gospels) and *Cod. Laudianus* (E$_2$*e*) and in St Paul's Epistles *Cod. Claromontanus* (D$_2$*d*) and *Cod. Boernerianus* (G$_3$*g*; without Hebrews). The origin of the Latin text, as clearly revealed by internal evidence, is precisely similar in all four MSS. A genuine (independent) Old Latin text has been adopted as the basis, but altered throughout into verbal conformity with the Greek text by the side of which it was intended to stand. Here and there the assimilation has accidentally been incomplete and the scattered discrepant readings thus left are the only direct Old Latin evidence for the Greek text of the New Testament which the bilingual MSS. supply. A large proportion of the Latin texts of these MSS. is, beyond all reasonable doubt, unaltered Old Latin : but where they exactly correspond to the Greek, as they do habitually, it is impossible to tell how much of the accordance is original and how much artificial ; so that for the criticism of the Greek text the Latin reading has here no independent authority. The Latin texts of Δ of the Gospels and F$_2$ of St Paul's Epistles are Vulgate, with a partial adaptation to the Greek."

According to Dr Hort the Latin text of the Sangallensis is merely Vulgate; but even if it had not been Vulgate, it would simply stand with *d, e* (of the Acts) and *g* and be condemned as an unreliable authority on account of its assimilation to the Greek, except in rare instances where it shews a textual divergence. As we have said above, the field for study does not seem to be a very promising one.

We remember, however, that our study of *D* and its companion *E* in the Acts brought us to quite different conclusions from those stated above, as to the value of the bilingual Latin: and we shall therefore begin our work on the Sangallensis by a suspicion as to whether the case does really stand exactly as it is given in the extract quoted above. Is it true, we ask, that the Latin text of the St Gall MS. is merely an accommodation of a Vulgate text to a parallel Greek text?

We will test the matter by taking a specimen chapter, say the twenty-first chapter of John: it will be unnecessary to discuss trivial spellings, nor the order of the words, as it is admitted that in an interlinear text like the St Gall MS. this follows the Greek; we will take a printed Latin Vulgate text and note the divergences from it with collateral references to the Cod. Sangallensis (δ); Cod. Vercellensis (*a*): Cod. Veronensis (*b*): Cod. Bezae (*d*): and the Codex Amiatinus of the Vulgate (*am*). The result is as follows: the Sangallensis stands apart from the Vulgate in the following positive variants.

> *v.* 3 ceperunt (*a*)
> *v.* 5 dicit (*am. b*)
> *v.* 6 + ipse autem
> + partem (*abd*)
> navis (*bd*)
> etiam (*b*) (probably for a primitive *retiam* which is found in *ab*)
> retrahere
> a multitudine (*am. d*)
> *v.* 7 dicit (*abd am.*)
> Simon itaque (*b*)
> audiens (*d*)
> investem .
> *v.* 8 a cubitis (*bd*)
> *v.* 10 An alternative reading
> cepistis (*ad*)   prendistis (sic! cum *am.* : prendidistis vg *b*)
> *v.* 11 trahit (*b*)
> *v.* 12 nemo autem

v. 14 discipulis eius (*d*)

v. 15 An alternative reading
    etiam (*d am.* vg)   utique (*ab*)

v. 16 iterum secundo
  oves meas (*ad*[*b*])

v. 17 omnia scis (*am. bd*)
  tu cognoscis
  (2°) dicit ei $\overline{\text{ihs}}$

v. 18 te ipsum (*ad*)
  ducet te (*a*)
  quo non vis (*am.*)

v. 19 An alternative reading
    qua (*bd* vg)   quali
  et hoc dicens

v. 20 conversus autem (*d*)

v. 21 An alternative reading
    cum vidisset (*b* vg)   videns (*ad*)

v. 23 An alternative reading
    venit   exiit (*abd* vg)
  quia non moritur

v. 24 om. ille (*am. abd*)

v. 25 om. posse (*am. bd*)
  scribendos libros

Here then are thirty-three variants, and five alternative readings to the Vulgate text. Only six of these thirty-three variants are supported by the Codex Amiatinus; and this shews at once that we are dealing with a text which is far removed from being a genuine Vulgate text: for, if we omit such points as variations of spelling, the Amiatinus does not on a similar calculation shew a third as many variants from the common Vulgate. Moreover the variants are real Old Latin readings: the St Gall text being supported eleven times by *a*, fifteen times by *b* and eighteen times by *d*.

Probably this will suffice to shew that the text is not a true Vulgate, and that it contains an Old Latin element which ought not to be neglected. Moreover, the unique readings of the MS. are very valuable, and some of them furnish us with suggestions as to the primitive Latin rendering.

For example, in v. 7 look at the curious translation of ἐπενδύτης by *investis*: a word for which it is difficult to find support, in the sense which the passage requires. Such a rendering can hardly fail to be early.

Or look at the combination in v. 12 where the text shews the singular union of two readings, viz. *discipulorum*, which is substantially the right reading, with the aberrant Vulgate reading *discumbentium*. Happily we know enough of the primitive Latin translation to be able to say how this error arose : for it is certain that the old translation read *discens* where we read *discipulus* : and this reading was a frequent perplexity to later scribes when they found it surviving in their copies. In our case then *discumbentium* is a mere conjectural correction for *discentium* and *discentium* is actually preserved in Veronensis ; a similar case will be found in Luke xix. 37 where some Old Latin texts have corrected *discentium* to *descendentium*. The cases of literal rendering of the participle in vv. 19 and 21 should also be noticed ; for though the Old Latin texts have usually replaced this primitive translation by a more periphrastic manner of speech (usually by the subjunctive with *cum*), yet there are many traces of its survival in good texts ; and in particular we find codd. *a* and *d* reading *videns* in v. 21. Even the seemingly trivial reading *iterum secundo* in v. 16 is not without meaning : we cannot support *secundo* from *a b d* or the Vulgate, but that it once stood in the text of Cod. Bezae appears from the fact that on the Greek side πάλιν has been displaced by δεύτερόν while in Δ both words are preserved. We suspect then that *secundo* or rather *iterum secundo* is the primitive Latin rendering.

We say then, that Old Latin traces are to be found in the Sangallensis, and that some of its rougher and less supported readings are archaic.

But this is not all : for it appears from the collation of this one chapter that the Latin text in the Codex is not a single text at all, but a combination of two texts : so that even if the scribe used one copy to match his Greek he must have consulted another, for there are very many double readings in the Latin, and even a few triple readings, usually separated by the disjunctive word *vel*. Now it is clear, that even on the hypothesis that the text is substantially vulgate these readings cannot be neglected ; for they constitute a selected body of Old Latin variants. We must, therefore, examine them carefully to see what light they can throw on the genesis of the successive forms of African and Italian texts.

CHAPTER II.

WE are invited, then, to test the St Gall text for Africanisms by which we here mean the body of forms and readings which constitute the primitive tradition of the Latin New Testament. Some of these forms have been discussed in our study of Codex Bezae though we do not pretend to have done more than touch the outside edge of a great subject. We will see whether any traces of such forms can be found here.

For instance when the scribe of Sangallensis in Matthew xxvii. 28 writes over the Greek word στέφανον the rendering

coronamentum vel coronam

we know that he found in one MS., probably his principal text, the word *coronamentum* and that he coupled with it, from some other source, probably another Latin text, for all his readings come from MSS., the alternative *coronam*.

Now of these two renderings, there can be no doubt which is the earlier one, or which replaced the other: *coronamentum* must be the African, or if we prefer it, the vulgar Latin form, and, in fact, we actually find in Tertullian's *De Corona* the St Gall form.

Or, again, let us take the case which we discussed in connection with the Codex Bezae, the African reduplicated form of the verb *habeo*. We shewed how often this curious reduplication occurred, the future *habebitis* appearing in place of the present *habetis*, and the imperfect turning up in the extravagant *habebebatis*. Paleographical causes being inadequate to explain such frequent phenomena, we resorted to the theory of a vulgar African form, which had held its own in the Bezan text in many places and had drawn the Greek text into a supposed closer agreement with it. Now if the St Gall text has a *bona fide* Old Latin base, we may expect to find some traces of this peculiar verb-form. Let us see.

Turn to Matt. v. 46 where the Bezan text reads

habebetis (= ἕξεται)

and Codd. *ab* read habebitis,

and we find the St Gall text out-heroding Herod by reading

habebebitis.

Next turn to Matt. vi. 1 where *ab* agree with *d* in reading

habebitis (= ἔχετε) ·

and here we find in the St Gall text the same reading.

It is true that in both cases the Vulgate agrees with the Old Latin reading, but that does not prevent us from calling it an African reading.

Or suppose we examine some of those passages where the original African rendering had expressed itself by using a superlative adjective where we should have expected what is given in later recensions of the text—the exact translation of the positive degree.

There are several of these amongst the readings in the St Gall MS., though they would pass for Vulgate readings on account of their absorption into the Vulgate text.

For instance in Matt. xii. 45 we have

πονηρᾷ = pessimae.

This is in the Vulgate, but it is archaic, as its attestation by *abd* shews. In the same verse *prioribus* for πρώτων is more natural and can hardly be called an irregular translation; here *ab* have *quam priora*, and *d prioribus*.

In Luke x. 42 we have two superlative renderings with alternatives

περὶ πολλὰ = circa multa vel plurima

and ἀγαθὴν μερίδα rendered alternatively by

bonam vel optimam partem.

In both of these cases the Vulgate takes up the superlative: but we suspect them again to be Old Latin renderings: for in the second instance we find that *ab* render by *optimam* while *cd* have *bonam*. These alternative readings probably represent a very early textual divergence which has been perpetuated along different lines of manuscripts. It is clear that the readings do not originate either with the Vulgate or the Sangallensis. The last case is perhaps due to a lost African superlative of the form *bonus bonus = optimus.*

Turn, in the next place, to the question of pleonasms in the archaic Latin text. It is well known that the African speech was fond of pleonastic renderings; that it used a substantive with another equivalent substantive in apposition with it, or with an equivalent substantive in the genitive, that it coupled verbs in the same way, and that even the pronouns, adverbs and conjunctions were employed pleonastically. Many traces of this are still extant in the Old Latin copies, and the irregular readings have left a deep mark on the Western text, both in Greek and in Latin. Sometimes the MSS. will bifurcate over a pleonastic rendering, one half of the reading going off on one line of transmission and the other on the other. At other times, the Latin text being found to be overweighted as against the Greek, either a new word was added in Greek, or a superfluous word was struck out from the Latin (and not always the right word but often an adjacent one). Instances of all these various corruptions of the Western text will be found at large in our notes on the Bezan text.

One of these pleonasms, and apparently a favourite one, is the rendering of κληρονομέω by *possidere* and *hereditare*; and similarly with κληρονομία, for which we actually find in the Bezan text (Acts vii. 5) the pleonasm *possessionem hereditatis.* It is interesting to see how this pleonasm breaks up into two readings in the Old Latin tradition, and how nearly it is reproduced in the conjunction of alternative readings in the Sangallensis. For example:

Matt. v. 4. κληρονομήσουσιν = hereditabunt vel possidebunt where *b* reads *possidebunt* and *d hereditabunt,* but *a* has the original pleonasm hereditate possidebunt[1].

Matt. xix. 29. κληρονομήσει = possidebit vel hereditabit where *ab* read *possidebit* and *d hereditabit.*

---

[1] The same pleonasm occurs in Irenaeus V. ix. 4, in quoting this passage, where the context shews it to be the true reading of the translator of Irenaeus and not a conflation by scribes: "ipsi haereditate possidebunt terram; quasi haereditate possideatur terra in regno, unde et substantia carnis est." Moreover in the paragraphs which follow, of which the Greek is fortunately preserved, the translator of Irenaeus gives us the pleonastic rendering no less than eight times.

Matt. xxv. 34. κληρονομήσατε = hereditate vel possidete where *ab* read *possidete* and *d* has preserved the primitive pleonasm *hereditate possidete* where, by the way, *hereditate* is not a verb as the scribes supposed.

In Luke x. 25 κληρονομήσω = possidebo vel hereditabo where *ab* have *possidebo* and *d hereditabo*.

Luke xviii. 18. κληρονομήσω = possideam vel hereditem where *ab* have *possidebo* and *d hereditabo*.

These instances will shew how the St Gall text brought the bifurcated readings together again and almost restored the primitive pleonasm.

Another similar case is the use of *perficio* and *consummare* in combination. We have reason to believe that the primitive rendering in Luke i. 17 was of this nature, since we find in

  a populum perfectum
  b plebem perfectam
  d plebem consummatam,

which looks like an original reading

  plebem perfectam consummatam.

Something of the same kind appears in Luke i. 45, where

  a quod erit consummatio
  b quoniam perficientur ea
  d quia erit consummatio,

the original reading being probably

  quia erit perfectio consummationis

or something not very different.

In these two cases the St Gall text does not shew any signs o the use of *consummatio* : in Luke i. 17 it reads

  plm̄ perfectum,

and in i. 45 it gives

  perficientur vel erunt vel fient perfecta.

If however we turn to John xvii. 23, where the Codex Bezae has preserved a primitive pleonasm

  ut sint perfecti consummati

and where *a* has *perfecti* and *b consummati*, we find in the St Gall text

  consummati vel perfecti definiti,

which almost restores the original pleonasm as well as introduces a new rendering.

In this passage the Vulgate preserves *consummati*, but not in the two places quoted from Luke.

Another instance may be taken from John v. 2 where the primitive translation rendered

κολυμβήθρα by natatoria piscina

or rather, as I suspect, by *natatoria piscinae*.

We find in cod. *a*

est autem Hierosolymis in inferiorem partem natatoria piscina,

and in cod. *b*

Hierosolymis in inferiorem partem natatoriae piscinae

where the change to the genitive in *b* may be due to the form suggested above. The words

in inferiorem partem

are meant to represent

ἐπὶ τῇ προβατικῇ.

In cod. *d* we have

est autem hierosolymis in natatoria piscina

where the pleonasm has been preserved but at the expense of προβατικῇ whose equivalent has been ejected.

If any doubt remained in our mind as to the antiquity of the pleonasm, we might set it at rest by turning to Irenaeus (II. xxiv. 4) where we find

natatoria piscina quinque habebat porticus.

We are sure then that this reading is archaic; and Scrivener cannot be right when he says[1] that the rendering is a "mere error of the translator who unites the two separate words used by the Vulgate for rendering κολυμβήθρα in the places where it is found (v. 2, 4, 7 *piscina*; ix. 7, 11 *natatoria*)." The fact is that the existence of the two separate words in the Vulgate is another proof of the original pleonasm: and it is needless to multiply words to prove that the Bezan text is an earlier recension than Jerome's revision.

Now turn to the St Gall MS.: and it is highly interesting to see that the rendering preserves both words, for it has *piscina* in v. 2, 7, and *natatoria* in v. 4, ix. 7, 11. The survival of the primi-

---

[1] *Cod. Bezae*, p. xliv., note 2.

tive pleonasm is seen to be suggested independently by the Vulgate and the St Gall text. The whole evidence in the five passages in question can be seen at a glance as follows:

	John v. 2	v. 4	v. 7	ix. 7	ix. 11
natatoria		$\delta\,ab$	d	vg $abd\,\delta$	vg δ
piscina	vg δ	vg	vg $\delta\,ab$		
natatoria piscina	abd Iren.				

It is clear that there is no reason for saying that in the rendering of this Greek word either d or δ follow the Vulgate: but we can see from the St Gall text renewed reason for believing in the existence of a primitive double rendering, at least in the fifth chapter of John.

The next case to which we wish to draw attention is Matt. xx. 34, where καὶ εὐθέως ἀνέβλεψαν is rendered alternatively by

aperti sunt vel viderunt.

The Greek text follows on with αὐτῶν οἱ ὀφθαλμοί with corresponding Latin; but it is pretty clear that these words are an addition to the text, and if so they are due to the reflex action of the translation or to the influence of a previous verse. The question then arises as to whether the original text did not shew a pleonastic rendering of the word ἀνέβλεψαν. The Latin texts do not shew as much variation as we should expect; cod. b reads *viderunt* and is followed by the Vulgate; cod. Bezae reads *re-spexerunt*: cod. q, however, has the other half of the reading as in the Sangallensis. We suspect then that the primitive text contained both expressions and that its common form of translation was "their eyes were opened and they saw." This supposition explains at once a perplexing point in the Old Syriac texts, which constantly give similar conjunctions. In the preceding verse, for example, the Cureton text has "that our eyes may be opened and that we may see Thee"; and the same account is given in the Tatian Harmony in the form

· Caecus autem dixit ei: Domine mi et praeceptor, ut aperias oculos meos et videam te.

And further the Cureton text in Luke xviii. 41 reads for ἵνα ἀναβλέψω *ut aperiantur oculi et videam* which shews the very pleonastic rendering of which we were in search.

In my notes on the Tatian Harmony[1] I have taken pains to shew from the Old Syriac literature the antiquity of this rendering; it appears now that its wide and early distribution in the Syriac may be reasonably referred to a previous pleonasm in the Western bilingual texts. The St Gall text helps us towards such a conclusion both by its Greek and its Latin.

In Mark ii. 17 we have an alternative reading in the sentence

ὅτι οὐ χρείαν ἔχουσιν οἱ ἰσχύοντες ἰατροῦ ἀλλ' οἱ κακῶς ἔχοντες,

which is rendered

quia non necesse habent sani medico sed male habentibus vel habentes.

The reading *habentibus* might conceivably be an attempt to translate the previous ἔχουσιν, but I incline to believe that it is all that is left of the old translation which ran

non est necessarius[2] sanis medicus sed male habentibus.

For Tertullian writing against Marcion quotes the passage Luke v. 31 in the form

Medicum sanis non esse necessarium

(cf. also *De Pudic.* c. 9, medicus languentibus magis quam sanis necessarius).

Moreover in Mark xi. 3 the expression χρείαν ἔχει is rendered by Cod. Bezae in the form

domino necessarius est,

and in the Syriac we have frequent cases of the same form (e.g. Mark xi. 3 in the Peshito is

ܪܟܐܘ ܡܪܢ),

and compare the Peshito and Cureton texts in Matt. vi. 8; xiv. 16; xxi. 3; xxvi. 65 (Pesh.): Mark xiv. 63 (Pesh.): Luke v. 31 (Pesh.); x. 42; xv. 7; xix. 31, 34; xxii. 71: John xiii. 29 (Pesh.).

It will be seen that it is possible to utilize for critical purposes the shreds of the older translations which lie in the variants of the Codex Sangallensis.

We will conclude this chapter by putting the St Gall text in evidence for a very early Western reading, of considerable critical importance.

---

[1] *The Diatessaron of Tatian.* Cambridge, 1890.

[2] Or perhaps *non est opus* would be more African, as in cod. *e*.

If the reader will turn to the treatise of Irenaeus against Heresies, he will find in the second book the passage[1]:

"Aut iterum si quis ob hoc quod dictum sit in Evangelio: *Nonne duo passeres asse veneunt? et unus ex his non cadet super terram sine Patris vestri voluntate*: enumerare voluerit captos ubique quotidie passeres etc."

Now in this passage which seems to be taken immediately from the Gospel (Matt. x. 29) we have the striking variant

sine Patris vestri voluntate,

and that it belongs to Irenaeus, and not to any translator or commentator, may be seen from the fact that in the fifth book of the same writer[2] we have

"Deinde quoniam dominatur hominibus, et ei ipsi Deus, et *nolente Patre nostro* qui est in caelis neque passer cadet in terram, illud igitur quod ait etc."

So that we again suspect the same variant in the New Testament of Irenaeus, perhaps with the added clause *qui est in caelis*. His Greek text must have been ἄνευ τῆς βουλῆς τοῦ πατρὸς ὑμῶν τοῦ ἐν τοῖς οὐρανοῖς.

The same reading is found over and over in Tertullian; Rönsch has collected the fragments of the New Testament which are embedded in the text of Tertullian, and gives five passages in which the text which we are working on is used. Unfortunately Rönsch omits to notice that in each case the words *sine voluntate* form a part of the text and he does not italicize them as he should have done. Correcting Rönsch's extracts for this oversight, we have the following passages from Tertullian:

"Siquidem *unus ex passeribus duobus non cadit in terram sine patris voluntate.*" Monog. c. 9.

"Subiungit exemplum quod *ex duobus non cadit alter in terram sine* dei *voluntate.*" Resurr. c. 35.

"Credas utique, si tamen in eum deum credis, *sine cuius voluntate nec passer unius assis cadit in terram.*" Fug. c. 3.

"Is, *sine cuius voluntate nec passerum alter in terram cadit.*" Scorp. c. 9.

"A deo domino *sine cuius voluntate* nec folium de arbore labitur nec *passer assis unius ad terram cadit.*" Cast. c. 1.

---

[1] *Haer.* II. xxvi. 2.   [2] *Haer.* V. xxii. 2.

From these five passages we know that Tertullian's text as well as Irenaeus' contained the word *voluntate*. It is certainly, then, part of the Old Latin translation.

We might confirm this by quotations from other early Latin fathers as Cyprian and Hilary, and by the testimony of the Old Latin codices, of which the most important are

Cod. *ab* which both read

sine voluntate Patris vestri.

The Codex Sangallensis reads

ΑΝΕΥΤΟΥ · ΠΡC͞ΥΜΩΝ

and writes over the Greek the words

sine voluntate patris vestri.

Now there is no reason to call this a Vulgate reading, it is genuine Old Latin and prae-Vulgate; and we may be sure that the Codex contains a great deal of the same sort.

Before leaving the point, we may draw attention to one more result that follows from the study of this reading. We can have no doubt that it is an early second century reading, from the combination of its attestation in texts and quotations. And it seems equally clear that it is a genuine Western reading, the gloss of the first translating hand, perhaps an African hand.

It is interesting, then, to observe that the text of Matthew x. 29 in its expanded Latinized form has been carried into the Clementine Homilies[1]. This is not the place to enter into a complete discussion of the sources of the Evangelical quotations in the Clementines, but the reader is advised to note the coincidence between the Clementine and Western text at this point.

---

[1] Clem. Hom. xii. 31.

CHAPTER III.

THE VULGATE HYPOTHESIS FURTHER TESTED FROM MATTHEW XXV.

WE will now examine the text of the Sangallensis with the Vulgate in another chapter, say Matt. xxv., in order to get a clearer idea of the divergence of the two texts. The result is as follows:

	VULG.	SANGALL.
	Matt. xxv.	
1	simile erit	similabitur (*d*)
	obviam (*ab*)	in obviam (*d*)
	sponso (*ab*)	sponsi (*d*)
	et sponsae (*abd*)	om.
2	fatuae (*b*)	fatuae *vel* stultae (stultae *d*)
3	sed quinque (*b*)	quae erant
	acceptis lampadibus (*b* + suis)	accipientes lampades suas (*d*)
	non sumpserunt (*b*)	non sumpserunt *vel* non acceperunt (*d*)
4	lampadibus	+ suis (*bd*)
5	moram faciente ([*b*])	morante
	dormitaverunt (*b*)	pausaverunt *vel* (nihil addidit)
	dormierunt (*b*)	dormitaverunt
6	factus est (*bd*)	factus
	exite *d*	venite *vel* exite
	obviam (*bd*)	in obviam
8	sapientibus (*bd*)	sapientibus *vel* prudentibus
9	responderunt (*b*)	+ autem (*d*)
10	dum autem irent	abeuntibus autem illis (*q*)
	ad nuptias (*d*)	in (*b*) *vel* ad nuptias
11	novissime (*bd*)	novissime *vel* iterum
12	at ille (*b*)	ille
	amen (*bd*)	vere
	nescio (*bd*)	nescio *vel* (?)[1]
13	itaque (*b*)	itaque *vel* ergo (*d*)
14	servos suos (*bd*)	servos proprios
16	et operatus est (*abd*)	operatus est *vel* egit
	lucratus est (*ad*)	fecit *vel* lucratus est
	alia quinque (*ab*)	+ talenta

[1] Rettig could not read the alternative word

17	lucratus est (*ab*)	et ipse (et ipse lucratus est *d*)
18	pecuniam (*ab*)	argentum *vel* pecuniam (argentum *d*)
19	multum temporis (*ab*)	tempus multum (*d*)
	posuit rationem (*ab*)	ratiocinatus est rationem
20	obtulit (*bd*)	obtulit *vel* attulit
	talenta (2°) (*abd*)	om.
	quinque (4°) (*ab*)	+talenta (*d*)
	superlucratus sum (*abd*)	lucratus sum super ea
21	ait (*abd*)	ait autem
	quia (*abd*)	om.
22	accessit (*b*)	accedens (*d*)
	acceperat (*bd*)	om.
	et ait (*b*)	ait
	duo (3°) (*b*)	+talenta (*d*)
	lucratus sum (*b*)	+super ea *vel* in eis
23	quia (*bd*)	om.
	super multa (*bd*)	super multa *vel* in multis
24	accedens (*abd*)	accedens *vel* accessit
	scio	+te
	durus es	+homo (*ad*)
25	abii et (*abd*)	abiens
	quod tuum est (*ab*)	tuum (*d* quod tuum)
26	male (*b*)	nequam *vel* male (nequa *ad*)
	semino (*ab*)	seminavi (*d*)
27	committere (*ab*)	mittere (*d*)
	pecuniam (*ab*)	argentum *vel* pecuniam (argentum *d*)
	recepissem (*ab*)	accepissem (*d*)
	utique (*d*)	om. (*ab*)
	quod meum est (*abd*)	meum
28	itaque (*ab*)	ergo (*d*)
	ei qui habet (*ab*)	habenti (*d*)
29	ei autem qui non habet (*ab*)	ab autem non habente
31	angeli (*abd*)	sancti angeli
	maiestatis (*ab*)	gloriae *vel* maiestatis (gloriae *d*)
32	ante eum (*abd*)	coram eo
	pastor segregat (*abd*)	separat *vel* segregat
34	his qui a dextris eius erunt (sunt *ab* om. sunt *d*)	a dextris sedentibus eius
	possidete (*ab*)	hereditate *vel* possidete (her. possid. *d*)
	a constitutione (*ab*)	ab origine (*d*)
35	dedistis mihi bibere (*a*)	potastis me (*d*)
36	infirmus (*b*)	infirmus *vel* infirmatus fui (*d* infirmatus sum)
	eram (*b*)	fui (*d*)
37	iusti (*bd*)	om.
	pavimus te (*b*)	pavimus (*d*)

	dedimus tibi potum (*b*)	potavimus *vel* potum dedimus (potavimus *d*)
38	collegimus te (*b*)	collegimus (*d*)
	cooperuimus te (*b*)	cooperuimus (*d*)
39	aut quando (*abd*)	quando autem
	aut in (*abd*)	in autem
40	amen (*abd*)	vere
41	his qui a sinistris erunt (his qui ad sinistris eius sunt *ab*), his qui a sinistris (*d*)	sinistralibus
	discedite (*ab*)	ite *vel* discedite (ite *d*)
	qui paratus est	paratum
43	eram (*ab*)	fui (*d*) *vel* eram
	infirmus (*abd*)	+fui
44	ei et ipsi	et ipsi (*abd*)
	aut in carcere (*ad*)	vel in carcere (*b*)
45	amen (*abd*)	vere
	minoribus (*b*)	minimis (*a*)

Here then are sixty-four variants from the Vulgate and twenty-three alternative readings in the space of the chapter, passing over variations in spelling and in the order of the words. It need scarcely be said that this is far too many for the Vulgate hypothesis to carry: for the text of the Amiatinus itself, which may be taken as the earliest type of a true Vulgate, would not shew more than about sixteen such variants as we have recorded, its aberrations being mostly in spelling and in the order of the words.

We shall say then that the Sangallensis is not to be slighted as to its Latin text, nor to be treated merely as accessory to the evidence of the Vulgate copies. It is true that the Codex Sangallensis has some Vulgate apparatus, such as the letter to Damasus, but this is merely external evidence ; the internal evidence of the text shews a strong non-Vulgate element from at least two quarters. If the scribe used a ground-text in inserting his Latin together with a second copy for reference, both of these copies were full of Old Latin readings.

The value of the St Gall Latin text is clearly not to be limited to the double readings, though these are of great value, and there are over 200 of them in St Matthew alone. Where it differs from the Vulgate it usually differs in company with a good Old Latin MS.: and where it differs from the best Old Latin texts, it often contains a reading which exceeds them all in antiquity.

For example in the fifth verse of this chapter we note the singular reading *pausaverunt*: this must be African; no one would introduce such a reading at a late period in the history of the Latin text, and no trace of it is to be seen in *abd*. Let us turn to Röusch *Itala und Vulgata* and see whether any similar forms can be found in the Old Latin texts or fathers.

Röusch does not seem to notice the case in the Sangallensis but he gives the following instances of the verb *pausare*.

"Pausare [durch παῦσις von παύειν] 4 Esdr. 2. 24 *pausa* et quiesce populus meus, Vulg.; Plaut. Trin. i. 2. 150; Cael. Aur. Acut. iii. 21. 212; Chron. i. 1. 16, v. 10. 116; Fulgent. Myth. 1. 6; Gruter. 1050. 9 fideliter *pausanti*; Keron, Interpr. vocabb. barb. (ap. Goldast, *rer. Alam.* II. p. 86), *pausent*, resten; *pausetur*, kirestit sin."

Rönsch also gives instances of the use of the related words *pausa, pausabilis, pausatio, pausatus*. The evidence is entirely in favour of ascribing the word to an African origin. And we say that the Codex Sangallensis at this point has preserved a fragment of the old second century translation.

That this translation was due to the first hand may I think be suspected from Luke xvi. 23 where the Codex Bezae shews signs of having once had a similar reading. At present the text stands

ΚΑΙ ΛΑΖΑΡΟΝ ΕΝ ΤΩ ΚΟΛΠΩ ΑΥΤΟΥ ΑΝΑΠΑΥΟΜΕΝΟΝ.

et lazarum in sinus eius requiescentem.

We suspect that this *requiescentem* is a correction for a primitive *pausantem*, and that the gloss of the Latin translator ultimately found its way into the Greek in the form ἀναπαυόμενον[1].

It is not then an unreasonable thing to maintain that in Matt. xxv. 5 the Sangallensis has preserved a primitive Africanism.

One other point may be noticed in support of our theory that the ground-text and commentary-text were not true Vulgates. The reader will find that the double readings to which we have drawn attention are almost nil in the Gospel of Mark. The reason of this is probably to be found in the fact that the scribe was working with Latin texts of which one at least had St Mark in the last place, which is the order of *Old Latin* copies. He wrote his Latin interlinear gloss in the Western order and grew tired of collating before he reached the end of the Gospels.

---

[1] The gloss in Luke was extant in Tertullian's time in the form *requiescentem*, if we may judge from *c. Marcionem* IV. 34 pauperis in sinu Abraham requiescentis; and *de Anim.* 57.

CHAPTER IV.

THE collation of the single chapter which we have given above
helps us to a better understanding with regard to the nature of the
divergence of the primitive Latin tradition. We see two things
pretty clearly, that where the St Gall text and the Vulgate dis-
agree the Vulgate usually follows the combined tradition represented by *ab* (what is often called the European Latin), and
the St Gall text usually some older form of text such as is
supported by what we may call, I suppose, the non-European
elements of the Codex Bezae and the great North-Italian copies.
Thus the Vulgate appears as an eclectically reformed European
text and the St Gall MS. as a text (possibly European) but with
very many forms belonging to earlier stages of the textual history.

Now it is not our object to write at this place the history of
the genesis of the Vulgate text, though it will be probably a
simple enough business when once the data are collected; but
with regard to the primitive Latin it is our most earnest wish to
recover every fragment, whether from the Vulgate, the St Gall
MS. or any other source. For we strongly suspect that this lost
version is responsible for the greater part of the existing aberrations in copies, versions and fathers. It is, therefore, peculiarly
unfortunate that it is lost; and the only thing to be done is to
recover it piecemeal and by critical work from the existing
materials. We have already shewn instances of the way this
should be done, and we will now collect some more cases.

For example in Matt. xxv. 41 we have the peculiar reading
sinistralibus. Nothing like it occurs in *abd*. The word is a
rare word; Rönsch only notes it in one author, not having de-

tected it in this text. But it is just because of its very rarity that we feel sure that it is a fragment of the primitive translation; and there is every reason, from the formation of the word, to regard it as an Africanism, or if we prefer to call it so, a vulgar Latinism. Accordingly we refer it to the first stage of the Latin text, perhaps before the stage of more exact Greek mimicry which we find in *his qui a sinistris* of Cod. *d*, which becomes expanded by the addition of *sunt* in *ab* and *erunt* in the Vulgate. Here then is one case in which we detect the original rendering.

The problem is seen to resolve itself into a series of smaller problems, almost all of the cases having to be considered on their own merits. For instance, keeping our mind, for convenience sake, on the same chapter, let us ask, which of the readings in v. 2 is to be regarded as primitive, *stultae* or *fatuae*. Note that for the divergent reading the St Gall text has the support of the Bezan text, which is usually early in character, when it diverges from the Italian reading.

Then turn to Irenaeus (II. xxiv. 4) "sapientes virgines a Domino sunt quinque dictae: et *stultae* similiter quinque"; and to Tertullian *De Anima* c. 18 "quinque *stultae* sensus corporales figuraverint...sapientes autem intellectualium virium notam expresserint." The combination shews that the variant reading *stultae* is very ancient and in view of its attestation by Cod. Bezae we suspect it to be the original translation at this point.

The word in question does not occur elsewhere than in Matthew in the four Gospels; the following table will give some idea of its translation.

		stultus	*fatuus*
Matt. v.	22		*abd* vg δ *k* Tert.
vii.	26	*ab* vg δ	
xxiii.	17	*abd* vg δ	
xxiii.	19	δ	
xxv.	2	*d* δ ⎫ Iren.	*b* vg δ
xxv.	3	*d* ⎬	*b* vg δ
xxv.	8	*d* ⎭ Tert.	*b* vg δ

I think we may say positively that in six of the seven places where μωρός occurs, its original rendering is by *stultus*. In Matt. v. 22 the evidence is all the other way. We will leave the rendering in this passage an open question; or the reader can prefer *fatuus*. But this starts another enquiry: what was the

original rendering of the word· φρόνιμοι in the same chapter?
Was it *prudentes* or *sapientes*? The passages already quoted from
Irenaeus and Tertullian suggest the latter; in v. 8 the St Gall
text intimates that there was a divergence in the tradition, for it
offers us both *sapientibus* and *prudentibus*; and so in Matt. x. 16.
Let us tabulate the attestation:

		sapiens	*prudens*
Matt. vii.	24	ab vg δ	
x.	16	d δ	ab vg δ
xxiv.	45	d	ab vg δ
xxv.	2	d ⎤ Iren.	b vg δ
xxv.	4	d ⎦	b vg δ
xxv.	8	bd vg δ ⎤ Tert.	δ
xxv.	9	d δ ⎦	b vg
Luke xii.	42	d	b vg δ
xvi.	8	d	ab vg δ

An examination of the table shews that the original reading
must have been *sapiens*. In the 25th of Matthew *d* shews this
reading .steadily, *b* has it once, the Vulgate once and δ twice;
and it has the combination of early Patristic attestation. We
therefore, regard it as original: and the fidelity with which this
reading is maintained in Cod. Bezae intimates that it is the
habitual form in the early translation.

Let us in the next place consider whether the old translation
read *sumpserunt* or *acceperunt* in v. 3.

In the translation of such a common word as λαμβάνω we
have no right to expect a uniformity of usage throughout the
Gospels; so we will confine ourselves to the Parable of the Ten
Virgins, where it occurs four times:

	sumo	*accipio*
Matt. xxv. 1		bd vg δ
xxv. 3		bd vg δ
xxv. 3	b vg δ	d δ
xxv. 4		bd vg δ

The evidence would seem to shew that the original reading
was uniformly *accipio*, in which case the alternative reading
is simply introduced to relieve the sentence from the repeated
word in v. 3. But it is a point that requires to be confirmed from
a further examination of cases. Perhaps as good a passage by way

of parallel as we can find, would be Matt. xvi. 5—10 λαβεῖν ἄρτους· κοφίνους ἐλάβετε etc.   Here we find

		sumo	accipio
Matt. xvi.	5		abd vg
xvi.	7		abd vg
xvi.	8		δ
xvi.	9	ab vg δ	d δ
xvi.	10	ab vg δ	d

The same suspicion arises as before, from the constancy of the Bezan text, and the double reading in δ, viz. that the use of *sumo* in vv. 9, 10 is a refinement on the original rendering.

If the reader will look now at the collated chapter in verses 36, 43, he will twice note the substitution of *fui* for *eram*.   This may seem a very trivial change of text.   But let us turn to Dr Sanday's discussion of the Africanisms in the Old Latin codex *k* and we shall find a number of similar readings.   Dr Sanday says[1], "It will not be difficult...to set down certain usages as really characteristic of *k*....The use of two co-ordinate verbs for participle and finite verb, of *cum* with subj....of *fui* for *eram*, of words like *adoratio, adora, claritas, clarifico*, of the compounds of *eo* (especially *introeo* for *intro*), of *excludo* and *expello* for *eicio* (in the phrase *excludere* or *expellere daemonia*), of *nequam* for *malus*, of *similitudo* for *parabola*, all rest on a very broad basis."

It will be seen that our single chapter shews some instances of the change of *fui* to *eram* mentioned by Sanday amongst the Africanisms of the period of Cyprian; so that we are working convergently in our search for the primitive rendering.   And other coincidences may be noted: we may be sure that *nequam*, of which he speaks, was in the old translation and the corresponding noun *nequitia*.   The following table will shew it.

		nequa[m]	malus	malignus
Matt. v.	11	k	b δ	d
v.	37		abdk δ	
v.	39	k (bis)	abd δ	
v.	45		abdk δ	
vi.	13		abk δ	
vi.	23	abk δ		
vii.	11	k	ab δ	vel *mali agentes* δ
vii.	17		abk δ	

[1] *Old Latin Biblical Texts*, p. cxxvi.

xii. 34		*k*	*abd*	nantes vel ma-ligni
xii. 39		*k*	*abd* δ	
xii. 45	*abdk* δ			
xii. 45		*k*	*abdk* δ	
xiii. 19		*k*	*ab* δ	*d* malignus
xiii. 38	δ nequam } *a* (nequitiae)}		*k*	{ *b* iniqui, { *d* maligni
xiii. 49			*bdk* δ	
xv. 19			*ad* δ	
xvi. 4			*abd* δ	
xviii. 32	*abd* δ			
xx. 15	*abd* δ			
xxii. 10			*abd* δ	
xxv. 26	*ad* δ		*b* δ	

We need not go further into the other Gospels, for it is abundantly clear that *nequam* was the original rendering: all the texts have it at some point, and some have it at many points. The substitutes for it are interesting: in xiii. 38 cod. *a* corrects the construction to *nequitiae*; while *d* substitutes *maligni*. This shews that *d* had *nequam* in v. 11 and in xii. 34 and in xiii. 19, where in fact it is preserved by cod. *k*. We may then go through the Bezan text and restore *nequam* for *malignus*. This *malignus* is evidently the same in origin as the three St Gall readings *malignantes*, *maligni cum sitis* and *mali agentes*, and in all these cases *nequam* may be restored. But it is by this time sufficiently clear that *nequam* was the original African rendering of πονηρός.

Dr Sanday's suggestion as to the use of *excludo* and *expello* for *eicio* is also borne out by the St Gall text. In Matt. ix. 33 the MS. shews the alternative reading expulso vel iecto (sic!). In Matt. x. 1 the word is *expellerent*, and no doubt other cases may be found.

Similitudo for *parabola* is found in Matt. xxiv. 32; Luke iv. 23, vi. 39, viii. 4, xii. 16, xiii. 6, xviii. 1, xix. 11, xxi. 29.

In Luke v. 36 we have the double rendering, comparationem vel similitudinem;

and in xx. 19, parabolam vel similitudinem.

It appears, then, that in the Gospel of Luke there are plenty of signs of an older form; rather we must say of two variant forms,

probably older, of the word *parabola*. The Bezan text seems
always to have *parabola*, which is a little surprising, if the original
reading were *similitudo* or *comparatio*: for it is seldom that the
older form is entirely corrected away.

Codex *b* in Luke shews *similitudinem* in iv. 23, v. 36, vi.
39, viii. 4, xii. 16, 41, xiii. 6, xv. 3, xviii. 9. Cod. *a* has no
trace of it in Luke, but has it in Mark, in two passages at least
(vii. 17, xiii. 28).

Of the early diffusion of the reading which is found so extensively in *abkδ* there can be little doubt. But we will not
finally conclude that it was the first reading of all; the defection
of *d* from contributing anything to the evidence makes us cautious.
A reading may be African and early African without being the
first translation; and in the present case we have a new variant
comparationem suggested by the St Gall text.

One more example from Matt. xxv. and we will conclude the
discussion of this group of readings. What are we to read as the
original rendering of καταβολή in verse 34? The word occurs
four times in the Gospels, always in the same sense: and the
Bezan text shews three translations; we have in fact

	initium	*origo*	*constitutio*
Matt. xiii. 35	*d*	*ek*	*ab* vg δ
xxv. 34		*d* δ	*ab* vg
Luke xi. 50		*a*	*bd* vg δ
John xvii. 24			*abd* vg δ

The later reading is certainly *constitutio*: and from the fact
that both in Matthew and Luke, we find four out of the six
authorities quoted wandering into another text, it seems likely
that in these two Gospels at all events, *origo* was the reading of
the first translation. It is not so easy to decide in cases where
both words are equally unexceptionable, as it is when one form can
be shewn to be archaic or vulgar or African. Still we have shewn
that in many cases we can recover the more venerable forms of the
translation by a little care and comparison of texts: and if we have
also shewn that the St Gall codex contains some valuable critical
material in its Latin version, that is what we began our enquiry
with, and the end justifies the beginning.

CHAPTER V.

A GENERAL VIEW OF THE DOUBLE TRANSLATIONS OF THE SANGALLENSIS.

Now that we have shewn that these double readings are corrections of one MS. from another, and not new translations; that they often relate to minutiae such as would never suggest themselves to a first translator; and that they are uniformly attested by early copies as true variants, it becomes a matter of interest to tabulate these variants for purpose of reference in the study of the Old Latin version. The major part of them, certainly all the important ones, will be found in the following tables. A few more may also be gathered from the translated titles of the Chapters: e.g. in Matt. we have

περὶ τῆς διδασκαλείας=de magisterio[1] vel doctrina,
περὶ τῶν ἰαθέντων=de curatis debilibus, }
ἀπὸ ποικίλων νόσων languidis vel a langoribus, }
περὶ τῶν παραβολῶν=de similitudinibus vel comparationibus,
περὶ τῶν μυσθουμένων (sic)=de mercenariis operatoribus vel operum,

where we notice again the alternative rendering for the word παραβολή. The following are the most important cases in the text, with the leading factors of the attestation and a few remarks. Trifling errors of spelling are not regarded in the analysis of the attestation. Where we have reason to believe the rendering to be primitive we print in capitals.

St Matthew.

i. 20	γυναῖκα	UXOREM (dk)	coniugem (ab vg)	
	γεννηθέν	NATUM est (d vg Tert.)	(k natum fuerit)	nascetur
	(ab)			

[1] Cf. Iren. III. xiv. 3, "Et in magisterio illud quod ad divites dictum est."

23 ἕξει   concipiet (*ab* Tert.)   habebit (*d* vg) (*k* pregnans erit)
(Cf. Gen. xvi. 11 in Cod. Lugd. *praegnans es*).   .

ii. 6 ἡγεμόσιν   DUCIBUS (*k* Tert.)   principibus (*abd* vg read inter
principes)
If the primitive reading was not *ducibus* it was something
more African ; perhaps *ducatoribus*.

10 χαρὰν μεγάλην   gaudio magno (*abd* vg)   GAUDIUM MAGNUM (*k*)

11 εἶδον   viderunt (*adk*)   invenerunt (*b* vg)
αὐτῶν   eorum   suis (*k*)
προσήνεγκαν   adduxerunt   ⁻obtulerunt (*abdk* vg Tert.)
δῶρα   DONA (*k*)   munera (*abd* vg)

12 δι' ἄλλης ὁδοῦ   ex alia via   per aliam viam (*abd* vg) (*k* per
aliam quam)
ἀνεχώρησαν   reversi sunt (*dk* vg)   recesserunt
αὐτῶν   eorum   suam (*abdk*)

13 ἐγερθείς   surge (*abk* vg)   SURGENS (*d*)
ζητεῖν   ut quaerat (*ab* vg)   quaerere (*d*) (*k* quaesiturus est)
τοῦ ἀπολέσαι   ut perdat (*dk*)   perdere (*ab*)

15 ὑπὸ Κυρίου   a domino (*abk*)   sub domino
διὰ τοῦ προφήτου   ex propheta   ad (?) propheta (*k* prophetam)

18 αὐτῆς   suos (*abk*)   eius

20 οἱ ζητοῦντες   QUERENTES   qui quaerebant (*abk* vg) qui
quaerunt (*d*)

iii. 1 μετανοεῖτε   PENITETE (*k* penitemini)   penitentiam agite (*ab* vg)
(cf. Tert. poenitentiam initote)

4 ἄγριον   silvestre (*abk* vg)   agreste

7 γεννήματα   progenies (*abk* vg)   GENIMINA (Tert.)
ὑπέδειξεν   demonstrabit   demonstrauit (*ab* vg)
μελλούσης   futura (*ak* vg)   ventura (*bd* vg^{nm})

9 ἐν ἑαυτοῖς   inter vos (*a*) (vg *k* intra vos)   IN VOBIS

15 πρέπον ἐστίν   oportet (*b*)   decet (*a* vg) (*d* DECENS EST)
ἀφίησιν   sinit   dimisit (*abd* vg)

iv. 2 ἡμέρας   DIES (*d*)   diebus (*abk* vg)

11 ἀφίησιν   sinit   reliquit (*ab* vg) (*d* dimisit) (*k* discessit)

16 ὁ καθήμενος   SEDENS (*k*)   qui sedebat (*d* vg) (*ab* qui sedebant)

24 προσήνεγκαν   duxerunt   obtulerunt (*abdk* vg)

v. 5 κληρονομήσουσι   hereditabunt (*dk*)   possidebunt (*b* vg) (*a*
HEREDITATE POSSIDEBUNT)

13 εἰς οὐδέν   IN NIHILUM   ad nihilum (*abd* vg) (*k* ad nihil)

19 τούτων   istis (*abk*)   his (*d* vg)

22 ὁ ὀργιζόμενος   qui irascitur (*abd* vg)   irascens (*k* qui pascitur)
εἰς τὴν γέενναν   ad gehennam   in gehenna (*k*) (*d* IN
GEHENNAM)

34 ἐν τῷ οὐρανῷ   IN CAELUM (*dk*)   per caelum (*ab* vg)
ἐν τῇ γῇ   IN TERRAM (*dk*)   per terram (*ab* vg) .
ὑποπόδιον   SUPPEDANEUM (*dk* Iren.)   scabellum (*ab* vg)

39 εἰς τὴν   IN (*abdk*)   super

στρέψον   praebe (*ab* vg)   CONVERTE (*dk*) (Tert. obverte)

    Tertullian's reading seems to be a refinement upon the harsh literalism of *converte*

40   λαβεῖν   ACCIPERE (*d*)   tollere (*b* vg) (*k* auferre)

    τὸ ἱμάτιον   VESTIMENTUM (*dk*)   pallium (*ab* vg Tert.)

41   ὅστις   quicunque (*b* vg)   quisquis (*adk* qui)

    μίλιον   mille (*abk* vg mille passus)   miliarium (*d* milium)

vi. 2   μὴ σαλπίσητε   ne tubicines   noli tubicinare (*dab* vg noli tuba canere) (*k* noli bucinare)

5   οὐκ ἔσῃ   non sitis   non eritis (*ab* vg) (*dk* non eris)

6   κλείσας τὴν θύραν σου   concludens ostium tuum (*d* cludens) *vel* concluso ostio tuo (*ab* vg cluso ostio) (*k* cludentes osteum)

14   δόξα   maiestas   gloria

    Probably these two forms are derived from an original pleonasm, MAIESTAS GLORIAE or MAIESTAS CLARITATIS; for compare Isaiah vi. 3 as quoted by the Te Deum in the Old Latin Version: "pleni sunt coeli et terrae maiestatis gloriae tuae": where the LXX. shews only τῆς δόξης.

25   μὴ μεριμνᾶτε   ne sollicit estis (sic !) (vg ne solliciti estis)   NE COGITATE (*ab* ne cogitetis, Tert. nolite cogitare)

    The Old Version seems always to have rendered μὴ by *ne* : this appears from the numerous variants where *ne* occurs on one side and *noli* on the other : often it is *ne* with the imperative.

29   τούτων   ex ipsis (*k* ex his)   ex istis (*ab*)

31   μεριμνήσητε   meditemini (*k* Tert. nolite cogitare)   solliciti estis (*ab* vg nolite solliciti esse)

    Probably the archaic rendering was NE COGITETIS ; for compare the forms given in the following verse.

34   μὴ μεριμνήσητε   NE COGITETIS (*k* nolite cogitare)   nolite solliciti esse (*ab* vg)

vii. 1   μὴ κρίνετε   NE IUDICATE   nolite iudicare (*abk* vg)

11   πονηροὶ ὄντες   cum sitis mali (*ab* vg) (CUM SITIS NEQUAM *k*) *vel* male agentes

    οἴδατε   nostis (*ab* vg)   scitis (*k*)

13   ἀπώλειαν   interitum (*k*) (vg *ab* perditionem)   mortem

    I can find no support for the reading *mortem* : all texts seem to settle finally on *perditio* : but *k* translates by EXTERMINIUM in Mark xiv. 4. I suppose this was the original word.

16   ἀπὸ   a (*ab*)   de (vg) ex (*k*)

23   ἐργαζόμενοι   qui operati estis (*bk* qui operamini)   operantes (*a* operarii)

26   προσέπεσαν   irruerunt (vg) (*k* inpegerunt)   ceciderunt (?) (*ab* offenderunt)

viii. 4   προσένεγκε   adduc   offer (*abk* vg Tert.) (*ab* offers)

9   πορεύθητι   vade (*abk* vg)   abi

    πορεύεται   vadit (*abk* vg)   it

    ἄλλῳ   alii (*k*)   alio (*ab* vg[am])

16 προσήνεγκαν   adduxerunt   obtulerunt (*abk* vg)
λόγῳ   verbo (vg *abk*)   SERMONE
Sermo seems to be the original African rendering, but it' must have been very early replaced by *verbum* (=*verbus* sometimes in *d*).

17 διὰ Ἡσαίου   ex Es.   per Es. (*abk*)

22 ἄφες   sine   *vel* dimitte (vg) (*abk* remitte) *vel* relinque

25 δὲ   vero   autem

31 ἐπίτρεψον   mitte (*abdk* vg)   concede

34 πᾶσα   omnis   tota (*dk*)
μεταβῇ   transiret (*abd* vg) (*k* transferret)   ascenderet
    I suspect an original rendering (agreeable to the circumstances of the history) ASCENDERET ET TRANSFRETARET, cf. Matt. ix. 1.

ix. 4 ἰδὼν   sciens (*d*)   videns (*bk* vg) (*a* cum vidisset)

12 εἶπεν   dixit (*ak*)   ait (*b* vg)
χρείαν ἔχουσιν   necesse habent (*d*)   indigent (*abk* vg non est opus)
    The original reading was probably NON EST NECESSARIUS.
ἰσχύοντες   fortes (*d*)   sani (*abk* Tert. sanis) vg valentibus

18 ἐλθὼν   VENIENS (*d*) (*k* venitens (sic !))   accedens (*ab* vg accessit)

20 ἥψατο   tetigit (*k*)   tangar (sic !)
ἄψωμαι   tetigero (*ab*)   tacta sim (?)
σωθήσομαι   SALVABOR (*dk*)   salva ero (*ab* vg)

25 (cf. 33) ἐξεβλήθη   expulsa est (*k* expulsa esset but in v. 33 exclusum esset)   eiecta est (*d*) (*ab* vg eiecta esset)

35 θεραπεύων   CURANS (*abdk* vg)   sanans

x. 16 φρόνιμοι   prudentes (*abk* vg)   SAPIENTES (*d*)

17 προσέχετε   attendite (*abd*)   cavete (*k*)

28 μὴ φοβεῖσθε   ne timete (ne timueritis *k*)   ne terreamini

28 δυνάμενον   qui potest (*abdk* vg)   potentem

31 διαφέρετε   meliores (*b* vg meliores estis) (*k* pluris estis)   praecellitis (*d* SUPERPONITE, Tert. antistatis)
    The variety of renderings intimates some primitive misunderstanding: the rendering of *d* which is repeated in xii. 12 is probably the cause of all the trouble.

xi. 11 ἐν γεννητοῖς   IN NATIS (*k*)   inter natos (*abd* vg)

16 προσφωνοῦσιν   clamantes (vg) (*b* clamantibus *a* adclamantibus *k* qui atclamant)   VOCIFERANTES (*d* respondentes)
    Vociferantes is probably the first translation of φωνέω and its compounds, for we find it again in Matt. xxvi. 74 as a variant.

21 μετενόησαν   peniterent (*k*) (*d* paenituissent)   penitentiam egissent (*ab* vg)

xii. 12 διαφέρει   praecellit (*ab* vg melior est)   differt (*k*) (*d* superponit)
    Probably we may take SUPERPONIT as the original rendering.

14 συμβούλιον   consilium (*abdk* vg)   COLLATIONEM
    The alternative word is so much rarer than the common

consilium that one would suppose it must be the original rendering.

25 μερισθεῖσα   divisum (*abd*) (*k* divisitum)   PARTITUM

The use of *partior* as a passive can be supported by African parallels; it would surely be corrected away. A trace of it is in *k*.

34 γεννήματα   GENIMINA (?) (*d* generatio)   progenies (*abk* vg)

42 κατακρινεῖ   iudicabit   condemnabit (*ab*[*d*] vg) (*k* damnavit)

43 διέρχεται   ambulat (*ab* vg)   graditur (?) (*d* circuit) (*k* pertransit)

44 σεσαρωμένον   scopis (*b* vg SCOPIS MUNDATAM)   scopatam (*ad* mundatam) (*k* emundatam)

The original reading was certainly *scopis mundatam*, but this gave two words in Latin for one in Greek: one word was then excised; one part of the tradition erased *mundatam*, hence the reading *scopis*, the other part erased *scopis*.

xiii. 13   συνίουσιν   sentiunt   intelligunt (vg) (*bdk* intelligant)

25   ζιζάνια   zizania (*abdk* vg)   lolia

xiv. 19   κελεύσας   iubens (*abd* vg cum iussissent)   confortans

λαβὼν τοὺς πέντε ἄρτους   acceptis quinque panibus (*ab* vg) ACCIPIENS QUINQUE PANES (accepit *d*)

25   φυλακῇ   vigilia (*abd* vg)   CUSTODIA

Although there seems no support for *custodia* here, yet it must have been the original rendering; for in Luke vi. 48 *d* which usually renders "a watch in the night" correctly by *vigilia* has *et si veniet vespertina custodia*.

31   εἰς τί   IN QUID (*d* vg)   quare (*ab*)

The harsh literalism is certainly original.

35   ὅλην   universam (*abd* vg)   totam

xv. 4   τελευτάτω   consummabitur   morietur (*ad* [*b* vg])

16   ἀσύνετοι   sine intellectu (*a* vg)   NON INTELLECTUALES (*d* insipientes)

The peculiar *non intellectuales* has probably given rise to the other two readings by correction.

32   προσμένουσιν   perseverant (*ab* vg) (*k* manente (sic !))   expectant (*d* SUSTINENT)

Sustineo is the common African substitute for *maneo* and its compounds; we can refer not only to the Latin gospels passim, but also to the Acts of Perpetua c. 4 "Sustineo te": and many other places in Rönsch.

34   ὀλίγα   paucos (*abdk* vg)   modicos

36   εὐχαριστήσας   gradulans (sic !)   gratias agens (*d* vg) (*ab* gratias egit)

xvi. 4   γεινώσκετε   noscitis (*d* scitis)   nostis (*ab* vg)

καταλείπων αὐτοὺς   relictis illis (*ab* vg)   relictus eos (*d* relinquens eos)

The original reading was, I suspect, an African accusative

absolute RELICTOS EOS : this at once explains the origin of the successive variants.

9 ἐλάβετε   sumpsistis (ab vg)   ACCEPISTIS (d)

xvii. 2 λευκά   alba (ad vg)   candida (b)

15 προσήνεγκα   attuli (abd vg obtuli)   adduxi

xix. 7 ἀποστασίου   repudii (abd vg)   recessionis

The original may have been ABSCESSIONIS : for the closely related word ἀποστασία is rendered by d in Acts by *abscessionem a Moysen ;* and Irenaeus' translation (III. xxiii. 2) explains *princeps apostasiae* by *princeps abscessionis.* If this was not the form, perhaps RECESSIO.

9 γαμήσῃ   nupserit   duxerit (abd vg)

12 ὁ δυνάμενος   qui potest (abd vg)   potens

20 νεανίσκος   IUVENIS (d)   adolescens (ab vg)

    ἐφυλαξάμην   conservavi   custodivi (abd vg)

25 σωθῆναι   SALVARI (d)   salvus esse (ab vg)

29 κληρονομήσει   possidebit (ab vg)   hereditabit (d)

The original rendering was HEREDITATE POSSIDEBIT.

xx. 7 ὑπάγετε   VADITE   ite (abd vg)

18 κατακρινοῦσιν   condemnabunt (abd vg)   iudicabunt

22 βαπτισθῆναι   baptizabimini   baptizari

34 ἀνέβλεψαν   aperti sunt   viderunt (b vg) (respexerunt d)

The original translation was pleonastic ; APERTI SUNT OCULI ET VIDERUNT.

xxi. 14 ἐθεράπευσεν   CURAVIT (d)   sanavit (b vg)

Curo seems to be the regular African form, in preference to *Sano.*

25 διελογίζοντο   cogitabant (ab vg)   disputabant (d altercabantur)

38 κατασχῶμεν   habebimus (ab vg)   habita... (?)

44 ὁ πεσών   qui ceciderit   cadens

xxii. 18 πονηρίαν   malitiam (d)   NEQUITIAM (ab [vg])

The prevalence of the form *nequam* for *malus* in the African text has been pointed out.

40 ὅλος   tota (d totum i.e. verbum)   universa (ab vg)

44 ὑποπόδιον   scabellum (a)   SUPPEDANEUM

xxiii. 27 ἀκαθαρσίας   spurcitia (ab vg)   inmunditia (d)

xxiv. 3 κατ᾽ ἰδίαν   secreto (ab vg)   seorsum (d)

9 μισούμενοι   odibiles (d) (odio ab vg)   exosi

26 ἐρήμῳ   ERIMO   deserto (abd vg)

Eremus is a good form for the Biblical Latin ; though it does not occur here in Cod. Bezae, yet it is found in Acts xxi. 38. And the word itself is found in most of the romance languages. Tertullian has it in a number of places.

30 δόξης   maiestate (ab vg)   gloria (d)

Probably another original pleonasm MAIESTATE CLARITATIS.

31 σάλπιγγος   tuba (abd vg)   tubicantione (?)

38 τρώγοντες   comedentes (vg)   cibantes ([a]bd MANDUCANTES)

39 παρουσία   adventus (abd vg)   adventio

43 φυλακῇ   vigilia (d)   vel hora (ab vg) vel CUSTODIA

    Cf. what was said above, Matt. xiv. 25.

    διορυγῆναι   perfodi (d perforari)   perfodiri (ab [vg])

47 τοῖς ὑπάρχουσιν   bona (ad vg)   subsistentia

xxv. 2 μωραί   fatuae (b vg)   STULTAE (d)

3 ἔλαβον   sumpserunt (b)   ACCEPERUNT (d vg)

8 φρονίμοις   SAPIENTIBUS (db vg)   prudentibus

18, 27 ἀργύριον   ARGENTUM (d)   pecuniam (ab vg)

20 προσήνεγκεν   obtulit (bd vg)   attulit (a posuit)

32 ἀφορίσει   separat (ab vg separabit)   segregat (d)

34 κληρονομήσατε   hereditate (d)   possidete (ab vg)

    The original was HEREDITATE POSSIDETE where *hereditate* is a noun ; but the word passes into *d* as a verb, and the complete reading breaks up.

37 ἐποτίσαμεν   POTAVIMUS (d)   potum dedimus (b vg)

41 πορεύεσθε   ite (d)   discedite (ab vg)

xxvi. 2 εἰς τὸ σταυρωθῆναι   ut crucifigatur (abd vg)   crucifigi

12 πρὸς τὸ ἐνταφιάσαι   sepeliri   ad sepeliendum (abd vg)

26 εὐχαριστήσας (l. εὐλογήσας)   benedixit ([a]b vg) (d benedicens)

    BENEGRATULATUS

27 εὐχαριστήσας   gratias egit (ab vg)   gratias egens (d)

44 ἀπελθών   abiit (abd)   abiens

    λόγον εἰπών   sermonem faciens (a sermonem iterato)   sermonem dicens (bd vg)

47 ξύλων   fustibus ([a]b[d] vg)   LIGNIS

    From the fact that *lignis* turns up again as a variant in Mark xiv. 43 where the Vulgate has actually preserved it, we infer that it was the first rendering.

51 ἀπέσπασεν   exemit (b vg) (d eiecit)   EVAGINAVIT

    The form *evaginare* will be found again in our MS. at John xviii. 10 with an alternative *eduxit*. It occurs also in Cod. Brixiensis in Mark xiv. 47 ; and in *d* vg in Acts xvi. 27. Cf. Rönsch p. 190.

65 χρείαν ἔχομεν   necesse habemus (d opus habemus)   egemus (b vg)

71 πυλῶνα   ianuam (ab vg)   portam

74 ἐφώνησεν   VOCIFERATUS   cantavit (ab vg)

    Compare what was said about this translation under Matt. xi. 16.

xxvii. 7 ξένοις   peregrinis (abd vg peregrinorum)   hospitibus

    The Codex Bezae shews *hospes* in Matt. xxv. 44 but nowhere else in the chapter : the St Gall text has *hospes* in Matt. xxv. in all four places where the word occurs, and so with *ab* and the Vulgate.

28 στέφανον   CORONAMENTUM   coronam (abd vg)

54 μετ' αὐτοῦ   secum   CUM EO (*bd* vg)
58 προσελθών   accessit (*abd* vg)   ACCEDENS
60 ἀπῆλθεν   discessit   abiit (*abd* vg)
66 ἠσφαλίσαντο   custodierunt   munierunt (*abd* vg)

xxviii. 9 ἀπήντησεν   occurrit (*abd* vg)   OBVIAVIT

The form *obviare* though not supported by our quoted authorities at this point occurs frequently in the tradition of the Latin Gospels and in other places.

10 μὴ φοβεῖσθε   NE TIMETE   nolite timere (*abd* vg)
12 ἀργύρια ἱκανά   ARGENTUM COPIOSUM   pecuniam copiosam (*abd* vg)
15 μέχρι τῆς σήμερον   USQUE AD IN HODIERNUM vel usque hodie (*ab*[*d*])   usque in hodiernum

The pleonastic form is to be preferred, as more African than any of the others.

16 ἐτάξατο   constituerat (*abd* vg)   praeceperat
19 μαθητεύσατε   docete (*abd* vg) vel DISCIPLINATE   vel discipulos facite

Here the last of the three readings is certainly not the original African form, for that has *discens* for *discipulus* uniformly: the choice then lies between the first two, and here the second has an African colour which is wanting in the first. We find a number of instances of the word *disciplinatus* in Rönsch: and Tertullian shews the comparative adjective *disciplinatior*. We therefore decide this to be the primitive rendering.

These, then, are the principal double readings in Matthew in the Codex Sangallensis; and the reader will see how helpful they are in the detection of primitive Africanisms, and in the tracing of the relations between the various lines of descent of the Latin tradition. As we have gone so far with the subject, it would be a pity not to examine the remaining Gospels, for every ray of light on such an obscure subject is helpful; we will, therefore, give a full selection from the double readings in Mark, Luke and John. Those in Mark, as we have said, are very few and will be easily disposed of.

CHAPTER VI.

A GENERAL VIEW OF THE DOUBLE TRANSLATIONS OF THE SANGALLENSIS.

PASSING on, then, to the Gospels of Mark, Luke and John, we must collect our instances of double translation as before, and endeavour to discriminate between them in the matter of antiquity. We must, however, be careful not to generalize too hastily as to the uniformity of a translation from one gospel to another, or even from one part of a gospel to another; for we have not proved that the first translator was the same person in all four Gospels, nor that he always used the same manner of interpretation in his work. But we shall get light on these points as our enquiry progresses. We turn, then, to the double readings in the Gospel of Mark and note as follows:

St Mark.

i. 28   ἐξῆλθεν   processit (*d* vg)   abiit (*b* exiit)

   31   εὐθέως (2°)   statim (*bd*)   denuo

   35   πρωΐ   deluculo (*bd* vg)   mane (*a* prima luce)

ii. 10   εἰδῆτε   sciatis (*abd* vg)   videatis

   12   δοξάζειν   honorificarent (*abd* vg)   glorificarent

     The original reading was probably CLARIFICARENT.

   17   κακῶς ἔχοντες   male habentes   MALE HABENTIBUS (*abd* vg qui male habent)

     (Note that the second reading implies an original text NECESSARIUS EST MEDICUS.)

   22   νέον (1°)   NÒVELLUM (*d*)   novum (*ab* vg)

     The French *nouveau* shews the displacement of *novum* in the Vulgar Latin.

iii. 12   φανερὸν ποιήσωσιν   manifestarent (*bd* vg)   manifestar facerent (?) (*a* palam facerent)

     The reading which we have given in the second place is

obscure; it may be MANIFESTARIUM FACERENT in which case it is probably original.

iv. 1 παρὰ   ad (*abd* vg)   iuxta

  11 γνῶναι   nosse (vg)   scire (vg^{am}) (*abd* cognoscere)

  13 ταύτην   istam   hanc (*ab* vg)

  18 σπειρόμενοι   seminantur (*d* vg)   seminati (*b* seminati sunt)

  19 ἀγάπη   deceptio (vg)   dilectio

     Here, apparently for the first time in our investigation, we strike a genuine Greek Variant, the well-known ἀπάτη (as in Matt. xiii. 22) for ἀγάπη. All the texts are in much confusion. Perhaps the original was OBLECTAMENTUM which Cod. *k* shews at this point.

  24 μετρεῖτε   MENSURABITIS   mensi fueritis (vg) (*bd* metieritis)

     Our MS. shews the same form *mensurare* in Matt. vii. 2, without an alternative.

vi. 3 πρὸς ἡμᾶς   nobiscum (*bd* vg)   ad nos (*a* aput nos)

  27 ἐνέγκαι   adferri (*ad* vg)   adduci (*b* auferri)

  32 ἀπῆλθον   ascendentes   abierunt (*b*) (*ad* vg ASCENDENTES....ABI-ERUNT)

vii. 22 πονηρὸς   malus (*bd* vg)   NEQUAM (*a* nequa)

  37 ἀλάλους   non loquentes   mutos (*a*[*bd*] vg)

x. 4 ἀποστασίου   RECESSIONIS   repudii (*abdk* vg)

     Cf. what was said under the parallel passage Matt. xix. 7.

xi. 4 εὗρον   viderunt   invenerunt (*abd* vg)

xii. 14 κῆνσον   censum   tributum (*abd* vg)

xiv. 3 πιστικῆς   spicati (vg) (*a* optimi)   pistici (*d*)

  40 πάλιν   denuo (vg)   iterum

  43 ξύλων   fustibus (*adk*)   LIGNIS (vg)

     Cf. Matt. xxvi. 47.

xv. 4 ἰδού   ecce (*a*)   VIDE (*k* vg) *d* vides

Under Mark ii. 12 we have the double translation of δοξάζω by *honorifico* and *glorifico*. This is a good place to examine whether the primitive translation shewed any unity on the subject of the rendering of δόξα and δοξάζω. The diversity of rendering has been remarked by Scrivener in the Codex Bezae (p. xxxiii note) "δοξάζω by *clarifico* Acts iii. 13. iv. 21. xi. 18. xxi. 20 but no where else. Yet in regard to δοξάζω we meet with just the same variation in the Gospels. In St Matthew it is *glorifico* four times, never in St Luke, but *honorifico* five times, *honoro* three times, in the passive *gloriam accipio* iv. 15: in St Mark we have *honorifico* once: in St John *glorifico* fourteen times, *honorifico* six. This precarious argument" (i.e. as to variety of hands in the rendering) "drawn from the use of different words in the several parts of the same work weighs far too much with some critics." No doubt Scrivener is right in entering a warning against precipitate conclusions in such a complex problem. Let us see whether there are, however, any indications of a primitive uniformity of rendering.

		clarifico	glorifico	honorifico	magnifico	honoro
Matt.	v. 16	k Iren.	d vg δ		ab	
	vi. 2	k	d δ	ab vg		
	ix. 8	k Iren.	d vg δ	ab		
	xv. 31	k	d δ		ab vg	
Mark	ii. 2		δ	abd vg δ		
Luke	ii. 20		vg d Iren.	d	ab	
	iv. 15				b vg (a honorem accipiens) (d gloriam accipiens)	
	v. 25		δ	ad	b vg	
	26		δ		b vg	
	vii. 16		δ	ad	b vg δ	
	xiii. 13		vg δ	ad	b	
	xvii. 15			a	b vg δ	d
	xviii. 43		δ	a	b vg	d
	xxiii. 47		vg δ	ad	b	
John	vii. 39		vg δ	b		ad
	viii. 54		a vg δ	b		d
	54		d vg δ	b		d
	xi. 4	b	d vg δ			
	xii. 16	b	ad vg δ			
	23	b vg	d vg^am δ	a		
	28	b vg δ	d			
	28	b vg δ	d			
	28	b vg δ	d	a		
	xiii. 31	b vg δ	d	a		
	31	b vg δ	d	a		
	32	b vg δ	d	a		
	32	b vg δ	d	a		
	32	vg δ				
	xiv. 13		d vg δ	ab		
	xv. 8	b vg δ	d	a		
	xvi. 14	b vg δ	d	a		
	xvii. 1	b vg δ	d	a		
	1	b vg δ		ad		
	4	b vg δ		ad		
	5	b vg δ Iren.		ad		
	10	b vg δ	d	a		
	xxi. 19	b vg δ		ad		
Acts	iii. 13	d	vg Iren.			
	iv. 21	d vg				
	xi. 18	d	vg			
	xxi. 20	d			vg	

Now, I apprehend, no one will scrutinize this table of various renderings without seeing that there is a method in the madness and disorder.   Even the Vulgate, where we should expect to trace a reviser's hand accomplishing uniformity at the expense of clearness of genealogical transmission, is seen to be a MS. tradition. It may be doubted whether any of its readings are arbitrary changes, and where they are eclectic, the number of sources is clearly limited.   In Matthew and in John the primitive reading must be *clarifico*; for in Matthew we have the decided African evidence of *k* followed by *d* which makes the trifling modification of hardly more than a letter to *glorifico*.   Where we find *glorifico* in *d*, then we may reasonably expect that the primitive was *clarifico*.   This is most decidedly the case in the last chapters of John where the evidence for the primitive *clarifico* is very strong. In Acts also this seems to be the ruling form.

In Luke, however, the evidence is much less decided, and is, amongst our quoted authorities, chiefly deducible from the occurrence of *glorifico* in the Sangallensis.   It is observable that *a* and *d* are very nearly related in this Gospel.   Note especially the agreement of *ad* in reading *honorifico* (with its variant *honoro*) and probably in the correction of *honorificatus* into

$$\left.\begin{array}{l} \text{honorem} \\ \text{gloriam} \end{array}\right\} \text{accipiens.}$$

It is not quite clear, then, whether we ought to restore *clarifico* uniformly.   We will see whether any light is thrown on the matter by the quotations in Tertullian or the translator of Irenaeus.

In Luke vii. 16 Tertullian uses *gloriam referre*: in xvii. 15 *gloriam reddere*; and in xviii. 43 *gloriam referre*.   These look like modifications of *glorifico* but we cannot be sure.

The evidence of Irenaeus which is inserted in our Table supports twice the reading *clarifico* in Matt. as in cod *k*; and once in John.   In two other places it gives *glorifico*; once in Acts iv. 13 where the primitive reading is surely *clarifico* and once in Luke where the matter is doubtful.   On the whole the evidence of Irenaeus favours the form *clarifico*, but it is best to leave a margin for a possible variation of translation in the Gospel of Luke.

But we may evidently reinforce the argument by a consideration of the noun-forms *claritas, gloria, honos, majestas* as renderings of δόξα.

We will make a table as in previous cases.

			claritas	gloria	honos	majestas
Matt.	iv.	8	k	ad δ	b	
	vi.	13		δ		
		29	k	ab δ		
	xvi.	27		d δ		ab
	xix.	28		d		ab δ
	xxiv.	30		d δ		ab δ
	xxv.	31		d δ		ab δ
Mark	viii.	38	k	abd δ		
	x.	37		abd δ		
	xiii.	26	k	ad δ .		
Luke	ii.	9	b δ	d		a
		14		abd δ		
		32		abd δ		
	iv.	6		abd δ		
	ix.	26		a		b δ
		31		ad		b δ
		32		ad		b δ
	xii.	27		abd δ		
	xiv.	10		abd δ		
	xvii.	18		d δ	a	
	xix.	38		ad δ		
	xxi.	27		ad		δ
	xxiv.	26		abd δ		
John	i.	14		a δ	b	
		14		ab δ		
	ii.	11		a δ	b	
	v.	41		ad δ	b	
		44		ad δ	b	
		44		ad δ	b	
	vii.	18		abd δ		
		18		abd δ		
	viii.	50		ad δ	b	
		54		ad δ	b	
	ix.	24		d δ	ab	
	xi.	4	b	ad δ		
		40		bd δ		a
	xii.	41		ad δ		b
		43		ad δ		b
		43		ad δ		b
	xvii.	5	b δ	ad		
		22	b δ	ad		
		24	b δ	ad		

vii.	2	*d*	
	55		*d*
xii.	23	*d*	
xxii.	11	*d*	

Now we notice that this table is in many ways similar to the one which we had before, as indeed was to be expected in part, for some verses contain both the noun and the verb in question side by side (e.g. "glorify me...with the glory etc."). So that we are not surprised to find that *b* gives evidence for *claritas* in the last chapters of John; nor that *k* which uses *clarifico* in Matthew should use *claritas* in the same Gospel. The evidence is internally harmonious. Moreover we have the new piece of evidence from *k* in favour of the use of *claritas* and therefore, presumably, of *clarifico* in Mark. We have also found one case of *claritas* in the Gospel of Luke. But one thing must, I think, be apparent; that the grouping of the authorities is much more simply made in the testimony for the noun forms than it is for the verb forms. We have still the four ways of expressing the idea in question, but there is not so much variation in the relation of the attesting groups. Confining our attention, then, for a few moments to the attestation for the noun, we see that in no case when the authorities divide, do we find an attestation for both *honos* and *majestas*. The authorities divide on *gloria* and *majestas*, and on *gloria* and *honos*, but not on *honos* and *majestas*. These two forms, then, are not alternative, nor did they coexist in a pleonastic translation; for in that case it is most likely that some codices would preserve the one and some the other. May it not be, however, that they came in separately out of pleonastic renderings of which *gloria* was the other member? We have already seen reason from a passage of the Old Latin of Isaiah preserved in the Te Deum to suspect a pleonastic rendering,

majestas gloriae.

And it seems that the primitive Latin texts were coloured with such pleonastic renderings as *honos gloriae* (or *honos claritatis*), *majestas gloriae*; of which later scribes erased one half, keeping the other. This explains most of the peculiar features of the attestation, as for example, why *b* should in John xi. 40 give *gloria* and *a majestas*; while on the other hand in John xii. 43 *b* should give *majestas* and *a gloria*. The common ancestry had both terms. Where the original reading was simply *claritas* without any addition, it was probably at once altered to *gloria* to which no codex in question shews any special aversion.

But if this be the right interpretation of the divergence in the attestation, we can turn it back from the nouns to the verbs; and we suggest that the complicated testimony is due to original pleonasms, which have been variously resolved in the transmission of the text by the scribes.

Moreover a review of the whole evidence shews a strong case for a primitive *claritas* with or without other expansions of interpretation. The case for *claritas* is weakest in the Gospel of Luke.

CHAPTER VII.

DOUBLE READINGS IN THE GOSPEL OF LUKE.

i. 6   πορευόμενοι   ambulantes (*d*)   proficiscentes (incedentes *b* Iren.)

  8   ἐναντίον τοῦ θεοῦ   ANTE DEUM (*b* Iren.)   coram Deo (in conspectu Dei *d*)

14   ἀγαλλίασις   exultatio (*ab*)   laetitia (*d*)
    Cod. *d* has laetitia again in v. 44.

19   ἐνώπιον τοῦ θεοῦ   in conspectu Dei (*ad*)   coram Deo (*b* ante Dominum)

21   λαός   populus (*a*)   plebs (*bd*)

29   ἡ δὲ ἰδοῦσα   quae vero audiens *vel* quae cum scivisset *vel* cum vidisset (*ab* ut vidit)

29   οὗτος   ista (vg)   haec (*d*)

30   εἶπεν   ait (*b*)   dixit

35   δύναμις   virtus (*abd* Tert. Iren.)   potestas

44   εἰς τὰ ὦτά μου   in auribus meis   in meis auribus
    ἐν ἀγαλλιάσει   in laetitia (*d*)   in gaudio (*b*)

45   ἡ πιστεύσασα   quae credidisti (*ab*)   QUAE CREDIDIT (*d*)

    ὅτι ἔσται τελείωσις   quoniam perficientur (*b*)   erunt / fient } perfecta

    (Note that *a* reads quod erit consummatio
      „   „   *d*   „   quia erit consummatio.)
    Perhaps an original QUIA ERIT CONSUMMATIO PERFECTIONIS.

48   ἐπὶ τήν   super (*d*) *vel* in *vel* ad
    δούλης   ancillae (*abd*)   famulae

50   εἰς γενεάς   in generatione (IN GENERATIONES *d*)   in progenies (*ab* in saecula saeculorum)

54   μνησθῆναι   MEMORARI (*b*[*d*])   recordari
    Certainly the African form: the form *Commemorari* is also very common.

57   ἐγέννησεν   genuit (*b*)   peperit (*ad*)

63   πάντες   universi   omnes (*abd*)
    Probably a pleonasm in the original UNIVERSI OMNES (cf. Sittl, *Die lokalen Verschiedenheiten* p. 97).

66   οἱ ἀκούσαντες   qui audierint (*abd*)   audientes

70   διὰ στόματος   per (*abd*)   ex

ii. 3 ἰδίαν   propriam   suam ([a]bd)

7 ἐσπαργάνωσεν   pannavit   pannis involvit (abd)

8 φυλακάς   vigilias (ab)   CUSTODIAS (d)

15 ἐγνώρισεν   innotuit   ostendit (ab) (d demonstravit)

18 περὶ τῶν λαληθέντων   de his quae dicta erant (bd [sunt])   de dictis (a de his quae locuti sunt)

21 ἐπλήσθησαν   consummati sunt (bd)   impleti sunt (a) vel implerentur

A primitive pleonasm is latent : cf. John xvii. 23 in Cod. Bezae *ut sint perfecti consummati*.

22 ἀνήγαγον   tulerunt (b) (Iren. imposuerunt)   duxerunt (a) (d adduxerunt)

27 εἰθισμένον   morem   consuetudinem (abd)

34 πτῶσιν   casum (b)   RUINAM (ad Tert. Iren.)

37 δεήσεσιν   obsecrationibus (b observationibus)   deprecationibus (ad orationibus)

The verb *obsecro* almost always appears pleonastically with *rogo*, and it seems that something of the same kind is to be found with the corresponding nouns : cf. v. 33 which suggests the form OBSECRATIONIBUS ET DEPRECATIONIBUS.

49 εἶπεν   ait   dixit

iii. 1 ἡγεμονίας   imperii (ab)   DUCATUS (d) (Tert. principatus)

Certainly *ducatus* must be the primitive African form ; whether another word should go with it is uncertain.

iv. 5 στιγμῇ   puncto   momento (abd)

14 ὑπέστρεψεν   reversus (a) (d conversus est)   regressus (b egressus)

15 δοξαζόμενος   glorificatur ($\begin{Bmatrix} a\ \text{honorem} \\ d\ \text{gloriam} \end{Bmatrix}$ accipiens)   glorificabatur (b magnificabatur)

18 συντετριμμένους   captivos   CONTRIBULATOS

(Probably some confusion in the comparison of the texts upon which the Scribe was working.)

19 ἀνάβλεψιν   videre   visum (abd)

23 πάντως   utique (bd)   omnino (a forsitam)

26 οὐδεμίαν   neminem (d)   nullam (ab)

σιδωνίας (cod. σίδωνος)   Sidoniae (bd) (a Sidonia)   Sidonis

38 συνεχομένη   tenebatur (b) (a detinebatur)   ligata (d conprehensa)

v. 2 ἀποβάντες   descenderant (b descendebant)   descendentes (a egressi) (d exientes)

8 γόνασιν   ad genua (b) (d ad pedes)   genibus (a)

15 διήρχετο   perambulabat (b) (a divulgabatur)   perveniebat (d transiebat)

17 διδάσκων   sedens   docens (ab) (d docente)

Probably an original SEDENS ET DOCENS.

ἰᾶσθαι   sanando (ab ad sanandum)   sanare (d ut salvaret)

20 ἀφέωνται   remittuntur (Iren.) (ab remissa sunt)   DEMIT-
TUNTUR (d Tert. demittentur)

25 παραχρῆμα   confestim (abd)   continuo

26 παράδοξα   MAGNALIA   mirabilia (bd) (a mirifica)

33 δεήσεις   obsecrationes (b)   orationes (a) (d precationes)
Cf. the renderings in ii. 37.

36 παραβολήν   comparationem (ad parabolam)   SIMILITUDINEM (b)

37 ἀπολοῦνται   peribunt (abd)   perditi sunt

39 χρηστότερος   suavius   melius

vi. 1 σπορίμων   sata (a)   seminata (bd segetes)

4 ὡς   quomodo (ab) (Iren. quemadmodum)   sicut

17 πεδινοῦ   campestri (bd) (a CAMPENSE)   pedestri
The rarer word has the greater claim to be regarded as
archaic.

21 πεινῶντες   ESURIENTES   qui esuriunt (bd) (a qui esuritis)

29 σιαγόνα   maxillam (abd)   GENAM (Tert.)

35 χρηστός   suavis (ad)   benignus (b)

42 ἄφες   sine (abd) (Iren. Tert. remitte)   dimitte (Tert.)
(N.B. There is no disjunctive vel between the readings.)

47 ὁ ἐρχόμενος   qui venit (abd)   VENIENS

48 προσέρρηξεν   illiserunt (?) (bd allisit)   · erupit (a impulit)

49 ἀκούσας   qui audit (ab) (d qui audivit)   AUDIENS

vii. 6 οὐδὲ ἠξίωσα   non sum dignus   non dignum arbitratus (?)

16 ἐδόξαζον   magnificabant (b)   glorificabant (d)

22 εἴδετε   videtis   scitis (?)

23 σκανδαλισθῇ   offenderit (bd non fuerit scandalizatus)   scanda-
lizaverit (a scandalizabitur)

39 εἶπεν ἐν ἑαυτῷ   dixit (ad)   ait (b)

45 καταφιλοῦσα   osculari (b)   osculans (d) (osculando a)

47 ὀλίγον   paucum   parvum minus (ab)

48 ἀφέονται   DIMITTUNTUR   remittuntur (a) (remissa sunt b)

viii. 5 παρά   super   SECUS (b)   .

8 ἐφώνει   clamabat (abd)   VOCIFERABAT
We have already had several instances of vocifero as a rendering of φωνέω. We suspect it to have been the first translation.

24 ἀνέμῳ   ventum   VENTO (abd)
The dative after increpavit is a Graecism.
κλύδωνι   tempestatem   tempestati (ab) (d undae)
Perhaps an original TEMPESTATI AQVAE (as in ab).

25 ὕδατι   mari (b)   aquae (ad)

40 ἐν τῷ ὑποστρέψαι   cum rediret i͞h͞s ([a]d cum reverteretur)   in
rediendo i͞h͞m

47 ἀπήγγειλεν   nuntiavit (d adnuntiavit)   indicavit (ab)

ix. 3 ἀργύριον   ARGENTUM   pecuniam (abd)

21 μηδενί   ne cui (ab Tert.)   nemini (d)

28 παραλαβών   accipiens   adsumens (d Tert.) (a adsumptis b
adsumpsit)

προσεύξασθαι   ut oraret (*ab*)   ORARE (*d*)

33   ἡμᾶς ὧδε   NOS HIC (*ab* Tert.)   nobis hic (*d*)

42   ἔρρηξεν   elisit (*b*) adlisit (*a*)   disipavit

    συνεσπάραξεν   disipavit (*b* discipavit)   elisit (*a* concarpsit *d* conturbabit)

There is some difficult word used here by the primitive translator which gives trouble to all the successive transcribers. The word is something like the form in *b* : for in the parallel passage in Mark Cod. *k* gives *dissupavit*. Dr Sanday equates this to *discarpo*, but the existence of the form *discipavit* in *b* shews that there is something of a different form latent.

47   ἐπιλαβόμενος   adpraehendens (*d*) (*a* ADPRAEHENSUM INFANTEM *b* adpraehendens puerum *d* adpraehendens infantem)   adpraehendente

Probably a confusion due to the appearance of an Accusative Absolute in the text.

x. 1   ἀνὰ δύο   simul duo   binos (*abd*)

Probably an original ANA DUO. Cf. *d* in Luke ix. 3 *ana duas tunicas*.

25   κληρονομήσω   possidebo (*ab*)   hereditabo (*d*)

Original reading was HEREDITATE POSSIDEBO.

30   περιέπεσεν   incidit (*abd*)   decidit

31   κατὰ συγκυρίαν   accidit (*a* fortuito *b* om. *d* forte autem)   contegit

The original was FORTE AUTEM ACCIDIT or something very like it.

34   τὸ ἴδιον κτῆνος   suum iumentum (*ab* in suo iumento)   suum asinum (*d* SUPER SUUM PECUS)

    ἐπεμελήθη   medelam egit   curam egit (*b*) (*ad* CURAM HABUIT)

35   ἐκβαλών   mittens (*d* eiciens)   proferens (*ab* protulit)

42   περὶ πολλά   multa   plurima

    ἀγαθήν   bonam (*d*)   optimam (*ab*)

Probably an original African Superlative BONAM BONAM.

xi. 8   ἀναστάς   surgere   surgens (*ad*)

13   πνεῦμα ἅγιον   spiritum bonum (*bd* BONUM DATUM)   spiritum sanctum

23   συνάγων   colligit (*b*)   congregat (*d*)

25   σεσαρωμένον   scopis vacantem   scopis mundatam (*b*) (*d* mundatum)

The original reading answered to

σεσαρωμένον σχολάζοντα

and was rendered

SCOPIS MUNDATAM VACANTEM.

Some texts erase *scopis* and some *vacantem*, and some lose both.

26   παραλαμβάνει   adsumit (*abd*)   accipiet

27   ἐν τῷ λέγειν   cum diceret (*ab*) (*d* in eo cum diceret)   dicendo eum

28 ἀκούοντες   qui audiunt (abd)   audientes
30 ταύτῃ   isti   huic (abd)
35 σκόπει   vide   intende
39 πίνακος   catini (ab) (d catilli)   disci
40 ἄφρονες   stulti (abd)   insipientes

xii. 2 κρυπτόν   absconditum (Tert.) (d ABSCONSUM)   occultum (ab)

7 διαφέρετε   praefertis (ad differtis)   praecellitis (b plures
estis)

15 ἐκ τῶν ὑπαρχόντων   ex his quae possidet (b)   ex possessis (a
de facultate sua d de substantia eius)

17 ποῦ   quo (b)   ubi (ad)

22 ἐνδύσησθε   induamini (abd)   vestiamini

24 ταμεῖον   cella vinaria (without a conjunction and probably a
single reading)   (ab cellarium d promptarium)

38 φυλακῇ   CUSTODIA (d)   vigilia (b Iren.)

45 χρονίζει   moratur (d tardat)   moram facit (b)

50 τελεσθῇ   perficiatur (b)   finiatur (d consummetur)
Cf. the readings in ii. 21.

xiii. 15 ποτίζει   ADAQUARE (b) (ad adaquat) (Tert. ducit ad potum)
potare

22 διεπορεύετο   ihat (b)   perambulabat (ad circuibat)

24 ἀγωνίζεσθε   certate (d CERTAMINI)   contendite (b)

28 ἐκβαλλομένους   expelli (b)   expulsandos (a Iren. proici d eici)

xiv. 4 ἰάσατο   sanavit (b) (d sanans)   curavit (a curatum)

31 ὑπαντῆσαι   occurre (sic !)   OBVIARE (ab) (d obviari)

33 τοῖς ἑαυτοῦ ὑπάρχουσιν   possessis suis (a facultatibus b quae
possidet d substantiae suae)   ea quae possidet
Cf. the readings in xii. 15.

35 ἔχων   habens   qui habet (ad) (qui habent b)

xv. 6 τὸ ἀπολωλός   quem perdideram   [quae] perierat (abd)

17 ἐλθών   veniens (d)   reversus (?) (a) conversus

28 ὠργίσθη   iratus est (ad)   indignatus (b vg)

28 παρεκάλει   vocavit   rogavit (ab coepit rogare d rogabat)

30 τὸν βίον   facultatem (a omnem facultatem)   substantiam (b)
(d omnia)

xvi. 6 τὸ γράμμα (a triple reading)   cautionem (a)   litteram (bd lit-
teras)   liniam (?)

16 εὐαγγελίζεται   BENE NUNTIATUR   evangelizatur ([a] b [d])

30 μετανοήσουσιν   PENITEBUNT (d paenitebuntur)   penitentiam
agent (a) (b persuadebit illis)

xvii. 2 μύλος ὀνικός   lapis molaris (ab) (d lapidem molae)   MOLA
ASINARIA

7 ἐξ ὑμῶν   vestrum (a)   ex vobis (d ex vestris)

11 ἐν τῷ πορεύεσθαι αὐτόν   dum iret (ab) (d cum iter faceret)
ingrediente eo

12 ἀπήντησαν   occurrerunt   OBVIAVERUNT

23 μὴ ἀπέλθητε   NE ITE (d ne ieritis)   nolite exire (ab nolite ire)

29 ἔβρεξεν πῦρ   pluit ignem   pluit ignis

xviii. 4 οὐκ 2°   non (d)   nec (ab)

13 ἱλάσθητί μοι   propitius esto (a) (b repropitiare)   propitiato mihi (d miserere mihi)

18 κληρονομήσω   possideam (ab possidebo)   hereditem (d hereditabo)
Original reading HEREDITATEM POSSIDEBO.

24 εἰσελεύσονται   intrabunt (ab) (d INTROIBUNT)   intrare
The fondness of the Old Latin for *introeo* as against *intro* has been noted by Dr Sanday.

31 παραλαβών   assumens (d adsumens b adsumpsit)   ACCIPIENS (a convocatis)

35 προσαιτῶν   mendicans (a) (mendicus bd)   petens

xix. 4 συκομορέαν   sycomorum arborem (a arborem sycomori b arborem sycomorum d morum)   (Probably a single rendering)

5 ἀναβλέψας   suspiciens   respiciens (a [b])

7 εἰσῆλθεν καταλῦσαι   introisset solvere (a introisset manere d introivit manere)   divertisset (b devertit)
The original rendering may well have been INTROIVIT SOLVERE.

11 διὰ τό   eo quod (ab)   propter (d propter quod)

15 and in 23 ἀργύριον   pecuniam (abd)   ARGENTUM

18 ὁ δεύτερος   alter (b) (ad alius)   secundus

21 αὐστηρός   austeris (abd)   asper

24 ἄρατε   tollite (d)   auferte (ab)

26 ἀρθήσεται   tolletur (d)   auferetur (a)

28 ἔμπροσθεν   ante   coram

29 τὸ καλούμενον   vocabulo (a qui appellatur)   vocatum (d qui vocatur)
Cf. Luke x. 39 where καλουμένη Μαρία is rendered *vocabulo Maria*.

30 ὑπάγετε   ite (ad)   VADITE

xx. 9 γεωργοῖς   colonis (a)   agricolis (d)
Colonus seems to be the common rendering, but d has *cultoribus* once in Matt., and *agricola* regularly in Luke. Cod. a has VINITOR regularly in Mark, the last is such a rare word that one would suppose it to be the archaic reading at least for this Gospel.

11 προσέθετο   adposuit (a)   addidit (d misit alium)

21 πρόσωπον   personam (ad)   faciem

26 θαυμάσαντες   mirantes (d)   mirati (a)

43 ὑποπόδιον   SUPPEDANEUM   scabellum

46 ἐν τοῖς δείπνοις   in conviviis   in caenis (d)

xxi. 7 magister (ad)   praeceptor
An original pleonasm of the translator; a number of parallel cases can be found in the Western text as John xx. 17 in Cod. Bezae "rabboni quod dicitur domine magister." The present instance MAGISTER ET PRAECEPTOR can also be paralleled from the Arabic Harmony of Tatian in Mark x. 51.

12   ἀγομένους   ducentes [*d* ducentur (*a* ducemini)]   tradentes (*a* tradent vos)

14   ἀπολογηθῆναι   quemadmodum respondeatis (*a* quomodo ratio- nem reddatis *d* respondere)   disputare

15   ἀντειπεῖν   resistere (*a*)   contradicere (*d*)

24   αἰχμαλωτισθήσονται   CAPTIVENTUR   captivi ducentur (*ad*)

29   πάντα τὰ δένδρα   · omnia ligna   omnes arbores (*ad*)

31   γινόμενα   fientia   fieri

33   λόγοι   verba (*abd*)   sermones

33 (fin.) παρέλθωσιν   transibunt (*ad* praeteribunt)   transient (*b*)

36   ἔμπροσθεν   ante (*a*)   · coram (*d* in conspecto)

37   ἐλαιῶν   olivarum   oliveti (*bd*) (*a* olivetum)

xxii. 2   λαόν   plebem (*b*)   populum (*ad*)

4   πῶς   QUOMODO (*d*)   quemadmodum (*ab*)

16   ἕως ὅτου   donec (*ab*)   usque quo (*d*)

17   διαμερίσατε   dividite (*b*)   PARTITE (partimini *ad*) ἑαυτοῖς   inter vos (*b*)   vobis (*d*) (*a* in vobis)

27   ὁ ἀνακείμενος   qui recumbit (*abd*)   recumbens

31   ἐξητήσατο   quaerebat (*a* Tert. postulavit)   expetivit (*bd*)

37   τελεσθῆναι   impleri (*ab*) (conpleri *d*)   finiri

xxiii. 4   οὐδὲν αἴτιον   nil causae (*bd* nihil causae)   nullam causam (*a* nullam culpam)

33 and 39 κακούργους   latrones (*ab*) (but in *v.* 39 *a* has malefici) NEQUAM (*d* malignos)

As we shewed before, *malignus* is a correction for *nequam*.

50   βουλευτής   decurio (*abd*)   consiliarius

53   οὗ   quo (*b* in quo)   ubi (*ad*)

xxiv. 13   ἀπέχουσαν   intervallo (*a* habentem *b* quod aberat *d* ITER HABENTIS)   spatio

14   ὡμίλουν   loquebantur (*a* tractabant)   FABULABANTUR (*bd*)

18   παροικεῖς   peregrinus es (*ab*) (*d* advena)   incola

20   οἱ ἀρχιερεῖς   summi sacerdotes (*a* pontifices)   principes sacerdotum (*bd*)

30   μετ' αὐτῶν   cum illis (*ab*) (*d* cum eis)   secum ἐπεδίδου   dedit (*d* dabat)   porrigebat (*ab*)

34   ὄντως   vere (*ad*) (*b* om.)   certe

43   λαβών   ACCIPIENS (*ad*)   sumens

49   ἐξ ὕψους   ex alto (*a* a summo *b* ab alto *d* de alto)   ex altis

51   ἀνεφέρετο   ferebat   ferebatur

CHAPTER VIII.

THIS Gospel should have been taken in the second place in dealing with a Western text, the Western order being Matthew, John, Luke, Mark; a fact which needs always to be kept in mind, since the order of the books has an influence upon the nature of the text. Any one who has worked in the collation of MSS. knows how often we find an early text in Mark following a conventional text in Matthew, and the reason is to be sought in the imperfect correction of copies. Scribes grow tired of making changes and correctors grow tired of making corrections before they reach the end of the volume of the Gospels, and hence it often happens that we have a different text at the end of the Gospels than at the beginning. Thus we may modify Jerome's saying, and maintain that the very order of the *books* is a sacred mystery! But this by the way: let us now take up some of the double renderings in the Gospel of John, as they have been preserved for us by the hand of the Scribes of the Sangallensis.

i. 1 λόγος   verbum (*ab* Iren.)   SERMO (Tert.)
   2 οὗτος   hoc (*ab* Iren.)   HIC (Tert.)
   6 αὐτῷ   cui (*ab*)   illi
   9 τὸ φῶς τὸ ἀληθινὸν ὅ   lux vera quae (*b* Tert.)   lumen verum quod (*a*)
   11 τὰ ἴδια   propria (*b* sua propria)   sua (*a*)
   14 λόγος   verbum (*ab* Tert.)   SERMO (Tert.)
   18 πώποτε   UNQUAM NISI (*ab* Iren.)   forte (?)
        Of this *nisi* Harvey notes in Iren. III. xi. 5 that it is "of no Scriptural authority"!
   23 εὐθύνατε   parate   dirigite (*ab*)
   29, 35 τῇ ἐπαύριον   altera die (*a*) (*b* postera die)   crastino
   37 αὐτοῦ   eum   illo (*a* illum)

38 μéνεισ   manes (*a*) (*b* manis)   habitas
40 των ακουσ´αντων   audientibus   qui audierant (*ab*)
48 Φιλιππον φωνησαι   Philippum vocantem   Philippus vocaret
     (*ab* Philippus vocarat)
50 ειπεν   dixit   ait
ii. 15 ποιησασ   faciens   cum fecisset (*ab* fecit)
16 αρατε   auferte   tollite (*ab*)
iii. 15 εισ αυτóν   in eum (*ab*)   ipsum
26 μετà σου   tecum (*abd*)   cum te
36 απειθων   incredulus (*a* INDICTO-OBAUDIENS   qui non credit
     (*bd* Tert. Iren.)

I think this is the only place where the forms *indicto-audiens*,
indicto-obaudiens have left a mark on the Latin Gospels : but the
words occur frequently in Irenaeus and in the Old Testament,
moreover we suspect a not uncommon *inobediens* to be derived
from the same source.

iv. 9 'Iουδαιοσ ων   Judaizans   cum sis Judaeus (*abd*)
25 ερχεται   venit (*bd*)   veniet (*a* venturus est)
37 λóγοσ   verbum (*abd*)   SERMO (Iren.)
40 ηρωτων   rogabant (*abd*)   interrogaverunt
47 ακουσασ   audiens   cum audisset (*abd*)
    ημελλεν   futurus erat (*a* erat moriturus)   incipiebat (*b*)
v. 4 πρωτοσ   prius (*ab* prior)   primus
14 γενηται   contingat (*ad*)   fiat (*b* Iren.)
35 φαινων   apparens (*a* inluminans)   lucens (*bd* Tert.)
38 λóγον   SERMONEM   verbum (*abd*)
vi. 22 τη επαυριον   crastina   altera die (*ab*)
    εστηκωσ   stabat (*ad* quae stabant *b* quae stabat)   stans
23 ευχαριστησαντοσ   gratias agente (*b* quem benedixerat)   grati-
    ficante
27 την απολλυμενην   quae perit (*abd*)   perientem
    την μενουσαν   quod permanet (*ad* quae manet *b* quae permanet)
    manentem
vii. 32 του οχλου γογγυζοντοσ   turbam murmurantem (*ad* turbas mur-
    murantes) (*b* populum mussitantem)   turba murmurante
35 'Eλληνων }
    Ελληνασ }   Graeci (*abd*)   gentes
37 τη εσχ´ατη ημερα   novissimo die (*bd*)   novissima... (*a*)
viii. 44 ψευδοσ   mendacium (*abd* Tert.)   falsum
ix. 8 γειτονεσ   vicini (*abd*)   parentes
    τυφλóσ (l. προσαιτησ)   caecus   mendicus (*abd*)
    προσαιτων   adpetens (?)   mendicabat (*abd*)
22 συνετεθειντο   conspiraverant (*a* constituerant *b* consiliati erant
    d cogitaverant)   consenserant
24 εκ δευτερου   ex secundo   rursu (*abd* iterum)
35 ευρων   inveniens   cum invenisset (*abd* invenit)
x. 2 θυρασ   ianuam (*ab*)   ostium (*d*)

  3 κατ' ὄνομα secundum nomen (d ad nomen) nominatim (ab)

 11 τίθησιν ponit (a Tert.) (tradet b) dat (d)

 13 μέλει pertinet (ab) curat (d cura est)

 16 ποίμνη ovile (abd grex) pastorale

 17 λάβω ACCIPIAM (d) sumam (ab)

 18 λαβεῖν ACCIPIENDI (d tollere) sumendi (ab)

 21 δαιμονιζομένου demoniaci demonium habentes (abd)

 25 εἶπον LOQUOR (b Tert.) dixi (a) (d dico)

 xi. 20 ὑπήντησεν occurrit (ab) OBVIAVIT (d obiavit)

  38 πάλιν iterum (d) rursum

  45 οἱ ἐλθόντες qui venerant (abd) VENIENTES

xii. 20 Ἕλληνες Graeci (abd) gentiles

xiii. 15 καθὼς sicut (ad) quemadmodum (b)

  The favourite African form seems to be QUOMODO, but from the recurrence of the pair of forms we may suspect a primitive pleonasm QUOMODO SICUT.

  26 βάψας τὸ ψωμίον intingens tinctum panem

  This is evidently a compound reading, made up from

       tinctum panem ⎫ dedero ⎫
         buccellam ⎭ porrexero⎭

  and   intingens panem ⎫ dedero ⎫
         buccellam⎭ porrexero⎭

  Observe a b intinctum panem
      d intincta buccellam.

  The reading is triply alternative according to the rendering of ψωμίον, of ἐπιδώσω which the St Gall text gives alternatively as
        didero porrexero (abd),
and according to the manner of translating the participial construction.

  The original rendering of ψωμίον clearly contained buccella, in fact the MS. has buccellam in vv. 27, 30, and in v. 30, while ad have panem, b has buccellam.

  Perhaps we may set the original rendering in the form INTINCTAM BUCCELLAM PANIS DEDERO.

  38 ἀπαρνήσῃ neges (b) (a abneges d negabis) negaveris

xiv. 2 πορεύομαι vado (b) abeo (ad eo)

xv. 13 ἀγάπην dilectionem (bd) karitatem (?) (a)

  14 ἐντέλλομαι praecipio (ab) mando (d)

  18 μεμίσηκεν odio habuit (b) odivit (d) (a odiit)

  19 ἐκ ex de (abd)

xvi. 8 ἐλθών VENIENS (d) cum venerit (ab)

  17 εἶπον dixerunt (abd) dicebant

  29 ἴδε vide ecce (abd)

xvii. 14 ἐμίσησεν odio habuit (b) odivit (ad odit)

  20 πιστευόντων CREDENTIBUS (b qui credunt) credituris (ad qui credituri sunt)

    23   τετελειωμένοι   consummati (*b* consummati in unum) (*d* PERFECTI
         CONSUMMATI)   perfecti definiti (*a* perfecti in unum)

xviii. 2   πολλάκις   MULTOTIES   frequenter (*ab*)

    3   σπεῖραν   cohortem (*ab*)   SPERAM
       ἐκεῖ   illuc (*b*)   ibi (*a*)
       λαμπάδων   lampadibus (*a*)   facibus (*b*)

    6   ὀπίσω   retro (*a*)   retrorsum (*b*)

   20   ὅπου   quo (*ab*)   ubi

   21   ἀκηκοότας   audientes   qui audierunt (*ab*)

xix. 12   ἐκ τούτου   ex inde (*b*)   ex hoc (*a*)

   13   λεγόμενον   qui dicitur (*b*) (qui appellatur *a*)   dictum

   41   οὐδείς   nemo   quisquam (*b*)

xx. 2   τρέχει   cucurrit (*ab*) (*d* currit)   festi[navit]
         The reading *festinavit* is peculiarly interesting : it does not
     belong here, but with the *cucurrit* of verse 4, where it represents a
     primitive rendering of προέδραμεν τάχειον, which is preserved in the
     Tatian Harmony (*festinavit et praecessit*).
       ἐφίλει   diligebat (*d*)   amabat (*b*)

   19   θυρῶν   ianuis (*abd* ostiis)   foribus

xxi. 10   ἐπιάσατε   cepistis (*ad*)   prendidistis ([*b*])

   12   μαθητῶν   discumbentium (*a* discipulis) (*b* discentium)   disci-
       pulorum
         The primitive reading was DISCENTIUM.

   15   ναί   etiam (*d*)   utique (*ab*)

   19   ποίῳ   qua ([*a*]*bd*)   quali

   21   ἰδών   cum vidisset (*b*)   videns (*ad*)

   23   ἐξῆλθεν   venit   exiit (*a*) (*bd* exivit)

We will conclude this chapter by an attempt to discover by means
of the Codex Sangallensis and associated copies how the primitive
translator rendered the particle ἄν when he found it in connection
with a verb in the indicative mood. We know that in spite of
occasional freedoms of speech and a few necessary paraphrases
the original rendering was slavishly, religiously literal; and it
appears that the old translation in the majority of cases attempted
an adverbial translation of ἄν, either by *forsitan* (a favourite word,
and usually, I think, in the spelling *forsitam*) or by *utique* which
may itself be sometimes a substitute for a primitive *forsitam*. The
reader will be interested in examining the following table, in
which the cases are collected, omitting a double reference where
ἄν occurs in two successive clauses, since it is hardly likely the
translator would give the word twice.

Matt.   xi. 21   πάλαι ἂν μετενόησαν   forsam *k*^corr

        23   ἔμεινεν ἄν   forte (*ab* δ vg)   utique (*d*)

	xii.	7	οὐκ ἂν κατεδικάσατε	
	xxiii.	30	οὐκ ἂν ἦμεθα κοινωνοί	
	xxiv.	22	οὐκ ἂν ἐσώθη	
	xxiv.	43	ἐγρηγόρησεν ἄν	utique (ab δ vg)
	xxv.	27	ἐκομισάμην ἄν	utique (d vg)
Mark	xiii.	20	οὐκ ἂν ἐσώθη	
Luke	vii.	39	ἐγίνωσκεν ἄν	(abd vg) utique
	x.	13	πάλαι ἂν μετενόησαν	fors (a)
	xii.	39	ἐγρηγόρησεν ἄν	(d δ vg) utique
	xvii.	6	ἐλέγετε ἄν	(bd) utique
	xix.	23	σὺν τόκῳ ἂν ἐπραξάμην	utique (b δ vg)
John	iv.	10	σὺ ἂν ᾔτησας forsitan (d vg) magis (b)	
			ἔδωκεν ἄν forsan (δ)	
	v.	46	ἐπιστεύετε ἄν (b δ vg) forsitan utique (δ)	
	viii.	19	ᾔδειτε ἄν utique (a) (δ vg) forsitan	
		39	ἐποιεῖτε ἄν forsitan (δ) (b) utique	
		42	ἠγαπᾶτε ἂν ἐμέ (bd δ vg) utique	
	ix.	41	οὐκ ἂν εἴχετε ἁμαρτίαν profecto	
	xi.	21	οὐκ ἂν ἐτεθνήκει	
		32	οὐκ ἂν ἀπέθανεν	
	xiv.	2	εἶπον ἄν (δ) forsitan	
		7	ἐγνώκειτε ἄν (δ vg) utique	
		28	ἐχάρητε ἄν (d vg δ) utique	
	xv.	19	κόσμος ἂν ἐφίλει (δ) utique	
	xviii.	36	ὑπηρέται ἂν ἠγωνίζοντο (δ vg [not am]) utique	

The persistent attempts to render the particle in question are evident from these instances. It is rarely found untranslated amongst our whole body of authorities, and these are evidently derived as to their rendering from a primitive form.

CHAPTER IX.

A FEW WORDS ON THE GLOSSES IN THE SANGALLENSIS AND ON THE COLOMETRY.

Now that we have discussed at length the double readings of the Sangallensis, we will add a few words about a series of occasional glosses which we find in the text and which throw some light on the manner of production and propagation of textual errors. At the first reading of the MSS. one naturally supposes that these are merely the expressions of the actual transcriber of the Codex who wishes to explain a hard word or construction to those who come after him. But the more we look into the matter the more sure we shall be that here too we have elements preserved from an earlier stage in the textual history. Our St Gall scribe is an ignorant person, as mechanical as most of his tribe in his own day and not likely to do much by the way of comment, when, as we can easily assure ourselves, the task of dividing his continuous Greek text into words was often too much for him. But let us take an example of the glosses in question.

In Mark ix. 23 the Greek text is in Cod. Δ

O ΔE · I̅C̅ · EIΠEN · AYTω · TO · EI · ΔYNH˙ ΠANTA....

which the scribe fits with Latin as follows,

—autē i̅h̅s̅ ait illi   si potes ·|· credere omnia etc.,

where the sign ·|· stands for *id est* or *scilicet*: apparently, then, we are to regard *credere* as a gloss of an explanatory nature: it is definitely excluded from the text by the sign that is placed before it.

Now was this the scribe's own doing? Let us turn to some of the old Latin texts and examine.

quid est si quid potes? si potes credere.

Here the original text in the preceding verse was clearly

si quid potes = εἴ τι δύνῃ,

but a marginal hand wrote an enquiry as to what this abrupt sentence might mean: and the question with the appropriate answer has found its way into the text. Nor are we surprised to find that Cod. *b* reads *si potes credere* and that Cod. *d* has the same and carries the added *credere* back into the Greek as πιστεῦσαι. In Codex *k* nothing of the kind has been added. We see then that the old Latin tradition started from a Greek text like that printed in Westcott and Hort's text, and ought not to be quoted in support of *credere*. Now turning back to the St Gall text, can we doubt that we have in its gloss a part of the very same as appears in Cod. *a*? It is extremely unlikely, at any rate, that we are here dealing with an emendation due merely to the scribes of the Sangallensis. We ought, then, to watch those places where the scribe introduces a reading with the explanatory sign ⊹, and to keep our senses alive to detect any traces of antiquity that may present themselves. For the organic unity of the Latin versions, as well as the primitive form from which they proceed, comes out strongly in just such enquiries as these.

Next let us turn to Luke iv. 13 where we have the text

ὁ διάβολος ἀπέστη ἀπ᾽ αὐτοῦ ἄχρι καιροῦ.

The passage is rendered very closely by the Latin, which gives, not as in the English Bible "for a season," but *usque ad tempus*, and then the question arises: what time is meant by the Evangelist? The answer is contained in a brief gloss which follows in the St Gall text

⊹ passionis.

The time meant is, then, the time of the Passion. We have not succeeded in finding any trace of this explanation in Latin Gospels. But it seems likely that traces of it may be found. Ephrem in his commentary on Tatian's Harmony appears at first sight to interpret differently, for we find him expounding as follows,

"Quod dixit: discessit ab eo ad aliquod tempus, donec scilicet se praeparat, ut per calumniam et invidiam Scribarum victoriam

Domini impediret. Sed sicut initio, ita et devictus est in fine, quia Dominus morte sua gloriosius de eo triumphavit."

But one is inclined to ask whether this *ad aliquod tempus* can really represent Tatian or Ephrem, and whether it does not stand for the same *usque ad tempus* as we find in the Old Latin and in the Vulgate: and if so, Ephrem's explanation is exactly like that of our glossator, for the time is clearly the time of the Passion, and the two stages of the temptation are marked off by the words "the beginning" and "the ending" in the sentence quoted from Ephrem.

In any case, the interpretation is an early one, and that being so, it is not *necessary* to regard the gloss in our text as being of late authorship.

In Luke v. 33 the MS. translates καὶ οἱ τῶν Φαρισαίων by et ⁝ discipuli Pharisaeorum. If we turn to Codex Bezae we shall find the gloss in the form of an actual reading in the Latin and from the Latin transferred to the Greek.

In Mark vii. 4 the Greek text ἀπ' ἀγόρας is rendered *a foro* ⁝ *redeuntes*. Let us turn to the Codex Bezae and we shall find that a very similar gloss has been added there, the Greek shewing the corresponding additional words ὅταν ἐλθῶσιν.

An interesting gloss will be found in Luke xxiv. 24 where the Greek καὶ ἀπῆλθάν τινες τῶν σὺν ἡμῖν ἐπὶ τὸ μνημεῖον is explained by a glossed translation of τινες .

quidam ⁝ petrus et iohannes.

Besides these exegetical glosses the MS. contains a number which belong merely to the transcriber or one of his followers; they are merely grammatical explanations of an elementary character; explanations of verb-forms, or distinctions between different words that might be confused by a tyro, e.g. Matt. ii. 11 πεσόντες is translated

procidentes ⁝ a cado

to explain the derivation of the verb *procido*. All of these points may be found noted by Rettig in his account of the MS.

There is one other direction in which I think the St Gall text deserves a further study: namely, the colometry: it was pointed out by Rettig that the Greek text was derived ultimately from a MS. written in short sentences or *cola*, and that the traces of such a subdivision were still apparent in the capital letters which form a conspicuous feature on the pages of the St Gall text. And Rettig acutely conjectured that there was some relation between these *cola* in the St Gall text and the line-division in Cod. Bezae, "Si operae praetium habueris, Cantabrigiensem evolvere Kiplingianum, consensum haud spernendum reperies. Caeterum haud constanter stichi ita per totum librum insigniti sunt."

The question opened up by Rettig is by no means an unimportant one: for many textual phenomena are explained by the circulation of such a conventional form of text as is here spoken of. Is the St Gall colometry, then, the same as we call elsewhere the great Western colometry? We are well prepared to believe it, in view of the strong Old Latin features of the text.

We have drawn attention in our study of Codex Bezae to this point; and have there suggested that the same colometry is to be traced in the punctuation of the Old Latin Cod. *k*, and in the red points of the Curetonian Syriac, which we take to have been made from a Western bilingual. By means of these four forms of colometric text, the Cod. Bezae, the Codex Bobbiensis, the Codex Sangallensis and the Cureton Syriac, we ought to be able to get some conclusive evidence as to whether a single colometry was evolved in the Western bilinguals of the second century.

As far as our examination of these texts goes, we have as yet found nothing seriously inconsistent with this belief in the existence of a common line-building. It is unfortunate that we have no evidence of the kind forthcoming with regard to the form of the two great North Italian Codices (*ab*): these were printed by Bianchini independently of the form in which they appear in the MSS.: nor do I think that any hint of a possible common colometry in these two MSS. has ever been given. If there had been any such signs, it would have been well to have preserved them, for the line-division is much more valuable critically in these early texts than in a late text like the St Gall MS.

It may seem to some that the examination of such a trifling point is almost beneath the dignity of a critic; but we have found reason to believe that there are certain textual omissions and certain interpretations which are immediately explained by the existence of a conventional line-divided text. And, although we are not in a position as yet to speak too positively on the matter, we strongly incline to believe that the colometric text was early, and was widely diffused.

In bringing our notes upon this interesting MS. to a conclusion, I desire to remind my readers that they do not constitute an exhaustive treatment of the text or of any subject connected therewith: I have never seen the MS. itself, and for this reason should be reluctant to speak positively upon any of its palaeographical details. But as the lithographed facsimiles published by Rettig in 1836 afford an admirable representation of the book, I am content, for once, to work on the textual history at second-hand, and to refer for further information to Rettig's own text and prolegomena, which are of permanent value.

Meanwhile my hope is that some suggestions which have been made in the previous pages with regard to the historical genesis of the Latin text of the Codex Sangallensis may be of use to those who are occupied with the Textual Criticism of the Old Latin Version (I refuse to say Versions) of the Gospels.

UNPUBLISHED INSCRIPTIONS OF ESARHADDON

BY

ROBERT W. ROGERS.

THE two inscriptions here published, for the first time, belong to a collection acquired for the Trustees of the British Museum by Dr E. A. Wallis Budge. The texts of Esarhaddon in that collection were kindly placed in my hands by him for study, and several of them I copied, these two being among that number.

These, and others still to follow, must be considered as preliminary to a full edition exhibiting the entire text gained from a comparison of various duplicate fragments already copied by me and from others which I expect to find in other collections.

The first here given is interesting as being partially a duplicate of the famous black stone published in I. R. 49, 50, while the second also repeats some of the phrases of that same text, but in a somewhat different style of writing. The others copied by me will throw some additional light upon that difficult text.

The work of deciphering was by no means easy, and for assistance in it I am greatly indebted to my good friends Dr Carl Bezold of the British Museum and Pater Strassmaier of London. In the translation I have profited by some kind hints from Dr W. Muss-Arnolt of the Johns Hopkins University, Baltimore, and later from Drs Bezold and Jensen.

BRITISH MUSEUM, LONDON,
August 17th, 1891.

BU. 88-5-12, 80.

TRANSLITERATION.

COLUMN I.

Ašur-aḫ-iddi-na

šar kiš-ša-ti

šar Aššur

šakkanak

5 Bâbilu

šar Šu-me-ri

u Akkadî,

ruba nû-a-du

pa-liḫ Nabû Marduk.

10 ul-la-nu-u-a

bêlu rabû Marduk

i-gu-ug,

î-ru-um-mà

...... E-sag-gil

BU. 88-5-12, 80.

TRANSLATION.

COLUMN I.

Esarhaddon

king of the world

king of Assyria

governor

5   of Babylon

king of Sumir

and Akkad,

exalted prince,

worshipper of Nebo and Merodach.

10 Before my day

the great lord Merodach

was angry.

I entered

...... E-sag-gil,

BU. 88-5-12, 80.

TRANSLITERATION.

Column II.

zu-ʾ-u-zu,

il-li-ku

ri-e-šu-tu

ina rêš šarru-ti-ia

5 ina maḫ-ri-e

palê-ia ša ina kussi

šarru-u-tu

ra-biš u-ši-bu

be-lu-ut mâtâti

10 u-mal-lu-u

ḳa-tu-u-a

lib-bi (*ilu*) bêlu rabu-u

Marduk

i-nu-uḫ-ma

BU. 88-5-12, 80.

TRANSLATION.

COLUMN II.

placed *

they had become

slaves (?).

At the beginning of my reign

5   in the first

year, when upon the throne

of royalty

I sat majestically,

with the dominion of countries

10 (he) filled

my hands,

the great lord

Merodach,

and was peaceful.

....

* See note at end.

BU. 88-5-12, 80.

TRANSLITERATION.

COLUMN VIII.

mu-sa-ru-u

si-ma-ti-ia

pa-si-su

e-piš-ti

5 (*ilu*) bêlu rabi-e

Marduk

ina nap-ḫar

ma-li-ki

lik-kil-me-šu-ma

10 šumi-šu zêri-šu

li-ḫal-liḳ-ma

BU. 88-5-12, 80.

TRANSLATION.

COLUMN VIII.

the tablet

(recording) my honors,

and destroys

my work,

5   may the great lord

Merodach

in the number *

of the kings

be angry at him

10   his name and seed

destroy

* *Lit.*, totality.

BU. 88-5-12, 101.

TRANSLITERATION.
Column II.

1 ....

....

u-šap-ši

uš-ta-bi-il

5   ka-bit-ti

lib-bi

ar-ḫu-uṣ-ma

ê-pi-šu

aḳ-bi

10   nišê mâtâti

ki-šit-ti

kâte-ia

u-pa-ḫi-ir-ma

(iṣ) al-lu

15   tup-šik-ku

u-ša-aš-ši-šu-nu-ti-ma

i-na

šamni ṭabi

diš-pu

20   ḫimeti

BU. 88-5-12, 101.

TRANSLATION.

COLUMN II.

I made up

5   my mind,

I made my heart

confident,

the execution of the work

I commanded

10   the people of the lands

the possession

of my hands [i.e. prisoners]

I assembled

chains

15   the badge of slavery

I caused them to wear.

With

good oil

honey

20   cream

BU. 88-5-12, 101.

TRANSLITERATION.

COLUMN I.

. . . .

ilâni-šu

ištâriti-šu

ip (b)-]ri-du-ma

5 . . . . ki-iṣ-]ṣi-šu-nu *

e-zi]-bu †-ma

e]-lu-u

ša]-ma-meš

niše] a-šib

10 kir]-bi-e-šu

a-n]a si-in-di

u] bir-ti

zu-'-]uz-zu

il]-li-ku

15 ri]-e-šu-ta

i]-na

rêš] šarru-ti-ia

i]-na

maḫ]-ri-i

---

* This line to be inserted in the autographed plate.
† Thus.

BU. 88-5-12, 101.

TRANSLATION.

COLUMN I.

....

the gods

and goddesses

.... (?)

5   their shrines

forsook,

they went

heavenward.

The people who dwelt

10   there

to bonds

and fetters

 · placed *

had become

15   slaves.

At

the beginning of my reign

in

the first

* See note at end.

NOTES.

BU. 88-5-12, 80.

This inscription is written upon soft friable clay, the height is five inches and the base one and three quarters inches. The angles of the base show plainly that it is the fragment of an octagonal prism. The autograph fac-simile aims to preserve in some measure the actual shape of the characters, but, as is well known to those who are familiar with the originals, no copy ever fully accomplishes that purpose.

Col. II., 1. Before *zu-'-u-zu* the words missing are of course *una si-in-di u bir-ti*. *Zu-'-u-zu* is from *za-'-a-zu*, not from *nazâzu* as might be suggested by the translation "placed." The original meaning seems to be " to divide," then to destine to some use or purpose.

2 and 3. *illiku ri-e-šu-tu*, had become slaves. *rêšu* = servant, chattel, from *râšu* to possess, like Greek κτῆμα from κτάομαι. Cf. Arnolt, *Hebraica*, July, 1891.

Col. VIII., 1. *musarû*. See Pognon: *Wadi Brissa*, 64 f. Heb. שׁוּר and שׁוּרָה, Arabic سُور; so Halévy, *ZK.* I. 268, 9.

3. *pa-si-su*. פסס to smash, to break. So Peiser, *Keilin-schriftliche Akten-Stücke*, 88 : 13.

BU. 88-5-12, 101.

This inscription is of hard baked clay dark brown in color, height three and three-eighths inches and the base two inches. The translation demands no comment.

CAMBRIDGE : PRINTED BY C. J. CLAY, M.A. AND SONS, AT THE UNIVERSITY PRESS.

88.5.12.80.

Column I.

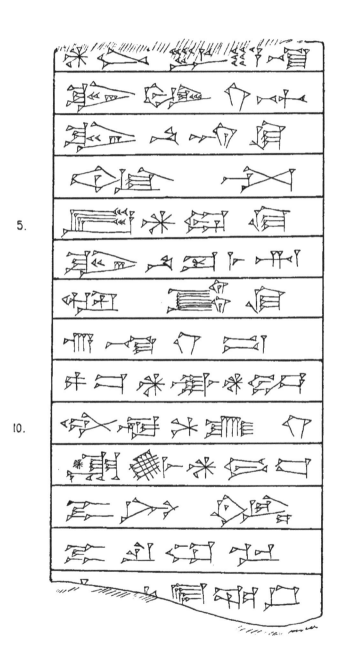

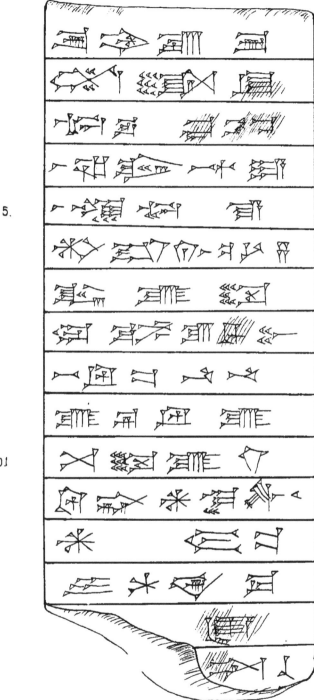

Column VIII.

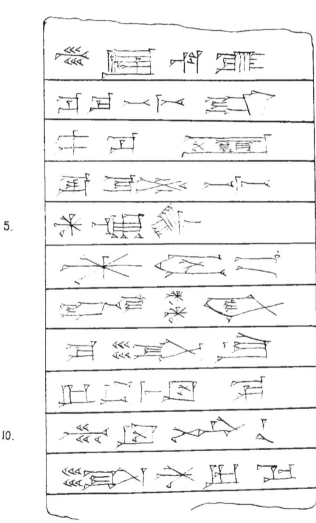

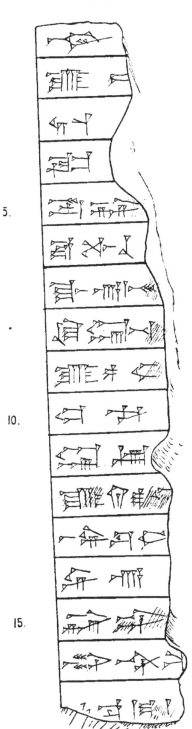

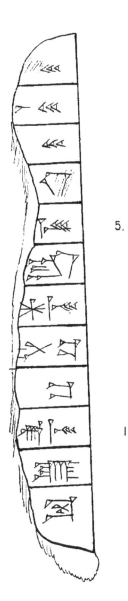

Column II.

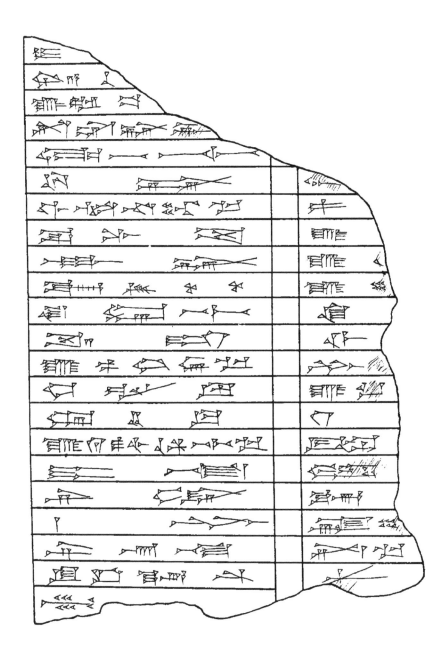

BU. 88. 5. 12.
101

Column I.

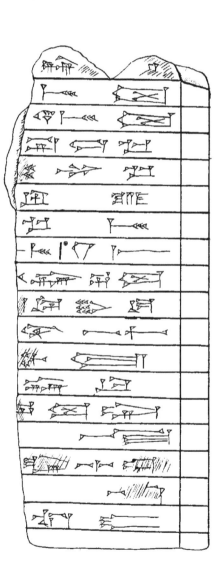

in / stroke

Haverford College Studies

Studies

Published by the Faculty of

HAVERFORD COLLEGE.

No. 10   Price $1.

CONTENTS.

To obtain copies of this publication address the Secretary of Haverford College, Haverford College P. O., Pa.

SOME INTERESTING SYRIAN AND PALESTINIAN INSCRIPTIONS

BY

J. RENDEL HARRIS.

ONE of the charms of Eastern travel consists in the constant appeal which is made to the historical conscience and archaeological instinct of the pilgrim. However carefully the countries visited may have been surveyed, their principal sites identified and their monuments copied and commented on, there is always something new to be seen amongst the remains of so long a sequence of centuries, and where so many and various populations have passed and repassed over the historical field of view. There are new inscriptions to be read, and old ones to be re-read with newer light and with greater accuracy: nor is the pleasure of the pursuit · diminished by the fact that here, as elsewhere, one has to be a "trusty money-changer" who knows how to tell good coins from bad, the fabricated antiques of the modern trader and stone-mason from the genuine legacies of ancient days.

During my Syrian rambles in the year 1888—1889 I made a point of copying such monuments as I could get access to, both those which were already in the hands of collectors, and those which were still lying amongst ancient ruins or built into modern walls. Many of these are well known and have been fully described in books of travel, in the Corpus Inscriptionum or in the supplementary Ephemeris Epigraphica which is so necessary an adjunct

to all these great collections; but there are one or two beautiful
inscriptions of which I have been able to make copies or pictures
which I cannot find in the works of reference; and even if it
should turn out that they have already been quoted, it will do no
harm to say a few words about them, and to indicate afresh their
historical value.

I. On a Sarcophagus at Bokfeya in the Lebanon.

In the modern house of the Emir of the village of Bokfeya in the
Lebanon, there may be seen built into the front of the dwelling
a portion of a beautiful carved sarcophagus. I visited the place
on October 24th, 1888. Upon enquiry I was told that the stone
had been brought from Byblos, apparently for the purpose of
decoration of the modern building: nor is there anything incon-
ceivable in the story, for the house has not been built many years,
and there was no special motive to be conceived for attributing
the monument to a false origin. But whether it came from
Byblos or not, it is now at Bokfeya, and is a lovely piece of
ancient carving, of a very early period. Our plates will shew
that we have not exaggerated either its age or its beauty[1].
Further, the carving is well preserved, except for the conventional
malady in Eastern monuments, where the Moslem hand has
defaced the representation of the human form[2]. In our sarcophagus there is a Greek inscription in the middle of the length,
flanked by two medallion portraits, viz. one of the person buried
(a lady) and the other of her husband. Both of these have been
hacked and chipped, so that the faces are hardly recognizable:
the inscription is however intact; and it is of the highest interest.
It runs as follows:

---

[1] From the Addenda to Boeckh, *Corp. Inscr. Gr.*, 4528 *e*, I see that this
inscription was originally extant "ad Libanum prope Botryn," which agrees very
closely with the account given me of its origin; and that it was published by
Matranga "ap. Diamillam, *Mem. Numism.* Fasc. ii., 1847, p. 55, n. 2," a work
to which I have no access.

[2] For the sake of archæological comparison we may refer to a somewhat
similar sarcophagus in the Museum of Roman Antiquities at Arles.

ΚΑCCΙΑ ΛΥCΙΑC
ΦΙΛΟΞΕΝΟΥ ΘΥΓΑ
ΤΗΡ Η ΚΑΙ ΚΛΑΥΔΙΑ
ΖΗCΑCΑ ΕΤΗ Μ̄Θ
CΩΦΡΩΝ ΚΑΙ ΦΙΛΑΝΔΡΟC

That is, it is the sarcophagus of a lady named Cassia Lysias, the daughter of Philoxenus; she is also called Claudia; she died at the age of forty-nine years; and her character is given in the words: "a discreet woman and one that loved her husband."

It seems reasonable then to assume that the two heads figured on the tomb are those of Cassia and her husband. He himself is not mentioned, unless it should turn out that his name is involved in hers. In the next place we are to notice the additional name that is given to her; for we are told, she is also called Claudia. This manner of expression ἡ καὶ Κλαύδια is common in inscriptions. Readers of patristic Greek will remember the similar instance in the opening words of the epistle of Ignatius to the Ephesians, and Dr Lightfoot's learned note thereon. This epistle begins with the words

$$\text{Ἰγνάτιος ὁ καὶ Θεοφόρος}$$

upon which Lightfoot remarks: "It has the character of a second name or surname, as the mode of introduction, ὁ καὶ Θεοφόρος, shows, comp. Acts xiii. 9 Σαῦλος, ὁ καὶ Παῦλος. This form of expression is extremely common in inscriptions; e.g. Boeckh *C. I.* 2836 Ἀριστοκλῆς ὁ καὶ Ζήνων, 2949 Μ. Αὐρ. Πετρώνιος Κέλσος ὁ καὶ Μένιππος, 3282 Καστρίκιος Ἀρτεμίδωρος ὁ καὶ ['Αμ]μιανός, 3309 Ἑρμείας ὁ καὶ Λίτορις, 3387 Φλαουΐα Τρύφαινα ἡ καὶ Ῥοδόπη, 3550 Μενέστρατον τὸν καὶ Τρύφωνα, 3675 Γάϊος ὁ καὶ Πίστος, 3737 Μάξιμα ἡ καὶ Ἡδονή, 4207 Ἑλένη ἡ καὶ Ἄφφιον and so frequently." It would be superfluous to add anything to this list of cases; the usage is clearly common in inscriptions; nor is it necessary to assume that the name is a late name added to the former. It may or may not be: but that is a point to be decided independently. In the present case, then, the name implies that a lady whose father bore a Greek name belonged to the Claudian family; she is therefore called Claudia; but her other name is Cassia. The first question that suggests itself is with reference to the conjunction of names, Claudia and Lysias;

was the lady related in any way to the Claudius Lysias mentioned
in the Acts of the Apostles as commandant of the garrison in
the castle of Antonia at the time when the mob at Jerusalem
attempted to kill Paul?

To the proposed question we may reply that there is nothing
resulting from the study of the sarcophagus to prevent us from
attributing it to a relative of the Claudius Lysias of the Acts:
for it is, as the artistic structure shews, of extreme antiquity.
But the Claudius Lysias in the Acts was the first, although, as
we shall shew, not the only one of that name. He had purchased
the Roman freedom and, as he confesses to Paul, paid no slight
sum for it. None of his family, then, had borne the name of
Claudius before him. The genuineness of the allusion to the
purchase of the Roman citizenship is borne out by the historical
allusions to the sale of the privilege, especially by freedmen and
others belonging to the gens Claudia who played the part of
broker to more distinguished people.

We infer then that there is a probability, and not necessarily
a slight one, that the Greek or Syrian who had bought himself
the rights of the gens Claudia and occupied an important military
position in the Roman army at Jerusalem, was an ancestor of the
very person who is commemorated on our sarcophagus.

That he was not a Jew may be seen from the fact that he was
willing to converse with St Paul, provided it was in Greek; and
that, when the mob tried to drown the voice of the Apostle
addressing them in Aramaic, Lysias proposed to apply torture
that he might find out why they so cried out upon him.

We can, however, get a little nearer to the determination of
the persons named on the tomb. For if we turn to the Corpus
Inscriptionum, we can find a votive inscription containing all three
names, Claudius, Philoxenus and Lysias in the compass of a single
family. The inscription is No. 435 in Boeckh's collection and
contains as follows:

Ἱερόφαντιν τῆς νεωτέρας Κλ. Φιλοξέναν, Τι. Κλαυδίου Πάτρωνος Μελιτέως θυγατέρα, ἀργυρώσασαν τὸν βωμὸν τῆς νεωτέρας
θεοῦ· ἐπιμεληθέντος τῆς ἀναθέσεως τοῦ υἱοῦ αὐτῆς Τι. Κλ.
Λυσιάδου Τι. Κλ. Πάτρωνος υἱοῦ Μελιτέως ἐπὶ ἱερείας Κλ.
Τιμοθέας.

This inscription was found at Eleusis, and shews us a family attached to the ritual of Demeter (= νεωτέρα θεός). The part of Demeter, in the Eleusinian worship of that goddess, was taken by some Roman lady of high position; and Boeckh follows Villoison in identifying the goddess of this inscription with Sabina, the wife of Hadrian[1].

Accordingly we have, for the early part of the second century, the following portion of the family tree, containing the same names as on the Syrian inscription.

Tib. *Claud.* Patronus Melitensis
|
Claud. *Philoxena* married Tib. Claud. Patronus
|
Tib. Claud. *Lysiades* Melitensis.

Note, in passing, the conjunction of the names Tiberius and Claudius, which is agreeable with the origin of the family from Claudius Lysias, whose real name must surely have been Tib. Claudius Lysias.

A generation or two later than the persons mentioned above, we find traces in an Eleusinian inscription (No. 397) of another stem of the family whom Boeckh connects as follows:

Tib. Claud. Lysiades Daduchus
|
Tib. Claud. Lysiades Daduchus
|
Tib. Claud. Sospis Daduchus
|
Claud. Demostratus
who married
Philiste the daughter of Praxagoras
|
Claud. Philippus Daduchus.

The sister of Tib. Claud. Sospis was Aelia Cephisodore, who married a certain sophist Julius Theodotus, whom M. Aurelius appointed to a professorship at Athens. This would seem to shew that we are here dealing with a later generation than those named above.

---

[1] "In Triopio Herodis Attici Ceres nova fuit Faustina ut videtur iunior; sed hic νεωτέρα sc. Δημήτηρ s. νεωτέρα θεὸς videtur Sabina Hadriani uxor esse, quae θεὰ Δημήτηρ dicitur in titulo Megarico n. 1073. Idem censet Villoison. De Julia Domna quae in Lampsaceno titulo νέα Δημήτηρ, ne cogites."

Now we have shewn good reason, from the coincidence in the names, for believing that the lady mentioned on the Syrian tomb is related to the family whom we find occupied as hierophants of Demeter in Attica at the beginning of the second century. Whether she is earlier or later than this, we have no means of determining.

Last of all, the tomb-inscription speaks of her virtues in laconic fulness: she has the title which, of all others, was most coveted by Greek married ladies. In the delightful picture which Xenophon, in his Economicus, draws of the first conversational amenities of a newly-married Greek pair, the lady confides to her husband that her mother had taught her that her business was to be σώφρων[1]. It is interesting to find that this untranslatable combination of domestic virtues was characteristic of the lady whose sarcophagus we have been studying; and, when we find that in addition she was devoted to her husband, we can only say that, since we have no definite clue to his name, we cannot do him wrong in calling him the Fortunate Anonymous.

II. On a Votive Inscription of the Tenth Legion at Jerusalem; with some notes on the Tenth Legion.

The next inscription to which I wish to draw attention, on account of its historical importance, is one which has certainly been described elsewhere, though I do not know where to put my hand upon it; and, in fact, much of the recent literature upon the subject is inaccessible to me. It will do no harm then to make a reference again to an inscription found within the past few years during excavations for building purposes at Jerusalem. Probably few travellers see it; although it is a conspicuous object enough: as one enters the City by the Jaffa gate, a few yards from the entrance stands what is known as the new Greek building, a kind of arcade with shops and a hotel. Right in the middle of this building stands a short pillar, which has been promoted to the dignity of a lamp-stand (to borrow a word from the Revised Version); and the reason for the conservation of the pillar, and

---

[1] Xen. Œc. vii. 14, ἐμὸν δ᾽ ἔφησεν ἡ μήτηρ ἔργον εἶναι σωφρονεῖν.

```
        M · IVNIO
        MAXIMO
        LEG AVGG
        LEG · X · FR            ANTONINIANA
        C DOM SERG
       · IVL HONORATVS
        STREIV
```

Such is my copy, and now for the description of it.

The inscription is in one hand except for the word Antoniniana which has been rudely scratched on the side of the first writing, something as we represent it in print, only more obliquely.

In the first place, then, we notice that this inscription is a votive inscription to a legate of the Tenth Legion, known also by the name of Fretensis (LEG . X . FR), and which in later days than those to which the inscription refers exchanged its name, as did so many other Roman legions, for another which should express more exactly their devotion to the Emperor Caracalla and the close relation in which they stood to him. We remember at once the important part which the tenth legion played in the siege of Jerusalem. They were brought from beyond the Euphrates[1] at the time of the commencement of the Jewish war[2], and we find that when Vespasian was sent into Syria to take the conduct of military affairs, he sent Titus his son to Alexandria[3] to fetch from thence the fifth and the tenth legions; and that Titus, using great expedition, brought these two legions to Ptolemais[4], where he met Vespasian and the fifteenth legion. So that the tenth legion must have been in winter quarters in Egypt in the winter of 66–67 A.D. The fifth and tenth legions, says Josephus in passing, were the most famous Roman regiments. Perhaps his judgment on this point was a little warped by the fact that in the early part of the war, while Vespasian was reducing Galilee[5] to order, and especially besieging the stronghold of Jotapata, Josephus

---

[1] According to Tacitus (*Ann.* ii. 57) the headquarters of the tenth legion in Augustus' time was at Cyrrhus on the Euphrates.

[2] *Bell. Jud.*, vii. 1. 3.   [3] *Ib.*, iii. 1. 1.

[4] *Ib.*, iii. 4. 2.   [5] *Ib.*, iii. 7—21, 22.

achieved some successes against these very legions. The commander of the tenth legion at this time was a certain Trajan[1], and
to him Vespasian committed the siege operations against the
fortress of Japho. When the Galilean campaign was now nearly
at an end, Vespasian, apparently in the belief that the country was
subdued, removed to Cesarea with two legions (the sixth and the
fifteenth) and placed the other two, viz. the fifth and tenth, across
the Jordan at Scythopolis[2], under the command of Titus. The
tenth legion, then, was at Scythopolis at midsummer of the year
67 A.D.

From this point the movement of the legions becomes a little
more difficult to follow. Vespasian, and a part of his army remove
to Northern Galilee, to visit Agrippa at Cesarea Philippi[3], as well
as to keep an open eye on the plans of the Galilean patriots. But
that a part of the army is still at Cesarea is seen by the fact that
a new revolt breaks out in Galilee, especially at Taricheae, and
Titus is despatched to Cesarea to bring up reinforcements. Three
legions are brought into camp on the shore of the lake of Galilee;
the tenth legion was one of them, for we find its commander
Trajan employed by Vespasian in negotiating the surrender of the
city of Tiberias. Shortly after this occurs the great naval battle
on the sea of Galilee, followed by the siege of Gamala and of the
remaining Galilean fortresses.

We are inclined to believe that the summer campaign in
Galilee cost the Romans much more labour than appears on the
surface. Titus was sent into Northern Syria to the legate
Mucianus, no doubt on business of important military exigency;
and we find the Roman army much dejected at having failed to
reduce the citadel of Gamala. When Titus returns he is indignant
at the losses the Roman army has met with[4]. However, Gamala
being reduced, and the season being regarded as now too advanced
for the campaign against Jerusalem (and this is another indication
of the weakened state of the Roman army), preparations are
made for going into winter-quarters, and the tenth legion is sent
to Scythopolis, while the other two return with Vespasian to
Cesarea.

In the beginning of the spring of A.D. 68, we find Vespasian
moving his forces about in Samaria and Judea, and after sundry

---

[1] *Bell. Jud.*, iii. 7. 31. [2] *Ib.*, iii. 9. 1.
[3] *Ib.* iii. 9. 7. [4] *Ib.*, iv. 1. 10.

raids over the country between Cesarea and Jerusalem we find the camp or head-quarters of the fifth legion at Emmaus: shortly after which we find Vespasian's forces in camp joined by the tenth legion[1] and their commander Trajan, who had come across the Jordan: the meeting-place was probably somewhere to the East of Nablous. But Josephus tells us that the day when Trajan's forces came into camp was the third day of the month Daesius, which means the Hebrew Sivan. It would seem that the Romans had been making haste slowly, not to have got further than this by the end of May. Nor did they do more at the first attempt upon Judea than throw garrisons into one or two strong positions, after which Vespasian returned to Cesarea, no doubt taking the greater part of his army with him. Here the military proceedings were stayed by news which arrived from Rome, of the death of Nero and subsequent unsettlement of the empire. After some watching of the course of events, it seemed as if Galba's star were in the ascendant, and Titus is despatched to Rome; it was now winter, and Titus returns soon after, without having accomplished his purpose, and bringing the news of the death of Galba. On the return of spring, A.D. 69, Vespasian seems to have resumed the work of reducing the Judean fortresses[2]; he leaves Cesarea on the fifth day of Daesius, and succeeds in reducing all the cities and strongholds except Jerusalem and the castles Masada, Machaerus, and the Herodium.

Returning again to Cesarea, he is declared Emperor by the soldiery, and the rest of the year is taken up with preliminary negotiations for securing the empire, and a part of the army is despatched to Rome under the generalship of Mucianus. A portion of the tenth legion took part in these movements, we may be sure; and it will be seen that the Roman military life had plenty of variety in it. The next thing we know is that Vespasian goes to Rome, by way of Beyrout and Alexandria, and that in the spring of the year A.D. 70 Titus returns from Alexandria with a part of the soldiery, and re-assembles his forces at Cesarea, in preparation for the final struggle with the Jews. Titus had with him the three legions which had formerly been under Vespasian's command[3], viz. the fifth, the tenth, and the fifteenth; to which was now added the twelfth legion, which had been in disgrace on

---

[1] *Bell. Jud.*, iv. 8. 1. [2] *Ib.*, iv. 9. 9.

[3] *Ib.*, v. 1. 6.

account of their flight under the leadership of Cestius Gallus at the very commencement of the war. The legions, however, had been depleted by the Italian expedition, and the thinned ranks were recruited by two thousand men whom Titus had brought with him from the Egyptian army.

The march upon Jerusalem was made from two directions; and I am inclined to believe, from the details in Josephus, that the legions in question were not all in winter quarters at Cesarea, as might at first sight be supposed; but that the depleted fifth was in camp at Emmaus, and the tenth at Scythopolis. The reason for this is that the troops are ordered to rendezvous at Scopus, the fifth legion going by way of Emmaus, and the tenth going by way of Jericho. Now, Emmaus was certainly the ancient camp of the fifth legion, and a force moving from Scythopolis would very naturally come up by way of Jericho. However that may be, it is clear that Titus planned the first camp for the twelfth and fifteenth legions on the ascent of Scopus[1] overlooking Jerusalem; so that these forces would come in by the great North-road: while the fifth legion was ordered to march by night, and a camp was pitched for them, three furlongs in the rear of the other two legions. The reason for this movement was that the forces at Emmaus might under cover of the night (and it is presumed that they were acquainted with the country), remove to the north of the city without giving any intimation of their plans to the besieged. The tenth legion, whose movements we are recording, were encamped on the Mount of Olives. If we may judge from a remark in Josephus[2], Trajan was no more their general, but in his place a certain Larcius Lepidus.

The story of the siege need not be repeated here, except in so far as it is possible to apply an archeological test to the singularly vivid pages in which the record of the doom of the city and the fall of the Holy House are recorded. I have no doubt that excavations at Scythopolis would disclose many traces of the sojourn of the tenth legion in that city; but I do not know that any such examinations have ever been made. With the Mount of Olives it is, however, quite different: here not infrequently are found the tiles of the old Roman camp, with the stamp of the legion LEG . X . FR and the figure of an animal (possibly a hog). A portion of one of these tiles is in my own possession; and there

---

[1] *Bell. Jud.*, v. 3. 2.   [2] *Ib.*, vi. 4. 3.

are a number of large ones in the new Greek convent which is just built on that part of the Mount of Olives which the ecclesiastical guides call by the name of the Viri Galilaei (or place where the men of Galilee stood gazing up into heaven). This Greek convent encloses in its boundary, without a doubt, a large part of the camp of the tenth legion. They occupied no other position until the fall of the city: the other legions were, by military advance, brought nearer and nearer to the north-west angle of the city. But no advance was possible on the eastern side, and no better position could have been found for a camp. It is true that in the first laying out of the camp, an unexpected sally on the part of the Jews almost led to the defeat of the famous legion, and to the capture of the Emperor himself, but after the camp was fully fortified no danger was to be apprehended, even from a desperate people, for the position is certainly a very strong one.

Now, passing over the well-known details of the siege, we find that when the city was taken, Titus left the tenth legion as a garrison amongst the ruins[1], instead of sending them again to their former station in the Euphrates valley (τῷ δεκάτῳ δὲ τάγματι τὴν τῶν Ἱεροσολύμων ἀπέστρεψε φυλακὴν, οὐκέτ᾽ αὐτοὺς ὑπὸ τὸν Εὐφράτην ἀποστείλας, ἔνθα πρότερον ἦσαν). The position of this new camp may be determined from the statements of Josephus, who says that Titus left a part of the west wall standing, that it might serve as a protection to the garrison; he also left the three great towers of Herod's fortification standing, which were known by the names of Hippicus, Phasael and Mariamne, probably for the use of the garrison, although Josephus suggests that it was with a view of impressing future ages with the strength of the city which he had conquered (πύργους μὲν ὅσοι τῶν ἄλλων ὑπερανεστήκεσαν καταλιπόντος, Φασάηλον, Ἱππικόν, Μαριάμνην, τεῖχος δὲ ὅσον ἦν ἐξ ἑσπέρας τὴν πόλιν περιέχον)[2].

It is just at this point that the recovered inscription comes in to verify Josephus' statement about the camp of the tenth legion inside the city: for the place where this inscription was found is just inside the west wall and under the very shadow of what is called the Tower of David, which in all probability is the ancient Hippicus.

The inscription, then, was written in honour of the Augustan

[1] *Bell. Jud.*, vii. 1. 3.   [2] *Ib.*, vii. 1. 1.

legate, Marcus Junius Maximus, presumably by the tenth legion, and in particular by his *strator* or equerry, Caius Domitius Sergius Julius Honoratus.

The military inscriptions will furnish plenty of parallel memorials; we will first give one from Mauretania (*C. I. L.* viii. 9370):

```
          C · OCTAVIO · PUDEN
         TI · CAESIO · HONORA
          TO · PROC · AVGGG
             A · CENSIBVS
         DEc · alaE · THRAC ·
           EX · strATORE ·
                EIVS
           PRAESIDI · IN
           NOCENTISSIMO
```

A similar one, and of some importance for the history of the tenth legion is *C. I. L.* 7050, at Constantine in Numidia. This is an inscription in honour of a former legate of the tenth legion inscribed by a primipilaris of the third legion (Cyrenaica) who records that he had been equerry to the legate in Arabia. The tenth legion would seem to have done military service in Arabia under the leadership of Pius Julius Geminius Marcianus. The inscription is as follows:

```
p · iVLIO · P · FIL · QVIR ·
geMINIO · MARCIANO
cos · SODALI · TITIO · PROCOS · PROVIN
ciaE · MACEDONIAE · LEG · AVGG · SV
per · VEXILLATIONES · IN · CAPPA
doCIA · LEG · AVG · LEG · X · GEMINAE
leg · PRO · PR · PROVINC · AFRICAE
praETORI · TRIB · PLEB · QVAESTORI
triBVNO · LATICLAVIO · LEG · X ·
frETENSIS · ET · LEG · IIII : SCY
thICAE · III · VIRO · KAPITALI
opTIMO · CONSTANTISSIMO
··· VRMIVS · FELIX · PRIMI
piLARIS · LEG · III · CYRENAICAE
stRATOR · IN · ARABIA · MAIORIS
teMPORIS · LEGATIONIS · EIVS
hON · CAVSA · D · D ·
```

Note that in this inscription the term LEG . AVGG . would seem to imply *legatus duorum Augustorum*: for there are two Greek inscriptions at Constantine (*C. I. L.* 7051, 7052) which were inscribed in honour of the same Marcianus by a grateful embassy sent from Adraa in Arabia Petraea, in memory of his benefactions to the people of that city: and in both of these inscriptions he is called

$$\pi\rho\epsilon\sigma\beta\epsilon\upsilon\tau\grave{\eta}\nu \; \Sigma\epsilon\beta\alpha\sigma\tau\hat{\omega}\nu.$$

It is possible then that a similar explanation may have to be made of the AVGG. in our Jerusalem inscription, and if so, the inscription would belong to the time of the Antonines. It would however be earlier than Caracalla, in whose reign the title Antoniniana began to be affected by the legions[1].

This title Antoniniana must be due to a later hand, of the first years of the third century, which added the word on the side of the inscription. This fondness for the name of Antonine in preference to the regular title of the legion is, as we have said, not confined to the legion Fretensis. We suspect that sometimes the soldiers went so far as to erase the early titles of their regiment, and add or leave only the term Antonine. A curious case of this will be seen amongst the famous Dog-River inscriptions, just north of Beyrout, where successive kings and emperors have left their records since the days of Rameses the Great and Esarhaddon. The inscription to which we refer is as follows, and the reader will see that in the last line but one all except the first word has been erased.

IMP · CAES · M · AVRELIVS

ANTONINVS · FIVS · FELIX · AVGVSTVS

PART · MAX · BRIT · MAX · GERM · MAXIMVS

PONTIFEX · MAXIMVS

MONTIBVS · INMINENTIBVS

LYCO · FLVMINI · CAESIS · VIAM · DELATAVIT

PER··

ANTONINIANAM · SVAM ·

---

[1] Marquardt, *Röm. Staatsverwaltung*, ii. 441.

"Was insbesondere den Kaisernamen betrifft, so scheint anfangs der Name Augusta und noch später die Beinamen Vespasiana, Trajana, und Commoda als ein Auszeichnung zugleich mit den Prädicaten *pia fidelis constans vindex aeterna felix victrix* Verliehen zu sein, allein die Flaviae, Ulpiae, Aeliae, führen diese Bezeichnung nach ihren Gründern, und von Caracalla an wird es Sitte, dass alle Legionen den Namen des regierenden Kaisers annahmen."

This is how the inscription stands in the Corpus (*C. I. L.* iii. 206);
and it relates to the cutting of a new road through the rocks that
overhang the river Lycus, (or as it is now called Nahr-el-Kelb or
Dog-River). This widening of the road was accomplished by
military aid under the orders of the Emperor Caracalla. No
doubt, then, we must fill in the blank space with the name of
some legion. My own efforts to read the erased letters of the
original inscription were not very successful. The editors of the
Corpus insert the name of the third legion: LEG . III . GALLICAM.
They base this upon the fact that the name of the third or
Gallican legion is found erased in an unaccountable way in an
inscription from Aradus, while the names of other legions mentioned on the inscription are not erased: amongst these other
names of legions stands that of the twin tenth legion. Possibly
there may be a reason for erasing the name: but it is very
doubtful. If it could be shewn that the tenth legion was in Syria
between the years 213—217 A.D. to which this Dog-River inscription is referred, I should not hesitate to read PER · LEG · X · FR ·
NVNC or simply LEG · X · FRETENSEM.

We do not know a great deal about the Roman regimental
histories; and, in particular, the history of the legion Fretensis is
often confused with that of the Gemino-Fretensis, or twin tenth
legion, whose province was upper Pannonia[1]. We do know, however, that the tenth legion continued to take part in military
operations in Judea after the fall of Jerusalem, and that they
were engaged in the capture of Machaerus and of Masada, the
last Jewish strongholds[2].

It does not seem likely that Larcius Lepidus, of whom
Josephus speaks as succeeding Trajan in command of the legion,
remained long in Judea; there is a fine inscription, discovered near
Antium, which contains a list of his military honours, set up to
his memory by his wife and daughter. I give it from Wilmanns[3].

From this inscription it will be seen that Larcius Lepidus was
promoted to the government of the combined provinces of Pontus
and Bithynia.

---

[1] Cf. Dion Cass. lv. 23, οἱ δέκατοι ἑκάτεροι, οἵ τε ἐν τῇ Παννονίᾳ τῇ ἄνω οἱ δίδυμοι
καὶ οἱ ἐν Ἰουδαίᾳ.

[2] *Bell. Jud.*, vii. 6. 1.

[3] No. 1146 = *C. I. L.* x. 6659. See also Renier, *Acad. des Inscriptions*, xxvi.
(1867), pp. 269—321.

a · larcio · a ·f· lepido
seviR · EQVIT · ROM · trib · mil · leg····X · VIR
stLITIB · IVDIC · QVAESt · pr · pR · PROVINCIAE
cRETAE · ET · CYRENARum · leg · IMP · VESPASIANI
cAESARIS · AVG · LEG · X · FRETENs · donato · DONIS · MILITARIBVS
·aB · IMP · VESPASIANO · CAESARe aug · et T · CAESARE · AVG · F ·
bELLO · IVDAICO · CORONA · MVRALI · VALLARI · AVREA · HASTIS · PVRIS
vEXILLIS · DVOBVS · TR · PL · PR · LEG · PROVINC · PONTI · ET · BITHYNIAE
cAECINIA · A · F · LARGA · VXOR · ET
laRCIA · A · F · PRISCILLA · FILIA · FECERVNT ·

This inscription seems to have been set up before the death of
Vespasian (who is styled *imperator* and not *divus,* while Titus is
not called *imperator*). So that it is probable that Larcius Lepidus
returned to Rome with Titus[1]. He was probably succeeded by
Terentius Rufus; for we find Rufus in command of the army at
Jerusalem after the departure of Titus, and the army now means
the tenth legion.

When Trajan made his expedition against Parthia, he took
this legion with him, as the following Roman inscription, given by
Gruter (p. ccclxvii) will shew.

D · M ·

A · ATINIO · A · F · PAL

PATERNO

SCRIB · AEDIL · CVR

HON · VSVS · AB · IMP

EQVO · PVBL · HONOR

FRAEF · COH · II̅ · BRACAR

AVGVSTAN · TRIB·· MIL

LEG · X̅ · FRETENS · A · DIVO

TRAIANO · IN · EXPEDITION

PARTHICA · DONIS · DONAT

PRAEF · ALAE · VII̅ · PHRYG · CVR

KAL · FABRATERNOR · NOVOR

ATINIA · A · F · FAVSTINA · PATRI

OPTIMO · FECIT

This monument was set up, then, by Atinia Faustina in honour
of her father Aulus Atinius Paternus who had been tribune of the

---

[1] *Bell. Jud.*, vii. 2. 2.

tenth legion in the Parthian war: and the inscription itself is
subsequent to the death of Trajan, as we see by the term *divus*.
Other inscriptions may be brought forward containing references
to the commanders of the legion Fretensis, but I strongly suspect
from the places where they are found that they belong to the
twin-legion in Pannonia, and not to the Fretensis, properly so-
called. There is however one inscription from Tibur to a legate
of the tenth legion who is said to have taken part in the military
movements against Judea in the Hadrianic war: this may furnish
another link in the fragmentary record of the history of the legion.
The inscription belongs to the reign of Antoninus Pius, and runs
as follows (Wilmanns, No. 1186):

C · POPILIO · C · F · QVIR · CARO
PEDONI · COS · VII · VIRO · EPVLON
SODALI · HADRIANALI · LEGATO
IMP · CAESARIS · ANTONINI · AVG
PII · PRO · PR · GERMANIAE · SVPER · ET · EX
ERCITVS · IN · EA · TENDENTIS
CVRATORI · VIAR · AVRELIAE · VETERIS · ET
NOVAE · CORNELIAE · ET · TRIVMPHALIS
LEGATO · LEGIONIS · X̄ · FRETENSIS
A · CVIVS · CVRA · SE · EXCVSAVIT · PRAETORI
TRIBVNO · PLEBIS · Q̄ · DIVI · HADRIANI · AVG
IN · OMNIBVS · HONORIBVS · CANDIDATO
IMPERATOR · TRIB · LATICLAVIO · LEG · III
CYRENEICAE · DONATO · DONIS MILI
TARIBVS · A · DIVO · HADRIANO · OB
IVDAICAM · EXPEDITIONEM · X̄ · VIRO
STLITIBVS · IVDICANDIS · PATRONO ·
MVNICIPI · CVRATORI · MAXIMI · EXEMPLI
SENATVS · P · Q · TIBVRS
OPTIME · DE · REPVBLICA · MERITO ·

We have not succeeded in finding any evidence in imperial
times of the presence of the tenth legion in the West, and it may
be presumed, until further evidence is forthcoming, that they were
an Oriental legion, whose head-quarters was at first on the
Euphrates, and afterwards at Scythopolis, and then Jerusalem or,
as it is now called, Aelia Capitolina; and that their military duties
were chiefly confined to the restraint of the Parthians and the

Arabians. Indeed I should have supposed that this Oriental character was the explanation of the mysterious name Fretensis, which I take to be a corruption of the word Euphratensis, and to have been applied to the legion on account of the province to which they were originally designated. The recently published Peregrinatio Silviae gives the name of the province as Augusto-fratensis ("et inde ingressa fines provinciae Augustofratensis, perveni ad civitatem Gerapolim[1]") which shews the name in composition in a form very like the current one.

III. On an inscription near Hebron.

In Robinson's Biblical Researches in the year 1838 will be found a good description of some important ruins which lie at a short distance north-east of Hebron, and are known to the Arabs as Ramet-el-Khalil or, which is nearly the same thing (el-Khalil being 'the Friend' i.e. Abraham), the place is called by the Jews the House of Abraham.

The following is Robinson's first account: (Vol. i. p. 215) "At one hour from Hebron a blind path went off to the right at right angles,.........and on it, about five minutes walk from our road, are the foundations of an immense building, which excited our curiosity. We ran thither on foot, leaving our beasts to proceed slowly; and found the substructures of an edifice, which would seem to have been commenced on a large scale, but never completed. They consist of two walls apparently of a large enclosure; one facing towards the south-west, two hundred feet long; and the other at right angles facing north-west one hundred and sixty feet long, with a space left in the middle of it as if for a portal. There are only two courses of hewn stones above ground, each three feet four inches high; one of the stones measured fifteen and a half feet long by three and one third feet thick. In the north-west angle is a well or cistern arched over, but not deep. There are no stones or ruins of any kind lying round to mark that these walls were ever carried higher. It is difficult to say, judging merely from the remains themselves, what could have been the object for which the building was intended. It may

---

[1] Gamurrini, *Peregrinatio S. Silv. Aquitanae*, p. 32.

have been a church: though it does not lie, like most ancient churches, in the direction from west to east.   Or it might possibly have been begun as a fortress : though there would seem to be nothing in the vicinity to guard.   At any rate these walls cannot have been constructed later than the first centuries after the Christian Era, and the size of the stones points rather to an earlier age.   The spot is called by the Arabs Ramet-el-Khalil.   The Jews of Hebron call it the House of Abraham, and regard this as the place of Abraham's tent and terebinth at Mamre.   May we not perhaps suppose that these massive walls are indeed the work of Jewish hands, erected here in ancient days around the spot where the founder of their race had dwelt?"

In a note Robinson suggests that, if this supposition be not admissible, the remains might perhaps be regarded as belonging to the church erected by Constantine, near the supposed place of Abraham's terebinth.

There can be little doubt that the latter supposition is far superior to the former, and we shall probably see reason to conclude that it is the right interpretation.   In 1852 Robinson visited the place again and speaks of it with much more confidence as the traditional site of Abraham's terebinth.   In Biblical Researches (iii. 279) he expresses himself to the following effect.

"Several items of ancient testimony go far to show that this spot, now called er-Râmet, is that which in the early centuries of the Christian Era was held, whether truly or falsely, to be the site of the terebinth of Mamre, near Hebron, where Abraham long ago pitched his tent.   The testimony of Eusebius and Jerome in the fourth century shows that the place was then pointed out near Hebron: while from that of Josephus, the Itinerarium Hierosolymitanum in the fourth century, Sozomen in the fifth, and Adamnanus in the seventh it is clear that it lay not far from Hebron towards Jerusalem.   The Itin. Hieros. and Sozomen agree in placing it *two* Roman miles from Hebron ; while Josephus says it was only *six* stadia distant from that city.   As the place during those centuries was well-known and frequented ; and as the specification of *two* miles agrees well with the actual distance from Hebron ; there can be little doubt that the notice of Josephus, though intended to refer to the same spot, is erroneous.

"Admitting then that this was the reputed place of Abraham's terebinth, we can account for the extensive vestiges of an ancient site. Eusebius relates, that the terebinth of Abraham, which was still standing in his day, had become an object of worship to Christians: as also to the Gentiles round about, who had set up here an idol and altars. To break up this idolatrous worship, the emperor Constantine gave orders to erect on the spot a Basilica or church; the oversight of which was entrusted to Eusebius himself. In the same connection it is likewise related that this had long been the seat of a celebrated mart or fair, whither the people of the country far and wide resorted to buy and sell: and that after the final overthrow of the Jews in the war with Adrian, A.D. 135, a great multitude of captives of every age and sex were here publicly sold as slaves. These facts show that not long after the time of Josephus, and for several subsequent centuries, this was a well-known and greatly frequented spot; and they are also sufficient to account for the existence here of a large town, the actual vestiges of which are still extant.

"In respect to the immense walls, which form the most imposing feature of the place, I find, as yet, no satisfactory explanation. They seem not to be Jewish; for they bear no resemblance to the walls of Jewish structures at Hebron or Jerusalem. If a church was actually erected here in accordance with the orders of Constantine; as indeed the testimony of later writers seems to imply; we should most naturally regard these as its foundation walls. Yet they exhibit none of the tokens of ecclesiastical architecture and do not of themselves suggest a church."

From Robinson's time to the present, nothing further seems to have been done in the investigation and identification of the ruins of Ramet el-Khalil. Baedeker's guide-book is entirely negative as to their origin: "what purpose the building served, and whether it was ever completed, cannot now be ascertained...The basilica which Constantine is said to have erected at Hebron cannot well have any connection with these ruins, as their style points to a much earlier period. About 50 yards to the East are the ruins of another building which is more likely to have been the basilica, and near it are two wine presses in the rock."

On August 1st, 1889 my friend Mr Hanauer, of the London Jews' Mission, was so fortunate as to detect some traces of an inscription amongst the remains of the great building at Ramet-el-Khalil. The sun was shining sideways upon the stones, and the following letters could easily be read:

ANE

On the next stone west of it, but at a higher level

ΔOMNA

ΔH ? O

and on another, a little further on, but built back in a sort of recess

EKN

It may seem rather presumptuous to draw conclusions from such scanty remains, but let us see what can fairly be deduced from them.

The inscription is Greek; this can be seen from the form of the letter Δ, followed by H, which last letter must clearly be vocalic. This immediately suggests that the first stone contains a part of the word ἀνέθηκεν. And the next stone suggests that the building and dedication are the work of Julia Domna.

Now the inscription in question does not seem to be an ordinary votive inscription *pro salute*, it is more like the record of a building, or the dedication of an altar. Now that Julia Domna and her two sons (Caracalla and Geta) travelled in the East, in Syria, Palestine and Egypt, may be regarded as certain. Consequently we suspect that the letters EKN are the remains of the sentence καὶ τὰ τέκνα αὐτῆς. The inscriptions do not usually present Julia Domna by herself, although there are a few cases of the kind; she is usually described as *mater Augustorum* and *mater Kastrorum*, μήτηρ τοῦ στρατοπέδου and the like: but in the present case I can find no trace amongst our few broken letters of either of these titles.

I think, however, we can determine something as to the time of Julia Domna's building by the following considerations; it is extremely likely that the ancient tourists (and they were in many ways as ardent travellers as people in our own day) followed much the same order of march as ourselves: and the presence of Julia Domna at Hebron is an indication that she was either going into Egypt from the North, or into the North from Egypt. Now we have significant traces of her presence in Northern Syria in the shape of religious buildings dedicated in honour of her visit.

We allude to the inscription over the great portico of the temple at Baalbek, recording that the brazen pillars had been dedicated in honour of the Emperor and his mother, and that the capitals of the pillars had been gilded. The inscription is (*C. I. L.* iii. 138) as follows:

M · DIIS · HELIVPOL · PRO · SALVT*e*
et · VICTORIIS · D · N · ANTONINI · PII · FEL · AVG · ET · IVLIAE · AVG ·
MATRIS · D · N · CAST·SENAT · PATR · AVR· ANTONINVS ·LONGINVS·
SPECVL · LEG · I ·
*an*TONINIANAE·CAPITA· COLVMNARVM· DVA · AEREA · AVRO · INLVMI-
NATA · SVA · PECVNIA · EX · VOTO · L · A · S ·

The inscription is not an easy one to read, being only reached by long ladders from below or by ropes from above; nor is it an easy one to explain at the first reading. But I think it must be clear that the dedication of these gilded columns must have had a motive, and it is difficult to see what the motive can have been except an imperial visit to Baalbek.

If we examine the inscription carefully, comparing with it the parallel terms which occur in other inscriptions such as *mater domini nostri et kastrorum et senatus et patriae* which occurs a number of times as a title of Julia Domna, we shall see the meaning of most of the imperial titles. The inscription then says that to the gods of Heliopolis for the safety and victories of our lord Antoninus Pius Felix Augustus and Julia Augusta the mother of our lord and of the camp, the senate and the fatherland, a certain Aurelius Antoninus Longinus who was attached to the first legion (which had taken the title of Antoniniana) dedicated the two brazen capitals of the columns which were gilded at his own expense. From this it is clear that the Emperor mentioned is not Antoninus Pius, as is sometimes stated in guide-books and itineraries but Antoninus the son of Severus, commonly known as Caracalla : and the date of the inscription must be later than the death of Severus. It will thus be seen that the decoration of the portico of the temple of Baalbek can be determined within a very few years, in the second decade of the third century: and it is to the same period that we propose to refer the inscription at Ramet el-Khalil. We will show later on another inscription which seems to belong to the same imperial journey through the Lebanon.

The next point we notice is that these inscribed stones at Ramet el-Khalil are not *in situ*. They have been displaced from their own building which was probably an altar or something of that kind, and now are rebuilt in another. Surely, then, we have here the key to what Eusebius means when he says that Constantine ordered a Christian church to be built at the site of the terebinth: this unfinished building must be the first attempt at replacing the idolatrous altars by orthodox structure.

But why was it never finished? That is a more difficult question. But if reference be made to my "Last Words of Baruch," abundant evidence will be found to show that there was a popular belief that no buildings could stand in the place where the great Theophany had occurred. It is not necessary to repeat the proofs of this, and it will be sufficient to suggest that perhaps popular clamour may have had something to do with the incompleteness of the building. At all events we have no reason to believe it ever was completed. The apparent antiquity of Constantine's attempted church is explained by the use made of materials from earlier buildings in the neighbourhood.

IV. On the Acropolis at Baalbek.

In the previous note we have alluded to the famous ruins at Baalbek, and have conjectured that a part of the decoration of the portico at the entrance to the buildings was a votive .work in honour of an actual visit paid to the great temples by the emperor Severus and his mother. How much more of the building is due to this period we will not undertake to say, but we are confident that a careful study would throw much light on this wonderful but perplexing, mass of ruins. Most travellers do not remain long enough at Baalbek to get their orientation; I was fortunate, however, to be snowed up there for a number of days, and so was able to study the architecture of the temples and Acropolis more carefully than I could otherwise have done.

For the assistance of other travellers I mention here a single point which will help them to understand the place: Baalbek is a true Acropolis, and the great central area, which is frequently called the fore-court of the larger of the two temples, is a place of assembly and of judgment. This may be proved in a very simple manner as follows: the northern wall of the great court consists of shell-shaped exedrae and a double row of niches separated by surmounting Corinthian pilasters. At the base of the wall the niches are divided by projecting stones, and these stones are either seats or mark the places of seats of the judges or councillors of Baalbek; for, underneath the niches and along the edges of the dividing stones the names of the persons entitled to sit in the separate places may actually be seen; in some cases they are worn quite away, in others the Greek letters can still be read by a keen eye. There are nine such stone seats in the total recess on the north wall, and two more in the wings of the recess. We are able to read on one stone

θρονοϲ ΔΝΔΔ...

and on an adjacent one

...νοϲ .. νεω...

both of which imply that these were the regular seats of officials. Further exploration ought to be made at Baalbek both above ground and below.

Some fragments of an inscription were brought me by the guardian of the ruins which were said to be from a small gateway at the side of the entrance of the lesser of the two great temples. The inscription had evidently been roughly removed from the lower courses of the temple wall. The fragments when put together did not furnish a complete inscription, but only the following :

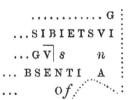

the italicised letters being doubtful.

There are inscriptions constantly turning up in the neighbourhood of Baalbek; at the entrance to the village from the south lie two stones, which are a part of the same Christian monument; for, on putting them together we have

✠ ει ω β ο αρχι
ΔιΔκ..ν...... ✠

which shews it to be the gravestone of Job the archdeacon. On a stone in a garden near the hotel are legible the letters

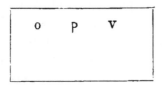

No doubt other inscriptions can be found in Baalbek, and some forged ones amongst the number.

V. A GROUP OF FUNERAL INSCRIPTIONS FROM SIDON.

The following inscriptions are from the collection of my friend Professor Porter of the American College at Beyrout.

(*a*)

ΔΙΟΔωΡΕΑΜΑ
ΡΑΝΤΟΥΧΡΗСΤΕ
ΚΑΙΕΠΙΠΟΘΟΥΜΕ
ΝΕΑωΡΕΧΑΙΡΕ

i.e. Διόδωρε Ἀμαράντου, χρηστὲ καὶ ἐπιποθούμενε, ἄωρε χαῖρε.
(Diodorus son of Amarantus, good and longed for, untimely, farewell!)

The connection of the adjectives is something like Philippians iv. 1, ἀγαπητοὶ καὶ ἐπιποθητοί.

(β)

ΑΡΤΕΜΙΔ
ωΡΟСΖΗ
СΑСΚΑΛω
СΕΤΗΝΕ

i.e. Ἀρτεμίδωρος ζήσας καλῶς ἔτη νε΄.
(Artemidorus, who lived well for 55 years.)

The lettering is peculiar; the μ in the first line is of the shape which occurs sometimes in early uncials and is called Coptic: while the η is very nearly the same as a modern h (the right-hand stroke not being carried above the middle of the line.

(γ)

ΝΕΙΚωΝ
ΧΡΗСΤΕΖΗ·
СΑСΕΤΗ
ΙΖ

i.e. Νείκων χρηστέ· ζήσας ἔτη ιζ΄.
(O good Nicon! who lived 17 years.)

(δ)
        ΓΗΡΟC
        ΤΡΑΤΕΕ
        ΟΔΟΜΟCΤΑ
        ΤΑΧΡΗCΤΕΧΑ[Ι
        ΡΕΖΗCΑC
        ΕΤΗΟ$\overline{\varsigma}$

Γηρόστρατε, ...στάτα, χρηστέ, χαῖρε. Ζήσας ἔτη οϛ΄.

(Gerostratus...farewell, good friend! who lived 76 years.)

The name Gerostratus is a famous one in Sidon, if we may judge from a splendid sarcophagus at the American Consulate at Beyrout, where a gymnasiarch of Sidon is commemorated, to which we will allude presently.

The official title of the present Gerostratus I am unable to read.

(ε)
        CΑΡΒΥ
        ΚΙCΧΡΗC
        CΤΕΖΗCΑ
        CΕΤΗΠ+

Σάρβυκις· χρηστέ· ζήσας ἔτη π...΄

(Sarbukis, good friend! who lived 80 years.)

(ϛ)
        ΦΛ.ΛΑΔΙ
        ΚΗΧΡΗC
        ΤΗΚΑΙ
        ΑΩΡΕ
        ΧΑΙΡΕ
        ΖΗCΑCΑ
        ....

Φλ(αουΐα) Λαδική· χρηστὴ καὶ ἄωρε· χαῖρε, ζήσασα...

(Flavia Ladike, good friend untimely taken! Farewell! She lived ... years.)

(ζ)
        ΦΙΛΙΠΠΕ
        ΧΡΗCΤΕΖ
        ΗCΑCΚΑΛ
        ΩCΕΤΗ
        ΜΑ

Φίλιππε χρηστέ, ζήσας καλῶς ἔτη .μα΄.

(Farewell! good Philip! he lived well for one and forty years)

In the last line the Μ has again the Coptic shape.

(η)   .ΔΟΖΕΤѠ

                        .ΥΤѠC

                        .ΝΕΤΟ

Probably ἔδοξε τῷ Θεῷ· οὕτως ἐγένετο.

(θ)   ...ΜΑΚΑΡΕΛΙC...

                        ...ΡΤΟΥ

?... μακάριε λίσσομαι ...

(ι)   ΗΣΤΗΛΗΚΕ...

         ΑΖΙΟΝΕΙΡѠΝΦ...

         ΤΗΝΧΡΗΣΤΗΝΚΔ...

         ΗΝΕC[ΤΕ]ΡΞΕΝΑΝ...

         ΚΑΙΤ[ΟΥ]ΤΕΝΚΑΤΕΓΡΑΨ...

         Σ...Β......ΗΧΑΙΡΟΙC...

(Ἡ στήλ...ἀξιονείρων...τὴν χρηστὴν...ἣν ἔστερξεν...καὶ τοῦτ'
ἐνκατέγραψε...χαίροις.)

Evidently from the ἣν ἔστερξεν, this inscription belongs to a
lady's tomb; and we may perhaps recognize in the last line σύμβιε
καλή, χαίροις.   Is the previous part of the inscription the remains
of verses ?

The next two inscriptions are of doubtful origin; we refer
them to Beyrout, for want of more accurate knowledge.

(ια) and (ιβ)   They consist of two long strips from the plinths
of some tomb; probably containing parts of the same inscription:
the first shews

         ...ΚΟΥΦΗ...

    ΛΥΠΑΙCΠΡΟΛΕΙΨΑCΙΛΑΡΕΚΑΙΔΑΙ...

    ΚΕΙCΕΤΙCΓΑΡΕΝΒΙѠ~ΜΑΘѠΝCΕΠΙΚΡѠ...

and the second

         ...CΟΙ............[C]ΤΕΡΗΘΕΙC

    ...ΟCΚΑΙΦΙΛΤΑΤΟC

Evidently a funeral inscription in verse.

VI. A GROUP OF INSCRIPTIONS IN THE GARDEN OF THE AMERICAN CONSULATE AT BEYROUT.

The following four inscriptions have certainly been published, but where? The finest is a magnificent sarcophagus from Sidon, of which we give a representation.

(*a*) It is the sarcophagus of Gerostratus, the gymnasiarch to which we alluded above: the inscription is very simple.

ΓΗΡΟϹΤΡΑΤΕ
ΓΥΜΝΑϹΙΑΡΧΕ
ΧΑΙΡΕ

(Farewell, gymnasiarch Gerostratus!)

The family of Gerostratus is famous in these parts. One of the name was king of Aradus, when Alexander made his invasion of the East in 333 B.C.; cf. Kenrick, *Phenicia*, p. 412 "Gerostratus was king of Aradus and the adjoining territory; the people sent his son to surrender the island to Alexander. The king himself was with the Persian fleet, but he deserted and came to Sidon in time to assist in the siege of Tyre." Perhaps we may trace in this account the origin of the Sidon family of Gerostrati.

(β) A square block surmounted by a carved lion; on one face of the block the inscription

D. ✠ M.
V I B I A E
A V R E L I A E
C O N I V G I
K A R I S S I M A E
A E L I V S   D I O S C V R V S
C O N S E C R A V I T

(i.e. Aelius Dioscurus dedicated this monument to his dearest wife
Vibia Aurelia.)

The monument probably belongs to Beyrout, as it would not be a very easy one to move[1].

---

[1] I see now that this inscription is given amongst the additamenta in *C. I. L.* iii. 6042. It is there stated that the stone was discovered at Beyrout in excavating for the foundations of Fachri Bey's house.

(γ) A portion of an inscribed altar, dedicated to the Sun.

....
Η Λ Ι Ο Υ
Β ω Μ Ο C

Some signs of the letters мо (?) in the line above ἡλίου and over the letters ηλ. Locality from which the inscription came unknown to me. Perhaps Baalbek ?

(δ)   Μ Ε Ρ Κ Ο Υ Ρ Ι [c]

               Υ Π Ε Ρ C ω Τ Η

               Ρ Ι Δ C Ν Ι Κ Η C

               Δ Ν Ε Θ Η Κ Ε Ν

               Δ Υ Τ Ο Κ Ρ Δ Τ Ο Ρ ω Ν

(i.e. Μερκούριος ὑπὲρ σωτηρίας [καὶ] νίκης ἀνέθηκεν αὐτοκρατόρων.)

A votive inscription for the safety and triumph of the Emperors by Mercurius. The inscription must be of the Antonine period. This seems to be the reverse of the previous inscription ; the altar being inscribed on two sides.

VII. FOUR INSCRIPTIONS FROM THE NEIGHBOURHOOD OF TYRE.

The next group of inscriptions consists of four which I obtained at Tyre. They are only small fragments and not much can be made of them.

(a) A fragment of a votive inscription.

...Ι Ο Σ...
...Υ Ρ Ι Ο Σ Ζ Ο...
...Δ Ι Π Δ Τ Ρ Ι Δ...
...Δ Ν Ε Θ Η Κ [Ε Ν...

(β)   ─────────

               Ι C Π Ο C...
               Ν Ο Ν Ν...
               Ο Υ Τ Ο C...

                    . . . Λ Ι ω Ν   . . .

                    . . . .

(a bar across the diphthongal sign, perhaps to represent the letters του)

(δ)   . . . .

                    . . . Δ Ο Υ Ι Ο Σ Σ Δ Λ . . .

                    . . . Ν Ι Δ Ν Ο Σ Ι Ο Υ Λ Ι . . .

                    . . . Λ Δ Ο Υ Ι Ο Σ Ε Κ . . .

                    . . . Ο Ι Σ Τ Ο Ε Φ Ο . . .

                    . . . C O S V I . . .

                    . . . V I R I S . . .

                    . . . E S D E . . .

                    . . . [s ι] . . .

                    . . . .

This inscription is bilingual; and although it is much muti-
lated some of the names can be made out; the first in the Greek
is Flavius Salvinianus, the next apparently is Julius Flavius.
This has a military appearance. But what they did, or dedicated
I am unable to determine.

VIII. On an inscription of Domitian.

Just below the village of Akoura in the Lebanon a road, which
has been artificially cut through the rocks in certain places,
diverges over the mountains towards Baalbek viâ Lake Yemouneh,
The ordinary road to Baalbek is over the ridge behind Akoura
and so by way of Besherreh and the Cedars and across the
Lebanon. But the divergent road of which we are speaking was
cut in early times, apparently with the view of obtaining a more
direct passage. The Corpus Inscriptionum (*C. I. L.* iii. 179)
gives from Renan a copy of an inscription which stands on the
face of the rock at the commencement of this road. It is as
follows:

           I M P D O M I T I A N I A' G . S . V . T

with the following explanatory note :

"In rupe prope Akuràm in loco q. d. Diradjet Mar Gervan (gradus s. Petri), ibi ubi aperit se via per rupes excisa Heliupolim versus: visusque est titulus Renano ad eam ipsam caesuram ratione pertinere."

Renan is perfectly right in saying that the inscription refers to the cutting of the road : for a careful examination in a good light will shew that there is a second line to the inscription ; viz.

$$\text{I V S S V} + + + \text{C V} + + + + +$$

where the lacunae may conjecturally be filled up so as to give the words "iussu et pecunia sua" (the last letter looks more like o than A). What is meant by the letters S . V . T, no one seems to know.

The reason why the place is known to-day by the name of S. Peter's stair, is that in the side of the mountain near the village is the cell of an ascetic named Peter, which cell is now rudely fitted with an altar and a wretched picture of the Virgin. It is really a very fine rock-tomb with deep-cut niches all round the cell for sarcophagi. Whether any monk of the name of Peter ever anticipated his dissolution by sleeping in one of these sarcophagi I leave an open question.

IX. On an inscription from the temple of Venus at Afka.

At Afka in the Lebanon may still be seen the remains of one of the most famous of the temples of the Adonis Tammuz cult: here, perhaps, even more than at Byblos was the place of weeping for Tammuz (of which Ezekiel speaks in language that implies that the popular Syrian Adonis worship had found a home even within the holy precincts of Jerusalem itself). There are few more lovely spots in the Lebanon than the site of this temple. From a deep cave in the hollow of the mountains comes a rushing stream, one of the sources of the Nahr Ibrahim. This stream when in flood detaches a stratum of purple earth from its banks, and colours its waters with it, thus giving rise to the story of the blood of the newly wounded Adonis. Close to the birthplace of the stream, in an eminent position is the temple of Venus-Apheca, whose ruins go back to the time of Constantine, and whose building must be dated many centuries before. This temple must have been one of the chief points of interest to the travellers of the first centuries of our era.

We are inclined to believe that this spot was visited by Julia Domna; the reader will remember that we attempted to find a motive for the gilding of the columns of the portico at Baalbek, by assuming an imperial visit to the great temples. But if we make such a hypothesis, the empress Julia Domna is hardly likely to have come into the Lebanon without visiting the temple at Afka, which was one of the most famous in Syria. The following inscription which is in the collection of Professor Porter at Beyrout, and which came from the temple referred to will throw some light on the question.

...[c] ωΤΗΡΙΑC...
...ΤωΝΕΥCΕΒΕ[?Υ]
...[ο?]Υ ΑΥΡΗΛΙΟC
[?εẓ]ωΔ+Η++ΠΟΛΕΙ

The inscription, especially in the last line is hard to read. But three things are clear: it is a votive inscription for the well-being of certain imperial personages (ὑπὲρ σωτηρίας = pro salute); that these persons are spoken of in the plural; and that the person to whom the inscription is due is named Aurelius. Now it is evident that this is very like the Baalbek inscription in all three points; and taking into account that Afka is the next point of interest to Baalbek for a traveller in these parts (unless we choose to go round by the Cedars), it does not seem unreasonable to infer that the Aurelius of the Afka inscription is the same as the one who gilded the columns at Baalbek.

In that case we can hardly avoid the conclusion that Aurelius of the first legion was not on military duty, in the strictest sense of the word, but that he was sight-seeing with an imperial party.

X. The inscription of Siloam[1].

The famous inscription of Siloam is known to all archæologists as one of the most precious monuments of the early history of our race; and its indisputable evidence has thrown much light on the state of civilization in the earliest times of the Jewish monarchy, on the development of the Jewish literature, and on the genesis of the Western alphabets from their common Semitic ancestral form.

When we say that all archæologists know the worth of the Siloam stone, perhaps we might go on to say that by the workings of a kindly Providence we are all of us becoming archæologists, especially in Oriental matters; for the right understanding of the Hebrew Scriptures, and the right estimation of the Jewish literature and ethics, are more and more seen to depend upon that revived sense of the life of past ages which comes to us more keenly in the study of archæology than by any other means. It may be assumed, then, that any new information, with regard to this important monument will be welcome, even though it should seem to be of the nature of a tragedy.

Up to the present time, the story of the Siloam stone has been rather of the nature of a romance; it often happens so in archæological work, and perhaps this makes the study so much more attractive to ordinary minds than that of philology. The romance of the search after a lost root or a lost linguistic form is nothing compared to the excitement provoked by the discovery of an inscribed stone from a vanished temple, or a piece of the wall of an ancient city. Imagine, for example, the emotion of M. Clermont Ganneau when he saw protruding from the ground the stone inscribed with Greek letters, which had once formed a part of the fence between the Court of the Gentiles and the Court of the Israelites in the Jewish temple. Or take the case of Mr Wood, the explorer of Ephesus, when he found the first tokens of that great temple of Artemis, which had been so long sunk deep below the surface of the marshy soil on which the first builders had placed it, that it might enjoy immunity from the shock of earthquake. No less interesting than these, nor less valuable from a

---

[1] Reprinted from the *Sunday School Times* (Philadelphia) Dec. 6, 1890.

scientific point of view, was the accidental discovery of the famous Siloam inscription, by the boys in Jerusalem, who wandered from the pool of Siloam into the southern end of the ancient tunnel that connects the pool with the Fountain of the Virgin in the Kedron Valley, and detected the incised letters upon the side of the tunnel not far from its entrance.

This was ten years ago. In February of 1881, Professor Sayce made his copy of the inscription by candle-light, and a paper squeeze of the inscription was taken, as well as a plaster cast. Finally, the inscription was treated with hydrochloric acid by Professor Guthe in order to dissolve out the lime which had settled in the deeply incised letters (an unfortunate proceeding, according to my judgment). Copies of the plaster cast of the inscription have found their way into the West; and the original mould from which they were made is in my possession (the artist who made it, caught a fever from working in the foul air of the tunnel). So that we can say that we are very well placed for a knowledge of the inscription, and may console ourselves over that fact, for now we come to the tragic part of the story,—the inscription itself has disappeared !

In order to explain more fully about this piece of vandalism, let me now communicate some bits of information which are not generally known.

For some time past there have been rumors in Jerusalem of the discovery of a new Hebrew inscription. As far back as the month of August, copies of it were in circulation, something to the following effect :

נעשית זה המרזיב על פי אמירת

תשעים ופעלים תשעים והוצאה

תשעים תזכור תמצא לפניך תשעים

ואחריך תשעים קח ותקם אותו

לנהר והתחיל המעשה מן הר קרחא

מפעולתך עד מקום שיומר ותזקור

שלוח

Now the meaning of this transcript is evidently as follows:

" This channel (or drain) was made at the command of ninety, and laborers ninety, and the outlay ninety : remember thou wilt find before thee ninety, and behind thee ninety: take it, and thou shalt raise it to a river, and the work is strengthened[1] from Mount Qarḥa from thy work to the place which men will call, and thou shalt remember it, Shiloah."

Now this inscription evidently has reference to the tunnel of Siloam. Further, it is a forgery. The author of it has fortified himself for the work by a study of the famous Moabite Stone, in which he found a word which has never yet been satisfactorily explained; namely, the word "Qarḥa." We find Mesha, king of Moab, recording that there was no cistern in the wall in Qarḥa; but no one seems exactly to know what "Qarḥa" means,—whether it was a place or a citadel, or something different from either. Accordingly the author of this inscription of which I have given the rough transcript, will have the doubtful word to represent a mountain connected with the Siloam tunnel in some mysterious manner, perhaps because of the mention of a cistern in Qarḥa.

The reports which were current in Jerusalem showed that the Moabite Stone had something to do with the "find"; for it was reported that the stone was a new Moabite Stone in the possession of a certain wealthy Greek. It may be doubted, however, whether the wealthy Greek wished the Moabite Stone to be mentioned in the matter. His object was something quite different. It is suggestive enough from the transcript that we have here an attempt to complete the Siloam inscription, which is known to be imperfect and illegible at the end, the concluding sentence being generally given as follows:

"And the waters flowed from the channel into the pool for a distance of one thousand cubits, and [a part of] a cubit was the height of the rock," etc.

Now, it would seem that the forger of the new stone, seeing that the tunnel inscription had ended incompletely with numerical details of the work, was disposed to fill up the lacuna with statements about the number of men employed, and other similar matter; all of which is very clever, but absolutely useless unless the actual Siloam inscription were removed from its place, so that no tests for the newly read letters might be employed. A horrible suspicion of vandalism thus rises in the mind. But we are moving too fast; let us return to sober history.

The reports current in Jerusalem said that the stone was in the ancient Phenician character. This was what might have been

---

[1] Or does he mean "the beginning of the work"?

expected. Phenician alphabets are a specialty amongst the forgers of inscriptions in Syria (only they make mistakes sometimes; I myself was offered some Phenician inscriptions by the youth of Sidon, in which the artist had mingled early forms of the Greek alphabet, evidently from some Western hand-book, in which the two languages were compared as to their early alphabetic forms).

To bring the matter to a point, a correspondent of mine succeeded, on the 18th of last October, in getting an introduction to the wealthy Greek of whom report had been speaking, and an invitation to examine the newly discovered stones. Accordingly, he paid a visit, and, by good luck, the Greek was away from home, and his wife was well pleased to show the inscriptions.

First and foremost (*horresco referens*), there was lifted on the table an ancient stone with Phenician characters, which a glance showed to be nothing more or less than the great inscription of Siloam. Next came the Phenician inscription of which we gave a copy above. An examination of this stone showed it to be a forgery. Where the copy has a Hebrew *p*, the stone had ·a *b*. The Arabs cannot pronounce a *p*; with them *Tripolis* becomes *Tarabulus*; and a steamboat (*vapore*) is *baboor*.

It was clear, then, that the stone was a forgery of some Arabic-speaking person, and was meant as a pendant to the Siloam inscription. My correspondent tells me he returned to Jerusalem, and lost no time in making the necessary visit to the tunnel of Siloam. Every evil suspicion was verified; the inscription had indeed been removed. As my correspondent was coming away from the examination of the tunnel, he met Fra Lièvin, the famous Franciscan archæologist, the authority of authorities on all Jerusalem antiquities. To him he communicated the discovery; and the reply which he received was "Mais c'est un vandalisme!" a sentiment in which I think I may assume that all scholars will join.

PARALLAX OF LALANDE 1196 = SOUTH 503,

BY

F. P. LEAVENWORTH.

A SERIES of measures has been made at this observatory on the double star S 503 in the hope that an appreciable relative parallax could be found. This star was selected because it was an optically double star with a large proper motion (about $0''\!\cdot\!65$), and because the distance between the components was very small (about $3''\!\cdot\!5$), and therefore permitted extreme accuracy of measurement.

Several faint companions at greater distances from the principal star can also be used as comparison stars, and it is our purpose to make use of them at some future time. On account of the small distance it was thought unnecessary to take into account the effect of change of temperature on the micrometer screw. This was more especially unnecessary as the parallactic displacement was almost entirely in position angle; and the measures of distance were used only in converting the measures of angle into arc.

METHOD OF OBSERVATION. The first observations were made with the head erect; but as the work progressed, large discrepancies appeared in the measures of position angle. For the purpose of determining their cause, if possible, the method of observation was changed. From October 17, 1888 until the end of the series each complete set of measures was made as follows:

1st. The zero of the position circle was determined.

2nd. Three measures of position angle were made with the eyes. First, normal; i.e. line through the eyes at right angles to line through the stars. Secondly, parallel; i.e. line through the eyes parallel to line through the stars. Thirdly, horizontal; i.e. line through the eyes parallel to the horizon.

3rd. The position circle was rotated through 180° and the observations repeated in the reverse order, so that the mean of the times of observation in each position of the eyes should be the same.

4th. The zero of the position circle was again determined.

5th. The distance was measured.

The sidereal time at which each measure was made was also recorded. In all cases a magnifying power of 375 was used with a bright field illumination.

PERSONAL EQUATION. It soon became evident that the discrepancies in position angle were due to personal error. By plotting on paper the observations corrected for proper motion, and drawing a smooth curve through them, it was found that the curves could be approximately represented by the equations

$$p_N = p_1 + a \sin^2 \tfrac{1}{2} q,$$

$$p_P = p_2 + b \sin^2 \tfrac{1}{2} (q + n),$$

$$p_H = p_3 + c \left(\frac{q^\circ}{90^\circ}\right)^3,$$

where p_N, p_P, p_H is the position angle obtained with eyes normal, parallel, and horizontal; q is the angle with the vertical; and a, b, c, and n are constants.

The position of the star for 1889·5 is

$$a = 5^h\ 49^m\ 45^s : \delta = +13^\circ\ 55'\ 37''$$

and the magnitudes 7·0 and 8·7.

The following are all the observations made with the exception of two normal observations which were accidentally omitted. In the column headed Position Angle, N, P, H mean that the observations were made with eyes respectively normal, parallel and horizontal.

No.	Date	Sid. Time	Position Angle			Dist.	Wt.
			N	P	H		
	1888	h. m.	°	°	°	''	
1	Sept. 13	2 38	...	...	14·30	3·155	2
2	14	3 8	...	...	13·06	3·125	4
3	26	4 55	...	...	9·00	3·198	3
4	28	3 2	...	...	13·48	3·116	2
5	28	4 29	...	...	12·10	...	2
6	Oct. 3	3 1	...	...	12·95	3·091	2
7	9	2 50	...	...	13·45	3·087	2
8	14	4 10	...	...	12·40	3·119	2
9	14	5 4	...	...	8·00	...	2
10	17	2 44	9·00	...	13·20	3·130	2
11	17	3 2	...	13·00	...	...	2
12	17	4 23	...	12·60	10·80	3·106	2

No.	Date	Sid. Time		Position Angle			Dist.	Wt.
				N	P	H		
	1888	h.	m.	°	°	°	"	
13	Oct. 21	3	42	9·20	11·80	11·20	3·077	2
14	24	7	5	9·45	9·80	...	3·140	2
15	28	5	45	8·20	11·80	7·80	3·190	2
16	30	4	4	8·85	11·20	9·00	3·172	5
17	Nov. 12	4	1	8·95	10·90	9·50	3·175	5
18	13	5	1	...	10·35	8·05	3·17	3
19	20	4	8	8·90	11·00	9·00	3·150	4
20	20	8	1	9·10	8·50	8·50	3·190	4
21	Dec. 15	3	20	8·8	9·00	...	3·20	1
22	19	3	39	...	8·70	...	3·224	4
23	19	4	30	8·50	...	...	...	4
24	19	5	23	...	8·90	...	...	4
25	20	1	47	8·10	11·70	...	3·220	2
26	20	8	13	7·20	7·60	...	3·267	2
27	24	2	20	8·31	10·60	...	3·254	2
28	24	3	25	...	9·70	...	3·302	2
29	28	2	38	8·00	9·26	...	3·241	4
30	28	5	16	7·34	9·17	...	3·271	4
	1889							
31	Jan. 18	4	10	7·70	9·10	8·60	3·350	2
32	22	3	35	7·70	10·05	9·40	3·237	4
33	22	8	55	7·40	8·20	5·90	3·326	4
34	Feb. 1	4	40	7·65	...	...	...	1
35	2	5	58	6·44	...	...	3·272	3
36	2	8	58	6·40	7·60	...	3·296	3
37	8	4	18	6·97	8·40	...	...	1
38	12	5	18	6·20	8·40	...	3·203	2
39	14	4	50	6·07	8·83	...	3·189	2
40	15	4	38	5·76	7·62	...	3·226	4
41	20	5	4	6·28	7·75	...	3·163	4
42	20	10	14	5·80	6·56	...	...	2
43	25	5	39	5·97	7·27	...	3·233	4
44	25	9	38	5·90	6·75	...	...	2
45	Mar. 7	7	9	5·84	6·79	...	3·255	2
46	11	7	18	5·56	6·12	...	3·289	3
47	12	9	12	5·55	5·99	...	3·293	4
48	26	7	52	5·70	6·06	...	3·314	4
49	Apr. 18	10	22	5·37	5·63	...	3·406	1
50	22	9	26	5·71	5·64	...	3·384	2
51	Sept. 21	3	48	2·73	3·68	3·90	3·71	1
52	23	2	42	2·74	4·91	3·72	3·462	2
53	Oct. 2	3	32	2·14	4·70	4·10	3·491	3
54	3	3	16	1·87	3·72	3·65	3·54	2
55	4	3	55	1·23	5·07	3·80	3·545	2
56	8	4	42	1·80	...	...	...	2
57	10	3	0	1·58	3·89	2·85	3·415	3
58	17	7	4	0·96	0·99	359·96	3·566	3
59	Nov. 3	6	15	1·13	1·52	0·99	3·636	3
60	15	3	1	0·50	2·74	2·95	3·570	3
61	25	5	7	0·53	2·71	0·49	3·649	2
62	25	8	50	1·30	1·10	357·92	3·725	2

No.	Date	Sid. Time		Position Angle			Dist.	Wt.
		h.	m.	N	P	H		
	1889			°	°	°	″	
63	Nov. 30	4	55	0·44	3·09	1·46	3·546	2
64	30	9	6	0·70	1·34	358·65	...	2
65	Dec. 21	2	58	0·87	2·79	1·83	3·604	3
66	21	7	38	1·19	1·31	359·13	...	3
67	22	5	34	0·55	1·42	0·83	3·644	2
	1890							
68	Jan. 12	7	7	359·88	1·13	359·40	3·711	2
69	24	5	20	0·04	0·45	359·93	3·649	2
70	24	8	27	0·20	359·80	358·35	...	2
71	28	6	41	359·03	0·08	...	...	3
72	Feb. 6	7	33	359·59	359·68	359·20	...	2
73	10	9	58	359·80	...	...	...	1
74	12	4	49	0·25	0·54	...	...	2
75	12	7	52	0·05	0·87	358·96	...	2
76	13	4	45	359·36	359·88	1·16	3·708	2
77	15	6	7	359·58	0·65	0·14	...	2
78	Mar. 18	7	46	0·04	0·24	358·70	3·772	2
79	29	8	9	359·94	359·94	358·13	3·829	2
80	29	10	12	359·81	358·70	355·09	...	2
81	Apr. 1	8	8	358·70	359·71	356·47	...	2
82	1	10	44	...	...	355·05	...	2
83	2	8	20	359·20	359·46	356·19	3·772	2
84	4	9	6	358·69	359·48	355·18	...	3
85	5	8	33	359·46	359·74	355·65	3·722	2
86	11	10	25	...	...	355·90	...	2
87	12	9	7	358·27	358·89	356·49	3·779	3

These observations were corrected for proper motion, precession and refraction. Nutation and aberration were neglected, as in no case could they amount to $0''·001$. From all the micrometrical observations, with the exception of South's measure in 1825, the yearly proper motion was computed to be

$$\Delta a = + 0''·438 ; \quad \Delta \delta = - 0''·490.$$

From these values was made the following table which gives the reduction for proper motion and precession of the position angles to 1889·5.

Year	Δp	Year	Δp
1888·6	$-7°·563$	1889·5	$0°·000$
8·7	6·630	9·6	+0·734
8·8	5·722	9·7	1·448
8·9	4·838	9·8	2·142
9·0	3·977	9·9	2·819
9·1	3·138	90·0	3·478
9·2	2·322	0·1	4·120
9·3	1·527	0·2	4·745
9·4	$-0·753$	0·3	$+5·354$

The correction for refraction was computed according to the formula found in the Dunsink Observations, Part I, page 15, except that they were put in the more convenient form

$$dp = - \kappa \, \text{tang}^2 \, \zeta \cos p \sin (p - 2\eta),$$

where ζ denotes the zenith distance of the star; η, the parallactic angle; and κ is taken from a table of refraction.

These corrections with the position angles reduced to 1889·5 will be found below.

No.	Date	Angle with Vertical	Proper motion to 1889·5	Refraction	Position Angle, 1889·5 N	P	H
	year	°	°	°	°	°	°
1	88·704	+59	−6·59	−0·02	...	...	7·69
2	8·707	+56	−6·57	−0·01	...	...	6·48
3	8·740	+33	−6·27	0·00	...	...	2·73
4	8·746	+56	−6·21	−0·01	...	...	7·26
5	8·746	+40	−6·21	−0·01	...	...	5·88
6	8·759	+57	−6·09	−0·02	...	...	6·84
7	8·776	+57	−5·94	−0·01	...	...	7·50
8	8·789	+45	−5·82	−0·01	...	...	6·57
9	8·789	+29	−5·82	0·00	...	...	2·18
10	8·798	+58	−5·74	−0·02	3·24	...	7·44
11	8·798	+56	−5·74	−0·02	...	7·24	...
12	8·798	+42	−5·74	−0·01	...	6·85	5·05
13	8·808	+53	−5·65	−0·01	3·54	6·14	5·54
14	8·817	−19	−5·57	+0·01	3·89	4·24	...
15	8·828	+12	−5·47	0·00	2·73	6·33	2·33
16	8·833	+45	−5·43	−0·01	3·41	5·76	3·56
17	8·869	+47	−5·11	−0·01	3·83	5·78	4·38
18	8·872	+31	−5·09	0·00	...	5·26	2·96
19	8·891	+45	−4·92	−0·01	3·97	6·07	4·07
20	8·891	−32	−4·92	+0·01	4·19	3·59	3·59
21	8·959	+53	−4·33	−0·01	4·46	4·66	...
22	8·970	+50	−4·24	−0·01	...	4·45	...
23	8·970	+38	−4·24	0·00	4·26	...	...
24	8·970	+21	−4·24	0·00	...	4·66	...
25	8·973	+60	−4·21	−0·02	3·87	7·47	...
26	8·973	−35	−4·21	+0·01	3·00	3·40	...
27	8·984	+58	−4·11	−0·02	4·18	6·47	...
28	8·984	+52	−4·11	−0·01	...	5·58	...
29	8·995	+56	−4·02	−0·02	3·96	5·22	...
30	8·995	+24	−4·02	0·00	3·32	5·15	...
31	9·052	+43	−3·54	0·00	4·16	5·56	5·06
32	9·063	+49	−3·45	−0·01	4·24	6·59	5·94
33	9·063	−41	−3·45	+0·02	3·97	4·77	2·47
34	9·090	+33	−3·22	−0·01	4·42	...	...
35	9·093	−3	−3·20	0·00	3·24	...	...
36	9·093	−41	−3·20	+0·02	3·22	4·42	...
37	9·110	+40	−3·05	−0·01	3·91	5·34	...
38	9·121	+20	−2·97	0·00	3·23	5·43	...
39	9·126	+31	−2·93	0·00	3·14	5·90	...

No.	Date	Angle with Vertical	Proper motion to 1889·5	Refraction	Position Angle, 1889·5		
					N	P	H
	year	°	°	°	°	°	°
40	89·129	+34	−2·90	0·00	2·86	4·72	...
41	9·142	+24	−2·79	0·00	3·49	4·96	...
42	9·142	−46	−2·79	+0·04	3·05	3·81	...
43	9·156	+11	−2·68	0·00	3·29	4·59	...
44	9·156	−44	−2·68	+0·03	3·25	4·10	...
45	9·184	−25	−2·45	0·00	3·39	4·34	...
46	9·195	−26	−2·36	0·00	3·20	3·76	...
47	9·197	−43	−2·35	+0·02	3·22	3·66	...
48	9·236	−33	−2·04	+0·01	3·67	4·03	...
49	9·299	−47	−1·53	+0·04	3·88	4·14	...
50	9·310	−45	−1·45	+0·02	4·28	4·21	...
51	9·726	+42	+1·63	−0·01	4·35	5·30	5·52
52	9·731	+52	+1·67	−0·02	4·39	6·56	5·37
53	9·756	+43	+1·84	−0·01	3·97	6·53	5·93
54	9·759	+45	+1·86	−0·01	3·72	5·57	5·50
55	9·761	+40	+1·87	−0·01	3·09	6·93	5·66
56	9·772	+29	+1·95	0·00	3·75	...	...
57	9·778	+49	+1·99	−0·01	3·56	5·87	4·83
58	9·797	−28	+2·12	+0·01	3·09	3·12	2·09
59	9·844	−9	+2·44	0·00	3·57	3·96	3·43
60	9·876	+42	+2·66	−0·02	3·14	5·38	5·59
61	9·903	+19	+2·84	0·00	3·37	5·55	3·33
62	9·903	−47	+2·84	+0·02	4·16	3·96	0·78
63	9·917	+25	+2·93	0·00	3·37	6·02	4·39
64	9·917	−48	+2·93	+0·02	3·65	4·29	1·60
65	9·975	+48	+3·32	−0·02	4·17	6·09	5·13
66	9·975	−37	+3·31	+0·01	4·51	4·63	2·45
67	89·978	+10	+3·34	0·00	3·89	4·76	4·17
68	90·035	−29	+3·70	+0·01	3·59	4·84	3·11
69	0·068	+13	+3·91	0·00	3·95	4·36	3·84
70	0·068	−45	+3·92	+0·01	4·13	3·73	2·28
71	0·079	−23	+3·99	0·00	3·02	4·07	...
72	0·104	−35	+4·14	+0·01	3·74	3·83	3·35
73	0·114	−51	+4·21	+0·03	4·04	...	...
74	0·120	+25	+4·25	−0·01	4·49	4·78	...
75	0·120	−40	+4·25	+0·01	4·31	5·13	3·22
76	0·123	+26	+4·26	0·00	3·62	4·14	5·42
77	0·128	−8	+4·30	0·00	3·88	4·95	4·44
78	0·216	−40	+4·84	+0·01	4·89	5·09	3·55
79	0·243	−43	+5·01	+0·01	4·96	4·96	3·15
80	0·243	−53	+5·01	+0·04	4·86	3·75	0·14
81	0·251	−43	+5·06	+0·01	3·77	4·78	1·54
82	0·251	−53	+5·06	+0·06	...	...	0·17
83	0·254	−45	+5·08	+0·01	4·29	4·55	1·28
84	0·260	−50	+5·11	+0·02	3·82	4·61	0·31
85	9·262	−47	+5·13	+0·01	4·60	4·88	0·79
86	0·279	−53	+5·23	+0·04	...	...	1·17
87	0·282	−50	+5·25	+0·02	3·54	4·16	1·76

EQUATIONS OF CONDITION. We have reduced the observations made in the three different positions of the eyes separately, and have introduced a term in each depending on the personal error. The equations were put in the form

$$\Delta p = \Delta p_0 + x + ay + bz + c\pi,$$

in which Δp_0 is an assumed value of the true position angle; x, the correction to Δp_0; y, the correction to the assumed proper motion; bz, the personal error, in which z is the constant term, and b

for eyes normal $\sin^2 \frac{1}{2} q$;

„   „   parallel $\sin^2 \frac{1}{2} (q + 30^{\circ})$;

„   „   horizontal $\left(\dfrac{q^0}{90^0}\right)^3$;

π is the annual parallax; and c is computed by the formula

$$c = Rm' \cos (\odot - M'),$$

where R and $\odot$ denote respectively the radius vector and the longitude of the sun; and m', M' are determined by the equations

$$m' \sin M' = \frac{1}{s} \left[- \cos \epsilon \cos a \cos p - \cos \epsilon \sin a \sin \delta \sin p \right.$$
$$\left. + \sin \epsilon \cos \delta \sin p \right],$$

$$m' \cos M' = \frac{1}{s} \left[- \sin \delta \cos a \sin p + \sin a \cos p \right],$$

where a and δ are the right ascension and declination of the star; ϵ, the obliquity of the ecliptic; and s, the distance. On account of the change in angle, m' and M' were not constant. Their values were

	log m'	M'
1889·0	9·9954	-1° 6'
90·0	0·0000	-2 21
91·0	9·9984	-3 21

Δp_0 was assumed to be for

eyes normal $3^{\circ}\cdot50$

„   parallel $4\cdot00$

„   horizontal $3\cdot80$.

In order to express the quantities $\Delta p - \Delta p_0$ in seconds of arc they were multiplied by $s \sin 1^{\circ}$, in which the values of s were obtained from the mean of all the observations of distance in table as follows:

	s sin 1°		s sin 1°
1888·7	0·0539	1889·7	0·0614
8·8	0·0546	9·8	0·0621
8·9	0·0554	9·9	0·0629
9·0	0·0561	90·0	0·0636
9·1	0·0569	0·1	0·0644
9·2	0·0576	0·2	0·0651
9·3	0·0584	0·3	0·0658

WEIGHTING THE OBSERVATIONS. Although different weights were assigned to the measures at the time of observation, they were given the same weight in the equations of condition and no observations were rejected.

No.	Date	Equations of condition. Normal.				Residuals with p.e.	Residuals without p.e.
	year				"	"	"
1	88·798	$x - 0·702\,y$	$-0·881\,\pi$	$+0·235\,z$	$+0·014=0$	$+0·028$	$+0·012$
2	8·808	$-0·692$	$-0·848$	$+0·199$	$-0·002=0$	$+0·007$	$-0·004$
3	8·817	$-0·683$	$-0·821$	$+0·027$	$-0·020=0$	$+0·036$	$-0·022$
4	8·828	$-0·672$	$-0·780$	$+0·011$	$+0·043=0$	$+0·028$	$+0·042$
5	8·833	$-0·667$	$-0·759$	$+0·153$	$+0·005=0$	$+0·008$	$+0·004$
6	8·869	$-0·631$	$-0·597$	$+0·159$	$-0·018=0$	$-0·012$	$-0·017$
7	8·891	$-0·609$	$-0·482$	$+0·147$	$-0·026=0$	$+0·022$	$-0·025$
8	8·891	$-0·609$	$-0·482$	$+0·076$	$-0·038=0$	$-0·044$	$-0·036$
9	8·959	$-0·541$	$-0·044$	$+0·199$	$-0·054=0$	$-0·038$	$-0·050$
10	8·970	$-0·530$	$-0·001$	$+0·106$	$-0·042=0$	$-0·040$	$-0·038$
11	8·973	$-0·527$	$+0·016$	$+0·250$	$-0·020=0$	$-0·004$	$-0·016$
12	8·973	$-0·527$	$+0·016$	$+0·091$	$+0·028=0$	$+0·028$	$+0·032$
13	8·984	$-0·516$	$+0·085$	$+0·235$	$-0·038=0$	$-0·015$	$-0·033$
14	8·995	$-0·505$	$+0·154$	$+0·221$	$-0·026=0$	$-0·005$	$-0·021$
15	8·995	$-0·505$	$+0·154$	$+0·024$	$+0·010=0$	$+0·001$	$+0·015$
16	89·052	$-0·448$	$+0·495$	$+0·147$	$-0·037=0$	$-0·024$	$-0·030$
17	9·063	$-0·437$	$+0·554$	$+0·179$	$-0·042=0$	$-0·024$	$-0·034$
18	9·063	$-0·437$	$+0·554$	$+0·122$	$-0·026=0$	$-0·017$	$-0·018$
19	9·090	$-0·410$	$+0·688$	$+0·081$	$-0·052=0$	$-0·048$	$-0·043$
20	9·093	$-0·407$	$+0·700$	$+0·001$	$+0·015=0$	$+0·007$	$+0·024$
21	9·093	$-0·407$	$+0·700$	$+0·122$	$+0·016=0$	$+0·027$	$+0·025$
22	9·110	$-0·390$	$+0·769$	$+0·117$	$-0·023=0$	$-0·013$	$-0·014$
23	9·121	$-0·379$	$+0·810$	$+0·030$	$+0·015=0$	$+0·013$	$+0·025$
24	9·126	$-0·374$	$+0·830$	$+0·071$	$+0·021=0$	$+0·025$	$+0·031$
25	9·129	$-0·371$	$+0·839$	$+0·085$	$+0·037=0$	$+0·043$	$+0·047$
26	9·142	$-0·358$	$+0·874$	$+0·043$	$+0·001=0$	$+0·001$	$+0·011$
27	9·142	$-0·358$	$+0·874$	$+0·153$	$+0·026=0$	$+0·043$	$+0·036$
28	9·156	$-0·344$	$+0·918$	$+0·009$	$+0·012=0$	$+0·008$	$+0·023$
29	9·156	$-0·344$	$+0·918$	$+0·141$	$+0·015=0$	$+0·030$	$+0·026$
30	9·184	$x - 0·316\,y$	$+0·967\,\pi$	$+0·047\,z$	$+0·006=0$	$+0·008$	$+0·017$

No.	Date	Equations of condition. Normal.				Residuals with p.e.	Residuals without p.e.
	year				$''$	$'$	$''$
31	89·195	$x - 0·305\,y$	$+0·979\,\pi$	$+0·051\,z$	$+0·017 = 0$	$+0·020$	$+0·029$
32	9·197	$-0·303$	$+0·981$	$+0·134$	$+0·016 = 0$	$+0·033$	$+0·028$
33	9·236	$-0·264$	$+0·981$	$+0·081$	$-0·010 = 0$	$-0·001$	$+0·003$
34	9·299	$-0·201$	$+0·859$	$+0·159$	$-0·022 = 0$	$-0·001$	$-0·009$
35	9·310	$-0·190$	$+0·823$	$+0·147$	$-0·046 = 0$	$-0·026$	$-0·032$
36	9·726	$+0·226$	$-1·001$	$+0·128$	$-0·053 = 0$	$-0·036$	$-0·036$
37	9·731	$+0·231$	$-1·000$	$+0·206$	$-0·055 = 0$	$-0·026$	$-0·038$
38	9·756	$+0·256$	$-0·976$	$+0·134$	$-0·029 = 0$	$-0·010$	$-0·011$
39	9·759	$+0·259$	$-0·971$	$+0·153$	$-0·013 = 0$	$+0·009$	$+0·005$
40	9·761	$+0·261$	$-0·967$	$+0·122$	$+0·025 = 0$	$+0·042$	$+0·043$
41	9·772	$+0·272$	$-0·947$	$+0·062$	$-0·015 = 0$	$-0·008$	$+0·003$
42	9·778	$+0·278$	$-0·935$	$+0·172$	$-0·004 = 0$	$+0·022$	$+0·014$
43	9·797	$+0·297$	$-0·884$	$+0·054$	$+0·026 = 0$	$+0·034$	$+0·045$
44	9·844	$+0·344$	$-0·709$	$+0·006$	$-0·004 = 0$	$-0·002$	$+0·017$
45	9·876	$+0·376$	$-0·547$	$+0·166$	$+0·022 = 0$	$+0·051$	$+0·046$
46	9·903	$+0·403$	$-0·394$	$+0·027$	$+0·008 = 0$	$+0·017$	$+0·031$
47	9·903	$+0·403$	$-0·394$	$+0·159$	$-0·041 = 0$	$-0·013$	$-0·018$
48	9·917	$+0·417$	$-0·180$	$+0·043$	$+0·008 = 0$	$+0·020$	$+0·032$
49	9·917	$+0·417$	$-0·180$	$+0·166$	$-0·009 = 0$	$+0·021$	$+0·015$
50	9·975	$+0·475$	$+0·050$	$+0·166$	$-0·042 = 0$	$-0·010$	$-0·017$
51	9·975	$+0·475$	$+0·050$	$+0·096$	$-0·064 = 0$	$-0·042$	$-0·039$
52	9·978	$+0·478$	$+0·067$	$+0·008$	$-0·024 = 0$	$-0·015$	$+0·001$
53	90·035	$+0·535$	$+0·418$	$+0·062$	$-0·006 = 0$	$+0·014$	$+0·022$
54	0·068	$+0·568$	$+0·599$	$+0·013$	$-0·029 = 0$	$-0·015$	$-0·001$
55	0·068	$+0·568$	$+0·599$	$+0·147$	$-0·040 = 0$	$-0·006$	$-0·011$
56	0·079	$+0·579$	$+0·653$	$+0·040$	$+0·031 = 0$	$+0·050$	$+0·060$
57	0·104	$+0·604$	$+0·763$	$+0·091$	$-0·017 = 0$	$+0·010$	$+0·013$
58	0·114	$+0·614$	$+0·806$	$+0·185$	$-0·035 = 0$	$+0·007$	$-0·005$
59	0·120	$+0·620$	$+0·825$	$+0·051$	$-0·064 = 0$	$-0·042$	$-0·034$
60	0·120	$+0·620$	$+0·825$	$+0·117$	$-0·052 = 0$	$-0·020$	$-0·021$
61	0·123	$+0·623$	$+0·835$	$+0·225$	$-0·004 = 0$	$+0·044$	$+0·027$
62	0·128	$+0·628$	$+0·854$	$+0·005$	$-0·024 = 0$	$-0·009$	$+0·007$
63	0·216	$+0·716$	$+0·995$	$+0·117$	$-0·091 = 0$	$-0·036$	$-0·060$
64	0·243	$+0·743$	$+0·974$	$+0·134$	$-0·095 = 0$	$-0·057$	$-0·061$
65	0·243	$+0·743$	$+0·974$	$+0·199$	$-0·072 = 0$	$-0·024$	$-0·038$
66	0·251	$+0·751$	$+0·966$	$+0·134$	$-0·018 = 0$	$+0·020$	$+0·016$
67	0·254	$+0·754$	$+0·962$	$+0·147$	$-0·052 = 0$	$-0·012$	$-0·018$
68	0·260	$+0·760$	$+0·952$	$+0·179$	$-0·019 = 0$	$+0·024$	$+0·015$
69	0·262	$+0·762$	$+0·947$	$+0·159$	$-0·072 = 0$	$-0·030$	$-0·038$
70	0·282	$x + 0·782\,y$	$+0·904\,\pi$	$+0·179\,z$	$+0·000 = 0$	$+0·044$	$+0·035$

No.	Date	Equations of condition. Parallel.				Residuals with p.e.	without p.e.
	year				$''$	$''$	$''$
1	88·798	$x - 0\cdot702\,y$	$- 0\cdot881\,\pi$	$+ 0\cdot465\,z$	$- 0\cdot177 = 0$	$- 0\cdot048$	$- 0\cdot074$
2	8·798	$- 0\cdot702$	$- 0\cdot881$	$+ 0\cdot312$	$- 0\cdot155 = 0$	$- 0\cdot064$	$- 0\cdot052$
3	8·808	$- 0\cdot692$	$- 0\cdot848$	$+ 0\cdot438$	$- 0\cdot117 = 0$	$+ 0\cdot005$	$- 0\cdot017$
4	8·817	$- 0\cdot683$	$- 0\cdot821$	$+ 0\cdot009$	$- 0\cdot012 = 0$	$+ 0\cdot003$	$+ 0\cdot088$
5	8·828	$- 0\cdot672$	$- 0\cdot780$	$+ 0\cdot117$	$- 0\cdot128 = 0$	$- 0\cdot086$	$- 0\cdot029$
6	8·833	$- 0\cdot667$	$- 0\cdot759$	$+ 0\cdot354$	$- 0\cdot097 = 0$	$+ 0\cdot004$	$+ 0\cdot001$
7	8·869	$- 0\cdot631$	$- 0\cdot597$	$+ 0\cdot387$	$- 0\cdot098 = 0$	$+ 0\cdot010$	$- 0\cdot006$
8	8·872	$- 0\cdot628$	$- 0\cdot583$	$+ 0\cdot250$	$- 0\cdot070 = 0$	$+ 0\cdot004$	$+ 0\cdot021$
9	8·891	$- 0\cdot609$	$- 0\cdot482$	$+ 0\cdot371$	$- 0\cdot114 = 0$	$- 0\cdot011$	$- 0\cdot026$
10	8·891	$- 0\cdot609$	$- 0\cdot482$	$+ 0\cdot000$	$+ 0\cdot023 = 0$	$+ 0\cdot034$	$+ 0\cdot111$
11	8·959	$- 0\cdot541$	$- 0\cdot044$	$+ 0\cdot439$	$- 0\cdot037 = 0$	$+ 0\cdot080$	$+ 0\cdot035$
12	8·970	$- 0\cdot530$	$- 0\cdot001$	$+ 0\cdot414$	$- 0\cdot025 = 0$	$+ 0\cdot086$	$+ 0\cdot045$
13	8·970	$- 0\cdot530$	$- 0\cdot001$	$+ 0\cdot185$	$- 0\cdot037 = 0$	$+ 0\cdot017$	$+ 0\cdot033$
14	8·973	$- 0\cdot527$	$+ 0\cdot016$	$+ 0\cdot500$	$- 0\cdot194 = 0$	$- 0\cdot062$	$- 0\cdot124$
15	8·973	$- 0\cdot527$	$+ 0\cdot016$	$+ 0\cdot002$	$+ 0\cdot033 = 0$	$+ 0\cdot041$	$+ 0\cdot102$
16	8·984	$- 0\cdot516$	$+ 0\cdot085$	$+ 0\cdot491$	$- 0\cdot138 = 0$	$- 0\cdot009$	$- 0\cdot071$
17	8·984	$- 0\cdot516$	$+ 0\cdot085$	$+ 0\cdot430$	$- 0\cdot088 = 0$	$+ 0\cdot089$	$- 0\cdot021$
18	8·995	$- 0\cdot505$	$+ 0\cdot154$	$+ 0\cdot465$	$- 0\cdot069 = 0$	$+ 0\cdot053$	$- 0\cdot005$
19	8·995	$- 0\cdot505$	$+ 0\cdot154$	$+ 0\cdot220$	$- 0\cdot064 = 0$	$- 0\cdot003$	$0\cdot000$
20	89·052	$- 0\cdot448$	$+ 0\cdot495$	$+ 0\cdot371$	$- 0\cdot088 = 0$	$+ 0\cdot009$	$- 0\cdot036$
21	9·063	$- 0\cdot437$	$+ 0\cdot554$	$+ 0\cdot405$	$- 0\cdot147 = 0$	$- 0\cdot032$	$- 0\cdot097$
22	9·063	$- 0\cdot437$	$+ 0\cdot554$	$+ 0\cdot009$	$- 0\cdot044 = 0$	$- 0\cdot038$	$+ 0\cdot006$
23	9·093	$- 0\cdot407$	$+ 0\cdot700$	$+ 0\cdot009$	$- 0\cdot024 = 0$	$- 0\cdot019$	$+ 0\cdot020$
24	9·110	$- 0\cdot390$	$+ 0\cdot769$	$+ 0\cdot330$	$- 0\cdot076 = 0$	$+ 0\cdot009$	$- 0\cdot034$
25	9·121	$- 0\cdot379$	$+ 0\cdot810$	$+ 0\cdot179$	$- 0\cdot082 = 0$	$- 0\cdot035$	$- 0\cdot042$
26	9·126	$- 0\cdot374$	$+ 0\cdot830$	$+ 0\cdot258$	$- 0\cdot110 = 0$	$- 0\cdot043$	$- 0\cdot071$
27	9·129	$- 0\cdot371$	$+ 0\cdot839$	$+ 0\cdot281$	$- 0\cdot041 = 0$	$+ 0\cdot029$	$- 0\cdot002$
28	9·142	$- 0\cdot358$	$+ 0\cdot874$	$+ 0\cdot207$	$- 0\cdot055 = 0$	$- 0\cdot002$	$- 0\cdot017$
29	9·142	$- 0\cdot358$	$+ 0\cdot874$	$+ 0\cdot019$	$+ 0\cdot011 = 0$	$+ 0\cdot018$	$+ 0\cdot049$
30	9·156	$- 0\cdot344$	$+ 0\cdot918$	$+ 0\cdot122$	$- 0\cdot034 = 0$	$- 0\cdot004$	$+ 0\cdot002$
31	9·156	$- 0\cdot344$	$+ 0\cdot918$	$+ 0\cdot015$	$- 0\cdot006 = 0$	$0\cdot000$	$+ 0\cdot030$
32	9·184	$- 0\cdot316$	$+ 0\cdot967$	$+ 0\cdot002$	$- 0\cdot020 = 0$	$- 0\cdot018$	$+ 0\cdot014$
33	9·195	$- 0\cdot305$	$+ 0\cdot979$	$+ 0\cdot001$	$+ 0\cdot014 = 0$	$+ 0\cdot016$	$+ 0\cdot047$
34	9·197	$- 0\cdot303$	$+ 0\cdot981$	$+ 0\cdot013$	$+ 0\cdot020 = 0$	$+ 0\cdot025$	$+ 0\cdot053$
35	9·236	$- 0\cdot264$	$+ 0\cdot981$	$+ 0\cdot001$	$- 0\cdot002 = 0$	$+ 0\cdot001$	$+ 0\cdot031$
36	9·299	$- 0\cdot201$	$+ 0\cdot859$	$+ 0\cdot021$	$- 0\cdot008 = 0$	$+ 0\cdot002$	$+ 0\cdot029$
37	9·310	$- 0\cdot190$	$+ 0\cdot823$	$+ 0\cdot017$	$- 0\cdot012 = 0$	$- 0\cdot003$	$+ 0\cdot026$
38	9·726	$+ 0\cdot226$	$- 1\cdot001$	$+ 0\cdot346$	$- 0\cdot080 = 0$	$+ 0\cdot036$	$+ 0\cdot018$
39	9·731	$+ 0\cdot231$	$- 0\cdot999$	$+ 0\cdot414$	$- 0\cdot157 = 0$	$- 0\cdot025$	$- 0\cdot059$
40	9·756	$+ 0\cdot256$	$- 0\cdot976$	$+ 0\cdot354$	$- 0\cdot156 = 0$	$- 0\cdot037$	$- 0\cdot059$
41	9·759	$+ 0\cdot259$	$- 0\cdot971$	$+ 0\cdot330$	$- 0\cdot097 = 0$	$+ 0\cdot016$	$0\cdot000$
42	9·761	$+ 0\cdot261$	$- 0\cdot967$	$+ 0\cdot330$	$- 0\cdot181 = 0$	$- 0\cdot068$	$- 0\cdot084$
43	9·778	$+ 0\cdot278$	$- 0\cdot935$	$+ 0\cdot405$	$- 0\cdot116 = 0$	$+ 0\cdot015$	$- 0\cdot021$
44	9·797	$+ 0\cdot297$	$- 0\cdot884$	$+ 0\cdot000$	$+ 0\cdot055 = 0$	$+ 0\cdot085$	$+ 0\cdot149$
45	9·844	$+ 0\cdot344$	$- 0\cdot709$	$+ 0\cdot033$	$+ 0\cdot002 = 0$	$+ 0\cdot040$	$+ 0\cdot089$
46	9·876	$+ 0\cdot376$	$- 0\cdot547$	$+ 0\cdot338$	$- 0\cdot087 = 0$	$+ 0\cdot025$	$- 0\cdot006$
47	9·903	$+ 0\cdot403$	$- 0\cdot394$	$+ 0\cdot134$	$- 0\cdot098 = 0$	$- 0\cdot038$	$- 0\cdot023$
48	9·903	$+ 0\cdot403$	$- 0\cdot394$	$+ 0\cdot022$	$+ 0\cdot003 = 0$	$+ 0\cdot036$	$+ 0\cdot078$
49	9·917	$+ 0\cdot417$	$- 0\cdot180$	$+ 0\cdot213$	$- 0\cdot127 = 0$	$- 0\cdot049$	$- 0\cdot059$
50	9·917	$+ 0\cdot417$	$- 0\cdot180$	$+ 0\cdot024$	$- 0\cdot018 = 0$	$+ 0\cdot013$	$+ 0\cdot050$
51	9·975	$+ 0\cdot475$	$+ 0\cdot050$	$+ 0\cdot396$	$- 0\cdot132 = 0$	$- 0\cdot009$	$- 0\cdot073$
52	9·975	$+ 0\cdot475$	$+ 0\cdot050$	$+ 0\cdot004$	$- 0\cdot040 = 0$	$- 0\cdot015$	$+ 0\cdot019$
53	9·978	$x + 0\cdot478\,y$	$+ 0\cdot067\,\pi$	$+ 0\cdot117\,z$	$- 0\cdot048 = 0$	$+ 0\cdot005$	$+ 0\cdot011$

No.	Date	Equations of condition. Parallel.				Residuals with p.e.	Residuals without p.e.
	year				$''$	$''$	$''$
54	90·035	$x+0·535\,y$	$+0·418\,\pi$	$+0·000\,z$	$-0·054=0$	$-0·033$	$-0·008$
55	0·068	$+0·568$	$+0·599$	$+0·134$	$-0·024=0$	$+0·029$	$+0·015$
56	0·068	$+0·568$	$+0·599$	$+0·017$	$+0·016=0$	$+0·040$	$+0·055$
57	0·079	$+0·579$	$+0·653$	$+0·004$	$-0·005=0$	$+0·016$	$+0·032$
58	0·104	$+0·604$	$+0·763$	$+0·002$	$+0·011=0$	$+0·030$	$+0·044$
59	0·120	$+0·620$	$+0·825$	$+0·206$	$-0·050=0$	$+0·020$	$-0·019$
60	0·120	$+0·620$	$+0·825$	$+0·007$	$-0·073=0$	$-0·052$	$-0·042$
61	0·123	$+0·623$	$+0·835$	$+0·221$	$-0·009=0$	$+0·065$	$+0·021$
62	0·126	$+0·626$	$+0·854$	$+0·036$	$-0·058=0$	$-0·030$	$-0·028$
63	0·216	$+0·716$	$+0·995$	$+0·007$	$-0·071=0$	$-0·051$	$-0·047$
64	0·243	$+0·743$	$+0·974$	$+0·013$	$-0·063=0$	$-0·041$	$-0·039$
65	0·243	$+0·743$	$+0·974$	$+0·040$	$+0·016=0$	$+0·045$	$+0·040$
66	0·251	$+0·751$	$+0·966$	$+0·013$	$-0·051=0$	$-0·028$	$-0·026$
67	0·254	$+0·754$	$+0·961$	$+0·017$	$-0·036=0$	$-0·012$	$-0·011$
68	0·260	$+0·760$	$+0·952$	$+0·029$	$-0·040=0$	$-0·013$	$-0·015$
69	0·262	$+0·762$	$+0·947$	$+0·022$	$-0·058=0$	$-0·033$	$-0·033$
70	0·282	$x+0·782\,y$	$+0·904\,\pi$	$+0·029\,z$	$-0·010=0$	$+0·018$	$+0·017$

No.	Date	Equations of condition. Horizontal.				Residuals	
						with p.e.	without p.e.
	year				″	″	″
1	88·704	$x - 0·796\,y$	$- 0·983\,\pi$	$+ 0·282\,z$	$- 0·209 = 0$	$- 0·001$	$- 0·108$
2	8·707	$- 0·793$	$- 0·985$	$+ 0·241$	$- 0·145 = 0$	$+ 0·023$	$- 0·044$
3	8·740	$- 0·760$	$- 0·983$	$+ 0·049$	$+ 0·058 = 0$	$+ 0·035$	$+ 0·157$
4	8·746	$- 0·754$	$- 0·979$	$+ 0·241$	$- 0·187 = 0$	$- 0·018$	$- 0·088$
5	8·746	$- 0·754$	$- 0·879$	$+ 0·088$	$- 0·113 = 0$	$- 0·097$	$- 0·014$
6	8·759	$- 0·741$	$- 0·964$	$+ 0·254$	$- 0·165 = 0$	$+ 0·018$	$- 0·068$
7	8·776	$- 0·724$	$- 0·935$	$+ 0·254$	$- 0·201 = 0$	$- 0·017$	$- 0·107$
8	8·789	$- 0·711$	$- 0·904$	$+ 0·132$	$- 0·151 = 0$	$- 0·088$	$- 0·060$
9	8·789	$- 0·711$	$- 0·904$	$+ 0·033$	$+ 0·089 = 0$	$+ 0·053$	$+ 0·180$
10	8·798	$- 0·702$	$- 0·881$	$+ 0·275$	$- 0·199 = 0$	$- 0·012$	$- 0·110$
11	8·798	$- 0·702$	$- 0·881$	$+ 0·132$	$- 0·068 = 0$	$- 0·004$	$+ 0·021$
12	8·808	$- 0·692$	$- 0·848$	$+ 0·204$	$- 0·095 = 0$	$+ 0·041$	$- 0·008$
13	8·828	$- 0·672$	$- 0·780$	$+ 0·004$	$+ 0·081 = 0$	$+ 0·019$	$+ 0·162$
14	8·833	$- 0·667$	$- 0·759$	$+ 0·134$	$+ 0·013 = 0$	$+ 0·082$	$+ 0·093$
15	8·869	$- 0·631$	$- 0·597$	$+ 0·142$	$- 0·032 = 0$	$+ 0·049$	$+ 0·035$
16	8·872	$- 0·628$	$- 0·583$	$+ 0·041$	$+ 0·046 = 0$	$+ 0·026$	$+ 0·112$
17	8·891	$- 0·609$	$- 0·482$	$+ 0·132$	$- 0·015 = 0$	$+ 0·058$	$+ 0·043$
18	8·891	$- 0·609$	$- 0·482$	$- 0·045$	$+ 0·011 = 0$	$- 0·093$	$+ 0·069$
19	9·052	$- 0·448$	$+ 0·495$	$+ 0·094$	$- 0·072 = 0$	$- 0·015$	$- 0·087$
20	9·063	$- 0·437$	$+ 0·554$	$+ 0·161$	$- 0·121 = 0$	$+ 0·005$	$- 0·141$
21	9·063	$- 0·437$	$+ 0·554$	$- 0·095$	$+ 0·075 = 0$	$- 0·055$	$+ 0·055$
22	9·726	$+ 0·226$	$- 1·001$	$+ 0·102$	$- 0·106 = 0$	$- 0·040$	$- 0·057$
23	9·731	$+ 0·231$	$- 0·999$	$+ 0·171$	$- 0·097 = 0$	$+ 0·038$	$- 0·048$
24	9·756	$+ 0·256$	$- 0·976$	$+ 0·109$	$- 0·132 = 0$	$- 0·058$	$- 0·086$
25	9·759	$+ 0·259$	$- 0·971$	$+ 0·134$	$- 0·105 = 0$	$- 0·005$	$- 0·059$
26	9·761	$+ 0·261$	$- 0·967$	$+ 0·081$	$- 0·115 = 0$	$- 0·068$	$- 0·070$
27	9·778	$+ 0·278$	$- 0·935$	$+ 0·161$	$- 0·064 = 0$	$- 0·064$	$- 0·021$
28	9·797	$+ 0·297$	$- 0·884$	$- 0·030$	$+ 0·106 = 0$	$+ 0·045$	$+ 0·144$
29	9·844	$+ 0·344$	$- 0·709$	$- 0·001$	$+ 0·023 = 0$	$- 0·003$	$+ 0·047$
30	9·876	$+ 0·376$	$- 0·547$	$+ 0·095$	$- 0·113 = 0$	$- 0·041$	$- 0·101$
31	9·903	$+ 0·403$	$- 0·394$	$+ 0·009$	$+ 0·030 = 0$	$+ 0·020$	$+ 0·030$
32	9·903	$+ 0·403$	$- 0·394$	$- 0·142$	$+ 0·190 = 0$	$+ 0·029$	$+ 0·190$
33	9·917	$+ 0·417$	$- 0·180$	$+ 0·019$	$- 0·037 = 0$	$- 0·034$	$- 0·052$
34	9·917	$+ 0·417$	$- 0·180$	$- 0·152$	$+ 0·139 = 0$	$- 0·027$	$+ 0·124$
35	9·975	$+ 0·475$	$+ 0·050$	$+ 0·152$	$- 0·084 = 0$	$+ 0·059$	$- 0·117$
36	9·975	$+ 0·475$	$+ 0·050$	$- 0·070$	$+ 0·085 = 0$	$+ 0·006$	$+ 0·052$
37	9·978	$+ 0·478$	$+ 0·067$	$+ 0·001$	$- 0·023 = 0$	$- 0·033$	$- 0·057$
38	90·035	$+ 0·535$	$+ 0·418$	$- 0·033$	$+ 0·044 = 0$	$+ 0·010$	$- 0·017$
39	0·068	$+ 0·568$	$+ 0·599$	$+ 0·003$	$- 0·003 = 0$	$+ 0·003$	$- 0·077$
40	0·068	$+ 0·568$	$+ 0·599$	$- 0·132$	$+ 0·097 = 0$	$- 0·032$	$+ 0·023$
41	0·104	$+ 0·604$	$+ 0·763$	$- 0·064$	$+ 0·029 = 0$	$- 0·028$	$- 0·058$
42	0·120	$+ 0·620$	$+ 0·825$	$- 0·088$	$+ 0·039 = 0$	$- 0·040$	$- 0·051$
43	0·123	$+ 0·623$	$+ 0·835$	$+ 0·024$	$- 0·105 = 0$	$- 0·072$	$- 0·198$
44	0·128	$+ 0·628$	$+ 0·854$	$- 0·001$	$- 0·041 = 0$	$- 0·035$	$- 0·135$
45	0·216	$+ 0·716$	$+ 0·995$	$- 0·088$	$+ 0·016 = 0$	$- 0·056$	$- 0·092$
46	0·243	$+ 0·743$	$+ 0·974$	$- 0·109$	$+ 0·042 = 0$	$- 0·051$	$- 0·066$
47	0·243	$+ 0·743$	$+ 0·974$	$- 0·204$	$+ 0·239 = 0$	$+ 0·051$	$+ 0·131$
48	0·251	$+ 0·751$	$+ 0·966$	$- 0·109$	$+ 0·148 = 0$	$+ 0·054$	$+ 0·040$
49	0·251	$+ 0·751$	$+ 0·966$	$- 0·204$	$+ 0·238 = 0$	$+ 0·050$	$+ 0·130$
50	0·254	$+ 0·754$	$+ 0·961$	$- 0·132$	$+ 0·165 = 0$	$+ 0·049$	$+ 0·057$
51	0·260	$+ 0·760$	$+ 0·952$	$- 0·171$	$+ 0·229 = 0$	$+ 0·074$	$+ 0·121$
52	0·262	$+ 0·762$	$+ 0·947$	$- 0·142$	$+ 0·197 = 0$	$+ 0·070$	$+ 0·089$
53	0·279	$+ 0·779$	$+ 0·910$	$- 0·204$	$+ 0·173 = 0$	$- 0·015$	$+ 0·067$
54	0·282	$x + 0·782\,y$	$+ 0·904\,\pi$	$- 0·171\,z$	$+ 0·134 = 0$	$- 0·021$	$+ 0·028$

By the method of least squares these equations were reduced to the following normal equations:

Eyes normal.

$$+70 \cdot 000 \, x + 1 \cdot 879 \, y + 15 \cdot 776 \, \pi + 8 \cdot 105 \, z - 1'' \cdot 169 = 0$$
$$+ 1 \cdot 879 \, x + 18 \cdot 195 \, y + 5 \cdot 288 \, \pi + 0 \cdot 194 \, z - 0'' \cdot 429 = 0$$
$$+15 \cdot 776 \, x + 5 \cdot 288 \, y + 38 \cdot 903 \, \pi + 1 \cdot 528 \, z - 0'' \cdot 471 = 0$$
$$+ 8 \cdot 105 \, x + 0 \cdot 194 \, y + 1 \cdot 528 \, \pi + 1 \cdot 249 \, z - 0'' \cdot 180 = 0$$

Eyes parallel.

$$+70 \cdot 000 \, x - 0 \cdot 568 \, y + 13 \cdot 149 \, \pi + 12 \cdot 367 \, z - 4'' \cdot 105 = 0$$
$$- 0 \cdot 568 \, x + 18 \cdot 842 \, y + 6 \cdot 558 \, \pi - 2 \cdot 718 \, z + 0'' \cdot 437 = 0$$
$$+13 \cdot 149 \, x + 6 \cdot 558 \, y + 37 \cdot 514 \, \pi - 1 \cdot 920 \, z + 0'' \cdot 518 = 0$$
$$+12 \cdot 367 \, x - 2 \cdot 718 \, y - 1 \cdot 920 \, \pi + 4 \cdot 243 \, z - 1'' \cdot 235 = 0$$

Eyes horizontal.

$$+54 \cdot 000 \, x + 3 \cdot 305 \, y - 7 \cdot 834 \, \pi + 1 \cdot 567 \, z - 0'' \cdot 062 = 0$$
$$+ 3 \cdot 305 \, x + 19 \cdot 776 \, y + 17 \cdot 501 \, \pi - 3 \cdot 131 \, z + 2'' \cdot 200 = 0$$
$$- 7 \cdot 834 \, x + 17 \cdot 501 \, y + 34 \cdot 108 \, \pi - 4 \cdot 555 \, z + 3'' \cdot 126 = 0$$
$$+ 1 \cdot 567 \, x - 3 \cdot 131 \, y - 4 \cdot 555 \, \pi + 1 \cdot 057 \, z - 0'' \cdot 822 = 0$$

The solutions of these equations give

	Normal	Parallel	Horizontal
x	$-0'' \cdot 002 \pm 0'' \cdot 005$	$+0'' \cdot 017 \pm 0'' \cdot 005$	$-0'' \cdot 028 \pm 0'' \cdot 005$
y	$+0'' \cdot 021 \pm 0'' \cdot 005$	$+0'' \cdot 017 \pm 0'' \cdot 006$	$+0'' \cdot 037 \pm 0'' \cdot 011$
π	$+0'' \cdot 004 \pm 0'' \cdot 0035$	$-0'' \cdot 010 \pm 0'' \cdot 0049$	$+0'' \cdot 016 \pm 0'' \cdot 0080$
z	$+0'' \cdot 150 \pm 0'' \cdot 036$	$+0'' \cdot 249 \pm 0'' \cdot 022$	$+0'' \cdot 999 \pm 0'' \cdot 052$

The equations were also solved with the personal equation terms omitted and the following results were obtained:—

	Normal	Parallel	Horizontal
x	$+0'' \cdot 015 \pm 0'' \cdot 003$	$+0'' \cdot 065 \pm 0'' \cdot 004$	$-0'' \cdot 005 \pm 0'' \cdot 010$
y	$+0'' \cdot 021 \pm 0'' \cdot 005$	$-0'' \cdot 009 \pm 0'' \cdot 008$	$-0'' \cdot 052 \pm 0'' \cdot 021$
π	$+0'' \cdot 003 \pm 0'' \cdot 0034$	$-0'' \cdot 035 \pm 0'' \cdot 0061$	$-0'' \cdot 066 \pm 0'' \cdot 0160$

These values were substituted in the equations of condition and the residuals placed in the last two columns. The sums of the squares of these residuals give

	Normal	Parallel	Horizontal
$[vv]$ with p.e.	$0'' \cdot 0505$	$0'' \cdot 0993$	$0'' \cdot 1135$
$[vv]$ without p.e.	$0'' \cdot 0604$	$0'' \cdot 1782$	$0'' \cdot 4458$

and from them the probable error of a single observation was computed to be

	Normal	Parallel	Horizontal
r with p.e.	$\pm 0''·019$	$\pm 0''·026$	$\pm 0''·032$
r without p.e.	$\pm 0''·020$	$\pm 0''·034$	$\pm 0''·063$

From this we conclude that the introduction of the personal error term materially improved the results in the parallel and horizontal series, but was of doubtful value in the normal series. This was to be expected as the plotted curve for normal observations was almost a straight line.

Combining, therefore, these personal error values of the parallax according to their respective weights, we obtain as the final value of the parallax

$$\pi = + 0''·001 \pm 0''·0027,$$

a result unexpectedly small. It indicates either that the star is at an immeasurable distance from us, or that the linear distance between the two stars is immensely smaller than the distance from us to the nearer one.

The variable part of the personal equation for 1889·5 is represented by the formulae

$$\Delta p_N = + 0''·150 \, \sin^2 \tfrac{1}{2} q \ = + 2^{0}·50 \, \sin^2 \tfrac{1}{2} q,$$

$$\Delta p_P = + 0·240 \, \sin^2 \tfrac{1}{2} (q + 30^\circ) = + 4·00 \, \sin^2 \tfrac{1}{2} (q + 30^\circ),$$

$$\Delta p_H = + 0·999 \left(\frac{q^\circ}{90^\circ} \right)^3 = + 16·7 \left(\frac{q^\circ}{90^\circ} \right)^3.$$

HAVERFORD COLLEGE OBSERVATORY.

NOTE ON CONFORM REPRESENTATION BY MEANS OF THE p-FUNCTION

BY]

F. MORLEY.

WHEN the z-plane is mapped on the w-plane by means of the equation

$$(1) \qquad dz = dw/\sqrt{Q},$$

where Q is a quartic in w, to lines in the z-plane parallel to the real or imaginary axis there correspond in the w-plane bicircular quartics whose real foci are the zeros of Q, provided that these zeros are concyclic or 'anticoncyclic.' See Greenhill, *Camb. Phil. Proc.*, t. iv.;. Franklin, *American Journal*, xi. 3 and xii. 4.

When we deal with Weierstrass's form

$$(2) \qquad dz = dw/\sqrt{4w^3 - g_2 w - g_3},$$

or

$$w = pz,$$

there is a focus at infinity and the curve is a Cartesian (in the extended sense of Salmon, *Curves*, § 280). And to the problem of reducing the form $dw/\sqrt{Q}$ to Weierstrass's form there is the geometric analogue of the reduction of the bicircular quartic to the Cartesian.

The object of the present note is to show that the leading properties of the Cartesian are direct interpretations of standard formulæ for the p- and σ-functions. For these formulæ the references are to Schwartz: *Formeln und Lehrsätze zum Gebrauche der elliptischen Functionen*. The results, so far as concerns the relations of the focal distances of a point, are given in the first section of a paper by Greenhill (*Proc. London Math. Soc.*, t. xvii., 1886); but it seems to me that by the introduction of the triple focus I have given to these relations a more final form.

In the cubic $4p^3 - g_2 p - g_3$ let g_2 and g_3 be real. We have two cases to consider, for the discriminant,

$$(3) \qquad \Delta = g_2^3 - 27g_3^2,$$

may be positive or negative.

First case. Let Δ be positive. The roots e_1, e_2, e_3 are now real. Let $e_1 > e_2 > e_3$, as in Schwartz, §§ 45 and 51. We have a real period $2\omega_1$ and a purely imaginary period $2\omega_3$; the parallelogram of periods is a rectangle. We write for symmetry

$$(4) \qquad \omega_1 + \omega_2 + \omega_3 = 0.$$

Let now z describe a line parallel to the axis of imaginaries; the equation of such a line is, in circular coordinates,

$$z + \bar{z} = 2a,$$

$\bar{z}$ and z being conjugate, and a being real.

In the plane of pz (which we call the p-plane) we have as circular coordinates the conjugate quantities pz, $p\bar{z}$; or shortly $p, \bar{p}$. Let c denote $p(2a)$.

We have then from the addition theorem, as in Halphen, t. ii. p. 335,

$$(5) \quad \{p\bar{p} + c(p + \bar{p}) + g_2/4\}^2 = 4(p + \bar{p} + c)(cp\bar{p} - g_3/4).$$

The equation is that of a Cartesian; for the highest power of p is multiplied by $(\bar{p} - c)^2$. The triple focus, having coordinates c, c, corresponds to the point $z = 2a$.

To obtain the foci of a curve in circular coordinates, we have the equations:

$$p\text{-discriminant} = 0,$$
$$\bar{p}\text{-discriminant} = 0.$$

In our case the $\bar{p}$-discriminant is

$$4p^3 - g_2 p - g_3 = 0.$$

Hence the single foci are e_1, e_2, e_3.

For an elementary account of the Cartesian, in this case when the collinear foci are real, see Williamson's *Differential Calculus.*

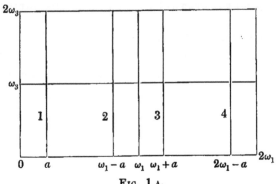

Fig. 1 A.

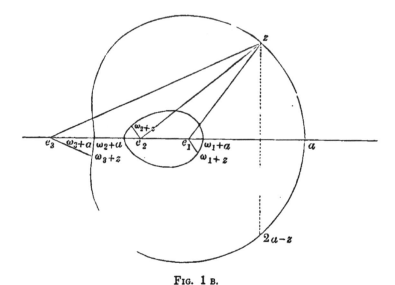

Fig. 1 B.

The curve depends on the single constant $p2a$. It will therefore include the representations of four lines in the rectangle; namely those which meet the real axis at the points (fig. 1 A)

$$a, \ \omega_1 - a, \ \omega_1 + a, \ 2\omega_1 - a.$$

For, if z is any one of these points,

$$p2z = p2a.$$

The first and fourth lines give the same values of pz, and give the outer oval (fig. 1 B).

The second and third lines give the same values of pz, and give the inner oval.

It is convenient to denote any point on the curve by the parameter $a + z$; so that for points on the outer oval z is a pure imaginary, and for points on the inner oval $z - \omega_1$ is a pure imaginary (periods of course not counting).

Now (Schwartz, p. 23, (5))

(6) $\quad \{p(z + \omega_\lambda) - e_\lambda\} \{pz - e_\lambda\} = (e_\mu - e_\lambda)(e_\nu - e_\lambda).$

Hence if we understand by quasi-inversion ordinary inversion + reflexion in the real axis, the point $a + z + \omega_\lambda$ is the quasi-inverse of the point $a + z$; and is the inverse of the point $a - z$. Thus *the curve is its own inverse with regard to any focus.*

It might at first be supposed that we could obtain any number of points on the curve from a given point by repeated quasi-inversion. But in fact we never get beyond a group of four points. For let e_λ, e_μ, e_ν be any three points (not necessarily collinear).

Let
$$(p_\lambda - e_\lambda)(p - e_\lambda) = (e_\mu - e_\lambda)(e_\nu - e_\lambda),$$
$$(p_\mu - e_\mu)(p - e_\mu) = (e_\nu - e_\mu)(e_\lambda - e_\mu),$$
$$(p_\nu - e_\nu)(p - e_\nu) = (e_\lambda - e_\nu)(e_\mu - e_\nu);$$

we readily deduce from the second and third equations

$$(p_\mu - e_\lambda)(p_\nu - e_\lambda) = (e_\mu - e_\lambda)(e_\nu - e_\lambda).$$

Thus if we say that p, p_λ are quasi-inverse as to e_λ, then also p_μ, p_ν are quasi-inverse as to e_λ; and the points p, p_λ, p_μ, p_ν form a group. It is easy to see that all such groups have a given Jacobian. Compare Russell, On the Geometry of the Quartic, *London Math. Soc.* t. xix.

In formulæ (3), p. 47 in Schwartz put

$$a = 0, \ b = 2a, \ c = a + z, \ d = a - z.$$

Therefore $\quad a' = 2a, \ b' = 0, \ c' = z - a, \ d' = a + z,$
$$a'' = a + z, \ b'' = a - z, \ c'' = 0, \ d'' = -2a.$$

Then A. (5) p. 48 becomes

(7) $\quad \Sigma(e_\mu - e_\nu)\sigma_\lambda 2a \cdot \sigma_\lambda(a + z)\sigma_\lambda(a - z) = 0.$

Now from (2) p. 21

$$\frac{\sigma_\lambda(a + z)\sigma_\lambda(a - z)}{\sigma(a + z)\sigma(a - z)} = \sqrt{\{p(a + z) - e_\lambda\}\{p(a - z) - e_\lambda\}}$$

$$= \rho_\lambda,$$

where ρ_λ is a focal distance.

Similarly $$\frac{\sigma_\lambda 2a}{\sigma 2a} = \sqrt{\overline{a_\lambda}},$$

where a_λ is the distance from the triple focus to a single focus.

Hence, dividing (7) by $\sigma 2a\sigma\,(a+z)\,\sigma\,(a-z)$,

$$\Sigma\,(e_\mu - e_\nu)\,\sqrt{\overline{a_\lambda}}\,\rho_\lambda = 0$$

or, since $$e_\mu - e_\nu = -(a_\mu - a_\nu),$$

(8) $$\Sigma\,(a_\mu - a_\nu)\,\sqrt{\overline{a_\lambda}}\,.\,\rho_\lambda = 0,$$

giving the values of the constants in the well-known linear relation of the focal distances.

Next, in Schwartz, (3) p. 47, put

$$a, b, c, d = a+z, a-z, 2a, 0,$$

so that $$a', b', c', d' = 2a, 0, a+z, a-z,$$

and $$a'', b'', c'', d'' = 2a, 0, a+z, z-a.$$

Then A. (4) p. 48 becomes

$$\sigma_\mu\,(a+z)\,\sigma_\mu\,(a-z)\,\sigma_\nu 3a - \sigma_\mu 2a\sigma_\nu\,(a+z)\,\sigma_\nu\,(a-z)$$
$$= (e_\mu - e_\nu)\,\sigma_\lambda 2a\sigma\,(a+z)\,\sigma\,(a-z).$$

Dividing by $\sigma 2a\,.\,\sigma\,(a+z)\,\sigma\,(a-z)$,

(9) $$\sqrt{\overline{a_\nu}}\,.\,\rho_\mu - \sqrt{\overline{a_\mu}}\,.\,\rho_\nu = (a_\nu - a_\mu)\,\sqrt{\overline{a_\lambda}}.$$

Two of the three such equations give

$$\sqrt{\overline{a_2\,.\,a_3}}\,\rho_1 - a_2 a_3 = \sqrt{\overline{a_3 a_1}}\,\rho_2 - a_3 a_1 = \sqrt{\overline{a_1 a_2}}\,\rho_3 - a_1 a_2,$$

and it is easy to show that each expression is equal to

$$.\ \tfrac{1}{2}\,(\rho^2 - a_2 a_3 - a_3 a_1 - a_1 a_2),$$

where ρ is the distance of the point from the triple focus.

This may be shown by a little ordinary algebra. Or, using σ-functions, from (1) § 11, p. 13 of Schwartz,

$$p\,(a+z) - p2a = \sigma\,(3a+z)\,\sigma\,(a-z)/\sigma^2\,(a+z)\,\sigma^2 2a,$$
$$p\,(a-z) - p2a = \sigma\,(3a-z)\,\sigma\,(a+z)/\sigma^2\,(a-z)\,\sigma^2 2a.$$

Hence $$\rho^2 = \{p\,(a+z) - p2a\}\,\{p\,(a-z) - p2a\}$$
$$= \sigma\,(3a+z)\,\sigma\,(3a-z)/\sigma\,(a+z)\,\sigma\,(a-z)\,\sigma^4 2a.$$

In (3) p. 47 put

$$a, b, c, d = 2a, 0, 3a+z, 3a-z\,;$$

then $$a', b', c', d' = 4a, -2a, a+z, z-a,$$

$$a'', b'', c'', d'' = a+z, a-z, 4a, -2a.$$

Then (2) p. 48 gives

$$\sigma_\lambda 2a\sigma\,(3a+z)\,\sigma\,(3a-z)-\sigma_\lambda 4a\sigma_\lambda 2a\sigma\,(a+z)\,\sigma\,(a-z)$$
$$-\sigma_\lambda\,(a+z)\,\sigma_\lambda\,(a-z)\,\sigma 4a\sigma 2a=0.$$

Therefore

$$\rho^2=\frac{\sigma 4a}{\sigma_\lambda 2a\sigma^3 2a}\,\rho\lambda+\frac{\sigma_\lambda 4a}{\sigma^4 2a},$$

or, since $\qquad\qquad\sigma 2u=2\sigma u\sigma_1 u\sigma_2 u\sigma_3 u$

and $\qquad\quad \sigma_\lambda 2u=-\sigma_\mu^2 u\sigma_\nu^2 u+\sigma_\nu^2 u\sigma_\lambda^2 u+\sigma_\lambda^2 u\sigma_\mu^2 u,$

(10) $\qquad \rho^2=2\sqrt{a_\mu a_\nu}\,\rho\lambda+a_\nu\alpha_\lambda+a_\lambda\alpha_\mu-a_\mu a_\nu.$

Subtracting any two of the three formulæ (10) we fall back on (9).

Second case. Let the discriminant Δ be negative. Let e_2 be the real root of the cubic $4p^3-g_2 p-g_3=0$, as in Schwartz, §§ 46 and 52. Then e_1, e_3 are conjugate. Let e_1 be in the positive half-plane.

The periods $2\omega_1$, $2\omega_3$ are now conjugate, and the parallelogram of periods is a rhombus.

Let $\qquad\qquad\qquad \omega_2=\omega_1+\omega_3,$

$$\omega_2'=\omega_3-\omega_1.$$

Then ω_2 is on the real axis, ω_2' on the imaginary axis.

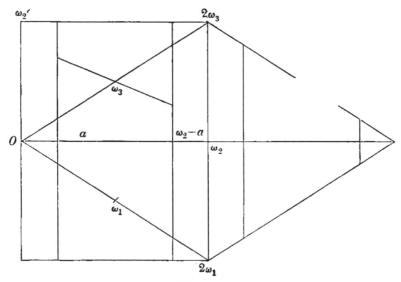

FIG. 2 A.

Fig. 2 b.

Equation (5) gives the curve in the p-plane corresponding to $z + \bar{z} = 2a$. But fig. (2 A) shows that the lines which meet the horizontal axis at the points a, $\omega_2 - a$ give, in different orders, the same values of p. Thus there is only one oval in the p-plane. We have in fact the Cartesian in which one real and two imaginary foci are collinear; the anticoncyclic case of Franklin's papers.

The points $\omega_1 + z$, $\omega_3 + z$ do not lie on the lines $z + \bar{z} = 2a$; for the real part of ω_1 or ω_3 is $\omega_2/2$. Therefore the abscissæ of the points differ from those of the lines by $\omega_2/2$.

Hence, exception being made of the special case when $a = \omega_2/4$, in which case $\omega_2/2 + a = \omega_2 - a$, the points $\omega_1 + z$, $\omega_3 + z$ give different curves in the z-plane.

Hence the property of inversion belong only to the focus e_2.

The limiting forms of the Cartesian of fig. 2 B, for vertical lines in the z-plane, are (1) when $a = 0$, the real axis from e_2 to $-\infty$; (2) when $a = \omega_2/2$, the smaller arc of the Jacobian circle which has its centre at e_2 and passes through e_1, e_3. The limiting forms for horizontal lines in the z-plane are (3) the remainder of the real axis and (4) the remainder of the circle. The curves (1) and (2), as well as (3) and (4), are quasi-inverse with regard to e_1 or e_3. (1) and (3), as well as (2) and (4), must be regarded as orthogonal.

Of the relations between the focal distances the only one which is free from imaginaries is

$$\rho^2 = 2\sqrt{\alpha_3\alpha_1}\rho_2 + \alpha_1\alpha_2 + \alpha_2\alpha_3 - \alpha_1\alpha_3,$$

ρ, ρ_2, α_2 having their former meaning, and α_1, α_3 being the conjugate quantities $p2a - e_1$ and $p2a - e_3$.

CAMBRIDGE: PRINTED BY C. J. CLAY, M.A. & SONS, AT THE UNIVERSITY PRESS.

SARCOPHAGUS AT DOKFEIA.

A.

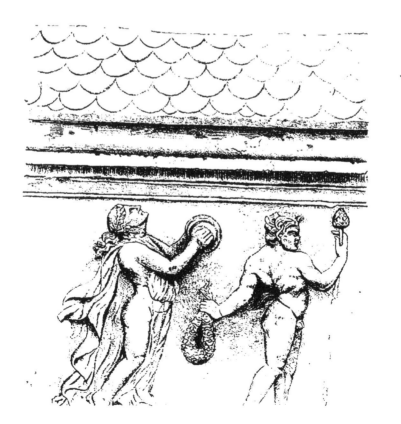

HAVERFORD COLLEGE STUDIES

STUDIES

Published by the Faculty of

HAVERFORD·COLLEGE.

COMMITTEE ON PUBLICATION:

ISAAC SHARPLESS   FRANCIS B. GUMMERE

FRANK MORLEY

FOURTH MONTH, 1892

No. 11   *$1.00*

CONTENTS.

To obtain copies of this publication, address the Secretary of Haverford Co
Haverford College P. O., Pa.

SOME FACTS ABOUT MUNICIPAL GOVERNMENT IN BIRMINGHAM, MANCHESTER AND LIVERPOOL.

THERE has been so much special legislation in the British Parliament that the student of local government in England has a complicated problem to solve. No two towns have exactly the same history or government. Through all ages, at the request of the locality interested, and to suit its special needs, acts have been passed applying to it alone. At intervals more general legislation has been effected, harmonizing certain provisions in cases where the conditions have been similar. "There is no labyrinth so intricate as the chaos of our local laws," says Mr. Goschen.

The three cities whose affairs we shall especially study, as well as many others, have been incorporated under the "Municipal Corporation Act of 1835," and, in the important elements of governmental life, possess many points in common.

The corporation of a town consists of a "mayor, aldermen and burgesses." If the corporation contains a cathedral and a bishop it becomes a city, and its legal title is "mayor, aldermen and citizens."

The burgesses (or citizens) are those who have a right to vote in municipal elections. This suffrage is more limited than for Members of Parliament, and embraces every man and woman who occupies a house, warehouse, shop or other building in the borough, on which he pays local taxes, and who resides within seven miles of the borough. It is thus based on occupancy of real estate, payment of taxes and near residence, and makes no distinction of sex. Women appear, however, to be ineligible to corporation offices, though they may serve on school boards, as overseers of the poor, and in other positions not directly under the purview of the corporation. They appear to exercise the right of suffrage accorded to them variously in different towns. In Birmingham, in a list of about 78,000 burgesses, about 10,000 are women, and they usually vote. In other places but few approach the polls.

It is very difficult to determine the number of adult males excluded from the suffrage by these qualifications. It varies with the town. Thus, Liverpool, with about 200,000 more inhabitants than Birmingham, has 3,000 fewer voters.

The Birmingham town clerk estimated the number excluded at 30,000; a prominent member of the Liverpool government gave as his estimate 100,000. In Manchester there were said to be very few. I do not place much reliance on any of these figures, and I have been unable to find any definite information on the subject. It doubtless has an important bearing on the efficiency of the government.

The population of the three cities especially under consideration and the number of men and women qualified to vote in municipal elections are as follows:

	Population.	Municipal Voters.	Voters per 1,000 of Population.
Birmingham	461,865	78,510	170
Manchester	484,937	79,998	165
Liverpool	613,463	74,145	121

It is probably safe to consider that ten to fifteen per cent. of the municipal voters are women.*

Any voter is eligible to the office of councillor, unless he is interested in some contract made with the Council, or is a minister. He is elected for a term of three years, one-third of the councillors retiring every year.

The number of councillors varies in different towns. In Manchester there are seventy. The number of aldermen is one-third the number of councillors. These aldermen are elected by the councillors, and when elected become a part of the Town Council, and have votes for succeeding aldermen. They hold office for six years, one-half retiring every three years. Their long term of office and their independence of the popular vote are supposed to give the Council stability

---

* According to the present registration there are in Philadelphia 266,065 voters. The population being 1,046,964, this implies that 254 out of every 1,000, or more than one out of four, have the right of suffrage.

and settled policy. The effect is sometimes to secure the continuance in power of a political party when in a minority of the burgesses. Thus in Liverpool, while the majority of councillors are Liberals, the Conservatives secure a majority in the Council by the aid of aldermen who vote their own party into all vacant aldermanic positions. In Manchester the relation of an alderman to Imperial politics is said not to be inquired into, and the advantage of the system is manifest.

The Mayor is also elected by the Council, is a member of it, and is usually, though not necessarily, an alderman.

He presides over the Council, can vote on all questions, and give the casting vote in case of a tie. He has no veto over the acts of the Council, and but little, if any, executive power. He is, *ex-officio*, a member of certain committees, but his main duty is to represent the borough on all public occasions. The Council may fix his remuneration. In Birmingham and Manchester they have fixed it at *zero*, and the necessary cost to the Mayor of performing the duties of his office has been estimated at $5,000, while much more is often spent. Aldermen and councillors are also unpaid.

Thus the Council is made up of mayor, aldermen and councillors. It is the real governing body of the town in all matters pertaining to the sphere of local government. Parliament and the Crown are allowed in general no interference. The burgesses, made so by a rather wide franchise, govern themselves through the Council, which has executive as well as legislative functions.

It manages all corporate property, maintains the police force, levies taxes, borrows money, regulates markets and burial grounds, and has general sanitary authority. Unless special acts provide otherwise, it is expected to have charge of paving, lighting and cleaning the streets and supplying the householders with gas and water. It can own land and erect buildings for municipal uses, and in case certain sections are adjudged insanitary, it can purchase these at a valuation, and erect houses or stores of its own thereon, and powers are also sometimes granted to make long leases to private parties. It has no control over the School Board or the Overseers of the Poor.

It does its work through committees. The following list of the Birmingham committees gives a fair idea of their special functions: Baths and Parks, Estates, Finance, General Purposes, Markets and Fairs, Health, Public Works, Watch (police force), Lunatic Asylums, Industrial Schools, Gas, Water, Improvements, Free Libraries, Museum and School of Arts, Art Gallery Purchases, Technical School.

These committees are the administrative bodies of the Council. A meeting of the Town Council of Manchester, which I attended, was devoted almost exclusively to the consideration of committees' reports. For convenience, the recommendations of the committees were printed and placed in the hands of the members in advance. Their adoption was moved, and, if no member had anything to say, the motion was quickly put and carried. In no case, I believe, was the recommendation of the committee reversed. One day per month suffices for meetings of the Councils. Parliamentary law requires it four times a year. Many of the committees meet weekly or oftener.

The Councils are composed of men of undoubted respectability. Their doings are often criticised, sometimes on the ground of conservatism, sometimes of extravagance; but suspicions of corruption, or of improper motive, rarely, if ever, exist. Most of the members are of such a standing that they would have but little temptation to enrich themselves discreditably. Several workingmen, at least in Birmingham, find seats in the Council and places on important committees, and all classes are fairly represented. In Birmingham, eleven members are classed as gentlemen, six as doctors or surgeons, thirteen as manufacturers, nine as merchants, and the remaining twenty-five are a miscellaneous collection of printers, chemists, bakers, glass-workers, silversmiths, etc., including only two lawyers.

MUNICIPAL TAXES.

Taxes for municipal purposes are levied on real property only, and are based on its estimated rentable value. An unoccupied lot of a great salable value, but producing no income to its owner, would not be taxed. This difference in the basis of taxation, viz., rentable rather than salable value, makes it difficult to make a comparison of the burden of taxation in Philadelphia and the English cities. Several English officials expressed a preference for our system.

From the estimated rental, a certain percentage (from ten to fifteen) is deducted for repairs and necessary expenditure, and the tax is levied on the remainder. This remainder is called the "rateable value," and is as follows:

Birmingham, £1,817,638 for 1890.

Manchester, £2,781,029 for 1890.

Liverpool, £3,068,617 for 1889.

The taxes are divided into two parts—those levied by the Overseers of the Poor and those levied by the Council. For convenience, these are collected by the same officers at the same time. As will be explained further on, but a little more than one-half of the total expense of the schools is borne by the taxes, and this is paid over to the School Board, a body not responsible to the Council, but is included in the Council rates.

The following table gives the tax rates, the first column as levied by the Overseers of the Poor, and the second by the Council:

	Poor rate per £.	Council rate per £.	Total per £.
	s. d.	s. d.	s. d.
*Birmingham	1 11	4 5	6 4
Manchester	(1 2½)?	3 5½	4 8?
Liverpool	1 4	3 4	4 8

Translated into American, this means that if a man owns buildings or lands of the net rental value of $100 he will pay in Birmingham in municipal taxes (excluding gas and water) $31, and in Manchester and Liverpool $23.

If it be true that six per cent. of the estimated selling value would represent the rateable value, this would make a tax rate in Birmingham of $1.86, and in Manchester and Liverpool of $1.38, but I should consider this supposition as very uncertain.

* For the main parish of the city.

CURRENT EXPENDITURES.

The following tables represent certain expenditures for 1889 (except in the case of Manchester, whose fiscal year ends March 31st, 1890). The different names under which accounts are kept make it impossible in all cases to make a comparison. Hence, only a few of the more important or interesting items are given. The numbers are given roundly and on the assumption that $5=£1.

	Birmingham.	Manchester.	Liverpool.
Police	$325,000	$305,000	$475,000
Free Libraries	50,000	60 000	40,000
* Public Baths	17,000	25,000	3,000
† Public Schools	350,000	190,000	250,000
Public Improvements	600,000	270,000	300,000

The total expenditures of the cities, including School Board and the Poor Law expenses, but excluding gas and water accounts, were about:

Birmingham $3,450,000
Manchester 2,950,000
Liverpool 5,600,000

The cost per head of population was about:

Birmingham $7 50
Manchester 6 10
Liverpool 9 10

The Liverpool expenses were greatly increased in the year under consideration by extraordinary payments, mainly in connection with their new water works. The actual ordinary expenses would bring the expenditure per capita about to the mark of Manchester.

The different methods of keeping accounts in the different cities, some giving gross and some net expenditures, and some placing items under different heads than others, make it impossible, without great labor, to make the above figures absolutely exact. It is believed, however, that the limit of error is not serious.

---

* Net expenditures.
† Less than half the total expenditure for schools.

The foregoing expenditure per capita is much less than most, if not all, of our large American cities. Manchester and Boston do not differ greatly in size, but their expenses are greatly different, as will be seen by a few items.

	* Boston.	Manchester.
Police	£222,000	£61,000
Fire Department	187,000	3,700
Parks	25,800	15,400
Libraries	28,000	12,000
Sewers and Highways	239,000	46,000
Health	169,000	103,000
Public Schools	382,000	38,000
Poor	164,000	120,000
Total	2,498,000	565,000

It will be thus seen that the total expenses of conducting the city of Boston were four and a half times as great as for the city of Manchester of the same population.

As a slight offset to this, it should be mentioned that the Imperial Government supports the Manchester jail and contributes to the maintenance of the schools.†

The increased economy of the English cities is largely explained by the lower price of labor; partly by the fact that in their older civilization they have been able to build things

* The Boston expenditures are from an estimate of the Boston *Herald* of February 28, 1890.

† Sir John Lubbock, the Chairman of the London Council, in a recent address, gives the following figures:

	Annual expenditure per head of population.	Amount of debt per head of population (exclusive of gas and water debt.)
London	$11 00	$46 00
Birmingham	14 00	50 00
Manchester	16 00	41 00
Vienna	15 50	38 00
Paris	26 00	161 00
Philadelphia	19 00	71 00
Boston	30 50	122 00
New York	31 00	83 .00

The figures in the first column probably embrace expenditures for gas and water, which are wholly recouped by the charges. I have been unable to make them agree with the official figures in several cities.

The best comparison between English and American cities in the matter of the burden of municipal government will probably be in the amount of tax levied per head.

In Philadelphia, in 1889, the taxes yielded $11,314,303.72, or about $11 per person. In Birmingham, they yielded $2,317,000.00, or about $5 per person.

more substantially; partly, also, by the fact that they are growing less rapidly; and yet, after making due allowance, there is probably something left which must be credited to efficiency. The Mayor of Manchester has been in America, and studied the problem in no unfriendly spirit. He showed me, as an illustration, the comparative expenses of his city and of Boston, Philadelphia and Baltimore in the matter of fire-extinguishment. Taking up the items of the Boston department, he pointed out that it had a much larger force, not only of firemen, but also of clerks, occupied many more buildings and rooms, and was a more complicated piece of machinery than theirs. The same was true of Philadelphia and Baltimore. And at the same time the loss from fires, and the loss per fire, was considerably less in Manchester.

Reasons for this, increased height of buildings, more wood used in construction, etc., will suggest themselves; but, making these and other allowances, the Mayor could not see the use of such cumbrous machinery.

In the same spirit a prominent member of the Liverpool government said to me that he could not understand the immense amount of detail that the American cities printed with their reports. He could not conceive that they would interest any one now or in the future. He did see that they might benefit the printer, but no one else.

These two matters may serve as illustrations. The English official is ever on the lookout for efficiency. His object is to get the best results by the smallest expenditure.

I apprehend an American would not begrudge expense if he secured desirable objects, streets well lighted, paved and cleaned, good and abundant water, favorable sanitary conditions, resources for recreation and instruction, and ample protection for life and property. In estimating the efficiency of any government, these, as well as the expense, must be taken into consideration. We will take them up under their appropriate headings.

DEBTS.

The corporations have debts as follows:

Birmingham	£7,724,634
Manchester	7,322,737
Liverpool	8,396,595

The average rate is three and a half per cent. National laws limit the borrowing powers of a corporation. Thus Manchester can borrow to the amount of £9,801,353 only. The "Local Government Board," a branch of the British Government, has to sanction all local borrowings and to decide the term of years (hardly ever exceeding sixty) during which the loan must be repaid by annual instalments.

Corporations may expend their annual incomes as they please, but they cannot (legally) borrow, or give a valid security for a loan, without the above sanction, which is generally preceded by a public local inquiry.

The debts have been mainly incurred by the erection of public improvements. In Birmingham over £2,000,000 of indebtedness has been incurred by the erection of the gas works; as much by the water works; over £1,000,000 by the purchase of an insanitary district and the opening of streets through it. The first two of these yield a profit to the city, and the third is expected to in the future, when the leases fall in. The burden of the debt is not, therefore, very heavy.

SCHOOLS.

The English system of public elementary education includes schools of two kinds: (1) *Voluntary* schools, supported by the religious denominations, teaching their tenets, receiving grants of money from the General Government, but having nothing from the local taxes, and (2) *board* schools, religious, but undenominational, also receiving Government grants as well as local tax support, and managed by an elected school board. The amount of the grant is dependent on the size and efficiency of the school as ascertained by an inspector appointed by the General Government.

Elementary education, as defined by the English laws, cannot continue beyond the age of 14, and there is, as yet, but little public provision for secondary education, an omission sadly felt and likely to be remedied.

The board schools, having more resources to draw from, are probably as a whole better taught and equipped than the voluntary schools, and are growing at their expense.

A recent act of Parliament practically makes the schools free, though public elementary schools are allowed to make a charge not exceeding ninepence (18 cents) a week per child.

The income of school boards from the three sources is seen below:

	Receipts from		
	Local Taxes.	School Fees.*	Government Grants.
Birmingham, year ending September 29, 1889 .	£65,000	£10,437	£36,636
Manchester, year ending September 29, 1888 .	41,250	19,135	29,517

The next table shows the attendance during the same years:

	No. on the Books.	Average Attendance.
Birmingham	45,553	38,453
Manchester	71,773	55,153

The annual cost of educating a child, based on average attendance, in Birmingham is £2 2s. 1¾d., or about $10.50, and at Manchester, £1 14s. 9d., or about $8.50.

Attendance is compulsory, and the laws are enforced with great strictness. The result is the number of illiterates among English children of 14 is practically zero.

The subjects required of all are reading, writing, arithmetic, English and geography. The boys take drawing, and the girls needlework. Special subjects, such as elementary science, mathematics, Latin, French, domestic economy and cooking, are also allowed.

After visiting a number of board and voluntary schools in England, I have no hesitation in pronouncing the instruction good and the results satisfactory. The work is very thorough. The children begin school early, at 4 or 5, and they soon learn to read fluently and to write a neat and regular hand. Everything attempted is thoroughly drilled into the pupils. A larger proportion of the teachers than with us have been trained in the normal school, and, in relation to the cost of living, the salaries are higher.

In the great majority of cases the education of the public school children stops at the ages of 10 to 14. There is no

* These fees will be largely extinguished another year by the new act.

chance to go further if they had the time, unless they can afford to pay the fees which private or endowed schools require, and this is impossible. In each of the two towns just mentioned, there is provision for some of their brightest boys and girls to continue their education by the aid of scholarships.

An ancient grant of land, coming down from the time of King Edward VI, yields for educational purposes to the city of Birmingham an income of about $160,000 a year. The trustees of this fund are appointed in part by the universities and in part by the Council of Birmingham. They maintain two high-schools, one for boys and one for girls, and seven grammar schools. The grammar schools do not fit for the high, but take children who expect to finish their education at an earlier age. The high-schools charge $60 a year for tuition, and the grammar schools $15, and one-third the whole number are admitted free on scholarships, which are granted by competitive examination to the best applicants. One-half the scholarships in the grammar schools are given to pupils of the public elementary schools, and the other half are open to them if they can get them.

The high-schools have a more ambitious curriculum and fit for the universities. They own a few scholarships, tenable at the universities, so that it is quite possible for a poor boy of Birmingham, if talented, to secure all that England has to offer in the way of education. There are comparatively few places in England of which this can be said. As a rule, the poor boy, whatever his talents, cannot rise.

As a crown to the educational system of Birmingham is Mason's College, founded in 1881–82 by Josiah Mason, who endowed it with about $1,000,000. Its trustees are also, in part, elected by the Council, and it is connected with the lower schools by a large number of free scholarships. It is thoroughly unsectarian, and the fees, which are small, are dependent on the number of courses taken by the boy. The practical and the scientific predominate in the courses.

There is also a large institute, whose courses are extensively advertised over the city, which gives evening lectures and courses to all applicants. The fee is usually a penny (two cents) a lecture. In some cases, where continuous attendance is important, it is a few shillings a term. It is largely patronized by artisans and shopkeepers.

There is also a School of Art, with several branches, supported by the corporation, in which excellent work is being done in drawing, painting, modelling, geometry, mechanics, architecture, the steam engine, etc. The fees vary from $5 to $40 a year, dependent on the course taken, with a liberal number of prizes and scholarships as the reward of good work. The School of Art also has supervision of the drawing taught in the board schools.

One cannot speak too highly of the educational provisions of Birmingham. With thorough teaching, every stimulus for exertion to the ambitious, facilities for evening work of great variety for those who are occupied through the day and for technical instruction in a variety of trades, the city authorities seem to have had the wisdom and the liberality to use their resources to the best advantage.

Much the same can be said of Manchester. The public elementary schools are efficient. They have an advanced public school of 1,000 boys and girls, and, what is rather unusual in England, they have adopted partial coeducation. The Manchester Grammar School of 1,000 boys is a connecting link with the universities, and Owens College, than which there is no more efficient institution for higher instruction in England, is situated in its midst.

Free Libraries and Museums.

The Reference Library of Birmingham contains about 105,-000 volumes, and is open to consultation by any one for twelve hours daily. There are large reading-rooms plentifully supplied with tables, and the attendants are numerous and obliging. A stranger, such as I, found every attention which a citizen would receive. Daily papers and periodicals are supplied in great abundance, and the rooms are continually full of a miscellaneous but orderly crowd, in which the working element predominates, especially in the evening.

The Lending Library, with five branches, free to the burgesses or any one recommended by them, loaned last year more than 500,000 volumes.

As Warwickshire, in which Birmingham is situated, is the native county of Shakespeare, an effort has been made to collect all the editions of his works. Probably the finest collection of Shakespeareana in the world is to be found in the Public Reference Library.

The nucleus of the libraries was given by public-spirited citizens, but the councils willingly appropriate the money necessary for their support and extension. They cost about $50,000 a year, and are an untold blessing to thousands of the citizens of Birmingham, being adapted alike to scholars and to laborers.

The city of Birmingham also contains a free art gallery and museum, supported by the corporation. The money was given for its origination by private citizens; but it is now maintained and enlarged at an expense of about $20,000 yearly. It contains valuable works of art, ancient and modern; a fine collection of Wedgewood ware, metal work, glassware and curiosities too numerous to mention. It occupies large rooms in the Town Hall, and is visited, especially on Sundays, by large numbers of people.

Manchester is equally liberal in the matter of public libraries. The number of books is larger, but the rooms are not so large and convenient. As I have tested, it is difficult at times to find an unoccupied seat in the large reading-rooms.

Liverpool also has large libraries and reading-rooms, supported liberally out of the public money, and also a fine art gallery, for which it expends large sums for works of the masters.

Baths and Parks.

All three cities have extensive arrangements for cheap bathing and washing. Birmingham has five bath houses, Manchester five, and Liverpool eight.

These have been erected by the corporation at considerable cost. The charges vary from twopence (four cents) to a shilling (24 cents), the larger amount procuring a Turkish bath, which, from experience in Birmingham, I can pronounce very good. These prices are not self-supporting. I give the yearly expenses and receipts below:

	Expenses.	Receipts.
Birmingham	£8,768	£5,340
Manchester	10,490	5,203
Liverpool	8,785	8,154

There are numerous and tasteful parks in the cities. Those in Birmingham are kept up at an annual cost of about £8,000; Manchester, £5,500, and Liverpool at £12,000.

Opening, Paving and Cleaning Streets.

Acts of Parliament allow the corporation to have charge of the opening of new streets and determining their level, width and construction. The opening is done at the expense of the owners, and, when satisfactorily completed, they are adopted by the city. There are in Birmingham 204 miles of street, in Manchester 518 miles, and in Liverpool 250 miles.

In Birmingham 7 miles are paved with wood, 24 with granite, and the remainder are macadamized.

The wood pavement which covers the streets most used in the heart of the city is made of 3 by 6 inch creosoted yellow deal blocks on 6 inches of Portland cement concrete. The first cost is 10s. 6d. ($2.62) per square yard.

The cost of maintenance is from 15 to 18 cents per year. They make excellent, smooth, quiet pavements. To prevent slipping in wet weather they are frequently sprinkled with gravel.

The granite roads are paved with blocks three inches in width and six inches in depth, on six inches of Portland cement concrete, and the first cost is about $3 per square yard. The repairs are practically nothing for the first seven years, six to twelve cents per square yard for the next seven, after which in the heaviest traffic streets the paving would require relaying at a cost of 37 cents a square yard.

For the new macadamized streets there are laid nine inches of ashes, eight inches of either gravel or broken slag, and six inches of broken stone. The first cost of such streets is about seventy-five cents per square yard. It is found economical to substitute pavement for macadam if two coatings of stone are required annually. [This information concerning Birmingham paving is obtained from a copy of a letter given the U. S. Consul, and furnished me by the City Surveyor.]

The specifications for paving first-class streets in Liverpool* are as follows: "The foundation when excavated shall be thoroughly consolidated by watering and rolling. A concrete foundation shall then be laid not less than six inches in thickness, composed of one part, by measure, of Portland cement (capable of bearing a tensile strain of 1,000 pounds on the section of $2\frac{1}{4}$ square inches) to six parts of gravel of approved quality, and eight parts, by measure, of clean, angular stone, or selected brickbats, broken to a $2\frac{1}{4}$-inch gauge; the whole to be mixed, incorporated and laid in accordance with the corporation standard.

"The paving shall consist of $3\frac{1}{4}$ inches by $3\frac{1}{4}$ inches syenite block sets, $6\frac{1}{4}$ inches in depth, laid in regular straight and properly bounded courses, breaking joints upon $\frac{1}{2}$ inch of bedding of suitable description. After the paving is laid the joints shall be filled with clean, hard, dry shingle or approved granite chippings passed through a $\frac{3}{4}$-inch riddle and retained by $\frac{1}{4}$-inch mesh. The sets shall be thoroughly rammed, and additional shingle or chippings added, until the joints are perfectly full, when they shall be carefully grouted with a mixture of hot asphalt of the best quality, composed of soft coal, pitch and creosote oil, melted together in a pitch boiler ·to the required temper, and finally the paving shall be covered with $\frac{1}{2}$ inch of clean, hard gravel."

The City Engineer considers that important sanitary benefits have been received from the above impervious pavements, and that the cost of maintenance has been greatly reduced.

Private companies are never permitted to cut through this pavement. Street car companies pay 10 per cent. for the use of the track laid and owned by the corporation.

---

* It is claimed that Liverpool streets are the best paved in the world.

The streets of most continuous traffic are cleaned by boys with brush and pan, the others are mainly swept at night by horse sweepers, and the refuse immediately removed. The smooth paving greatly facilitates the cleaning.

Even the casual traveller returning to New York or Philadelphia is struck by the great inferiority of the paving and cleaning of most of the streets to those of European cities, and the American, who examines critically these three cities, will be still more forcibly impressed with the finely laid and cleaned pavements. In company with a citizen of Manchester I visited the courts of the worst "slums" of that city. The people were dirty, and the houses sometimes insanitary; but the parts under the charge of the municipality were scrupulously clean and smoothly paved.

In Birmingham, also, in order to retain control of the streets, the city builds the street railways and rents them to the chartered companies, charging sufficient to defray interest on the cost of construction, and a little more.

DRAINAGE AND HEALTH.

Within the last ten years Liverpool has gone over her sewers in a systematic way. They were rudely constructed and unevenly laid. By a lining of cement concrete around the lower interior surface they have been made smooth and of uniform gradient. New plans for frequently flushing them, and private drains, have been adopted. They have been thoroughly ventilated. The new "impervious" pavement of hard material and the frequent sweeping of the streets have prevented the entrance of much solid material. The sewers empty into the river Mersey, which skirts the city, so that no attention is paid to the disposal of the sewage.

The effect of these and other improvements on the health of the city has been striking.

The average death rate for four years ending 1869 was 32.3 per 1,000. For four years ending 1879 it was 27.5 per 1,000. For four years ending 1889 it was 22.3 per 1,000.

Manchester has hitherto emptied its sewage into the Mersey, but the new ship canal prevents the continuance of this, and she is now engaged in the erection of works for the care of the refuse on a farm at some distance from the city.

As Birmingham has this plan in operation, it will be better to describe its works.

Birmingham has no large river to receive its sewage, and the residents along the small ones objected to the pollution of the water.

After considerable study of the situation the city joined with a few surrounding villages in the formation of a Drainage Board. They bought a farm of 1,227 acres, costing, with the works, £403,000, and conveyed the sewage for about 2¾ miles by an 8-foot drain. By the use of pans, frequently emptied with the ashes and converted into poudrette, they prevent much of the solid matter from passing down the sewers.

When the sewage reaches the farm it is mixed with lime to assist the precipitation of the solids. The liquid is distributed over the soil by a system of drain pipes. The subsoil being also thoroughly drained, the liquid finally passes off into the river nearly clear water.

The solid matter is, after drying, dug into the soil, which is thus rendered very fertile.

The annual cost is about £54,000, and the income from the farm £20,000. Sanguine prophets promised the return of the whole outlay. This is probably impossible. What is accomplished is to dispose of the sewage at the least possible expense, and to avoid the pollution of the rivers.

The death rate of Birmingham is a little over 19 per 1,000, making it one of the healthiest large cities in the world.

That of Manchester is considerably larger, probably 23 or 24 per 1,000. This is partly due to the fact that many of the inhabitants of Manchester are operatives in large mills, and through miles of street live closely packed in poorly constructed houses. Those of Birmingham work in smaller establishments, and many of them have houses independent of their employers. Manchester manufactories probably also pollute the air with injurious gases to some extent.

GAS.

Both Birmingham and Manchester own their gas works. Liverpool does not. Birmingham charges from 2s. 3d. to 2s. 7d. (54 to 62 cents) per 1,000 feet, and Manchester 2s. 6d. (60 cents) per 1,000 feet of 20-candle power gas. After paying dividends and interest and providing for the sinking fund, the profit to the Birmingham corporation in 1889 was £70,000 ($350,000). Manchester made in the same way about £45,000 ($225,000).

The streets are well, but not brilliantly, lighted. The ownership of the gas works and the fear of overhead wires make the cities slow about the introduction of electricity. The cheapness of the gas is partly due to proximity to coal fields, as well as the low price of labor. Common laborers in gas works receive about 2½ to 3 shillings a day.

WATER.

All the three cities own their water works, and Manchester and Liverpool are now engaged in the construction of reservoirs and aqueducts to bring themselves water from long distances, where they own large tracts of land, practically the whole watersheds which supply their lakes.

The new Manchester water works bring the water from Lake Thirlmere, between Keswick and Ambleside, in the lake district of Cumberland, a distance of about 95 miles. The corporation there owns about 11,000 acres, the whole watershed. They are thus secure of a sufficient and unpolluted supply through all time. For their new and old water works they have accumulated a debt of about £4,000,000 ($20,000,000).

The charge to dwelling houses is 9d. on each pound of rental (18 cents on every $5) per year. For manufacturing purposes the charge is by the meter, and varies with the amount taken, from 2s. for 1,000 gallons to £60 for 3,000,000 gallons. These rates bring a slight profit to the city after paying current expenses and interest on the investment.

Liverpool is also engaged in the construction of expensive water works. It has bought the watershed of the river Vyrnwy in North Wales, and has brought the water, tunnelling through mountains and under rivers, a distance of about 70 miles, at an expense of nearly £2,000,000. They have met with unexpected difficulties in passing under the river Mersey, or they would now have the pure water of the mountains in their pipes. They have dammed the valley so as to create a great lake, destroying a little village by the process, put in works for filtering the water, and built reservoirs along the way for storing it. In the meantime the old works and numerous wells keep the city supplied with water. The future, rather than the present, demands the improvement.

IMPROVEMENT SCHEMES.

An act of Parliament allows a city or town to purchase an insanitary district, making a fair compensation to the owners, and sell or lease the land to new owners or build on it itself. The most striking case of taking advantage of this permission has been in the city of Birmingham. In the midst of the city near the railway stations and public buildings was a large area of mean and unwholesome buildings which, about the year 1875, the city purchased at an expense of about £1,500,000, and through its midst opened a fine broad street. They leased to private parties lots on either side for 75 years, reserving to themselves the right to pass on all buildings erected. The result has been a beautiful street, which, when the leases run out, will be a great source of revenue to the city. It was figured out in advance that about this time the rents would pay the interest. This expectation has not been verified, the city still having to pay about £25,000 out of its treasury yearly to avoid increase of debt. As an investment it cannot be said to be very successful, though after about 1950 the city will doubtless reap a large revenue. As a sanitary measure it must receive its justification.

Having still some of this land on its hands, the Council has recently decided to erect buildings to rent to workingmen as dwellings. A number put up to let at 5s. 6d. ($1.32) a week were eagerly taken. Others are now talked about. With its sewage farm, water works, public buildings and property acquired by purchase and the falling in of leases, Birmingham will be a great owner of real estate.

Liverpool has made the same experiment. A block of insanitary buildings has been bought, and perfectly hygienic five-story dwellings have been erected, which the city lets to artisians and laborers in single rooms, or in suites of two or three, at about two shillings per room per week. The death rate in these buildings is only 17 per 1,000, while in other parts of the city not yet dealt with it has been 46 per 1,000. It has had in contemplation, and probably has completed, sanitary buildings to rent for 1s. 3d. (30 cents) per room per week.

An auxiliary advantage of this is that it affords models for other builders who desire to build healthy dwellings. Nothing could seem more commendable than the care exercised in all the details of their construction. The whole ground was covered with an impervious layer of cement. The streets around were made impervious. The plumbing, of which there was a sufficiency, was done in a thorough way. The windows were large, and the sash opened from top to bottom. Ventilators were inserted in all the rooms, and water and gas were supplied. The investment, I believe, yields a profit of four and one-half per cent. to the city.

The density of population in Liverpool is greater than any other city of the United Kingdon, being 116 per acre, and encouragement for the adoption of sanitary measures may be drawn from the fact that its death rate has been reduced from 27 per 1,000 in 1880 to 20 per 1,000 in 1888 by a steady decrease.

POLICE AND CRIME.

The police in all the cities are very efficient and very accommodating. A young lady of my acquaintance in Manchester felt no hesitation in going into the worst parts of the city at night alone on philanthropic work. The records of Manchester police returns give the following particulars: In 1890 there were 22,239 arrests for all crimes, of which number 52 per cent. of the men and 57 per cent. of the women were drunk, when arrested. The total number of robberies reported was 2,845. There are 488 houses licensed to sell spirits, and 2,094 to sell beer and wine. 161 of the owners of these were convicted of offences against the licensing acts.

The amount of drinking and drunkenness seems to a stranger to be greater than in an American city. Women are seen at many of the bars, drinking with the men. It is probable, also, that prostitutes are more numerous and prominent than with us.

The impression one gets is that they have a worse population than we have in Philadelphia, but that their machinery for managing it is very efficient.

CONCLUSION.

Birmingham has been said to be the "best governed city in the world." If this title is well earned, it must be due to the fact that its municipal government does so much for its citizens at so small a cost, and to the strength of the municipal life and spirit which seem to pervade all clases, including munificent gifts of land and money for corporate purposes, and the expenditure of an immense amount of intelligence and time gratuitously in the management of its affairs. Manchester is more economically governed, and there is all reasonable security for life, property and health, and perfect honesty and efficiency in its Council. There is less that is striking in its affairs, less of splendor and publicity in its management.

For the $7.50 which, on an average, Birmingham charges its inhabitants per year, it gives them conditions of hygiene as nearly perfect as modern science can furnish—streets smootly paved and promptly cleaned, schools for all classes at a trifling cost, great free reference and lending libraries, and reading-rooms scattered about the city; numerous and well-kept parks; baths of all kinds, many of them free; the privilege of enjoying good gas and pure water at a minimum cost of production; good public buildings, not extravagant, but all-sufficient; a police force devoted to the interests of the people, and, through all its ranks, efficient and obliging officials. It is needless to say that official thievery and bribery do not exist, and that the members of the Council are above suspicion of using their places for private aggrandizement.

It has not always been so. For perhaps twenty years previous to about 1870, the city was largely managed for private rather than public good by politicians and liquor dealers... Good men found the atmosphere too uncongenial for a very close interest in corporate affairs. The government was costly and inefficient. There were no libraries, no museums, no good schools except denominational ones; no baths, but few parks; streets and sidewalks were poorly paved; private gas and water companies charged extravagantly for poor products; great insanitary areas existed, breeding disease and death, and municipal loyalty was largely absent.

From this state of affairs the city has been rescued in the last twenty years. Under the mayoralty of Joseph Chamberlain, M.P., the gas and water works were purchased, unhealthy areas were bought and new streets opened, the libraries and museums were originated, and baths and parks established. Private munificence was the origin of many of these improvements. Many of the parks were given. Private subscription originated the libraries, and thousands of pounds of private property went into the art gallery and museum. This stream of munificence is still unchecked. ·Rich citizens of Birmingham prefer their own corporation to other demands in making out their charities.

To induce such a change in any other city it seems to me two things are necessary. First, an active and continuous interest in the affairs of the city by men of responsibility, wealth and ability. They must meet the foes of good government, not by unscrupulous means, but by as much shrewdness and political generalship as they themselves show. At the same time their motives must be unselfish and devoted to the good of all classes. They must be ever ready to make sacrifices of business and pleasure, and esteem it an honor to serve the public in official positions. This participation of business and professional men of standing in city government, not necessarily without salary, is, it seems to me, an indispensable condition of good government.

Secondly, the limiting of municipal franchise even to the extent it is done in England is probably an impossibility in America. Government must be "by the people" as well as "for the people." This being the case, the education of the people in thoroughly efficient schools becomes doubly important. Every voter should have a complete elementary education, and as many as possible should carry it on in advanced schools in which political methods and ethics, the history of good government in their own and other cities, and practical science should have a prominent place.

The great difficulty is to get the people to have a high standard of government. When it is granted they appreciate it, but they do not always believe that certain means will produce ends which they have never experienced, and hence they are conservative. If they saw the smoothly paved streets of Europe they would not tolerate cobble-stones. If they saw reading-rooms filled with workingmen, they, too, would, as Birmingham did, raise $75,000 at a single public meeting to establish them. If they knew that the lowering of the death rate three or four per 1,000 meant the abolition of a vast amount of suffering, and the great increase of the wage-earning power of the people, they would be willing to adopt means which experience has shown will inevitably produce this effect. If all these and many more things of a similar character were properly impressed on the people by various educational means, schools, lectures, literature, etc., they would support and demand good government. The double problem is to give the people, by the assistance of men of knowledge and business capacity and unselfishness, all the good government they will have, and educate them to demand continually something better. The two processes can go on together—in fact, they cannot well be divorced.

ISAAC SHARPLESS.

Haverford College, Tenth Month, 1891.

MYTH AND ALLEGORY.

What Tennyson calls the " rich procemion " of Lucretius, those opening lines to the "mother of Rome, delight of gods and men," which we all know, or should know but for the modern crusade against the humanities, and the notion that it is better to study the brain of a rabbit in its actuality than the brain of a poet in its products,—this invocation of Venus by the denier of gods offers us a very pretty starting-point for our inquiry about the real nature and origin of a myth. It shows us what we are so fatally apt to forget, the distinction between myth and cult, between religious poetry and religion. What a wealth of fervor is bestowed upon the goddess of budding spring, the mythical source of life and beauty and love! What deft application of the legends about her love for Mars—

> quoniam belli fera mœnera Mavors
> armipotens regit, in gremium qui sæpe tuum se
> reicit æterno devictus Vulnere amoris,
> atque ita suspiciens tereti cei vice reposta
> pascit amore aVidos inhians in te, dea, Visus—

Mars, who, by her intercessions, shall grant peace to troubled Rome! Now let us turn a page, and listen to the same Lucretius talking, not about a myth, but a cult, about *illa Religio*—where the *illa* must have sounded like blasphemy to a pious Roman's ear—and the sacrifice of Iphigenia. The poet who just now lavished the pomp and splendor of his verse to glorify the goddess, here calls on the resources of rhetoric and the satiric genius of his race in order to pour indignant scorn on the miserable and blind superstition which could slay a daughter for the sake of a ceremonial rite:—

> tantum religio potuit suadere malorum.

For this is another matter; we are no longer dealing with Venus of the myth, but with Diana of the temple.

It is the purpose of this paper to ask a few questions about the tests and criteria of a genuine myth, and to put forward one or two considerations in regard to the critical treatment of myths in general. First and foremost, let us bear in mind this distinction so plainly shown in the verse of Lucretius. We see one side of a divinity when it is the object of worship, and we see quite another side of it when it is the subject of myth. Myth and cult are not to be confused, as, in spite of repeated warnings, people will insist upon confusing them. Smart phrases are still current, as when one calls the myth a "bit of fossil religion." A myth must stand in connection with religion; it is a statement about some supernatural person or event; but it is not necessarily the offspring of religious rites, and it is hardly ever the parent of such a ceremony. Hence the folly of an attempt to restore historically the ceremonial religion of a race on the basis of its mythology. Suppose a man, ignorant of the religious rites of the Roman Catholic Church, undertaking to get a notion of those ceremonies by a diligent reading of the *Legenda Aurea*, or any such body of sacred legends! Even Herodotus, as a German writer has reminded us, recognized how little the mythology of his day corresponded to the popular belief and the popular worship. The myth is lacking in one important element of the cult—the ethical element; and in many cases a myth is without another element, which, for later phases of religious ceremonies at any rate, is of great importance—the element of emotion. Strip religion of its ethics and its emotion, and what has one left? Strip a myth of its ethics and its emotion, and one has failed to mar its essential character. The myth is largely a child of fancy. In one of the sonnets on the River Duddon,[1] Wordsworth, thinking perhaps of an often quoted phrase of Petronius, "Primos in orbe fecit deos timor," speaks of "Sacred Religion, mother of form and fear;" and if we made prose of it by reading "daughter of fear and mother of form," we should come yet closer to the true meaning of this commonplace of critics. But the myth is no child of fear; it is rather a child of curiosity, born of that old

[1] XVIII, "Seathwaite Chapel."

union between inquisitiveness and imagination. A later age put these two asunder, giving one of them to science and the other to poetry; but the genuine myths were all born before that divorce was brought about.

So evident is this distinction between the rigid rite and the fugitive myth, that a certain school of anthropologists, reckoning with primitive history, must fain do away with myths altogether. The myth is not, say they, the fountain head of religion, nor is it found at the source of the stream; long after this has become a sturdy brook, leaping down the rocks or hurrying through the uplands, men like to listen to the plash and murmur of it; and plash and murmur are the myth, accidental and variable, by no means the watercourse itself. Often, indeed, a myth is invented to explain a ceremony no longer intelligible, just as popular etymology is ready with its little story to serve as explanation for a misunderstood name.[1] Something of this is true, but we are justified in pushing the origin of heathen myth as far back as the origin of heathen religious ceremony. The latter is an act of inference, of reason; the former is a product of fancy. A mind capable of one was certainly capable of the other. Thus we come to the great question about the origin of myths. If we grant, as we surely must grant, that a myth is not necessarily fossil religion in the strict sense—that a story about a deity comes of a very different source from that whence primitive men derived the rites and ceremonies of worship, then we must admit that the nature of myth, as a matter of fancy or imagination, has a very close bearing upon the question of origins. To what supernatural material would the fancy earliest turn? To the processes of nature, answers one; to human legends and stories of ancestral deeds, says another; and so we are fairly embarked on the troubled sea of controversy. That myths are shadows of actual men and events, projected on the past and magnified into supernatural proportions, or what we call Euhemerism, is really the theory of

---

[1] Lippert, *Kulturgeschichte*, III, 71 ff. Tylor, *Primitive Culture*, II, 395 f. Brinton, *Hero-Myths*, p. 22.

Herbert Spencer and many of the anthropological school.
It explains myths as rising quite within humanity and not
originating outside of humanity. The myth of Hercules is
explained by Lippert[1] as the type or deification of a hero
and "woman-hater," who freed the world from the yoke of
the sex in those old days of Amazons and the *Mütterrecht*, and
in addition helped the higher organization of his race. " Especially is the image of the many-headed Hydra well calculated to characterize unorganized bands." According to these
gentlemen, then, myths are history, and where they are not
history they are entertaining fiction. Myths of nature are of
this origin, says Lippert,[2] mere tales to divert a childish time.
A stable-boy tells a story in one fashion, Hawthorne tells it
in another fashion : hence the difference between a New
Zealand myth and the more artistic stories of the Hellenic
Olympus. So far the anthropologist.

There seems, however, to be a general tendency to divest
the myth of its old majestic, sacred and mystic character. So
strict a philologist as the late Professor Scherer[3] makes an
attempt to cover by one theory the space between his old
masters and the representatives of modern science; he would
not abandon Müllenhoff, but he would include Darwin. He
agrees with Müllenhoff in making myths a part of poetry;
he follows Darwin when he makes them poetry in service of
the scientific instinct. Poetry, said Scherer, is no Jove-born
and majestic art; it began with coarse animal instincts, and
only after long ages succeeded in working out the brute. It
did not begin with tragedy, but with erotic songs; it distinctly
aimed to amuse, and "by origin and tradition, by centuries
of custom," was "associated with pleasant conceptions." Its
four primitive forms were "the didactic poem, the myth,
prayer or hymn, magic songs." And what was the myth?
An answer, says Scherer, to human curiosity, an interesting

---

[1] III, 211. Saxo Grammaticus is the chief of Euhemerists. The whole matter of Euhemerism, or *Exanthropismus*, is well treated so far as older times are concerned, in Creuzer's *Symbolik*, I[3], 105 ff.

[2] III, 216 ff. and in his *Religion d. europ. Culturvölker*, 214.

[3] Scherer, *Poetik*, 76 ff. 114, 116 f.

little explanatory tale. Imagine an assembly of primitive men, with a not too imminent thunder-storm in sight and hearing. "What," asks a saner and happier Lear, "what is the cause of thunder?" And the philosopher, poet and myth-maker of the assembly, remembering that loud noises are associated with fighting, tells a tale of some celestial warfare: "The gods are fighting." Paint out the sketch, add figure, incident, background, and we have a myth.

We may notice that all these theories of the nature and origin of a myth touch the domain of poetry; poetry, of course, in the widest sense, the work, as Ben Jonson defines, of "a poet. . . that feigneth and formeth a fable, and writes things like the truth." The notion that a myth belongs to poetry is best and most seriously developed by Müllenhoff in the unfinished preface to Mannhardt's *Mythologische Forschungen*.[1] Müllenhoff tells us that he never ceased "to regard mythology as an essential part of poetry;" and this notion we find expanded into a definition in his *Deutsche Alterthumskunde*.[2] "By mythology we understand the complete round of imagery and poetry (*dichtungen*) in which a race has coined its religious and poetical impressions of the natural world which lies about it, and of the forces regarded as personal beings, which operate within that world." That is, in a a myth we have poetry as the wider fact and animism as the narrower fact. With the wider fact our friends quoted above would probably agree. Poetic fancy acting on natural observation is the source of myths. But to what a rout of fables and legends does such a statement open an inviting door! Müllenhoff knows this well enough; and in another place[3] he speaks of *mythi qui a fabulis epicis caute distinguendi sunt*. We must exclude evident additions, such as poets made to the great epics which dealt with this or that old myth. We are not to think of the early myth-maker coining pretty tales after the fashion of a modern poet, even if the work of a poet be analogous to the work of early mythical fancy.[4] The

---

[1] *Quellen und Forschungen*, LI, Strassburg, 1884.
[2] V. 1, 157.
[3] *De antiq. German. poesi*, p. 5.
[4] Insisted upon by Tylor, *Primitive Culture*, I, 315.

latter was limited and conditioned by the nature of its material; the poet may wander at will into the perilous freedom of allegory. Of the many paths of investigation or comment upon which we are invited by the consideration of Müllenhoff's definition and the statements of Lippert or Scherer, we shall choose this particular matter of the relations of myth and allegory.

Critics are apt to treat the myth as a riddle, and the guessing at its meaning is òne of the pleasantest if most intricate of their tasks. The comparative mythologists are particularly gleeful in this regard; and when, like Schwartz, or Max Müller, or Sir George W. Cox, they annex to the world of natural phenomena the world of linguistic possibilities, the whole reach of etymology and word-origin, what a royal chase they have! Even in narrower bounds, the hunt is an exciting one. Thus we have the explanation, or interpretation, of our Germanic myths as carried on, say, by Simrock in his *Mythologie*. Jacob Grimm would have none of this; he collected, compared, commented; but'he rarely explained. Holtzmann, too, refused to join the guessing-match; "we lack," said he sturdily enough, "the proper understanding of these things."[1] As usual in such feats, no two interpreters of our Germanic myths coincide in a given explanation; and when, by chance, two or three of a school agree touching this matter, then they part company in handling single myths. To one the cloud is a camel, while to the other it is indubitably a whale. Some seè all myths in sun and tempest, some in the water, some in fog and mist; others make an Olympus of the funeral-pile, and call every myth a mere ghost come back from the grave; while, witness Bacon and his *Wisdom of the Ancients*, some earlier critics have actually believed the myth to be a pretty framework and flourish for some doctrine or sentiment of human sapience.

Nobody denies that myths had a definite origin, and hence have in them somewherè, evident or hidden, a kernel of meaning. What we must do is to make clear the difference between

---

[1] Holtzmann, *Deutsche Mythol.*, pp. 50, 53.

free, allegorical myth, and myth which runs parallel to cult, and is held down to definite data. Both of these are to be distinguished, again, from allegory pure and simple, as well as from unhampered poetic invention of new material. Myths about the doings of gods in their Olympus—serious, as in certain Homeric myths, or ironical and jocular, as in the Norse *Lokasenna*—are mostly to be ascribed to free-footed fancy, scouring unhampered over old mythic territory; but the myths which bring a god into contact with human interest are probably of clearer title, as they are of deeper meaning. Such are the myths of a culture-god, the god who introduces useful arts among his people. In other myths, as Scherer hints, we may doubtless find the scientific meaning. Such are the cosmogonic myths, which, though belonging to poetry and myth, are scientific, because they seek to make a reasonable explanation of phenomena in the outer world. Our ancestors loved such myths. Tacitus tells us that they had songs in which they sang the origins of the race itself; while commentators have not hesitated to see a cosmogonic lay, slightly touched by the new theology, in that short passage of *Beowulf* (vv. 86 ff.) where the King's minstrel sings—

> tales of far-off times of man ;
> how the Almighty made the earth,
> fairest fields, enfolded by water,
> set, triumphant, sun and moon
> for a light to lighten the land-dwellers,
> and braided fair the breast of earth
> with limbs and leaves : gave life to all,
> to everyone that walks and lives.[1]

We may note, as is well known, that none of our Germanic myths ever advances the idea of creation as an act of single power working of and in itself; materials were always supposed,[2] and a word for " creator " is *metod*, one who lays down

---

[1] Bugge, Paul-Braune *Beitr.*, XII, 366, compares this with the so-called *Wessobrunner Gebet*, which in its German setting has preserved a few traces of heathenism.

[2] Germanic myths lay stress on the symbol or weapon of the godhead (as Thor's hammer), while Greek myths attribute supreme and all-absorbing power to the godhead itself. See Wilhelm Müller, *System d. Altd. Rel.*, p. 151.

the boundaries, a measurer; *metod markŏda,* runs the Old
Saxon alliterating (and therefore ancient) phrase. This gives
us a glimpse, nothing more, into the old myths; the glimpse
is, however, a direct one, and we need not worry too much
over the "meanings."

How different is the case when we come to the so-called
myths of nature, the myths which described in terms of personality the physical processes of the outer world. Here are
the happy hunting-grounds of the comparative mythologist
and the interpreter. The school of Herbert Spencer would
deny these myths altogether. A dog, they say, does not
interest himself in a sunset or attribute personality to a
distant swaying bough. True; but neither does a dog,
waking from dreams of ancestral dogs, institute a canine
manes-worship. One negative argument is as good as the
other, and common sense must admit the great fact of
original and primitive nature-myths. It is the interpretation with which we are concerned.

Let us examine a few Germanic myths which have called
forth the interpreting talents of a scholar like Simrock or a
poet like Uhland. The former[1] takes a Norse myth about
the "Norns," the coming of three giant daughters out of
Monster-Land to the home of the happy gods. These Norns,
as the names imply, are Past, Present and Future; and
Simrock proceeds to interpret the myth, that is, to tell what
the makers of the myth had in mind when they made it,
by explaining that with the advent of the three, the blissful
golden age of the gods was over, because, forsooth, "happi-
ness is not conscious of the flight of time." There is arti-
ficiality in every syllable; it is no better than one of Bacon's
explanations, beginning "This fable seems invented to
show . . ." and we are justified in declaring that if this
is an old myth, it is impossible that such a meaning was
put into it; or else, if the meaning is correctly guessed, then
we are dealing with a bit of fantastic allegory, and not at
all with a myth. Again, when the Norse myth or distorted
Christian story of the World-Ash, the Yggdrasill—let the

---

[1] *Mythol.,* p. 50 f.

doctors decide its origin—tells us that the tree is watered by the well of the oldest Norn, the Past (our Wyrd), Simrock "explains" this as intended to convey the lesson that the life of a race needs to be refreshed from time to time at the wells of its own past history.[1] Mild, indeed, is Bugge's protest against this: "the thought seems modern."[2] We could quote example after example of this serious interpretation of such shards and scraps from old Scandinavian myth. But let us turn to a greater than Simrock, to Uhland, whose *Mythus von Thor* is the work of a scholar, a lover and a poet, and is full of interest even after all these years, but yet shows so many proofs of love's labor lost. Attractive to any one, doubly so to a poet like Uhland, is the myth of Idun. Idun, darling of the gods, has been beguiled by the mischievous Loki to hunt for apples in a grove far away from Asgard. Here she is seized by the giant Thiassi, who comes in the shape of an eagle, and bears her away to his home. The gods, deprived of Idun, all wax gray-haired and old; Asgard is desolate. Loki undertakes to bring her back, provided he may have the falcon-robe of Freyja. With this he flies to the land of giants, while Thiassi is out at sea, turns Idun into a nut, takes her in his claws, and flies swiftly back to Asgard. Thiassi, returning and missing Idun, assumes his eagle-shape, and pursues them. The gods from lofty burg watch the falcon close-pressed by the eagle, and heap up light wood before Asgard. As the falcon flies into the burg, they set fire to their heap, and so burn the eagle's wing; sinking helplessly among them, he is killed, and Idun is restored.

So runs the myth, and a very pretty little myth it is. But critics, intent upon the wisdom of the ancients and the meaning of their legends, proceed to interpret it. Uhland, in his admirable book, explains Thiassi as a storm-god, for winds are naturally to be represented as huge birds, and Idun as "the fresh summer-green of grass and leaf;" the wind of autumn whirls away the leaves. Loki, the waning, decaying, treacherous element in nature, "betrays the summer-goddess to the

[1] Ibid., p. 40.
[2] *Studier*, p. 402, note.

winter-giant;" but the other gods force him to make good
their loss. With the early breezes of spring, Loki must fly to
giant-land in search of her. Thiassi is properly on the sea in
these equinoctial times. Loki brings back Idun, and how?
In shape of a nut. Chops and tomato-sauce, gentlemen! This
nut, says Uhland, means the seed, the kernel, out of which a
dead plant-world will blossom forth again.[1] The gods light a
fire, the heat of summer; and in this fire the god of wintry
storms very properly ends his life.

Grace and lucidity are in Uhland's interpretation. Unfortunately, however, there are as many answers to these
myth-riddles as there are bright guessers among the mythologists. Mannhardt sees in Idun a goddess of the cloud
whose waters are the quickening and healing agency of nature.
Her apples which she gathers, the nut in which she is carried,
are symbols of life and life-giving power. Bragi, her husband,
god of poesy, is the thunder, and aptly enough is mated with
a cloud; so the muses, Orpheus, Apollo, the music-loving
centaurs, and other song-deities, all owe their origin to one of
the celestial sounds—to thunder, wind or rain.[2] This, too, has
grace and lucidity; it is plausible enough. Mannhardt will
hear nothing of grass and leaves. With Kuhn, he is among
the clouds of heaven, and is fain to drag most Germanic myths
up after him.[3] Later, Mannhardt abandoned some of these
vivacious interpretations. "I am very far," he writes to
Müllenhoff, "from regarding with Kuhn, Schwartz and Max
Müller . . . all myths as psychical reflections of natural
phenomena, still less as celestial (solar or meteoric); and
I have learned[4] *to value poetical and literary production as an essential factor in the formation of mythology.*" We express our
admiration of this sentiment by feeble italics; and we could
wish a like mind were to obtain among the modern school of

---

[1] Work quoted, p. 123. Mannhardt gives an erotic interpretation of this
symbolism.

[2] *Germanische Mythen*, p. 195 f.

[3] He makes the Ladybug (*Marienkäfer*) a mythical heroine of sky and cloud,
quoting in support the English rhyme: "Lady, Lady Landers, Fly away to
Flanders," and approving Pott's etymology of Landers = Laundress!

[4] Presumably from Müllenhoff.

interpreters in Germany. May the writer be pardoned for re-
calling a scene in a university lecture-room some few years
ago. The professor, lecturing on Germanic Mythology, has
come to Idun, or Freyja, or some such young person of the
older days; and, after giving all the myths, is face to face
with the interpretation. "Gentlemen," he says, "this goddess
is either a star or the early summer grass; I am not quite
certain which. Permit me to suspend decision until to-morrow
morning. I shall ponder the matter carefully, and I think I
can then give you a positive answer." This sort of thing is
hardly robust.

Let us try another of these exquisite interpretations. A
lay of the Edda,[1] dealing with the same persons, tells us that
Idun in an evil time came to dwell in valleys and shadowy
places beneath the tree Yggdrasill. It is a heavy season
among the gods, dull, full of omens. Odin sends Heimdall,
Bragi and Loki down to Idun to ask her concerning fate; but
she will not answer. Heimdall and Loki return; Bragi,
god of song, stays with her—and why? Because, says
Uhland, we know that poets are most fain to sing in the
spring-time; and since the earth has ceased to blossom, song,
grown dumb, lingers in exile by the withered green of summer.[2]

Surely, an exquisite solution! Yet, are we dealing with a
myth? The lay itself is admitted to be of comparatively
recent origin; and one scholar—Dietrich—has very shrewdly
called it a "Machwerk später Aftergelehrsamkeit," parlous
state indeed. It is extremely obscure. An Icelander of the
seventeenth century spent ten years upon it without understanding its meaning; and for precisely that reason it is any-
body's property so far as the interpretation goes. Yet thus we
proceed through all this group of myths. Tyr, who goes with
Thor to get that famous kettle for the god's banquet, is the son
of Hymir, owner of the kettle, a giant grim and stark, and of
a mother gentle, "all golden and white-browed." Tyr, says

---

[1] *Hrafnagaldr Odins*, Odin's Raven-Charm. Simrock, in a note to his translation of this lay (*Edda*, 30 ff. 368 ff.) agrees with Uhland's interpretation.

[2] Uhland. *Thor*, p. 128 f. He makes the interesting suggestion that in our
Scottish ballad of *Hind Etin* (= Jötun), Margaret takes the place of Idun.

Uhland, typifies the bold man who is always at home in the land of terrors and dangers. "This fair, white mother who welcomes her son and offers him the strengthening draught, appears as the noble, ambitious Hero-Nature, whose offspring is Courage. She draws her son to the house of danger, makes him familiar there, and gives him strength."[1] If that is myth, then *The Faery Queene* is a myth. Thor marries Sif, the corn. Their daughter is Thrûd, strength, "die Nährkraft die im Korne liegt." Thrûd is promised to a dwarf; that is, the seedcorn is sown in the ground. But her father comes in the spring and rescues her—Thor, with his warmth and fertilizing rains—and the corn shows itself above the ground, a tender blade.[2] Let us turn to a Scottish "myth" of a somewhat similar character. Some rustic named Burns has put it into verse and called it " John Barleycorn," and most of us know it.

It would seem like slaying the slain to go over these things, were it not for the fact that admirable and keen-sighted scholars are still keeping up the practice of interpreting such doubtful myths. Where we have a definite deity known to cult, with definite myths told about him among different races, it is in order to study these myths and arrive, if possible, not at their meanings, but at their origins. But to take some natural phenomenon, like a cloud, and use it as a key to unlock the "meaning" of a host of myths, is surely putting one's self in close proximity to Mr. Casaubon of "Middlemarch" renown. Laistner has done something like this in his *Nebelsagen ;* and he follows Uhland in a mist-interpretation for the familiar figure of Grendel in *Beowulf.* We began this paper by laying emphasis on the fact that myth and cult are distinct; we conclude by insisting that while they are distinct and separate phases of primitive culture, they are connected by a common bond of sacred tradition. They both have reference to a deity, to a deity believed in and worshipped. The creed, if we thus name so loose a system of early sacred poetry, is expressed in myths; the worship is expressed in ceremonial rites. When the elements of a genuine

---

[1] *Ibid.,* p. 163.

[2] *Ibid.,* p. 81 ff.

old myth have drifted so far away from living faith as to be no longer coherent, and have so ceased to have any connection with worship that the poet or narrator may shift the names about at will, change the situation, add or invent as he sees fit, then we are no longer dealing with myth at all, but with poetry based on loose mythic material. If the poet uses his material in allegorical fashion, as we know he often did use it, then we have a right to guess the riddle as we can. But we must not attribute the riddle to early myth-makers. What primitive men ever went about with such thin-spun notions in their heads? For the interpretation, as Simrock and Uhland see it, must have existed before the story; the story is there for the sake of the interpretation. Where is any belief or active religious feeling about this sort of thing? A myth which no one ever believed is not a myth at all. A myth is poetry, yes; but it is the poetry of men who expressed belief in terms of the imagination.

We have two stages of myths. First comes the myth with the awe of belief upon it; then the myth regarded as material of the poet. There are other divisions, of course, such as Meyer's distinction between the pandemonium and the pantheon; nor are the stages of any such myth to be regulated by a definite law. But let us insist upon the separation of fanciful allegory, of the Idun sort, from any scheme of primitive and genuine myths. Let us think soberly on the mental capacity of earliest myth-makers, and then reflect whether they would invent little tales to illustrate the true "hero-nature" or the idiosyncrasies of a poet-god like Bragi. What did primitive man care for the beauties of nature? The bolt of lightning that struck down his relative or friend, set his forest in flames, or else brought the warmth and rain for which he pined,—these things would leave their marks upon his earliest myths. But for the glimmer of the star, the laughter of sunlight on the waves, the shifting shapes of the cloud,—what did he care for these? He was no lotos-eater. He passed the hours of day in chasing game, and the hours of darkness in hiding from beasts of prey. His religion was severely practical. It claimed his time and thought only so

far as it offered him a definite return in good or a promise of
shelter from the evil; and as the evil about him was so im-
measurably vaster than the good, his religious exercises were
almost wholly those of propitiation. Assuming that his fancy
was quite as much awake as his reason, we may be sure that
he not only inferred the necessity of a propitiatory rite or sacrifice, but he imagined something about the vague being he
was about to cajole or hire or reward. Myths of that early
time must have dealt with those forces which struck into the
heart of everyday life,—the bolt of lightning, the redeeming
and quickening power of springtide, sunshine and light.
Wherever the round of daily life was touched with seemingly
superhuman agency, there was a myth.

For the rest, sheer allegory, pretty mythic fancy and such
forms of poetry familiar enough to later time, must have slum-
bered utterly in the midst of a fierce struggle for existence.
When the gods touched man's life with vindictive or benignant
insistence, he fancied something about them and told the tale
to his children. For the doings of those vast gods among
themselves, what did he care? If he could have put his sentiment into a thought, and the thought into words, he would
have anticipated the words of Goethe:[1]

> Ach, Ihr Götter, grosse Götter,
> In dem weiten Himmel droben!
> Gäbet Ihr uns auf der Erde
> Festen Sinn und guten Muth:
> O, wir liessen Euch, Ihr Guten,
> Euren weiten Himmel droben!

Only his demand would have been less ideal; he would have
asked for plenty of meat and a chance to kill his enemies.
Not till he felt a certain supremacy in his own world did he
send spiritual voyages of discovery to the world that lay
beyond the grasp of his senses. The allegorical and delicately-
fanciful myths of later time were no more possible among
such conditions than the sculpture of a Phidias.

The value of a more precise chronology in these matters

---

[1] " Menschengefühl."

was pointed out long ago. In 1861 Wilhelm Schwartz insisted on the distinction between the origin and the historical development of a myth.[1] E. H. Meyer has recently accepted the conclusions of anthropology with regard to ancestor-worship and the priority of demonic myths; first the pandemonium, he says, and then the pantheon.[2] Mr. Andrew Lang, as we all know, has rung many changes[3] upon the stories "cruel, puerile and obscene, like the fancies of the savage myth-makers from which they sprung." These earlier myths we may call marble from the quarry; choosing, polishing, carving, idealizing, is the work of the religious poets; and in the last stage of all, allegorical or satirical 'επίγονοι make free with the fragments. For the purposes of mythology, this third stage is only valuable so far as it helps us to a restoration of the earlier state of things; to spend energy on the "meaning" and put forth interpretations of such material seems to be a sheer waste of time and a more than ordinarily wanton throwing about of brains. This is only an additional reason for caution in our dealings with Norse mythology. The myth-making instinct is surely dead in a race which, by the conception of a *götterdämmerung*, as Felix Dahn reminds us,[4] had virtually "condemned its gods to death."

FRANCIS B. GUMMERE.

---

[1] *Zeitschrift für Gymnasialwesen*, Berlin, November, 1861, p. 837.

[2] *Indogermanische Mythen*, I., pp. 87, 210 f.

[3] *Custom and Myth*, p. 28. Schwartz (as above, p. 835) would satisfy Lang himself in this regard when he says, "Die rohesten Zeiten spiegeln sich in den rohesten Formen der Auffassung ab."

[4] *Bausteine*, I, 119.

PROFESSOR EWING'S THEORY OF MAGNETISM.

FROM THE "ELECTRICAL WORLD."

THE "Theory of Induced Magnetism" which Professor Ewing published in the *Philosophical Magazine* for September, 1890, is at once so beautifully simple and comprehensive that we have thought that some magnetization curves actually obtained from the model which he suggests might be interesting as testing, in some degree, the efficiency of the hypothesis. With this end in view, the accompanying curves were determined by the writer, under the direction of Dr. Henry Crew, of Haverford College.

The magnets used were similar to those described by Prof. Ewing, about two inches long and balanced on sewing needles set in lead bases. They were 68 in number, and were placed in three layers or tiers on glass plates, which slipped into the magnetizing coil. The coil was 32 inches long and 12 in diameter, and was wound from end to end with 76 turns of wire. It was set with its axis east and west.

The magnetic moment of the model was measured by a magnetometer 34 inches from the middle of the coil. To eliminate the magnetic effect of the current in the coil, an opposing coil was adjusted on the other side of the magnetometer at such a distance that it just balanced the large coil when the magnets were out. The maximum strength of field used was about 2.7 C. G. S. units, or 15 times the horizontal component of the earth's field.

The method of obtaining the curves was simply to put in the magnets, stir them up and let them come to rest by themselves, then to vary the magnetizing current through a cycle and read the magnetometer deflections at intervals. As no attempt was made to get anything but the *shape* of the curves, the tangents of the magnetometer and galvanometer deflections were plotted on a convenient scale, without regard to the absolute values of current and magnetic moment.

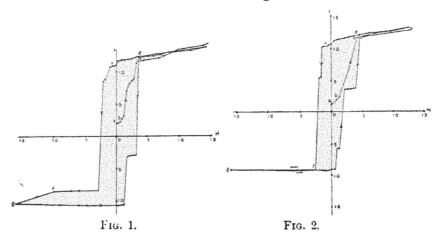

Figs. 1 and 2 show curves obtained with the magnets as close together as they could be placed without striking. They illustrate well the different results that may be caused by different initial directions of the magnets. The magnet *centres* were in almost the same positions in the two cases, but in Fig. 1 the magnets took the directions shown in Fig 3, while for the curve of Fig. 2. the original state is shown by Fig. 4. Both curves show beautifully the small susceptibility at first (*a* to *b*, Figs. 1 and 2), where the magnets are deflected through small angles, but have not yet passed through an unstable position. From *b* to *c* the magnets turned rapidly with small increase of current, and from *c* to the right they were brought more and more nearly into the direction of the axis of the coil, giving the flat part of the curve. On decreasing the current the curves almost retrace themselves to the point *d* directly above *c*, where stability begins. But here it leaves the ascending branch, because it takes less strength of field to *hold* them in this position than it required to *put* them there. This state continues until the field is of nearly zero strength, when two or three magnets turn, giving the small drop at *e*. A slight negative increase turns many more, and another reverses every remaining magnet except four, which are almost exactly opposite to the direction of the field. In Fig. 1 the

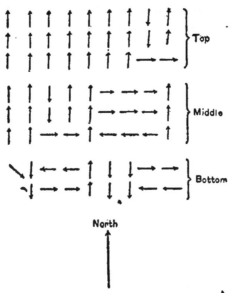

FIG. 3.—DIRECTION OF MAGNETS CORRESPONDING TO THE CURVE IN FIG. 1.

increase from *f* to *g* turned these four, but in Fig. 2 they were
not affected by the strongest current that could be used. Consequently the curve of Fig. 2 is almost horizontal between

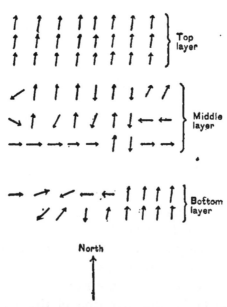

FIG. 4.—DIRECTION OF MAGNETS CORRESPONDING TO THE CURVE IN FIG. 2.

f and g. The difference was probably due to a slight change in the position of the plate which supported these magnets. Completing the cycle, the upward branch of Fig. 1 is seen to consist of two main steps, while Fig. 2 has three, and both curves are to the right of the origin.

These curves may possibly represent one group of molecules in a steel bar. Since the mean density of steel is nearly the same as that of iron, it appears that the large hysteresis of the former is due to the molecules in individual groups being nearer, the groups themselves being further apart than in soft iron. To diminish the hysteresis of the model, the magnets must be placed further apart in order to lessen the stability of their positions. The area of the curve can thus

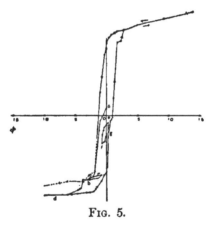

FIG. 5.

be decreased indefinitely. The curve of Fig. 5 was taken with the magnet centres $2\frac{1}{2}$ inches apart—that is, with the magnet ends $\frac{1}{2}$ inch apart at the closest. In this curve the cycle was performed in the opposite direction to that of the others. The last downward branch is dotted to distinguish it from the first. The area of the curve suggests at once that if Figs. 1 and 2 represent the case of steel, Fig. 5 represents soft iron—that is, the case in which there is a less intimate connection of the molecules in their respective groups.

At b a small cycle[1] was superposed upon the main cycle, as shown by the small loop. At c the loop returns to the main

---

[1] Lord Rayleigh, *Philosophical Magazine*, March, 1887.

curve. If one of these minor cycles be performed at a point like *d*, which represents a stable position of the magnets, the curve merely retraces itself, illustrating the fact that there is no hysteresis without passing through a position of instability. On the contrary, at a point like *e*, where nearly half of the magnets have just turned, the area is very large. It is interesting to note that the curve took a new track at *g* instead of returning to *e*.

These are a few of the curves which have already been obtained from the model. They are necessarily very imperfect, largely on account of the relatively small number of magnets used. They suffice to show, however, the close resemblance of the model to actual magnetic metal, as far as the most important properties are concerned, which was all that was originally expected.

ARTHUR HOOPES.

Haverford College, April, 1891.

ON A NEW METHOD FOR OBTAINING A CONSTANT TEMPERATURE.

THE following work was suggested by an attempt on the part of the writer to determine the coefficient of expansion of water by the areometric method of Matthiessen, using, instead of a solid piece of glass, the hollow glass bulb of a weight thermometer.

It was very soon found, however, that the errors introduced by temperature variation of the water in which the bulb was weighed, far surpassed all other errors involved.

The problem which must be solved, before this or any other method yet devised is available for accurate work, is to produce, throughout a certain limited space, a constant temperature, and to maintain this temperature for a time sufficient for one to make his observations. The writer offers the following solution :

Take the body within which it is desired to produce a constant temperature, and wrap it very closely with a fine covered wire having a high specific resistance. The wire should not be of iron or any substance which is liable to suffer large permanent changes of resistance by oxidation or heat. The body having been wrapped as completely, as closely and as uniformly as possible, a constant electric current is now passed through it. By this means can be practically developed the same amount of heat per second over every unit of surface of the body.

If now the body is surrounded by another and larger surface of lower constant temperature, the amount of heat which is radiated to it per second will keep on increasing until it is just equal to the amount produced per second by the electric current.

Between the inner heating wall and the outer cooling surface we shall then realize the condition of steady flow, while *within* the heating surface, thus held at a practically constant temperature, we shall have exceedingly small variations in the reading of the thermometer.

An experimental test of the method was made as follows:

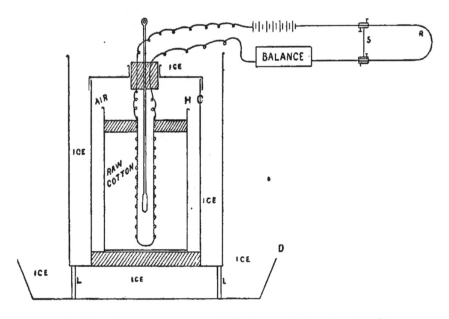

A cylindrical copper vessel C, about 10 inches in diameter, and having double walls, was mounted on three legs, two of which (L, L) are shown in the figure. C can thus be packed in a cylindrical wall of ice.

The whole is then set in a small dish-pan D, which allows ice to be easily packed under the bottom of C. If an ordinary double bottom be used it will be found difficult to keep ice there, and the temperature of the water is liable to rise to 4° C.

Within C is placed another copper vessel H, containing whatever is to be heated to constant temperature. In this experiment I used a large glass test tube, wrapped with No. 22 German silver wire. Some cork feet were waxed on to the bottom of H, and the test tube was suspended in H by means of a cork top. Cork in the figure is indicated by diagonal shading.

A little raw cotton placed about the test tube in H will stop convection currents and much improve the steadiness of the temperature.

On C is next placed a metallic cover, through which the terminals of the wire wrapping are led out and connected to the battery. This metal cap is covered with crushed ice, and the whole inside region is thus surrounded by a wall at zero.

The test tube was filled with water, whose temperature was measured with a sensitive Baudin thermometer on which the degrees (Centigrade) were 10 mm. long, so that with a telescope there was no difficulty in reading to $\frac{1}{100}$ of a degree.

In series with the storage battery (in this case 12 cells) is placed a loop, r, of German silver wire on which are strung two wire connectors. A copper shunt, s, soldered across these two connectors, as in the figure, makes of the whole a simple and excellent rheostat, by means of which changes in the E. M. F. of the batteries or temperature changes in the resistance of any part of the circuit may be compensated. A duplicate slider, parallel to S, should be added in order that one may be clamped while the other is moved, thus never breaking the current. A simple rheostat, devised by Mr. Bedell, and occupying much smaller space, is made by ploughing a number of longitudinal grooves in a piece of $\frac{7}{8}$ stuff and connecting by U-shaped copper connectors. These grooves are then filled with mercury and the resistance varied by sliding the connectors.

As a source of constant current, I have used Julien storage cells and find that they leave little to be desired.

One does not need a large current, even for the production of comparatively high temperatures; for the final temperature of the enclosed space increases as well with the thermal conductivity of the packing between the hot and cold walls as with the current strength, or the resistance of the wrapping, the steady flow of heat obeying Ohm's law.

For the *recognition* of a constant current one cannot use an ordinary tangent galvanometer, since while variations in the *direction* of H can be eliminated by commuting the current through the galvanometer, the variations in the *intensity* of H cannot be so eliminated. Neither is a D'Arsonval galvanometer available; for there is a time variation in the rigidity of the wire suspension and a temperature variation in the field of the permanent magnet. Not only so, but such an instrument must be used with a shunt; and unless the shunt has the same temperature coefficient as the suspension wire and coil of the galvanometer, the shunt ratio will vary with the temperature. However, if one has no better instrument at his disposal, fair results may be obtained with this. A Thomson centi-ampere or milli-ampere balance, being independent of thermal and magnetic changes, and needing no shunt for ordinary purposes, is an ideal instrument for this work.

The rheostat, r, should be placed immediately in front of it for convenience.

An additional convenience is obtained by putting a relatively small resistance in series with the Thomson balance, so arranged that it can be shunted out at will. In this way the current can be temporarily increased. Otherwise it will take a long time for the condition of steady flow to be reached.

A temporary increase of this kind is what is meant, in the observations which follow, by the note, "*current temporarily increased.*"

OBSERVATION I.

Time of Observation.	Reading of Thermometer.	Current on D'Arsonval.
H. M.	DEGREES.	DIV.
3.10	38.10	8.350
3.20	38.10	"
Current Interrupted.		
3.47	37.87	8.350
3.57	37.86	"
4.05	37.87	"
4.15	37.87	
4.25	37.87	
4.31	37.87	
4.49	37.875	"

OBSERVATION II.

Time of Observation.	Reading of Thermometer.	Current on Thomson's Balance.
H. M.	DEGREES.	C.-AMPERES.
7.04	25.37	36.00
7.16	25.38	"
Current Temporarily Increased.		
7.29	25.57	36.00
7.33	25.57	"
7.53	25.57	"
8.03	25.575	"
8.13	25.58	
8.20	25.585	"
Current Temporarily Increased.		
8.29	25.67	36.00
8.33	25.67	"
8.43	25.67	"
8.53	25.67	
9.03	25.67	
9.13	25.675	"
9.23	25.68	
9.33	25.685	"

These observations were made during the past summer in the Physical Laboratory of Haverford College. From the first set it will be seen that the temperature was held constant within $\frac{1}{100}$ of a degree for three-quarters of an hour; in this case no cotton packing was used.

In the second set of observations it will be seen that the condition of steady flow has not quite been reached, for the temperature continues to rise slowly. Nevertheless, there are two separate intervals of more than forty minutes each, during which the variation does not exceed $\frac{1}{100}$ of a degree.

I regret having had to leave the laboratory before I could make some further experiments, for I feel confident the method is able to give much greater constancy.

Its chief advantages are that it can be applied to a vessel of almost any shape, in almost any position. This feature makes it especially valuable for the determination of coefficients of expansion by the method of Boguski, described in the *Zeitschrift f. Phys. Chem.*, Bd. 2, S. 482; in fact, it was for use in this problem that the method was devised.

Unlike the methods of vapor baths, it will give any temperature desired. This temperature can be obtained by trial very quickly, without previous experiment, or the calorimeter can be calibrated and the ampere balance set for the correct current at once.

HENRY CREW,
Professor of Physics in Haverford College.

Lick Observatory, October, 1891.

ON THE ERRORS PRODUCED IN NUMERICAL CAL-
CULATIONS BY THE USE OF DECIMALS.

In making numerical calculations of any kind, whether for the determination of the position of an astronomical body from given observations or for the solution of a triangle from given numerical values of its sides and angles, it almost always happens that the quantities we want are expressible only by numbers whose values are to be obtained correct to a certain number of places of decimals. It therefore becomes of importance to know what degree of accuracy the results obtained by using these given quantities possess; that is to say, to know to how many places of decimals our result is perfectly correct or what error there is in the last place. And it is of still greater necessity, in order to shorten our work as much as possible, to be able to find out to what number of places our given quantities must be carried in order to obtain the results perfectly correct to a given number of decimal places.

For instance, suppose we wish to find the third side of a right-angled triangle, whose sides about the right angle are given correct only to three places of decimals each say, .346, .066. The first question is, "To how many places of decimals is the result correct, and what is the greatest possible error in the next place calculated?" And the second question, "To how many places of decimals must the sides be given to obtain the third side correct to a given number of places of decimals?" There are three operations involved here, firstly, squaring .346 and .066; secondly, adding these squares; thirdly, taking the square root of the result.

Now nearly all calculations reduce themselves finally to three classes of operations (a) additions and subtractions, (b) multiplications and divisions, (c) extracting roots. It will be seen further on that (c) being the converse of a particular kind of multiplication, *i. e.*, of equal quantities, can be brought under the heading (*b*).

In the first class we can very easily see to what extent our results are correct. Take an example: The two parts AB, BC of a straight line are exactly .346, .066 inches respectively, what is the length of AB correct to two places of decimals? We have .346 + .066 = .412, and therefore to two places of decimals AC = .41 inches. Suppose, however, we had used the values of AB, BC correct to two places of decimals only, that is, .35 and .07; these would have given AB = .42. The result so obtained would have been wrong by one unit in the second place of decimals. From this example it is easy to see that the following rule holds, remembering that if the last digit of a decimal is to be neglected, the preceding digit is increased by unity when the last digit is greater than 5.

"If 2*r* or 2*r*—1 numbers each carried correctly to *m* places of decimals be (algebraically) added, the result cannot be wrong by more than *r* units in the *m*th place."

As a general rule when r is greater than 2, the result is seldom so much as *r* units wrong in the *m*th place. This is evident since in the decimals, it is probable that the neglected digits greater than five put equal to 10, counteract those less than 5, put equal to zero. It should be noted that if some of the given numbers be carried to more places than others, we may, by using the full value of each decimal, diminish the greatest possible error of units in the required place by one-half the number of such quantities. This, however, is not of value practically, for the greatest probable error is seldom great and the greatest possible error increases in proportion to the number of fractions used.

Ex.	To 4 places.	To 3 places.
	+ 3.0776	+ 3.078
	+ 26.0537	+ 26.054
	— .0944	— .094
	— .0006	— .001
Alg. sum	+ 29.0363	29.037

Correct sum to 3 places, 29.036.

Here $r = 2$, $m = 3$. The greatest possible error by the rule is 2 units in the third place. In the above example it is only one unit.

With regard to the multiplication of decimals, I shall suppose the worst possible case, *i. e.*, that in which the digits following the last given one may have any value from 00.. to 999.., and deduce general rules. If we multiply .9 by .9 we get .81. The worst possible case is that in which both the correct values should be .999.., the product of which would be unity. Hence the result produced by neglecting the succeeding digits after the first is wrong by nearly two units in the first place. Similarly $(.9)^3 = .729$, $(.\dot9)^3 = 1$, the error being three units in the first place. By proceeding in this way we get the following rules: It is assumed, unless stated to the contrary, that there are no figures to the left of the decimal point, and that when a fraction is said to have i zeros, it means that there are i zeros to the right of the decimal point before the first significant figure. Thus .00032 has 3 zeros and 2 significant figures.

(I) If two decimal fractions be multiplied together and if in the one fraction there be i zeros, and in the other j zeros, the product will not be wrong by more than two units in the rth place, all the digits after the mth significant figure in each being neglected; where

$$r = i + j + m.$$

(II) Hence, if we want the product true to the rth place each decimal must be carried to m significant figures where

$$m = r - i - j + 1$$

(III) When the decimal with i zeros is divided by that with j zeros, (I) and (II) hold if we put $-j - 1$ for j.

(IV) If either of the decimals has numbers to the left of the decimal point, put $-i$ for i where i is now the number of figures to the left of the decimal point. If r become negative put $-r + 1$ for r and read "that the error will not be more than one unit in the rth figure reckoning from the decimal point to the left."

Since in the product of two decimals there is an error of

not more than 2 units in the $(i + j + m)$th place, neglecting the figures in each after the mth place, we can obtain the product true to the $(i + j + m)$th place without calculation by merely observing the $(m + 1)$th figures in each of the given decimals. If a, b be the first significant figures, h, k the $(m + 1)$th significant figures, it will be found that to get the $(i + j + m)$th place in the product correct

> add 2 to its digit of $hb + ka > 100$
> " " 1 " " $hb + ka < 100$ and > 30
> " 0 " $hb + ka < 30$

For this purpose it must be remembered that such a number as .077 must be written .07 and not .08.

(V) Generally: If we have n decimal fractions to be multiplied together having $i, j, k, \ldots$ zeros before their first significant figures, and we neglect all figures after the mth significant figure in each, we obtain the following: The product will be wrong by not more than P units in the rth place, P being the nearest integer to Q, where

$$Q = 10^m \left[1 - \left(1 - \tfrac{1}{10^m}\right)^n\right]$$

and

$$r = m + i + j + k + \ldots$$

Expanding Q (m being always made positive in Q whether it is so in r or not)

$$Q = n - \frac{n(n-2)}{2!} \cdot \frac{1}{10^m} + \frac{n(n-1)(n-2)}{3!} \cdot \frac{1}{10^{2m}} - \cdots$$

In calculations where the application of this might be of advantage, the number of significant figures is greater than 2. Suppose $m = 3$. Then as long as n is less than 30, the terms in Q after the first being less than $\frac{1}{2}$ can be neglected and hence the greatest number of units the product is wrong in the rth place is equal to the number of component fractions.

(VI) I have in (V) supposed the worst possible case. In all numerical calculations, the errors in the last place taken of the component fractions are never greater than half a unit, we now get

$$Q = 10^m\left[1 - \left(\frac{1}{2 \times 10^m}\right)^n\right] = \frac{n}{2} - \frac{n(n-1)}{4 \cdot 2!} \cdot \frac{1}{10^m} + \cdots$$

Hence if n is less than 63, the greatest possible number of units that the product can be wrong in the rth place is equal to one-half of the number of fractions multiplied together. If n be odd, we must take the integer next below $\frac{n}{2}$.

As an example of this last result, suppose that we want

$$(.09938745)^7$$

correct to 5 significant figures. If we omit the last two figures we get $m = 5$, $i = 1$, $n = 7$ and therefore the greatest number of digits which the decimal is wrong in the rth place is the integer next below $\frac{7}{2}$, that is 3. And $r = 5 + 7 \times 1 = 12$. By means of logarithms

$$(.099387)^7 \quad = .000,000,095,787,1$$
$$(.09938745)^7 = .000,000,095,790,0$$

The error is 3 digits in the 12th place, that is, the error produced is the maximum error. From this example we see that by a simple inspection we may often be able to supply the error without further calculation.

The rules (II) (III) and the first part of (IV) are easily seen to be immediately applicable also to the general case.

(VII) Lastly, as nearly all calculations ultimately reduce to operations of the form

$$a_1 a_2 \ldots a + b_1 b_2 \ldots b_s + c_1 c_2 \ldots c_t + \ldots$$

and that in each of these products as long as the number of significant figures of each member of the products is greater than 2, we have for the greatest errors, in the

1st product, $(R + A)$th place of decimals, $\frac{r}{2}$ units.
2d   ' $(S + B)$th   "   " $\frac{s}{2}$ "

where R is the sum of the number of zeros in $a_1 a_2, \ldots a_r$; S that in $b_1, b_2, \ldots b_s$; $A, B, \ldots$ the least number of significant figures in each member of the respective products. It usually happens that $R + A = S + B = \ldots = M$ suppose. This means that all the products must be carried to the same number of decimal places. The greatest error of the whole in the Mth place is then

$$\frac{r + s + t + \ldots}{2}$$

that is, it is equal to one-half of the number of quantities $a_1, a_2 \ldots b_1, b_2 \ldots c_1, \ldots$ used.

If some of the products are capable without trouble of being carried to a higher order of accuracy, take these to one or two places of decimals further, the greatest error will then be one-half the sum of the members of those products which are capable only of being carried to the lowest order.

Thus we have a limit for the error in the last place of decimals in a calculated result. In any calculation where the numbers go on some systematic plan, this might be of advantage, for in such a case the errors are far more likely to be of the same sign, and to gradually accumulate, thus producing a large error in the result. If the number of quantities involved be less than ten, we can be sure that the result is correct to the last figure but one, and in most other calculations to the last figure but two. Hence in complicated calculations it becomes necessary to carry the results two places further than what we actually require.

Ernest W. Brown.

Haverford College, January, 1892.

PARALLAX OF DELTA HERCULIS.

THE first complete observation of this double star Σ 3127 was made by Herschell in 1781. Since then the distance between the two stars has diminished 18″. The accompanying diagram shows the motion to be rectilinear (if, as appears likely, the first observation by Herschell be in error by 5° of angle), with a velocity of 0″.184 equal to a proper motion of —0″.080 in right ascension and of +0″.166 in declination. The proper motion of the principal star, according to the *Berliner Jahrbuch*, is △a—0″.038, △δ—0″.153. The effect of this motion from the year 1821 to 1891 is indicated on the diagram by the line *A B*. If the above proper motion be correct, the companion itself must be affected by a proper motion of —0″.118 in right ascension and +0″.013 in declination.

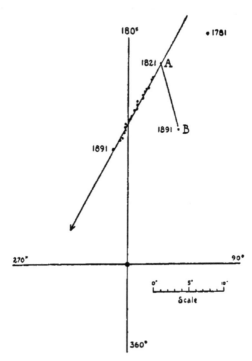

Motion of Σ 3127.

(56)

Notwithstanding this motion, I have thought it worth while to make a series of measures on this double star. For if the star proved to be a binary, the observations would be of value in determining its orbit. If the motion were not binary, but due to proper motion, there might be sufficient absolute distance between the stars to give a measurable parallax. Finally, if there were no parallactic displacement, I hoped the observations might still be of value in the investigation of personal equation, according to the method used by me on similar measures of the double star South 503.

VALUE OF A REVOLUTION OF THE MICROMETER.—A new set of observations was made by Mr. Collins and myself to determine the value of a revolution of the micrometer screw. Those stars were selected from the American Ephemeris whose declinations were greater than sixty degrees, preference being given to those between seventy and eighty.

After the wires were placed at right angles to the direction of motion of the star, and the movable wire placed five revolutions to the right of the fixed wire, ten transits were observed. The movable wire was then placed five revolutions to the left of the fixed wire, and ten more transits were taken. The observations were corrected for clock rate and for differential refraction, and reduced to equatorial interval by the formula

$$i = \frac{I \cos \delta}{k}.$$

The observations and results are shown in the following table:

Date.	Star.	Apparent Position.		Temp.	Hour Angle.	I	Dif. Refraction.	Clock Rate.	One Revolution.	Obs.
		a	δ							
		h m	° ′ ″	°	h m	s	s	s	″	
1889.										
Oct. 21.	α Ceph.	21 16	62 7 21	50	0 0	24.74	−0.010	0.000	17.345	L.
Nov. 5.	δ Ceph.	22 46	65 37 28	38	0 0	28 13	−0.015	0.000	17.408	L.
1891.										
July 9.	ε U. Mi.	16 57	82 13 3	67	−0 27	85.45	−0.023	+0.002	17.352	C.
" 9.	226 Ceph.	22 30	75 39 41	60	+0 24	46.69	−0.013	+0.001	17.341	L.
" 10.	δ U. Mi.	18 8	86 36 44	67	−0 20	195.93	−0.053	+0.003	17.363	L.
" 10.	226 Ceph.	22 30	75 39 42	62	−0 27	46.66	−0.013	+0.001	17.329	C.
" 21.	κ Ceph.	20 13	77 23 0	70	−0 27	52 87	−0.013	+0.001	17.319	L.
" 21.	Companion.	20 13	77 22 56	70	−0 27	52.97	−0.013	+0.001	17 354	L.
" 24.	11 Ceph.	21 40	70 48 31	68	−0 29	35.23	−0.010	+0.001	17.367	C.
" 25.	50 Drac.	18 50	75 18 23	71	−0 17	45.57	−0.012	+0.001	17.335	C.
" 27.	226 Ceph.	22 30	75 39 47	61	−0 4	46.82	−0.013	+0.001	17.387	C.
Aug 22.	δ U. Mi.	18 8	86 36 54	80	+0 8	196.02	−0.051	−0.007	17.356	C.
Sept. 2.	12 Y. C.	20 53	80 8 46	70	+0 6	67.60	−0.018	−0.005	17.347	C.
" 18.	κ Ceph.	20 13	77 23 15	80	−0 24	52.99	−0.014	−0.002	17.353	C.
" 18.	Companion.	20 13	77 23 11	80	−0 24	52.88	−0.014	−0.002	17.318	C.
" 23.	κ Ceph.	20 13	77 23 16	79	−0 9	52.85	−0.014	−0.002	17.306	C.
" 23.	Companion.	20 13	77 23 12	79	−0 9	53.03	−0.014	−0.002	17.367	C.
" 23.	38 Cass.	1 23	69 42 19	70	+0 30	33.25	−0.009	−0.001	17.294	L.
" 23.	Companion.	1 23	69 42 11	70	+0 30	33.34	−0.009	−0.001	17.342	L.
" 26.	κ Ceph.	20 13	77 23 17	81	+0 3	53.06	−0.014	−0.001	17 375	C.
" 26.	Companion.	20 13	77 23 13	81	+0 3	52.91	−0.014	−0.001	17.327	C.
" 27.	50 Cass.	1 54	71 53 42	70	+0 6	37.15	−0.010	−0.001	17.312	L.

Date	Star										C./L.
Oct. 28.	22 Cam.	6 7	69 21 17	30	—0 20	32.75	—0.010	0.000	17.315		C.
" 30.	β Ceph.	21 27	70 5 21	58	—0 5	33.79	—0 09	0.000	17.256		L.
" 30.	Companion.	21 27	70 5 16	58	—0 5	33 97	—0.009	0.000	17.349		L.
Nov. 2.	κ Ceph.	20 13	77 23 20	44	—0 24	53.01	—0.015	0.000	17. 38		L.
" 2.	α Cam.	4 43	66 9 26	32	—0 24	28.54	—0.008	0.000	17. 99		C.
" 4.	β Ceph.	21 27	70 5 21	38	+0 50	33.83	—0.010	0 000	17.252		L.
" 4.	Companion.	21 27	70 5 17	38	+0 50	33.78	—0 010	0.000	17.276		L.
" 5.	40 Cass.	1 54	71 53 56	33	+1 0	37.29	—0.011	0.000	17.376		C.
" 6.	226 Ceph.	22 30	75 40 20	41	+0 26	46.73	—0.013	.0 0	17.341		L.
" 6.	48 Ceph.	3 7	77 20 12	34	+0 48	52.56	—0.016	0.000	17.279		C.
" 7.	51 Cass.	1 56	74 3 26	42	+0 52	41 99	—0.012	0.000	17. 30		C.
" 13.	1 Drac.	9 22	81 48 2	36	—0 24	80.86	—0. 03	+0.002	17.296		L.
" 19.	48 Ceph.	3 7	77 20 17	28	+1 22	52.79	—0. 06	+0.002	17.357		L.
" 30.	226 Ceph.	22 30	75 40 23	24	+1 12	46.74	—0.015	+0.002	17.344		L.
" 30.	21 Cass.	0 39	74 24 3	22	—0 10	43.03	—0.013	+0.002	17.351		C.
" 30.	50 Cass.	1 54	71 54 3	21	—0 2	37.18	—0.011	+0.001	17.321		C.
Dec. 1.	γ Ceph.	23 35	77 1 58	32	+0 47	51.60	—0.015	+0.002	17. 84		C.
" 1.	Gb. 9 6.	5 25	74 58 17	27	+0 52	44.63	—0.014	+0.002	17. 83		L.

From these were obtained the equations of condition of the form

$$x + by - n = 0,$$

where x is the error of the assumed value of a revolution; y is the change in value of a revolution for a change of one degree of temperature; b is the difference between the observed temperature and 50°; n is the difference between the observed value of a revolution and the assumed value 17″.340.

No.	Equations of Condition.	Residuals.
	″	″
1	$x + 0y - 0.005 = 0$	−0.011
2	$x - 12y - 0.068 = 0$	−0.077
3	$x + 17y - 0.012 = 0$	−0.014
4	$x + 10y - 0.001 = 0$	−0.005
5	$x + 17y - 0.023 = 0$	−0.025
6	$x + 12y + 0.011 = 0$	+0.007
7	$x + 20y + 0.021 = 0$	+0.019
8	$x + 20y - 0.014 = 0$	−0.016
9	$x + 18y - 0.027 = 0$	−0.029
10	$x + 21y + 0.005 = 0$	+0.003
11	$x + 11y - 0.047 = 0$	−0.051
12	$x + 30y - 0.016 = 0$	−0.016
13	$x + 20y - 0.007 = 0$	−0.009
14	$x + 30y - 0.013 = 0$	−0.013
15	$x + 30y + 0.022 = 0$	+0.022
16	$x + 29y + 0.034 = 0$	+0.035
17	$x + 29y - 0.027 = 0$	−0.027
18	$x + 20y - 0.002 = 0$	−0.004
19	$x + 20y + 0.046 = 0$	+0.044
20	$x + 31y - 0.035 = 0$	−0.035

No.	Equation of Condition.	Residuals.
	"	*"*
21	$x + 31y + 0.013 = 0$	$+0.013$
22	$x + 20y + 0.028 = 0$	$+0.026$
23	$x - 20y + 0.025 = 0$	$+0.015$
24	$x + 8y + 0.084 = 0$	$+0.080$
25	$x + 8y - 0.009 = 0$	-0.013
26	$x - 6y - 0.018 = 0$	-0.025
27	$x - 18y + 0.041 = 0$	$+0.031$
28	$x - 12y + 0.088 = 0$	$+0.079$
29	$x - 12y + 0.064 = 0$	$+0.055$
30	$x - 17y - 0.035 = 0$	-0.046
31	$x - 9y - 0.004 = 0$	-0.012
32	$x - 16y + 0.061 = 0$	$+0.051$
33	$x - 8y + 0.040 = 0$	$+0.032$
34	$x - 14y + 0.044 = 0$	$+0.035$
35	$x - 22y - 0.017 = 0$	-0.023
36	$x - 26y - 0.004 = 0$	-0.015
37	$x - 28y - 0.011 = 0$	-0.023
38	$x - 29y + 0.019 = 0$	$+0.007$
39	$x - 18y - 0.024 = 0$	-0.034
40	$x - 23y - 0.013 = 0$	-0.024

From these were obtained the normal equations:

$$+ 40.000x + 162.00y + 0''.213 = 0$$
$$+ 162.00x + 16256.y - 2.520 = 0$$

The solution of these equations gives:

$$x = -0''.0062 \pm 0''.0038$$
$$y = +0''.000215 \pm 0''.000187$$

The probable error of a single observation is

$$r = \pm 0''.0233$$

The value of the $[vv]$ is

by elimination $0''.0455$
by substitution $0.0459.$

The value of a revolution of the micrometer, therefore, is

$$R = 17''.3338 \pm 0''.0038 + (0''.000215 \pm 0''.000187) (\tau° - 50°).$$

The value of R, which has previously been used, was $17''.333$. As this is a very convenient number for use, it has been retained, and a table constructed giving the constant correction and the correction for temperature for every ten degrees of the thermometer.

METHOD OF OBSERVATION.—The telescope used was the 10-inch Clark refractor. A complete set of measures was made, as follows:

(1) The zero of the position circle was determined by causing a star to " thread " the wire of the micrometer.

(2) The wires were separated by exactly two-thirds of a revolution of the screw, and the position angle measured in three ways, viz.: First, normal; *i. e.*, with the line through the eyes at right angles to the line through the stars. Secondly, parallel; *i. e.*, with the line through the eyes parallel to the line through the stars. Thirdly, horizontal; *i. e.*, with the line through the eyes parallel to the horizon.

(3) The position circle being rotated through 180°, the observations were repeated in the reverse order, so that the means of the times of observations in each position of the eyes should be the same.

(4) The zero of the position circle was again determined.

(5) Four double distances were measured.

The sidereal time at which each measure was made was recorded, as was also the temperature. In all cases a magnifying power of 375 was used with a bright field illumination.

THE OBSERVATIONS.—The following list contains all the observations made. The weights are on a scale of five:

No.	Date.	Hour Angle.	Position Angle.			Distance.	Tem.	Wt.
			Normal.	Parallel.	Horizontal.			
		h m	°	°	°	''	°	
1	1889 June 20	—2 56	186.42	186.97	. . .	16.282	76	2
2	July 4	+3 6	187.06	186.46	. . .	16.189	66	2
3	5	—3 0	187.52	186.40	185.68	16.190	75	2
4	8	+1 2	186.39	187.14	. . .	16.223	80	2
5	12	—0 48	186.8	185.7	185.3	. . .	77	1
6	15	—0 59	186.96	186 57	186.40	16.163	64	2
7	16	—1 15	187.00	186.78	185.95	16.229	72	3
8	16	+4 21	186.79	186.90	186.53	16.232	64	2
9	Sept. 23	+3 11	187.59	187.07	186.73	16.085	63	3
10	28	+4 17	187.23	186.79	186.62	. . .	58	2
11	Oct. 2	+4 0	187.66	187.32	186.19	16.398	54	2
12	5	+3 16	187.39	187.27	186.00	16.094	56	2
13	Nov. 4	+4 37	187.09	186.66	186.16	. . .	50	2
14	6	+4 35	187.10	186.96	184.86	16 153	42	2
15	1890 Apr. 11	+0 19	186.96	186.65	186.35	16.041	42	4
16	Nov. 14	+5 14	187.62	188.23	187.50	. . .	60	2
17	1891 Jan. 22	—2 55	188.3	185.9	186.5	. . .	32	1
18	Feb. 10	—2 41	188.30	186.17	·186.37	16.025	26	3
19	13	—2 41	188.12	186.08	187.28	. . .	28	2
20	22	—3 2	187.86	186.74	187.19	15.958	27	4
21	23	—3 50	188.53	185.97	186.57	16.064	29	2
22	Mar. 5	—1 44	187.83	187.33	186.91	16.012	18	2
23	17	—2 57	187.90	185.68	186.68	16.040	29	2

No.	Date.	Hour Angle.	Position Angle.			Distance.	Tem.	Wt.
			Normal.	Parallel.	Horizontal.			
	1891	h m	o	o	o	"	o	
24	Mar. 29	−0 17	187.62	186.74	187.44	16.058	35	2
25	Apr. 12	+1 7	187.72	188 14	188.44	15.949	38	3
26	15	−2 43	188.53	186.03	186.38	16.043	61	3
27	May 12	−2 42	188.90	186.78	186.52	16.034	53	3
28	17	−1 45	187.95	187.92	185.65	16.157	54	2
29	30	−1 23	188.25	186.25	. . .	. . .	60	1
30	June 1	+1 44	187.65	186.70	184.75	. . .	62	1
31	1	+3 15	187.78	186.68	186.20	15.986	62	3
32	8	+0 9	187.32	186.45	187.60	15.990	60	2
33	9	+0 14	188.25	186.98	187.45	. . .	68	1
34	10	+0 9	187.83	187.50	187.65	15.960	62	3
35	13	−0 13	187.57	186.39	187.45	16.022	68	2
36	24	+0 31	187.83	187.35	188.05	16.143	68	2
37	Aug. 31	+3 59	187.25	188.07·	186.50	15.941	62	3
38	Sept. 3	+3 11	187.47	187.90	186.65	15.893	68	2
39	9	+4 59	187.30	188.05	186.45	15.936	57	2
40	10	+4 23	187.53	188.35	188.53	15.865	62	3
41	Oct. 24	+3 18	187.99	188.59	186.43	15.757	52	3
42	Nov. 2	+5 5	187.27	188.40	186.00	15.773	38	2
43	6	+4 35	. . .	. . .	. . .	15.707	41	2
44	11	+5 7	· 188.60	189.75	187.80	15.792	52	2
45	30	+4 25	188.01	189.14	188.74	15.614	26	2

These observations were corrected for proper motion, precession and refraction. The yearly change due to proper motion of the stars was computed to be

$$\Delta a - 0''.018; \Delta\delta + 0''.166.$$

The yearly variation for precession, $-0°.006$, was combined with this proper motion, and the whole formed into a table which gives the reduction for proper motion and precession to 1891.0 expressed in angle and distance.

Date.	Δp	Δs
	°	''
1889.5	+0.518	−0.231
1890.0	+0.346	−0.154
1890.5	+0.174	−0.077
1891.0	0.000	0.000
1891.5	−0.181	+0.077
1892.0	−0.363	+0.154

The correction for refraction was computed by the formulæ

$$\Delta p = -\kappa \tan^2 \zeta \cos p \sin (p - 2\eta)$$
$$\Delta s = s \kappa \sec^2 H$$
$$\tan^2 H = \tan^2 \zeta \cos^2 (p - \eta),$$

where ζ denotes the zenith distance of the star; η the parallactic angle; and κ is taken from a table of refraction.

These corrections, with the observations reduced to 1891.0, will be found below.

No.	Precession and Proper Motion.	Refraction.	Position Angle 1891.0.			Proper Motion.	Refraction.	Distance 1891.0.
			Normal.	Parallel.	Horizontal.			
	°	°	°	°	°	"	"	"
1	+0.53	—0.01	186.94	187.49	. . .	—0.236	+0 005	16.051
2	+0.51	+0.01	187.58	186.98	. . .	—0.230	+0.006	15.965
3	+0.51	—0.01	188.02	186.90	186.18	—0.229	+0.005	15.966
4	+0.51	0.00	186.90	187.65	. . .	—0.228	+0.005	16.000
5	+0.51	0.00	187.31	186.21	185.81	. . .	. . .	. . .
6	+0.50	0.00	187.46	187.07	186.90	—0.225	+0.005	15.943
7	+0.50	0.00	187.50	187.28	186.45	—0.225	+0.005	16.009
8	+0.50	+0.03	187.32	187.43	187.06	—0.225	+0.009	16.016
9	+0.44	+0.02	188.05	187.53	187.19	—0.195	+0.006	15.896
10	+0.43	+0.03	187.69	187.25	187.08	. . .	. . .	. . .
11	+0.43	+0.03	188.12	187.78	186.65	—0.192	+0.007	16.213
12	+0.43	+0.02	187.84	187.72	186.45	—0.191	+0.006	15.909
13	+0.40	+0.05	187.54	187.11	186.61	. . .	. . .	. . .
14	+0.39	+0.04	187.53	187.39	185.29	—0.177	+0.010	15.988
15	+0.24	+0.01	187.21	186.90	186.60	—0.111	+0.005	15.935
16	+0.04	+0.07	187.73	188.34	187.61	. . .	. . .	. . .
17	—0.02	—0.01	188.27	185.87	186.47	. . .	. . .	. . .
18	—0.04	—0.01	188.25	186.12	186.32	+0.017	+0.005	16.047
19	—0.04	—0.01	188.07	186.03	187.23	. . .	. . .	. . .
20	—0.05	—0.01	187.80	186.68	187.13	+0.022	+0.005	15.985
21	—0.05	—0.03	188.45	185.89	186.49	+0.022	+0.007	16.093
22	—0.06	0.00	187.67	187.27	186.85	+0.028	+0.005	16.045
23	—0.07	—0.01	187.82	185.60	186.60	+0.032	+0.005	16.077

No.	Precession and Proper Motion.	Refraction.	Position Angle 1891.0.			Proper Motion.	Refraction.	Distance 1891.0.
			Normal.	Parallel.	Horizontal.			
	°	°	°	°		"	"	"
24	−0.08	0.00	187.54	186.66	187.36	+0.037	+0.004	16.099
25	−0.10	0.00	187.62	188.04	188.34	+0.043	+0.005	15.997
26	−0.10	−0.01	188.42	185.92	186.27	+0 044	+0.005	16.092
27	−0.13	−0.01	188.76	186.64	186.38	+0.055	+0.005	16.094
28	−0.14	0.00	187.81	185.78	185.51	+0.059	+0 005	16.221
29	−0.15	0.00	187.10	186.10	. . .	. . .	. . .	. . .
30	−0 15	+0.01	187.51	186.56	184.61	. . .	. . .	. . .
31	−0.15	+0.02	187.65	186.55	186.07	+0.065	+0.006	16.057
32	−0 16	0.00	187.16	186.29	187.44	+0.068	+0.005	16.063
33	−0.16	0.00	188.09	186.82	187.29	. . .	. .	. . .
34	−0.16	0.00	187.67	187.34	187.49	+0.068	+0 005	16.033
35	−0.16	0.00	187.41	186.23	187.29	+0.070	+0.004	16.096
36	−0.17	0.00	187.66	187.18	187.88	+0.074	+0.005	16.222
37	−0.24	+0.03	187.04	187.86	186.29	+0.104	+0 007	16.052
38	−0.24	+0.02	187.25	187.68	186.43	+0.106	+0.006	16.005
39	−0.24	+0.06	187.12	187.87	186.27	+0.108	+0.011	16.055
40	−0.25	+0.04	187.32	188.14	188 32	+0.108	+0.009	15.982
41	−0.29	+0.02	187.72	188.32	186.16	+0.125	+0.006	15.888
42	−0.29	+0.06	187.04	188.17	185.77	+0.129	+0.014	15.916
43	. . .	. . .	. . .	. . .	. . .	+0.130	+0.010	15.847
44	−0.30	+0.06	188.36	189.51	187.56	+0.132	+0.012	15.936
45	−0.32	+0 03	187.72	188.85	188.45	+0.142	+0.011	15.767

EQUATIONS OF CONDITION.—I have thought it best to reduce the observations first without introducing personal equation; for the results should show whether personal equation exists to any great extent. The equations of condition were put in the form

$$\Delta p = \Delta p_0 + x + ay + b\pi;$$
$$\Delta s = \Delta s_0 + x_1 + ay_1 + b_1\pi.$$

Δp_0 is an assumed value of the true position angle; and $-x$, its error; Δs_0 is an assumed value of the true distance, and $-x_1$, its error; y is the correction to the assumed proper motion as it affects the angle; and y_1 is the correction as it affects the distance; a is the time interval between the time of observation and 1891.0; π is the annual parallax and b and b_1 are computed by the formulæ

$$b = Rm_1 \cos(\theta - M_1)$$
$$b_1 = Rm \cos(\theta - M)$$
$$m_1 \sin M_1 = \frac{1}{s}[-\cos\epsilon \cos a \cos p - \cos\epsilon \sin a \sin\delta \sin p + \sin\epsilon \cos\delta \sin p]$$
$$m_1 \cos M_1 = \frac{1}{s}[-\sin\delta \cos a \sin p + \sin a \cos p]$$
$$m \sin M = -\cos\epsilon \cos a \sin p + \cos\epsilon \sin a \sin\delta \cos p - \sin\epsilon \cos\delta \cos p$$
$$m \cos M = \sin\delta \cos a \cos p + \sin a \sin p;$$

where R and θ denote respectively the radius vector and longitude of the sun; a and δ, the right ascension and declination of the star; and ϵ, the obliquity of the ecliptic. On account of the change in position angle, M and M_1 were not constant. Their values, with the values of m_1 and m, were computed to be

Date.	Log. m_1	M_1	Log. m.	M.
1889.0	0.0000	343° 36′	9.8690	73° 51′
1890.0	0.0000	343 20	9.8690	73 23
1891.0	0.0000	343 4	9.8690	72 55
1892.0	0.0000	342 48	9.8690	72 27

Δp_0 was assumed to be for

> eyes normal,   187°.68
> eyes parallel,   187.12
> eyes horizontal, 186.74.

Δs_0 was assumed to be 16″.014.

In order to express $\Delta p - \Delta p_0$ in arc they were multiplied by $s \sin 1^0$.

WEIGHTING THE OBSERVATIONS.—All the observations were given the same weight in the equations of condition excepting those which are marked 1 at the time of observation. These have been given half weight.

No.	Equations of Condition.—Normal.		Residuals.	
			Without p. e. Term.	With p. e. Term.
1	$1.0x - 1.529y - 0.289\pi + 0.210 = 0$	$-0.586z$	$+0.188$	$+0.204$
2	$1.0 - 1.491 - 0.506 + 0.027 = 0$	$+0.620$	-0.003	-0.012
3	$1.0 - 1.488 - 0.521 - 0.096 = 0$	-0.600	-0.132	-0.114
4	$1.0 - 1.480 - 0.564 + 0.221 = 0$	$+0.206$	$+0.182$	$+0.186$
5	$0.7 - 1.028 - 0.433 + 0.074 = 0$	-0.114	$+0.043$	$+0.069$
6	$1.0 - 1.460 - 0.658 + 0.062 = 0$	-0.196	$+0.016$	$+0.031$
7	$1.0 - 1.458 - 0.671 + 0.051 = 0$	-0.250	$+0.004$	$+0.020$
8	$1.0 - 1.458 - 0.671 + 0.102 = 0$	$+0.870$	$+0.053$	$+0.049$
9	$1.0 - 1.269 - 0.954 - 0.105 = 0$	$+0.636$	-0.172	-0.174
10	$1.0 - 1.255 - 0.924 - 0.003 = 0$	$+0.857$	-0.069	-0.070
11	$1.0 - 1.244 - 0.892 - 0.124 = 0$	$+0.800$	-0.186	-0.188
12	$1.0 - 1.236 - 0.868 - 0.045 = 0$	$+0.653$	-0.104	-0.104
13	$1.0 - 1.154 - 0.500 + 0.040 = 0$	$+0.923$	$+0.005$	-0.004
14	$1.0 - 1.148 - 0.485 + 0.042 = 0$	$+0.916$	$+0.007$	-0.001
15	$1.0 - 0.721 + 0.959 + 0.133 = 0$	$+0.063$	$+0.195$	-0.188
16	$1.0 - 0.127 - 0.342 - 0.014 = 0$	$+1.047$	-0.034	-0.046
17	$0.7 + 0.043 + 0.528 - 0.116 = 0$	-0.408	-0.082	-0.077
18	$1.0 + 0.114 + 0.922 - 0.159 = 0$	-0.537	-0.097	-0.095
19	$1.0 + 0.122 + 0.941 - 0.109 = 0$	-0.537	-0.044	-0.043
20	$1.0 + 0.147 + 0.978 - 0.034 = 0$	-0.610	$+0.034$	$+0.035$
21	$1.0 + 0.150 + 0.981 - 0.215 = 0$	-0.767	-0.147	-0.142
22	$1.0x + 0.177y + 0.993\pi + 0.003 = 0$	$-0.346z$	$+0.072$	$+0.070$

No.	Equations of Condition.—Normal.		Residuals.	
			Without p. e. Term.	With p. e. Term.
23	$1.0x + 0.210y + 0.954\pi - 0.011 = 0$	$-0.590z$	$+0.055$	$+0.059$
24	$1.0 + 0.242 + 0.896 + 0.039 = 0$	-0.057	$+0.100$	$+0.095$
25	$1.0 + 0.281 + 0.768 + 0.017 = 0$	$+0.223$	$+0.071$	$+0.061$
26	$1.0 + 0.289 + 0.734 - 0.206 = 0$	-0.543	-0.155	-0.150
27	$1.0 + 0.363 + 0.360 - 0.301 = 0$	-0.540	-0.277	-0.266
28	$1.0 + 0.377 + 0.279 - 0.036 = 0$	-0.350	-0.015	-0.009
29	$0.7 + 0.288 + 0.043 + 0.113 = 0$	-0.194	$+0.117$	$+0.123$
30	$0.7 + 0.293 + 0.020 + 0.034 = 0$	$+0.243$	$+0.036$	$+0.034$
31	$1.0 + 0.418 + 0.028 + 0.008 = 0$	$+0.650$	$+0.011$	$+0.003$
32	$1.0 + 0.437 - 0.091 + 0.145 = 0$	$+0.030$	$+0.143$	$+0.145$
33	$0.7 + 0.308 - 0.076 - 0.080 = 0$	$+0.032$	-0.084	-0.081
34	$1.0 + 0.442 - 0.125 + 0.003 = 0$	$+0.030$	-0.004	$+0.001$
35	$1.0 + 0.451 - 0.175 + 0.075 = 0$	-0.040	$+0.064$	$+0.072$
36	$1.0 + 0.481 - 0.339 + 0.006 = 0$	$+0.103$	-0.015	-0.005
37	$1.0 + 0.667 - 1.006 + 0.178 = 0$	$+0.797$	$+0.112$	$+0.116$
38	$1.0 + 0.675 - 1.008 + 0.120 = 0$	$+0.637$	$+0.054$	$+0.061$
39	$1.0 + 0.692 - 1.003 + 0.156 = 0$	$+0.877$	$+0.090$	$+0.092$
40	$1.0 + 0.694 - 1.002 + 0.100 = 0$	$+0.660$	$+0.034$	$+0.040$
41	$1.0 + 0.815 - 0.657 - 0.011 = 0$	$+1.017$	-0.033	-0.057
42	$1.0 + 0.839 - 0.530 + 0.178 = 0$	$+0.917$	$+0.144$	$+0.140$
44	$1.0 + 0.864 - 0.390 - 0.188 = 0$	$+1.023$	-0.213	-0.219
45	$1.0x + 0.918y - 0.070\pi - 0.011 = 0$	$+0.883z$	-0.015	-0.022

No.	Equations of Condition.—Parallel.		Residuals.	
			Without p. e. Term.	With p. e. Term.
1	$1.0x - 1.529y - 0.289\pi - 0.105 = 0$	$-0.586z$	-0.148	-0.319
2	$1.0 - 1.491 - 0.506 + 0.040 = 0$	$+0.620$	$+0.047$	$+0.147$
3	$1.0 - 1.488 - 0.521 + 0.062 = 0$	-0.600	$+0.073$	-0.131
4	$1.0 - 1.480 - 0.564 - 0.150 = 0$	$+0.206$	-0.138	-0.152
5	$0.7 - 1.028 - 0.433 + 0.181 = 0$	-0.114	$+0.205$	$+0.122$
6	$1.0 - 1.460 - 0.658 + 0.014 = 0$	-0.196	$+0.057$	-0.077
7	$1.0 - 1.458 - 0.671 - 0.050 = 0$	-0.250	-0.003	-0.154
8	$1.0 - 1.458 - 0.671 - 0.088 = 0$	$+0.870$	-0.041	$+0.094$
9	$1.0 - 1.269 - 0.954 - 0.116 = 0$	$+0.636$	$+0.009$	$+0.027$
10	$1.0 - 1.255 - 0.924 - 0.037 = 0$	$+0.857$	$+0.084$	$+0.161$
11	$1.0 - 1.244 - 0.892 - 0.187 = 0$	$+0.800$	-0.074	-0.004
12	$1.0 - 1.236 - 0.868 - 0.170 = 0$	$+0.653$	-0.062	-0.027
13	$1.0 - 1.154 - 0.500 + 0.003 = 0$	$+0.923$	$+0.032$	$+0.196$
14	$1.0 - 1.148 - 0.485 - 0.076 = 0$	$+0.916$	-0.060	$+0.114$
15	$1.0 - 0.721 + 0.959 + 0.062 = 0$	$+0.063$	-0.212	-0.022
16	$1.0 - 0.127 - 0.342 - 0.341 = 0$	$+1.047$	-0.279	-0.100
17	$0.7 + 0.043 + 0.528 + 0.244 = 0$	-0.403	$+0.122$	$+0.077$
18	$1.0 + 0.114 + 0.922 + 0.279 = 0$	-0.537	$+0.071$	$+0.046$
19	$1.0 + 0.122 + 0.941 + 0.304 = 0$	-0.537	$+0.092$	$+0.070$
20	$1.0 + 0.147 + 0.978 + 0.123 = 0$	-0.610	-0.095	-0.131
21	$1.0 + 0.150 + 0.981 + 0.343 = 0$	-0.767	$+0.124$	$+0.050$
22	$1.0x + 0.177y + 0.993\pi - 0.042 = 0$	$-0.346z$	-0.262	-0.230

No.	Equations of Condition.—Parallel.		Residuals.	
			Without p. e. Term.	With p. e. Term.
			$''$	$''$
23	$1.0x + 0.210y + 0.964\pi + 0.424 = 0$	$-0.590z$	$+0.214$	$+0.174$
24	$1.0 \ + 0.242 \ + 0.896 \ + 0.128 = 0$	-0.057	-0.063	$+0.021$
25	$1.0 \ + 0.281 \ + 0.768 \ - 0.257 = 0$	$+0.223$	-0.418	-0.283
26	$1.0 \ + 0.289 \ + 0.734 \ + 0.335 = 0$	-0.543	$+0.183$	$+0.115$
27	$1.0 \ + 0.363 \ + 0.360 \ + 0.134 = 0$	-0.540	$+0.072$	-0.060
28	$1.0 \ + 0.377 \ + 0.279 \ + 0.373 = 0$	-0.350	$+0.327$	$+0.213$
29	$0.7 \ + 0.288 \ + 0.043 \ + 0.199 = 0$	-0.194	$+0.206$	$+0.123$
30	$0.7 \ + 0.293 \ + 0.020 \ + 0.109 = 0$	$+0.243$	$+0.120$	$+0.132$
31	$1.0 \ + 0.418 \ + 0.028 \ + 0.159 = 0$	$+0.650$	$+0.177$	$+0.289$
32	$1.0 \ + 0.437 \ - 0.091 \ + 0.231 = 0$	$+0.030$	$+0.276$	$+0.212$
33	$0.7 \ + 0.308 \ - 0.076 \ + 0.059 = 0$	$+0.032$	$+0.093$	$+0.049$
34	$1.0 \ + 0.442 \ - 0.125 \ - 0.061 = 0$	$+0.030$	-0.008	-0.078
35	$1.0 \ + 0.451 \ - 0.175 \ + 0.248 = 0$	-0.040	$+0.313$	$+0.215$
36	$1.0 \ + 0.481 \ - 0.339 \ - 0.017 = 0$	$+0.103$	$+0.086$	-0.009
37	$1.0 \ + 0.667 \ - 1.006 \ - 0.206 = 0$	$+0.797$	$+0.063$	$+0.030$
38	$1.0 \ + 0.675 \ - 1.008 \ - 0.155 = 0$	$+0.637$	$+0.116$	$+0.040$
39	$1.0 \ + 0.692 \ - 1.003 \ - 0.208 = 0$	$+0.877$	$+0.064$	$+0.048$
40	$1.0 \ + 0.694 \ - 1.002 \ - 0.283 = 0$	$+0.660$	-0.011	-0.082
41	$1.0 \ + 0.815 \ - 0.657 \ - 0.333 = 0$	$+1.017$	-0.133	-0.089
42	$1.0 \ + 0.839 \ - 0.530 \ - 0.291 = 0$	$+0.917$	-0.117	-0.049
44	$1.0 \ + 0.864 \ - 0.390 \ - 0.662 = 0$	$+1.023$	-0.518	-0.400
45	$1.0x + 0.918y - 0.070\pi - 0.479 = 0$	$+0.883z$	-0.406	-0.271

No.	Equations of Condition.—Horizontal.		Residuals.	
			Without p. e. Term.	With p. e. Term.
			$''$	$''$
3	$1.0x - 1.488y - 0.521\pi + 0.159 = 0$	$-0.600z$	$+0.101$	$+0.041$
5	$0.7 \ -1.028 \ -0.433 \ +0.185 = 0$	-0.114	$+0.162$	$+0.135$
6	$1.0 \ -1.460 \ -0.658 \ -0.050 = 0$	-0.196	$-0 107$	-0.145
7	$1.0 \ -1.458 \ -0.671 \ +0.082 = 0$	-0.250	$+0.025$	-0.018
8	$1.0 \ -1.458 \ -0.671 \ -0.090 = 0$	$+0.870$	-0.147	-0.114
9	$1.0 \ -1.269 \ -0.954 \ -0.127 = 0$	$+0.636$	-0.171	-0.175
10	$1.0 \ -1.255 \ -0.924 \ -0.096 = 0$	$+0.857$	-0.140	-0.122
11	$1.0 \ -1.244 \ -0.892 \ +0.025 = 0$	$+0 800$	-0.019	-0.004
12	$1.0 \ -1.236 \ -0.868 \ +0.082 = 0$	$+0.653$	$+0.038$	$+0.043$
13	$1.0 \ -1.154 \ -0.500 \ +0.037 = 0$	$+0.923$	-0.003	$+0.038$
14	$1.0 \ -1.148 \ -0.485 \ +0.410 = 0$	$+0.916$	-0.294	$+0.411$
15	$1.0 \ -0.721 \ +0.959 \ +0.040 = 0$	$+0.063$	$+0.019$	$+0.062$
16	$1.0 \ -0.127 \ -0.342 \ -0.243 = 0$	$+1.047$	-0.129	-0.187
17	$0.7 \ +0.043 \ +0.528 \ +0 053 = 0$	$-0 408$	$+0.079$	$+0.055$
18	$1.0 \ +0.114 \ +0.922 \ +0.117 = 0$	-0.537	$+0.140$	$+0.130$
19	$1.0 \ +0.122 \ +0.941 \ -0.137 = 0$	-0.537	-0.114	$+0.122$
20	$1.0 \ +0.147 \ +0.978 \ -0.109 = 0$	-0.610	-0.084	-0.093
21	$1.0 \ +0.150 \ +0.981 \ +0.070 = 0$	-0.767	$+0.095$	$+0.073$
22	$10 \ +0.177 \ +0.993 \ -0.031 = 0$	-0.346	-0.007	$+0.003$
23	$1.0x + 0.210y + 0.964\pi + 0 040 = 0$	$-0.590z$	$+0 068$	$+0.056$

No.	Equations of Condition.—Horizontal.		Residuals.	
			Without p. e. Term.	With p. e. Term.
24	$1.0x + 0.242y + 0.896\pi - 0\overset{''}{1}73 = 0$	$-0.057z$	$\overset{''}{-0}.144$	$\overset{''}{-0}.157$
25	$1.0 \ + 0.281 \ + 0.768 \ - 0.446 = 0$	$+0.223$	-0.414	-0.379
26	$1.0 \ + 0.289 \ + 0.734 \ + 0.131 = 0$	-0.543	$+0.163$	$+0.143$
27	$1.0 \ + 0.363 \ + 0.360 \ + 0.100 = 0$	-0.540	$+0.137$	$+0.101$
28	$1.0 \ + 0.377 \ + 0.279 \ + 0.343 = 0$	-0.350	$+0.381$	$+0.355$
30	$0.7 \ + 0.293 \ + 0.020 \ + 0.415 = 0$	$+0.243$	$+0.454$	$+0.450$
31	$1.0 \ + 0.418 \ + 0.028 \ + 0.187 = 0$	$+0.650$	$+0.227$	$+0.267$
32	$1.0 \ + 0.437 \ - 0.091 \ - 0.195 = 0$	$+0.030$	-0.153	-0.173
33	$0.7 \ + 0.308 \ - 0.076 \ - 0.107 = 0$	$+0.032$	-0.066	-0.090
34	$1.0 \ + 0.442 \ - 0.125 \ - 0.209 = 0$	$+0.030$	-0.166	-0.187
35	$1.0 \ + 0.451 \ - 0.175 \ - 0.153 = 0$	-0.040	-0.110	-0.138
36	$1.0 \ + 0.481 \ - 0.339 \ - 0.317 = 0$	$+0.103$	-0.272	-0.297
37	$1.0 \ + 0.667 \ - 1.006 \ + 0.125 = 0$	$+0.797$	$+0.171$	$+0.163$
38	$1.0 \ + 0.675 \ - 1.008 \ + 0.086 = 0$	$+0.637$	$+0.142$	$+0.117$
39	$1.0 \ + 0.692 \ - 1.003 \ + 0.131 = 0$	$+0.877$	$+0.187$	$+0.183$
40	$1.0 \ + 0.694 \ - 1.002 \ - 0.439 = 0$	$+0.660$	-0.382	-0.396
41	$1.0 \ + 0.815 \ - 0.657 \ + 0.161 = 0$	$+1.017$	$+0.223$	$+0.240$
42	$1.0 \ + 0.839 \ - 0.530 \ + 0.269 = 0$	$+0.917$	$+0.333$	$+0.348$
44	$1.0 \ + 0.864 \ - 0.390 \ - 0.227 = 0$	$+1.023$	-0.163	-0.161
45	$1.0x + 0.918y - 0.070\pi - 0.474 = 0$	$+0.883z$	-0.407	-0.370

No.	Equations of Condition.—Distance.		Residuals.	
			Without p. e. Term.	With p. e. Term.
1	$1.0z - 1.529y + 0.721\pi - 0.037 = 0$	$-0.586z$	-0.005	$+0.016$
2	$1.0 - 1.491 + 0.653 + 0.049 = 0$	$+0.620$	$+0.077$	$+0.048$
3	$1.0 - 1.488 + 0.647 + 0.048 = 0$	-0.600	$+0.076$	$+0.093$
4	$1.0 - 1.480 + 0.627 + 0.014 = 0$	$+0.206$	$+0.040$	$+0.027$
6	$1.0 - 1.460 + 0.574 + 0.071 = 0$	-0.196	$+0.092$	$+0.095$
7	$1.0 - 1.458 + 0.566 + 0.005 = 0$	-0.250	$+0\,025$	$+0.032$
8	$1.0 - 1.458 + 0.566 - 0.002 = 0$	$+0.870$	$+0.018$	-0.015
9	$1.0 - 1.269 - 0.228 + 0.118 = 0$	$+0.636$	$+0.057$	$+0.053$
11	$1.0 - 1.244 - 0.332 - 0.199 = 0$	$+0.800$	-0.271	-0.280
13	$1.0 - 1.154 - 0.632 + 0.105 = 0$	$+0.923$	$+0.013$	-0.007
14	$1.0 - 1.148 - 0.638 + 0.026 = 0$	$+0.916$	-0.076	-0.084
15	$1.0 - 0.721 + 0.467 + 0.079 = 0$	$+0.063$	$+0.120$	$+0.074$
18	$1.0 + 0.114 - 0.259 - 0.033 = 0$	-0.537	-0.064	-0.033
20	$1.0 + 0.147 - 0.108 + 0.029 = 0$	-0.610	$+0.003$	$+0.043$
21	$1.0 + 0.150 - 0.095 - 0.079 = 0$	-0.767	-0.103	-0.058
22	$1.0 + 0.177 + 0.033 - 0.031 = 0$	-0.346	-0.040	-0.015
23	$1.0 + 0.210 + 0.185 - 0.063 = 0$	-0.590	-0.048	-0.025
24	$1.0 + 0.242y + 0.329\pi - 0.085 = 0$	$-0.057z$	-0.062	-0.057

No.	Equations of Condition.—Distance.		Residuals.	
			Without p. e. Term.	With p. e. Term.
			"	"
25	$1.0x + 0.281y + 0.479\pi + 0.017 = 0$	$+0.223z$	$+0.057$	$+0.006$
26	$1.0 + 0.289 + 0.508 - 0.078 = 0$	-0.543	-0.035	-0.015
27	$1.0 + 0.363 + 0.700 - 0\ 080 = 0$	-0.540	-0.016	$+0.002$
28	$1.0 + 0\ 377 + 0.720 - 0.207 = 0$	-0.350	-0.153	-0.131
31	$1.0 + 0.418 + 0.750 - 0.043 = 0$	$+0.650$	$+0.027$	-0.003
32	$1.0 + 0.437 + 0.748 - 0.049 = 0$	$+0.030$	$+0.021$	$+0.015$
34	$1.0 + 0.442 + 0.745 - 0.019 = 0$	$+0.030$	$+0.051$	$+0.045$
35	$1.0 + 0.451 + 0.740 - 0.082 = 0$	-0.040	$-0\ 013$	-0.015
36	$1.0 + 0.481 + 0.708 - 0.208 = 0$	$+0.103$	-0.141	-0.149
37	$1.0 + 0.667 + 0.536 - 0.038 = 0$	$+0.797$	-0.024	$+0.065$
38	$1.0 + 0.675 + 0.156 + 0.009 = 0$	$+0.637$	$+0.020$	$+0.005$
39	$1.0 + 0.692 - 0.060 - 0.041 = 0$	$+0.877$	-0.052	-0.062
40	$1.0 + 0.694 - 0.073 + 0.032 = 0$	$+0.660$	$+0.019$	$+0.009$
41	$1.0 + 0.815 - 0.555 + 0.126 = 0$	$+1.017$	$+0.068$	$+0.010$
42	$1\ 0 + 0.839 - 0.608 + 0.098 = 0$	$+0.917$	$+0.032$	$+0.023$
43	$1.0 + 0.850 - 0.647 + 0.167 = 0$	$+0.920$	$+0.096$	$+0.092$
44	$1.0 + 0.864 - 0.674 + 0.078 = 0$	$+1.023$	$+0.004$	$+0.048$
45	$1.0x + 0.918y - 0.728\pi + 0.247 = 0$	$+0.883z$	$+0.169$	$+0.167$

By the method of Least Squares these equations were reduced to the following normal equations:

Eyes Normal.

$$+ 41.450x - 7.720y - 5.382\pi + 0.266'' = 0$$
$$- 7.720x + 32.576y + 8.545\pi - 0.553 = 0$$
$$- 5.382x + 8.545y + 20.361\pi - 1.351 = 0$$

Eyes Parallel.

$$+ 41.450x - 7.720y - 5.382\pi - 0.489 = 0$$
$$- 7.720x + 32.576y + 8.545\pi - 0.340 = 0$$
$$- 5.382x + 8.545y + 20.361\pi + 4.018 = 0$$

Eyes Horizontal.

$$+ 37.960x - 3.422y - 4.053\pi - 0.538 = 0$$
$$- 3.422x + 25.742y + 6.502\pi - 1.254 = 0$$
$$- 4.053x + 6.502y + 19.701\pi - 0.228 = 0$$

Distance.

$$+ 36.000x - 4.307y + 6.521\pi - 0.056 = 0$$
$$- 4.307x + 28.835y - 4.501\pi - 0.085 = 0$$
$$+ 6.521x - 4.501y + 10.767\pi - 0.958 = 0$$

The solutions of the equations give:

	Normal.	Parallel.	Horizontal.	Distance.
x	$+ 0.002'' \pm 0.013''$	$- 0.005'' \pm 0.021''$	$+ 0.019'' \pm 0.024''$	$- 0.016'' \pm 0.010''$
y	$- 0.001 \pm 0.015$	$+ 0.069 \pm 0.019$	$+ 0.052 \pm 0.030$	$+ 0.017 \pm 0.011$
π	$+ 0.067 \pm 0.018$	$- 0.228 \pm 0.031$	$- 0.002 \pm 0.034$	$+ 0.106 \pm 0.018$
r	± 0.076	± 0.129	± 0.146	± 0.056

PERSONAL EQUATION.—Since the probable errors of π are small, we must conclude that the great difference in the values of the parallax is due to personal error. We must also conclude that the personal error varies with the different positions of the eyes: for the observations were made under exactly the same conditions in all other respects.

I have made a rough examination of the personal error by plotting the observations to scale. The hour angle was taken as the X co-ordinate; and the difference $p - p_0$, expressed in seconds of arc, was taken as the y co-ordinate. The observations were plotted separately for each position of the eyes, and a curve drawn to represent them. Observations made on the double stars South 503 and Σ 2877 were treated in the same manner. From a comparison of the curves it was found that the personal error might be considered to vary with the hour angle, since the curves are approximately straight lines. But, since the parallax coefficient may also be considered to be a function of the hour angle, if a sensible parallax exists the curves will be affected by it. On account of this relation, the effect of personal error appears more in π than in any of the other unknown quantities. It is necessary, therefore, in observations of this kind, to break up as much as possible this relation between the parallax coefficient and the hour angle by observing always at the same hour angle; or, where this is impossible, occasionally to measure the angle twice on the same night, at widely different hour angles.

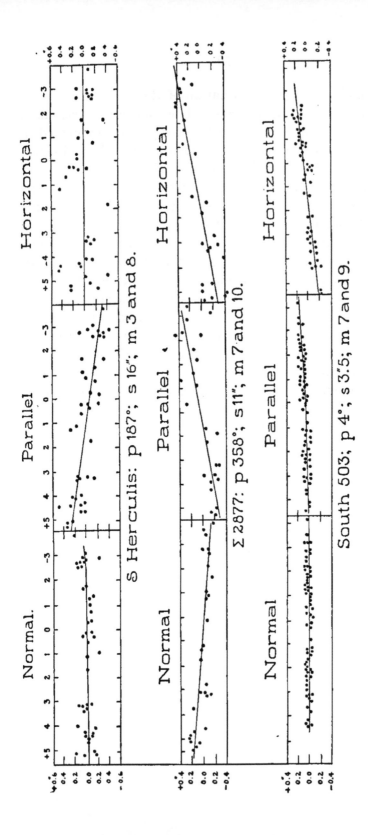

Horizontal   Parallel   Normal.

S Herculis: p 187°; s 16″, m 3 and 8.

Horizontal   Parallel   Normal

Σ 2877: p 358°; s 11″, m 7 and 10.

Horizontal   Parallel   Normal

South 503; p 4°; s 3″.5; m 7 and 9.

It is of interest to notice, from the drawings, that the Normal observations are most accurate and least affected by personal error.

PERSONAL EQUATION TERM.—To express the personal equation I have introduced a term in the equations of condition of the form dz, where d is the hour angle expressed in hours and divided by five. The values for d will be found in column seven of the equations of condition. The normal equations obtained from the equations of condition with this term added are:

Eyes Normal.

$$+ 41.450x - 7.720y - 5.382\pi + 8.584z + 0.266'' = 0$$
$$- 7.720x + 32.576y + 8.545\pi - 1.216z - 0.553 = 0$$
$$- 5.382x + 8.545y + 20.361\pi - 12.736z - 1.351 = 0$$
$$+ 8.584x - 1.216y - 12.736\pi + 16.406z + 0.960 = 0$$

Eyes Parallel.

$$+ 41.450x - 7.720y - 5.382\pi + 8.584z - 0.489 = 0$$
$$- 7.720x + 32.576y + 8.545\pi - 1.216z - 0.340 = 0$$
$$- 5.382x + 8.545y + 20.361\pi - 12.736z + 4.018 = 0$$
$$+ 8.584x - 1.216y - 12.736\pi + 16.406z - 4.540 = 0$$

Eyes Horizontal.

$$+ 37.960x - 3.422y - 4.053\pi + 8.478z - 0.538 = 0$$
$$- 3.422x + 25.742y + 6.502\pi - 0.828z - 1.254 = 0$$
$$- 4.053x + 6.502y + 19.701\pi - 12.468z - 0.228 = 0$$
$$+ 8.478x - 0.828y - 12.468\pi + 15.599z - 0.561 = 0$$

Distance.

$$+ 36.000x - 4.307y + 6.521\pi + 7.783z - 0.056 = 0$$
$$- 4.307x + 28.835y - 4.501\pi + 1.526z - 0.085 = 0$$
$$+ 6.521x - 4.501y + 10.767\pi - 4.298z - 0.958 = 0$$
$$+ 7.783x + 1.526y - 4.298\pi + 14.431z + 0.914 = 0$$

The solutions of these equations give:

	Normal.		Parallel.		Horizontal.		Distance.	
x	$+ 0.005 \pm 0.013$		$- 0.044 \pm 0.019$		$+ 0.007 \pm 0\,026$		$- 0.003 \pm 0.011$	
y	$+ 0.003 \pm 0.015$		$+ 0.025 \pm 0.022$		$+ 0.041 \pm 0.032$		$+ 0.018 \pm 0.010$	
π	$+ 0.055 \pm 0.026$		$- 0.060 \pm 0.038$		$+ 0.043 \pm 0.052$		$+ 0.082 \pm 0.021$	
z	$- 0.018 \pm 0.029$		$+ 0.255 \pm 0.042$		$+ 0.068 \pm 0.059$		$- 0.039 \pm 0.018$	
r	± 0.076		± 0.109		± 0.146		± 0.054	

Combining the different values of the parallax, we obtain as the final value

$$\pi = + 0''.050 \pm 0''.014.$$

The values of the position angles for the different positions of the eyes and for the distance are for 1891.0:

Normal	$187°.70$	$\pm 0°.05$
Parallel	186.96	± 0.07
Horizontal	186.76	± 0.09
Distance	$16''.011$	$\pm 0''.011$

The variable part of the personal equation for 1891.0 is

$$\Delta p_a = (- 0''.0036 \pm 0''.0058)\, \theta = (- 0°.013 \pm 0°.021)\, \theta$$
$$\Delta p_p = (+ 0.0510 \pm 0.0084)\, \theta = (+ 0.183 \pm 0.030)\, \theta$$
$$\Delta p_h = (+ 0.0136 \pm 0.0118)\, \theta = (+ 0.049 \pm 0.042)\, \theta$$

where θ is the hour angle expressed in decimals of an hour.

F. P. Leavenworth.

Haverford College Observatory, January, 1892.

DOUBLE STAR OBSERVATIONS.

The double star observations given below are a continuation of the work published in Haverford College Studies No. 1.

The telescope was the ten-inch Clark equatorial, with the micrometer and magnifying power of 375, as before. When not too inconvenient, the observer made the measures of angle with the head so inclined that the line through his eyes was at right angles to the line through the stars. Four measures of angle and two double distances were usually made.

The number of observations is not great, as the telescope was used during most of the time in the observation of stellar parallax.

The greater part of the measures were made by Mr. Wm. H. Collins, the assistant in the observatory. The remainder, with a few exceptions, were made by students of Practical Astronomy.

The following is a list of abbreviations and observers:

ABBREVIATIONS.

β. denotes Burnham.
A.C.   "   Alvan Clark.
A.G.C.   "   A. G. Clark.
H.C.   "   Harvard College Observations.
H.A.H.   "   H. A. Howe.
F.P.L.   "   F. P. Leavenworth.
Schj.   "   Schjellerup.
O.S.   "   Ormond Stone.
Σ "   Struve.
O Σ "   Otto Struve.

OBSERVERS AND ABBREVIATIONS.

B. denotes L. M. Byers.
Car.   "   W. H. Carroll.
C.   "   W. H. Collins.
D.   "   J. H. Dennis.
H.   "   J. W. Hutton.
J.   "   G. L. Jones.
L.   "   F. P. Leavenworth.

Σ 3062 0ʰ 0ᵐ : + 57° 49′.

	°	″	wt	m	m	h	
1891.609	325.1	1.52	...	...	...	1.0	C
1.672	326.0	1.71	...	...	...	22.0	C
1891.640	325.6	1.62					

Σ 23 0ʰ 12ᵐ : — 0° 27′.

1891.617	343.5	6.87	...	...	...	1.0	C
1.688	343.6	6.64	...	...	...	22.7	C
1891.652	343.6	6.76					

β 777 0ʰ 15ᵐ : — 0° 52′.

1891.688	163.5	4.27	...	...	...	23.5	C
1.853	166.8	3.89	...	...	...	1.5	C
1.965	167.8	4.07	2	8	10	2.5	C
1891.835	166.0	4.08		8	10		

β 395 0ʰ 31ᵐ : — 25° 23′.

1891.757	115.2	0.69	3	...	...	0.7	L

Σ 51 0ʰ 38ᵐ : + 16° 47′.

1891.773	128.6	3.38	...	8.0	9.1	0.2	D
1.829	129.6	3.79	...	7.5	9.5	1.7	C
1891.801	129.1	3.58		7.8	9.3		

Σ 60 0ʰ 42ᵐ : + 57° 14′.

1891.563	193.5	4.83	...	...	...	23.0	C
1.609	193.0	4.59	...	...	...	23.5	C
1891.586	193.2	4.71					

O. S. 0ʰ 46ᵐ : — 23° 13′.

1891.724	270.2	2.28	...	...	...	1.5	C
1.815	270.8	2.19	...	7.0	8.0	0.5	C
1891.770	270.5	2.24		7.0	8.0		

Σ 73 0ʰ 49ᵐ : + 23° 2′

1891.563	7.2	1.56	...	...	...	23.5	C
1.609	9.6	1.46	...	...	...	0.0	C
1891.586	8.4	1.51					

O Σ 20   0ʰ   49ᵐ : + 18°   35′.

	°	ʺ	wt	m	m	h	
1891.784	341.8	0.4	4	. . .	. . .	. . .	L

Distance estimated.

β 233   0ʰ   50ᵐ : — 18°   3′.

1891.724	91.7	1.38	. . .	. . .	. . .	2.0	C
1.815	92.2	1.24	. . .	9	11	1.0	C
1891.770	92.0	1.36		9	11		

Σ 86   0ʰ   59ᵐ : — 6°   2′.

1891.688	158.7	12.74	. . .	. . .	. . .	0.7	C
1.708	157.7	12.60	. . .	. . .	. . .	0.0	C
1891.698	158.2	12.67					

Σ 87   1ʰ   0ᵐ : + 14°   49′.

| 1891.826 | 196.8 | 6.81 | . . . | . . . | . . . | . . . | J |

H. A. H. 2.   1ʰ   11ᵐ : — 23°   49′.

1891.724	286.9	7.82	. . .	. . .	. . .	2.5	C
1.815	287.6	8.07	. . .	8.5	10.5	1.5	C
1891.770	287.2	7.94		8.5	10.5		

Σ 147   1ʰ   35ᵐ : — 11°   52′.

| 1891.829 | 88.2 | 3.64 | . . . | . . . | . . . | . . . | J |

Σ 180   1ʰ   47ᵐ : + 18°   47′.

1890.928	3.4	. . .	. . .	. . .	. . .	3.0	B
1.829	0.0	8.53	. . .	4.0	4.2	1.2	C
1891.378	1.7	8.53		4.0	4.2		

Σ 186   1ʰ   50ᵐ : + 1°   19′.

| 1891.741 | 230.8 | 0.35 | . . . | . . . | . . . | . . . | L |

Distance estimated.

Σ 202   1ʰ   56ᵐ : + 2°   13′.

1890.843	322.6	. . .	. . .	. . .	. . .	2.5	B
0.843	319.9	3.28	. . .	. . .	. . .	3.3	D
1890.843	321.2	3.28					

Hastings 2^h 11^m : $-$ 18° 44'.

	°	''	wt	m	m	h	
1889.757	340.2	...	2	...	...	2.2	L
9.975	340.5	2.22	2	...	...	1.8	L
9.980	340.9	2.34	2	...	...	2.3	L
90.079	840.5	2.51	2	...	...	4.3	L
0.835	340.2	2.34	...	...	...	3.5	D
0.851	341.0	2.21	...	...	...	2.0	L
1.117	340.8[1]	2.21	2	8.5	9.0	4.6	L
1.117	339.1[2]	...	2	...	...	4.6	L
1.691	341.9	2.40	...	...	...	2.2	C
1.713	340.7	2.18	...	...	...	2.0	C
1.760	342.6	2.09	2	...	...	3.3	L
1.760	340.9[3]	...	2	...	...	3.3	L
1889.904	340.3	2.28		8.5	9.0		
1890.588	340.6	2.35					
1891.526	341.0	2.22					

[1] Eyes normal. [2] Eyes horizontal. [3] Eyes parallel.

Σ 262 2^h 20^m : $+$ 66° 55'.

A : B.

1890.944	260.3	1.90	...	...	...	4.5	B

A : C.

1890.944	111.3	6.85	...	...	...	4.5	B

Σ 299 2^h 38^m : $+$ 2° 46'.

1890.843	297.6	2.63	...	...	...	3.5	D
0.867	294.5	2.64	...	.	...	2.2	D
1890.855	296 2	2.64					

β 261 2^h 39^m : $-$28° 23'.

1801.724	100.1	2.77	...	...	...	3.0	C

β 83 2^h 40^m : $-$5° 25'.

1891.713	114.4	0.97	...	...	...	2.5	C
1.853	119.8	1.09	...	8.5	10.5	2.0	C
1891.783	117.1	1.03		8.5	10.5		

Σ 311 2^h 43^m : $+$ 17° 2'.

A : B.

1890.867	119.2	3.19	...	...	...	1.6	D
1.869	119.3	3.41	...	...		4.2	D
1.872	120.8	3.28	...	4.0	7.5	1.7	C
1891.536	119.8	3.29		4.0	7.5		

	°	″	wt	m	m	h	
			A : C.				
1891.869	109.7	25.86	...	...	...	4.2	D

β 11 2ʰ 57ᵐ : — 8° 8′.

1891.724	83.2	2.56	...	...	...	3.5	C
1.872	86.4	2.71	...	4.5	8.5	3.0	C
1891.798	84.8	2.64		4.5	8.5		

O Σ 50 3ʰ 2ᵐ : + 71° 7′.

1890.958	201.9	1.45	...	...	...	2.2	B

Σ 355 3ʰ 2ᵐ : + 7° 58′.

1891.691	146.1	2.78	...	...	...	3.5	C
1.694	146.9	2.85	...	...	...	2.5	C
1.869	144.3	2.63	...	...	...	3.0	D
1891.751	145.8	2.75					

β 528 3ʰ 3ᵐ : — 4° 1′.

1891.724	195.4	1.00	...	...	...	4.0	C

Σ 494 4ʰ 1ᵐ : + 22° 49′.

1891.943	187.2	5.30	...	...	...	4.7	D
2.055	188.0	5.09	3	8.0	8.0	4.7	C
1891.999	187.6	5.20		8.0	8.0		

Σ 495 4ʰ 1ᵐ : + 14° 52′.

1890.944	220.9	...	...	...	...	5.7	B
2.055	220.4	3.78	4	8.0	9.5	4.8	C
1891.500	220.6	3.78		8.0	9.5		

Σ 516 4ʰ 9ᵐ : —10° 32′.

1890.944	151.7	...	...	...	...	6.0	B
1.864	148.6	6.49	...	...	...	4.7	C
1891.404	150.2	6.49					

β 402 4ʰ 18ᵐ : — 1° 32′.

1891.826	76.7	7.37	...	8	11	4.2	C
92.056	73.6	...	2	8	11	4.5	C
92.069	73.2	...	2	8	11	4.3	C
92.075	73.7	...	2	8	11	5.3	L
1892.006	74.3	7.37		8	11		

88

β 311   4ʰ 22ᵐ : — 24° 20′.

	°	″	wt	m	m	h	
1891.721	146.2	0.87	2	7.3	7.4	4.5	L
1.724	148.8	1.09	...	...	...	4.5	C
1891.722	147.5	0.98		7.3	7.4		

β 184   4ʰ 23ᵐ : — 21° 44′.

1891.721	259.2	1.09	2	7.4	7.6	4.2	L

β 404   4ʰ 50ᵐ : + 8° 59′

	°	″			:	h	
1891.790	108.6	1.97	...	...	...	5.0	C
1.864	110.5	1.92	...	8.5	8.5	5.2	C
1891.827	109.6	1.94		8.5	8.5		

Σ 622   4ʰ 52ᵐ : + 1° 30′.

1891.965	172.9	2.31	...	...	...	5.8	D
2.055	172.2	2.55	2	8.5	8.5	6.2	C
1892.010	172.6	2.43		8.5	8.5		

OΣ 93   4ʰ 55ᵐ : + 4° 54′.

1891.826	57.5	0.88	...	8.0	8.5	5.0	C

OΣ 98   5ʰ 2ᵐ : + 8° 21′.

1891.793	189.3	0.98	2	...	...	6.0	L
2.055	186.0	0.99	2	8.0	8.0	5.3	C
1891.924	187.6	0.98		8.0	8.0		

Σ 774   5ʰ 35ᵐ : — 2° 1′.

1891.116	157.7	...	...	...	...	...	H
1.831	153.9	2.71	...	2.5	4.5	5.5	C
1.883	154.7	2.64	...	3.0	5.0	7.7	C
1891.610	155.4	2.68		2.8	4.8		

β 568   6ʰ 19ᵐ : — 19° 43′.

1891.883	154.2	0.86	...	7		.0	C

Σ 948 6ʰ 36ᵐ : + 59° 32′.

A : B.

	°	″	wt	m	m	h	
1891.100	122.2	1.59	. . .	. . .	. . .	7.5	B
1.793	120.2	1.80	. . .	. . .	. . .	3.5	C
1.864	124.3	1.64	. :.	5.0	6 0	8.4	C
1.883	124.6	1.61	. . .	5.0	6.0	8.2	U
1.92	122.6	1.56	2	. . .	. . .	5.2	L
1891.712	122.8	1.64		5.0	6.0		

A : C.

1891.92	306.4	8.64	4	. . .	. . .	5.5	L

Σ 1037 7ʰ 6ᵐ : + 27° 26′.

1891.190	307.8	1.35	. . .	. . .	. . .	8.0	B
1.231	308.5	1.13	. . .	. . .	. . .	. . .	D
1.790	305.1	1.63	. . .	. . .	. . .	6.0	C
1.883	306.9	1.29	. . .	7	7	9.2	C
1891.523	307.1	1.35		7	7		

Σ 1110 7ʰ 27ᵐ : + 32° 7′.

1891.191	231.3	5.41	. . .	. . .	. . .	9.5	B
1.883	229.6	5.95	. . .	2	3	9.5	C
1891.537	230.4	5.68		2	3		

Σ 1196 8ʰ 6ᵐ : + 17° 59′.

A : B.

1891.191	33.3	1.44	. . .	. . .	. . .	8.5	B
1.210	37.1	1.25	. . .	. . .	. . .	11.0	B
1.790	34.1	1.59	. . .	. . .	. . .	6.7	C
1.993	31.9	1.32	. . .	. . .	. . .	6.5	C
2.023	31.0	1.22	2	5.0	6.0	6.2	C
1891.641	33.5	1.36		5.0	6.0		

A : C.

1891.314	122.2	5.97	. . .	. . .	. . .	. . .	C
1.993	116.8	5.33	2	5.0	6.0	6.5	C
1891.654	119.5	5.65		5.0	6.0		

Σ 1356 9ʰ 22ᵐ : + 9° 33′.

1890.881	101.5	0.64	. . .	6.5	7.0	9.7	L
1.210	103.6	. . .	. . .	. . .	. . .	10.0	B
1891.046	102.6	0.64		6.5	7.0		

OΣ 215   10^h 10^m : + 18° 17′.

1891.209	o 213.5	″ ...	wt ...	m ...	m ...	h 10.5	B

Σ 1424   10^h 14^m : + 20° 25′.

1891.160	112.2	3.30	...	...	...	8.5	B
1.306	112.2	3.74	...	...	...	...	C
1.327	114.8	3.78	...	...	...	...	D
1891.264	113.1	3.61					

Σ 1523   11^h 12^m : + 32° 9′.

1891.177	o 204.9	″ 1.62	...	...	...	h 8.0	B
1.231	201.3	1.72	...	...	...	...	D
1891.204	203.1	1.67					

Σ 1670   12^h 36^m : + 0° 50′.

1891.160	329.6	5.90	...	...	...	9.0	B
1.284	334.6	5.64	...	...	...	...	C
1.385	331.4	...	...	...	...	...	H
*1.442	332.7	5.73	2	...	...	14.0	C
*1.445	333.3	5.57	2	...	...	14.5	C
1891.343	332.3	5.71					

* Bright field.

Σ 1757   13^h 29^m : + 0° 16′.

1891.442	70.9	2.71	2	...	...	15.2	C
1.445	70.4	2.57	2	...	...	15.5	C
1891.444	70.6	2.64					

Σ 1819   14^h 10^m : +3° 39′.

1891.445	4.8	1.62	2	8	8	16.0	C
1.478	6.6	...	...	...	...	15.0	C
1891.462	5.7	1.62		8	8		

Σ 1888   14^h 46^m : + 19° 33′.

1891.418	240.6	...	...	...	...	...	H
1.440	241.2	3.13	...	...	...	...	C
1.445	242.7	3.35	2	...	...	16.5	C
1891.434	241.5	3.24					

Σ 1998 15ʰ 58ᵐ : — 11° 4′.

A : B.

	°	″	wt	m	m	h	
1891.440	21.3	1.24	2	5.0	5.0	. . .	C
1.483	19.8	1.30	. . .	. . .	. . .	15.5	C
1891.462	20.6	1.27		5.0	5.0		

$$\frac{A + B}{2} : C.$$

1891.483	63.4	7.51	. . .	. . .	. . .	14.7	C

Σ 1999 15ʰ 58ᵐ : — 11° 9′.

1891.478	101.2	11.16	. . .	. . .	. . .	17.5	C
1.483	100.8	11.29	. . .	. . .	. . .	16.5	C
1891.480	101.0	11.22					

Σ 2055 16ʰ 25ᵐ : + 2° 14′.

1891.480	37.3	1.82	. . .	. . .	. . .	18.5	C
1.483	39.0	1.64	. . .	. . .	. . .	17.0	C
1.541	43.3	1.92	. . .	. . .	. . .	18.7	C
1891.501	39.9	1.79					

Σ 2130 17ʰ 3ᵐ : + 54° 37′.

1891.478	147.8	2.17	. . .	. . .	. . .	16.2	D

Σ 2262 17ʰ 57ᵐ : — 8° 10′.

1891.521	254.1	2.06	. . .	. . .	. . .	17.0	C
1.691	256.3	1.91	. . .	. . .	. . .	19.0	C
1891.606	255.2	1.98					

Σ 2272 18ʰ 0ᵐ : + 2° 32′.

1891.521	328.4	2.48	. . .	. . .	. . .	18.2	C
1.598	329.8	2.39	. . .	. . .	. . .	19.7	C
1891.560	329.1	2.44					

Jacb. 201 18ʰ 19ᵐ : —‍20° 33′.

1891.694	291.0	2.08	. . .	. . .	. . .	19.0	C

β 247 18ʰ 26ᵐ : — 9° 27′.

1891.642	167.2	7.26	. . .	. . .	. . .	18.5	C
1.686	166.4	8.12	. . .	. . .	. . .	19.5	C
1891.664	166.8	7.69					

O. S. 18^h 38^m : — 20° 0'.

	°	"	wt	m	m	h	
1891.694	105.2	1.78	...	9.0	9.0	19.5	C
1.735	108.8	1.78	...	...	...	19.7	C
1891.714	107.0	1.78		9.0	9.0		

H. C. 150 18^h 55^m : — 30° 3'.

1891.571	253.7	0.57	4	...	...	...	L

H. A. H. 93 19^h 8^m : — 16° 10'.

1891.691	160.0	5.55	...	...	...	20.0	C
1.694	160.8	5.28	...	...	...	20.5	C
1891.692	160.4	5.42					

Hough 103 19^h 13^m : — 3° 39'.

1891.691	247.4	3.25	...	9.0	11.0	20.7	C

β 248 19^h 13^m : + 22° 50'.

1891.691	123.6	1.98	...	...	...	21.0	C
1.729	130.1	1.85	...	...	...	20.7	.C
1891.710	126.8	1.92					

β 827 19^h 38^m : — 11° 28'.

1891.642	249.8	1.46	...	...	...	19.0	C
1.807	253.9	1.23	...	8.5	9.5	20.5	C
1891.724	251.8	1.34		8.5	9.5		

O. S. 19^h 40^m : — 22° 6'.

1891.642	3.9	1.62	...	...	...	20.5	C

Σ 2579 19^h 42^m : + 44° 52'.

1891.563	310.7	1.79	...	...	...	22.5	C
1.738	310.2	1.73	...	...	...	22.0	C
1891.650	310.4	1.76					

A. C. 12 19^h 53^m : — 2° 31'.

1891.735	322.2	1.27	...	...	...	20.2	C
1.738	326.1	1.38	...	...	...	20.0	C
1891.736	324.2	1.32					

Σ 2626   20^h 0^m : + 30° 9′.

	o	″	wt	m	m	h	
1891.710	124.4	1.44	...	...	...	23.0	C
1.738	124.8	1.29	...	...	...	21.5	C
1891.724	124.6	1.36					

Σ 2666   20^h 14^m : + 40° 24′.

1891.710	244.2	2.80	...,	...	...	22.5	C
1.795	244.7	2.77	...	...	...	1.0	C
1891.752	244.4	2.78					

Σ 2735   20^h 30^m : + 4° 7′.

1891.642	284.8	2.07	...	...	...	21.5	C
1.702	285.5	2.22	...	...	...	23.5	C
1.807	286.4	1.85	...	7.0	8.5	22.7	C
1891.717	285.6	2.05		7.0	8.5		

Σ 2737   20^h 53^m : + 3° 51′.

A : B.

1891.609	285.9	0.86	3	...	...	20.5	L
1.617	286.2	0.91	2	...	...	...	L
1.617	284.4	1.31	...	...	...	23.2	C
1.738	285.3	1.20	...	...	...	22.5	C
1.795	287.2	1.16	...	...	...	0.2	C
1.807	285.7	1.06	...	6.0	6.5	21.0	C
1891.697	285.8	1.08		6.0	6.5		

$$\frac{A + B}{2} : C.$$

1891.609	74.4	10.79	3	...	...	20.7	L
1.617	75.0	10.82	2	...	...	...	L
1.807	74.4	11.08	...	6.0	8.0	21.5	C
1891.678	74.6	10.90		6.0	8.0		

β 252   21^h 13^m : — 27° 46′.

| 1891.735 | 279.2 | 2.67 | ... | ... | ... | 21.5 | C |

Schj. 33   21^h 22^m : — 13° 54′.

1891.735	133.1	2.98	...	...	...	22.0	C
1.807	133.6	2.85	...	8.5	9.5	21.0	C
1891.771	133.4	2.92		8.5	9.5		

β 165   21^h 28^m: — 3° 56′.

	o	″	wt	m	m	h	
1890.772	179.3	4.96	. . .	. . .	. . .	. . .	B

F. P. L.   21^h 37^m: — 11° 38′.

1891.815	271.0	. . .	2	8.5	10.5	21.0	L
1.815	269.2	1.44	. . .	9.0	11.0	21.7	C
1.829	269.4	1.36	. .	8.5	10.0	21.5	C
1891.820	269.9	1.40		8.7	10.5		

Σ 2847   21^h 52^m: — 4° 1′.

1891.617	301.0	1.40	. . .	. . .	. . .	0.2	C
1.713	300.8	1.29	. . .	. . .	. . .	23.0	C
1891.665	3(0.9	1.34					

Σ 2856   22^h 0^m: + 4° 18′.

1891.729	197.1	1.21	. . .	. . .	. . .	22.0	C
1.735	˙ 197.7	1.20	. . .	. . .	. . .	22.5	C
1891.732	197.4	1.20					

Σ 2863   22^h 1^m: + 64° 4′.

1890.799	282.5	6.46	. . .	. . .	. . .	22.7	B
0.799	285.6	6.74	. . .	. . .	. . .	24.5	Car
0.799	285 2	. . .	. . .	. . .	. . .	22.9	D
1.713	283.4	6.79	. . .	. . .	. . .	0.0	C
1.738	281.9	6.94	. . .	. . .	. . .	23.2	C
1.793	280.8	6.98	. . .	. . .	. . .	2.5	C
1891.274	283.2	6.78					

O. S.   22^h 8^m: — 20° 37′.

1891.735	96.7	10.26	. . .	. . .	. . .	23.0	C
1.795	95.0	9.82	. . .	8.5	10.0	22.5	C
1891.765	95.8	10.04	. . .	8.5	10.0		

Σ 2900   22^h 18^m: + 20° 17′.

1891.773	178.3	1.82	2	6.0	10.0	23.8	L
1.790	179.5	. . .	2	6.0	10.5	. . .	L
1.795	178.9	1.89	2	6.0	10.5	20.7	L
1.796	177.8	1.79	2	6.0	- 10.5	23.8	L
1891.788	178.6	1.83		6.0	10.4		

H 41   22ʰ · 21ᵐ : — 17° 18′.

	°	″	wt	m	m	h	
1891.675	307.2	6.96	. . .	. . .	. . .	22.5	C
1.688	308.2	7.26	. . .	. . .	. . .	22.0	C
1.713	306.7	7.24	. . .	. . .	. . .	22.0	C
1891.692	307.4	7.15					

Σ 2909   22ʰ   23ᵐ : — 0° 36′.

1890.788	323.7	3.30	. . .	. . .	. . .	1.3	B
1.524	322.2	3.67	. . .	. . .	. . .	22.5	C
1.563	324.9	3.28	. . .	. . .	. . .	22.0	C
1.571	323.8	3.21	. . .	. . .	. . .	23.0	C
1891.361	323.6	3.36					

Σ 2947   22ʰ   46ᵐ : + 67° 58′.

1891.713	66.7	3.74	. . .	. . .	. . .	0.5	C
1.738	64.4	3.52	- . . .	. . .	. . .	0.0	C
1.793	65.4	3.59	. . .	. . .	. . .	3.0	C
1891.748	65.5	3.62					

O Σ 489   23ʰ   5ᵐ : + 74° 47′.

1891.713	37.4	1.56	. . .	. . .	. . .	1.0	C
1.795	31.7	1.05	. . .	. . .	. . .	0.7	C
1.826	28.2	1.38	. . .	5.0	7.0	2.5	C
1891.778	32 4	1.33		5.0	7.0		

Σ 3008   23ʰ   18ᵐ : — 9° 4′.

1890.774	250.5	4.48	. . .	. . .	. . .	0.3	B
1.815	247.8	3.98	. . .	. . .	. . .	0.0	C
1891.294	249.2	4.23					

A.G.C. 14   23ʰ   38ᵐ : + 28° 45′.

1891.672	197.6	1.44	. . .	. . .	. . .	22.0	C
1.713	194.5	1.59	. . .	. . .	. . .	1.5	C
1891.692	196.0	1.52					

85 Pegasi   23ʰ · 56ᵐ : + 26°   30′.

1889.773*	358.4	22.88	3	. . .	. . .	3.0	L
9.781	358.3	22.52	2	. . .	. . .	22.0	L
9.844	358.4	. . .	2	. . .	. . .	4.5	L
9.904	358.7	. . .	2	. . .	. . .	3.3	L
1889 826	358.4	22.70					

* Bright field.

OBSERVATIONS OF COMET WOLF (b 1891).

Made at the Haverford College Observatory with the 10-inch equatorial.

By F. P. LEAVENWORTH AND WM. H. COLLINS.

Haverford M. T.	*	No. Comp.	Comet—*		Comet's apparent		log pΔ		Obs.
			Δα	Δδ	α	δ	for α	for δ	
1891			m s	′ ″	h m s	° ′ ″	s	″	
mo d h m s									
9 25 12 10 34	1	20, 5	+0 6.32	+2 0.0	4 19 38.86	+16 27 58.4	n9.600	0.643	C
25 16 16 38	1	5, 3	+0 20.72	−2 33.4	4 19 53.26	+16 23 25.0	8.593	0.857	L
25 16 17 12	2	6, 4	+0 20.99	−1 30.1	4 19 53.53	+16 23 22.0	8.526	0.546	L
30 16 47 34	3	5, 4	+2 25.64	−0 57.2	4 26 30.56	+14 3 31.4	9.194	0.591	L
11 2 12 38 15	4	12, 6	−0 23.70	−6 23.4	4 40 35.56	− 3 15 14.9	n9.219	0.779	C
6 14 21 50	5	9, 4	−4 42.90	−2 46.9	. . .	. . .	. . .	. . .	C
11 16 1 43	6	10, 6	+2 3.28	−1 47.4	4 36 45.63	− 7 27 16.9	9.486	0.796	C
12 5 10 19 16	7	10, 5	−2 15.40	−7 23.5	4 21 44.37	−14 1 14.2	n9.109	0.855	C

MEAN PLACES FOR 1891.0 OF COMPARISON STARS.

	α	Red. to app. place	δ	Red. to app. place	Authority.
	h m s	s	° ′ ″	″	
1	4 19 30.45	+2.09	+16 25 46.8	+11.6	} Positions obtained by comparing with Weisse's Bessel 391.
2	4 19 30.45	+2.09	+16 24 40.5	+11.6	
3	4 24 2.74	+2.18	+14 4 16.0	+12.6	Weisse's Bessel 453.
4	4 40 56.38	+2.87	− 3 9 5.1	+13.6	Karlsruhe.
5	4 43 57. .	. .	− 5 10 7. .	. .	S. D. M. −5, 1046.
6	4 34 39.37	+3.06	− 7 25 42.9	+13.4	Seeliger, Vol. II, 887.
7	4 23 56.41	+3.36	−13 54 1.7	+11.0	Schjellerup 1438.

The $\Delta\delta$ of 11mo. 2 was changed by 8 rev. $= -138''.7$, the record being obscure.

SUN-SPOT OBSERVATIONS.

Made at the Haverford College Observatory with the 8-in. Equatorial.

By F. P. LeAvenworth.

1890.	Time	Grs.	Spots	Fac Grs.	Def. and size.	1890.	Time	Grs.	Spots	Fac Grs.	Def. and size.
April 1	10	0	0	1	good	May 1	12	1	2	2	good
2	10	0	0	0	fair	2	11	0	0	0	poor
3	10	0	0	0	poor	3	10	0	0	2	fair
4	3	0	0	0	fair	5	10	0	0	1	fair
5	9	0	0	2	good	7	12	1	3	1	fair; small
6	10	0	0	1	fair	8	2	1	8	1	good; small
7	10	0	0	1	fair	9	10	1	22	2	fine; small
10	9	0	0	2	good	12	9	2	11	1	fair
11	12	2	10	3	fine; small	13	12	1	10	1	fair
12	10	2	18	3	fine; 1 lar	14	9	1	14	2	good; small
13	10	2	11	3	fine; small	15	4	0	0	0	fair
14	10	0	0	1	good	17	10	3	9	3	fair; large
15	11	0	0	0	bad	18	10	2	9	3	poor
16	9	1	3	0	fair; small	19	10	3	6	2	fair
17	12	0	0	2	fair	20	4	3	4	1	fair
18	5	0	0	0	fair	21	9	2	3	1	poor
19	11	0	0	0	poor	22	3	1	2	2	poor; small
20	12	0	0	0	fair	23	4	1	3	1	fair
21	10	0	0	0	fair	24	4	0	0	2	fair
22	10	0	0	0	poor	27	4	1	3	3	bad; small
23	10	0	0	0	good	28	9	0	0	1	fair
28	9	1	3	1	good; small	29	10	0	0	0	fair
29	10	1	19	1	fine; small	31	10	0	0	1	poor
30	11	2	11	0	fair; small						

SUN-SPOT OBSERVATIONS.

Made at the Haverford College Observatory with the 8-in. Equatorial.

By F. P. LEAVENWORTH.

1890.	Time	Grs.	Spots	Fac Grs.	Def. and size.	1890.	Time	Grs.	Spots	Fac Grs.	Def. and size.
June 1	1	0	0	1	good	Jun. 29	10	0	0	2	good
2	10	0	0	1	good	30	10	0	0	0	fair
3	10	2	5	2	good; small	July 1	10	0	0	0	fair; 2 lar
4	10	1	1	1	good	4	10	2	11	1	good; 4 lar
5	10	1	7	1	fair	5	5	1	22	3	good
6	10	1	11	0	poor; small	6	5	1	25	3	fair ·
7	10	1	15	1	good; 1 lar	7	12	1	33	2	fine; 2 lar
8	10	1	4	1	bad; 1 lar	8	11	3	32	0	good; 3 lar
9	9	1	6	1	poor; small	9	11	2	48	0	. . .
10	9	2	3	1	good	10	11	2	28	0	fair
11	9	1	3	0	fair	11	3	2	10	1	fair
12	12	0	0	1	fair	12	11	2	5	0	poor
13	10	0	0	1	fair	14	12	1	4	2	fair
14	9	1	4	3	good; small	15	11	1	2	2	good; small
18	10	0	0	1	good	16	10	0	0	1	poor
19	10	0	0	0	fair	17	11	1	1	0	fair; small
20	10	0	0	0	good	18	5	0	0	1	good
22	12	0	0	0	poor	19	5	0	0	1	good
23	9	1	1	1	good; small	20	5	0	0	0	good
24	5	0	0	1	good	21	10	0	0	0	poor
25	10	0	0	1	good	22	10	1	3	1	bad
26	10	0	0	1	fair	23	12	2	9	2	fair; 1 lar
27	10	0	0	1	poor	26	5	1	20	0	good; 1 lar
28	11	0	0	0	fair	27	5	1	12	1	good

SUN-SPOT OBSERVATIONS.

Made at the Haverford College Observatory with the 8-in. Equatorial.

By F. P. LEAVENWORTH.

1890.		Time	Grs.	Spots	Fac Grs.	Def. and size.	1890.		Time	Grs.	Spots	Fac Grs.	Def. and size.
July	30	11	4	13	1	good; 1 lar	Aug.	28		2	96	1	good; 2 lar
	31	10	6	11	2	good; 1 lar		29		1	60	0	fair; 2 lar
Aug.	1	12	3	22	2	poor; 1 lar		30		1	10	4	good; 2 lar
	2	5	3	4	2	1 lar		31	3	2	88	0	fair
	3	5	1	2	0	bad	Sept.	1	3	2	65	1	poor; 3 lar
	4	5	1	5	1	fine; 1 lar		2	10	2	59	1	fair; 2 lar
	5	5	2	9	1	poor		3	9	2	54	2	fair; 2 lar
	6	5	2	14	1	good		4	10	3	52	1	good;1 v lar
	7	4	2	3	1	. . .		6	5	5	37	5	good; 1 lar
	9	5	0	0	1	good		7	4	5	44	8	fair; 1 lar
	11	9	1	2	1	fair		8	10	4	20	4	poor; 1 lar
	13	5	0	0	1	fair		9	3	4	34	2	fair
	14	3	1	2	1	fair; small		10	11	2	34	0	fair; small
	15	4	0	0	0	good		12	11	2	25	0	poor
	16	1	1	3	0	poor; small		13	10	1	6	1	fair
	17	11	0	0	0	good		15	3	2	14	5	poor; 1 lar
	18	3	0	0	0	poor		17	12	1	17	1	fair; 2 lar
	19	12	0	0	1	good		18	11	2	28	1	fair; 2 lar
	20	6	0	0	0	fair		19	12	3	35	3	fine; small
	22	.5	2	3	1	good; small		20	10	1	7	2	fair
	24	4	3	8	1	fair		21	3	2	4	1	fair
	25	3	2	21	1	good; 1 lar		23	11	3	24	5	fine; v small
	26	11	1	24	1	poor; sev'l l		24	10	1	13	3	fair
	27	3	2	78	2	good; 1 v lar		25	12	1	30	4	good

SUN-SPOT OBSERVATIONS.

Made at the Haverford College Observatory with the 8-in. Equatorial.

By F. P. LEAVENWORTH.

1890.		Time	Grs.	Spots	Fac Grs.	Def. and size.	1890.		Time	Grs.	Spots	Fac Grs.	Def. and size.
Sept.	28	4	1	37	2	fair; small	Nov.	4	10	1	1	1	fair; veiled
	29	10	1	17	2	poor		5	10	0	0	0	good
	30	10	1	23	0	poor		6	11	0	0	0	fair
Oct.	1	9	1	28	0	fair; small		7	12	1	6	1	good; 1 lar
	3	11	0	0	2	fair		8	11	1	10	1	fair; 1 lar
	4	16	1	2	5	good		10	10	1	5	1	poor
	5	3	2	14	2	good; small		13	2	3	8	0	good
	8	9	1	1	2	good; small		14	10	1	2	1	good; small
	9	9	0	0	1	bad		18	10	0	0	3	fair
	10	11	1	1	2	fair		19	10	0	0	2	fair
	11	10	2	8	2	fair		20	12	0	0	2	fair
	14	4	1	2	1	poor		21	10	1	1	3	fair
	15	10	0	0	2	poor		22	10	1	4	2	poor; 1 lar
	17	9	0	0	2	fair		23	10	1	19	1	fair; 1 lar
	18	10	0	0	1	good		24	10	1	65	1	fine; 1 lar
	25	10	1	50	...	poor; 1 lar		25	10	1	47	0	good; 3 lar
	26	9	1	40	1	poor; 1 lar		26	12	1	53	2	fair; 4 lar
	27	2	1	24	0	fair; 1 lar		27	12	1	35	2	poor
	28	9	1	8	2	poor; large		28	11	1	30	2	poor
	29	2	1	16		1 lar		29	10	1	65	0	good; 2 lar
	30	10	1	2		fair; 1 lar		30	3	2	29	1	good; 1 lar
	31	10	1	4		fair	Dec.	1	10	3	13	2	fair; 2 lar
Nov.	1	11	2	2		1 lar		2	11	2	8	1	good; 1 lar
	3	9	0	0	2	fair		4	11	0	0	2	fair

SUN-SPOT OBSERVATIONS.

Made at the Haverford College Observatory with the 8-in Equatorial.

By F. P. LEAVENWORTH.

1890.		Time	Grs.	Spots	Fac Grs.	Def. and size.	1890.		Time	Grs.	Spots	Fac Grs.	Def. and size.
Dec.	9	2	1	4	1	good	Dec.	18	3	2	21	0	bad
	10	10	1	3	1	good; small		19	10	3	24	2	poor; 1 lar
	11	11	1	2	1	good; small		20	1	3	31	2	good
	12	11	0	0	0	poor		22	10	0	0	1	fair
	13	11	2	15	2	fair		23	10	1	2	2	poor
	14	12	2	32	1	fair		24	10	1	6	2	poor; small
	15	9	2	32	2	fair							

SUN-SPOT OBSERVATIONS.

Made at the Haverford College Observatory with the 8-in. Equatorial.

By F. P. LEAVENWORTH.

1891.	Time	Grs.	Spots	Fac Grs.	Def. and size.	1891.	Time	Grs.	Spots	Fac Grs.	Def. and size.
Jan. 2	3			1	bad	Feb. 2	9	3	10	1	good ; small
3	10			1	poor	4	9	0	0	1	poor ; small
4	10			1	poor	5	9	1	1	1	poor ; small
5	12	0/0	0/0	3	fair; small	6	9	1	2	2	fair; small
6	9	3	7	2	fair	8	10	2	2	1	good ; small
7	9	1	5	2	poor	10	10	2	33	0	fair
8	4	2	4	1	poor	11	11	3	65	0	fair
9	10	2	3	1	poor	13	3	3	26	1	good ; lar
12	10	0	0	2	fair	14	9	4	32	1	fair ; lar
13	9	0	0	0	good	15	9	4	54	2	good ; lar
14	10	0	0	0	poor	18	9	5	36	4	fair ; 2 lar
15	3	1	4	1	fair; 1 lar	19	11	4	14	1	bad
16	10	1	9	1	fair; 1 lar	22	9	6	55	3	good; { 1 lar lar fac
18	3	3	19	1	fair; 1 lar	23	4	4	45	1	good; 1 lar
19	10	3	21	1	fair; 1 lar	24	10	3	28	1	fair; 1 lar
21	10	1	1	0	bad; 1 lar	25	10	2	46	3	fair; 1 lar
22	4	2	13	0	fair; 1 lar	27	9	2	25	1	good ; small
23	10	2	23	0	fine; 1 lar	28	9	1	18	1	good ; small
24	10	4	28	2	good; 1 lar	Mar. 1	10	1	9	1	poor ; small
26	2	4	36		fair; 1 lar	2	9	1	5	1	bad
27	9	4	40	3	fair; sev lar	4	12	2	4	3	1 lar
28	9	4	45	3	fair; sev lar	5	10	3	6	3	fair; 1 lar
30	...	3	28	1	fair; 1 lar	6	10	2	2	0	bad
Feb. 1	2	2	22	0	fair; small	10	9	1	18	0	fair

SUN-SPOT OBSERVATIONS.

Made at the Haverford College Observatory with the 8-in. Equatorial.

By F. P. LEAVENWORTH.

1891.	Time	Grs.	Spots	Fac Grs.	Def. and size.	1891.	Time	Grs.	Spots	Fac Grs.	Def. and size.
Mar. 11	9	1	19	1	fair	Apr. 21	10	4	32	1	good; 1 lar
14	9	2	3	3	good; 1 lar	22	10	5	36	2	good; 2 lar
15	9	1	1	3	poor; 1 lar	23	10	3	92	1	fine; 1 lar
16	9	3	8	1	poor; 1 lar	24	10	3	62	1	fair; 1 lar
17	9	2	9	1	poor; 1 lar	25	10	4	42	3	good; 2 lar
18	10	3	17	2	good; 1 lar	26	10	4	34	4	fair; 1 lar
23	3	2	7	1	. . .	27	...	4	52	0	fine; 2 lar
24	3	1	1	2	poor; large	28	9	4	58	1	fine; 2 lar
25	9	1	1	5	fair	29	9	3	25	1	fair; 1 lar
29	3	4	20	2	fair; 1 lar	30	10	3	26	1	fine; 1 lar
30	9	3	8	2	poor; large	May 1	10	4	29	2	good
Apr. 5	9	1	15	2	fair; 1 lar	2	10	3	13	2	good; 1 lar
6	10	1	1	1	fair; 1 lar	3	2	1	2	2	fair
7	10	2	6	2	good; 1 lar	4	10	4	12	4	poor; 1 lar
8	12	1	1	1	good; 1 lar	5	12	2	9	2	poor; 2 lar
9	12	2	9	1	fair; 1 lar	6	9	2	16	2	poor; 2 lar
12	3	2	18	0	1 near pole	7	9	3	10	2	poor; 1 lar
13	9	3	14	2	fair; small	8	12	4	35	2	good; 1 lar
14	9	3	32	1	good; small	9	9	4	44	3	good
15	9	3	37	2	good	10	8	4	77	0	good; 1 lar
16	9	4	29	2	poor	11	4	6	40	4	fair; 4 lar
17	9	3	40	2	good	12	10	6	37	3	fair; 2 lar
19	9	5	32	3	good; small	13	10	6	16	4	poor; 3 lar
20	11	3	22	1	poor	17	10	4	24	1	fair; 1 lar

SUN-SPOT OBSERVATIONS.

Made at the Haverford College Observatory with the 8-in. Equatorial.

By F. P. LEAVENWORTH.

1891.	Time Grs.	Spots	Fac Grs.	Def. and size.	1891.	Time Grs.	Spots	Fac Grs.	Def. and size.
May 18	10	4	32	3	good; 4 lar	Jun. 12	3	5	66	3	fine; 1 lar
19	9	5	55	3	fine; 5 lar	13	11	4	24	3	good; 2 lar
20	11	5	40	1	fair; 4 lar	14	10	5	39	2	good; 2 lar
21	9	7	59	2	fair	15	10	6	47	3	good; 2 lar
22	9	9	81	2	fair	16	9	6	88	2	good; 2 lar
27	1	4	18	0	bad	17	9	5	100	2	fair; 1 lar
28	12	5	46	3	poor; 1 lar	22	9	9	69	5	good;' 2 lar
31	9	3	30	1	fair; 2 lar	23	9	7	48		good; 3 lar
June 1	10	5	32	2	fair; 3 lar	24	9	9	43		good; 3 lar
2	11	6	38	4	good; 2 lar	25	9	8	54		{ fair; 2 lar / im'nse fac
3	9	4	33	3	fair	26	9	7	108		good; 4 lar
4	11	3	20	1	fair	27	8	6	56	2	poor; 4 lar
8	11	1	11	1	poor	28	9	7	70	2	fair; 4 lar
9	11	2	17	0	poor	29	9	6	61	1	good; 3 lar
10	10	3	29	2	poor; 1 lar	30	9	7	35	2	good; 1 lar
11	9	3	19	2	poor; 1 lar					

SUN-SPOT OBSERVATIONS.

Made at the Haverford College Observatory with the 8-in. Equatorial.

By WM. H. COLLINS.

1891.		Time	Grs.	Spots	Fac Grs.	Def. and size.		1891.		Time	Grs.	Spots	Fac Grs.	Def. and size.	
July	1	4	8	30	0	fair		July	31	10	2	14	1	poor	
	3	3	6	38	4	fair;	5 lar	Aug.	1	9	3	11	1	poor;	1 lar
	4	8	3	21	2	fair;	2 lar		2	9	2	6	1	bad;	1 lar
	5	8	7	50	1	fair;	2 lar		3	10	3	9	0	bad;	1 lar
	6	8	6	62	2	fair;	1 lar		4	2	5	25	0	poor	
	7	8	6	57	2	fair;	3 lar		6	9	6	26	1	fair;	3 lar
	9	8	8	62	4	fair;	4 lar		7	10	5	27	1	fair;	3 lar
	10	9	9	129	5	fair;	2 lar		8	2	5	13	2	fair;	4 lar
	11	9	7	69	1	fair;	5 lar		10	8	5	9	2	fair;	1 lar
	12	9	8	99		fair;	7 lar		11	9	4	18	1	fair;	2 lar
	13	7	8	60	8 0	bad			12	9	4	5	2	fair;	2 lar
	14	11	7	83	1	poor;	4 lar		13	9	4	9	1	good;	2 lar
	15	8	7	48	1	poor;	5 lar		14	8	3	6	1	good;	2 lar
	16	11	5	35	1	bad;	5 lar		15	8	6	17	1	fair;	2 lar
	17	8	5	32	1	poor;	5 lar		16	9	4	13	0	fair;	2 lar
	19	9	6	28	1	bad			17	11	2	4	1	bad	
	21	8	4	42	1	fair;	1 lar		19	2	0	0	1	bad	
	22	8	6	45	1	fair;	1 lar		20	11	0	0	0	fair	
	23	10	6	25	1	bad			21	4	1	8	2	poor	
	24	4	6	11	2	bad			22	9	3	16	2	good	
	25	9	5	11	3	poor			23	12	1	8	0	fair	
	26	9	1	12	0	poor			27	2	1	4	1	fair	
	27	9	3	9	2	bad			28	11	2	7	1	fair	
	29	3	4	16	1	poor			29	9	1	6	0	poor;	1 lar

SUN-SPOT OBSERVATIONS.

Made at the Haverford College Observatory with the 8-in. Equatorial.

By Wm. H. Collins.

1891.	Time	Grs.	Spots	Fac Grs.	Def. and size.	1891.	Time	Grs.	Spots	Fac Grs.	Def. and size.
Sep. 1	11	3	44	0	fair	Sep. 26	10	2	25	2	fair ; 1 lar
2	9	4	59	1	good ; 1 lar	27	12	3	23	1	fair ; 1 lar
3	9	5	60	1	fair ; 1 lar	28	11	4	40	2	fair
4	9	5	58	0	poor	29	9	3	9	1	bad ; 3 lar
5	3	4	56	0	bad	Oct. 5	4	6	36	1	poor
6	11	6	75	0	bad	9	9	7	55	2	poor ; 3 lar
7	10	6	106	0	bad	11	1	4	22	2	poor
9	10	7	47	0	fair ; 3 lar	13	1	7	19	2	bad
10	10	7	15	0	fair ; 4 lar	14	2	4	9	1	poor
11	10	4	4	1	poor ; 4 lar	15	12	4	9	0	poor
12	10	5	8	0	poor ; 4 lar	16	10	5	23	1	fair
13	10	6	26	0	fair ; 3 lar	17	12	3	16	1	bad
14	9	4	26	1	fair ; 1 lar	20	2	2	21	5	poor
15	9	4	40	0	fair ; 1 lar	21	9	2	14	2	fair
16	10	3	64	0	fair ; 1 lar	23	11	4	18	2	poor
17	9	3	41	0	poor ; 2 lar	24	10	4	14	1	fair
18	11	3	60	0	fair ; 2 lar	25	9	4	5	1	fair
19	9	4	52	2	fair ; 2 lar	26	12	2	17	1	fair
20	9	5	44	3	poor	27	12	3	20	0	fair
21	10	6	37	1	poor	28	10	3	13	2	poor
22	10	4	29	2	poor ; 1 lar	29	2	3	27	3	fair
23	9	2	12	2	poor ; 1 lar	30	9	3	13	2	poor
24	9	2	15	2	poor ; 4 lar	31	11	4	22	2	fair
25	10	2	20	0	poor ; 2 lar	Nov. 1	2	5	30	3	fair

SUN-SPOT OBSERVATIONS.

Made at the Haverford College Observatory with the 8-in Equatorial.

By Wm. H. Collins.

1891.		Time Grs.	Spots	Fac Grs.	Def. and size.	1891.		Time Grs.	Spots	Fac Grs.	Def. and size.
Nov.	2	9	4	31	2	fair	Dec.	2	10	3	11	0	bad
	3	9	4	24	2	fair		3	10	2	2	0	bad
	4	10	4	26	1	poor		5	10	1	9	0	bad
	6	10	2	29	0	fair		6	10	3	15	1	bad
	7	9	2	22	2	poor		8	11	2	15	2	fair
	8	10	3	29	3	good		9	11	3	3	0	bad
	9	11	4	36	1	good		10	1	2	4	1	bad
	11	1	3	15	1	fair		11	9	2	2	0	fair
	12	11	4	16	1	good ; 1 lar		12	2	2	4	0	poor
	13	9	2	7	2	fair		13	10		4	1	fair
	14	10	3	14	2	fair ·		16	10		19	1	poor
	15	10	2	7	1	poor		17	10	2/3	17	0	poor ; 2 lar
	18	10	4	19	0	fair		18	10	3	12	1	poor ; 3 lar
	19	11	5	52	1	v good; 1 lar		19	9	2	12		poor ; 3 lar
	20	10	5	63	0	fair; 5 lar		21	11	4	37		poor ; 4 lar
	21	9	5	79	0	v good; 1 lar		22	12	4	39		poor ; 1 lar
	24	2	5	59	1	good ; 4 lar		23	12	4	64		fair
	25	1	4	48	1	good ; 3 lar		28	11	6	58		fair ; 2 lar
	27	10	4	18	0	fair; 1 lar		29	10	5	16		bad
	30	12	3	14	0	bad		30	10	7	47		poor
Dec.	1	10	3	16	0	poor		31	10	7	54	0/0	fair ; 1 lar

HAVERFORD COLLEGE
STUDIES

Published by the Faculty of

HAVERFORD COLLEGE.

COMMITTEE ON PUBLICATION:

ISAAC SHARPLESS   FRANCIS B. GUMMERE

FRANK MORLEY

FIFTH MONTH, 1893

No. 12   *$1.00*

CONTENTS.

To obtain copies of this publication, address the Secretary of Haverford College, Haverford College P. O., Pa.

Now is the Iudgement of this World, now shall the Prince of this World be cast out. *Iohn.12*

Now is comè salvation, and strength and the Kingdome of our God, and the power of his Christ.
Apoca: 12

THE FAMILY OF LOVE, OR THE FAMILISTS.

A STUDY IN CHURCH HISTORY.

AMONG the many sects which sprung up during the century following the Protestant Reformation, one of the most singular is the Family of Love. Few religious bodies of similar size have attracted more attention during so brief an existence, and few have dropped so completely out of notice. Hardly any sect has been so libelled, both by contemporaries and by historians, and but few have been so misunderstood, for though fundamentally wrong in many points, it is now clear that its members apprehended much that the church around them ignored or failed to comprehend.

In any discussion of religious questions pertaining to the sixteenth and sevententh centuries it must always be remembered that whether the matter related to Roman Catholic or to Protestant such a thing as toleration did not exist, and generally was considered absolutely sinful. Religious liberty and toleration are of recent growth and have been won, where they do exist, at the expense of much suffering, sometimes even of death.

It will be interesting as well as helpful, in our endeavor to give a true estimate of a well-nigh forgotten sect, to quote from a book celebrated in its day, which reflects not only the views of the author, but also of most of those who called themselves "orthodox."

"A Toleration is the grand designe of the Devil, his Masterpeece and cheif Engine he works by at this time to uphold his tottering Kingdom; it is the most compendious, ready, sure way to destroy all Religion, lay all waste, and bring in all evil; it is a most transcendent, Catholicke, and Fundamental evil, for this Kingdom of any that can be imagined: As original sin is the most Fundamental sin, all sin;

having the seed and spawn of all sin in it: So a *Toleration*
hath all Errors in it, and all Evils, it is against the whole
stream and current of Scripture both in the Old and New
Testament, both in matters of Faith and manners, both general
and particular commands; it overthrows all relations, both
Political, Ecclesiastical, Oeconomical; and whereas other evils,
whether Errors of judgement or practice, be but against some
one or few places of Scripture or Relation, this is against all,
this is the *Abaddon, Apollyon*, the destroyer of all Religion,
the Abomination of Desolation and Astonishment, the Liberty
of Perdition (as *Austine* calls it) and therefore the Devil follows
it night and day, working mightily in many by writing books
for it, and other ways, all the Devils in Hell, and their Instru-
ments, being at work to promote a Toleration."[1]

Such a condition of public opinion makes it extremely hard
to arrive at the truth, regarding theological questions. The
testimony on both sides is often violently prejudiced, while on
the side of those dissenting from the common views, statements of doctrine frequently seem purposely obscure and
indefinite, the result being that the investigator is tempted
again and again to give up his work in despair of reaching
any satisfactory conclusion.

Many of the doctrines which came prominently into notice
soon after the Protestant revolution were not new, but had
been held by individuals in secret, or by obscure sects, even
from the earliest days of the Christian Church. For instance,
in 1646, Edwards in his " Gangræna," already quoted from, in
his catalogue of 176 errors which call for especial condemnation, includes the following number: "101. That the Scriptures
nowhere speak of Sacraments, name or thing." "103· That
Baptism is not a seal nor sign of the Covenant of grace."
"119· That there ought to be no distinct order of Ministers,
nor such calling of some persons distinct and separated from
the people." "124. That 'tis lawful for women to preach, and
should they not, having gifts as well as men? and some of

---

[1] Gangræna, Part I, Observations, pp. 58, 59. By Thomas Edwards, Minister
of the Gospel. The third edition, corrected and much enlarged. London,
MDCXLVI (sm. 4to.)

them actually do preach, having great resort to them."[2] It should be remembered that this book was published before George Fox began to preach. It is true that the Family of Love were anticipated in many of their doctrines, and it will also appear that they anticipated others in some points, which are often supposed to have had a later origin.

THE LIFE OF HENRY NICHOLAS, OR NICKLAES, AND THE ESTABLISHMENT OF THE FAMILY OF LOVE.

HENRY NICHOLAS, or Niklaes, was born January 9th or 10th, 1501 or 1502, in Münster, Westphalia. His father, according to the accounts which have come down to us, was a devout Roman Catholic, who "daily prayed to God in the temple." Up to his fifth year the little Henry, who was a weak, delicate boy, was educated by his mother, but he was then sent to school to a Priest, Cornelius by name. At this school he was very diligent, and his zeal for learning so injured his health that he had to be taken away. In the meantime the lad read much concerning the passion of Christ.

It is said that he greatly resembled his father and that the latter did his best to inculcate in him a reverence and love for the Catholic ceremonies. It soon became a custom for the child to go daily to the Mass and to preaching, and naturally he talked much with his father about their meaning, asking many questions that his father was unable to answer. When the boy was eight years old a striking example of this occurred on one occasion after the household worship. The boy asked his father why he thanked God. The reply was, "for forgiveness of sins in Jesus Christ and that so, a true life of godliness might be established." The boy quickly replied with an intelligence beyond his years, that he could not see that sin in man *was* bettered and that he was brought back to true godliness. The father had nothing to say to this, except, that one should not doubt the grace of God in Christ Jesus, but must simply believe.

To this the lad rejoined that he did not doubt that through

---

[2] Gangræna, Part I, pp. 24, ff.

the death of Christ an entrance into God's kingdom was opened for us, and that if we followed him in his sufferings we should attain the true righteousness. But he went on to say that he could not but see that the rent which sin had made ought to be closed up, that it had not been, and therefore God must have intended it to be removed in some way which man did not yet understand. To this the father could only reply that he would consult his confessor and see what he would say, telling his son also, "thou art yet too young to be able to comprehend such things." His confessor, a Franciscan, told him "Bring your son to me and I will hear what the boy has to say." At a convenient time the father and son came; "the confessor looked on the child, who was very young and little, and said to the father, 'Is that the lad thou toldst me of, that hath such strange whimsies in his head? Surely he is too childish yet as to trouble himself with such things as you told me of. Thou shouldst of right with a rod chastise him from the same, and neither to hear nor answer him in his sayings, for it is not otherwise than the madness of a child.'" On this the boy said it was very true he was a child and under the instruction of his father, but if he could not understand what his father taught, should it not be allowed him to ask for the sense and true meaning? This reasonable statement so far mollified the confessor that he said, "That is true, but you are yet much too young and too small of capacity to search into the deep, profound mysteries of the godly things, or to fathom them." "Therefore," the boy replied, "am I the most inclined for that reason to ask and not to search thereafter out of my own power." A long conversation followed, in which the child repeated, in greater fulness, what he had said to his father; the burden being if Christ had died to redeem mankind, ought not man to attain to the righteousness which was in Adam before he fell, and if so why were men so far from being righteous. The confessor was puzzled how to reply, but a brother Franciscan, who stood by, came to his aid, ridiculing the whole matter; so, after speaking many harsh words to the child, making him weep, the Franciscans departed and the boy and his father returned home. The child was not satisfied however, but revolved the matters in his mind, "going up and down with a sad heart."

In his ninth year, it is said, he had a wonderful vision which explained what had been so dark to him before. He thought he was surrounded by the glory of God, like a great mountain, which presently united itself with him and illuminated his whole spirit and mind. And it was shown him that this unity with God is " the true accomplishment of the godliness in Jesus Christ." He fell asleep again, and saw that there were many saints of God who were to be with him in this experience, and that he was to call men to this "transcendent worthy nobleness of man and the most peaceable life of godliness to which God hath created man and chosen him thereto through Jesus Christ." He further saw that many men did oppose him and hardened their hearts against his sayings, and were " changed into terrible hurtful and tearing wolves," which " bellowed and foamed " against him and the saints of God. So frightened was he that he called out so loudly that his parents came running up to see what was the matter; but, fearing ridicule, in answer to their questions he only said, " A little weakness is come upon me," and kept all these things to himself.

How far this account is to be accepted as truthful, it is impossible to say. The mere fact of the visions being described does not necessarily stamp it with improbability, for it was customary in those days to expect visions, and many honestly believed in their reality. Nor does it follow that a child could not have imagined such things. A knowledge of these real or supposed visions is necessary to a clear understanding of the after-life of Henry Niklaes.

During the rest of his youth he was zealous in attendance upon the service and ceremonies of the Church. On the completion of his ninth year he went to a Latin school where he surpassed all his fellows. After three years he left school and joined his father in business. It appears that he was acquainted with Luther's writings, but objected to them because of "their calumnies against the priesthood of the Roman church," and also because he considered they did not "teach the ground of true righteousness and the fulfilment of godliness in Jesus Christ, and that common people were not restrained by a good and orderly discipline."[3] The effect of reading these writings of Luther was to make him desire to read the Bible, with which at that time he does not seem to have been acquainted. He accordingly asked his father to give him a copy in the German language; his father at first refused, fearing that his son might be led thereby into some error, but the young man telling him that he believed it to be his duty to read it, he procured a copy, gave it to his son, and was moreover much pleased with the book himself. Henry Nicklaes subsequently became well acquainted with the Bible, as his writings show very clearly, but his familiarity with it does not seem to have lessened his hostility to the principles of Protestantism in the slightest degree. It appears, however, that he was always ranked with heretics by his fellow townsmen, and we find that he was, in his twenty-seventh year, arrested on the charge of heresy, but after a severe examination, acquitted and discharged.

When he was twenty years old his parents chose a " virtuous young lady, of a plain and simple family, who had no sympathy with frivolity, to be his wife," and at the same time he undertook an independent mercantile business, in which he was very successful.

On account of the imprisonment just mentioned, he concluded to change his place of residence, which he accomplished a year later (1529 or 1530), removing to Amsterdam with his family. He soon associated himself with some " who had fallen away from the Catholic Church, but who sought earnestly after righteousness." This again brought him under suspicion, and in his thirtieth year he was arrested and brought before the magistrates of Amsterdam, who were not able to find him guilty of any heresy, and offered to release him if he would promise to avoid going with suspicious persons; on his refusal to do this he was remanded to prison, and was finally taken before the high council of Holland, by which he was,

---

[3] Zeitschr. f. die histor. Theologie, 1862, p. 349.

after a further examination, set at liberty without the exaction of any promise.

After such a youth and such experiences as he had passed through, it is only natural that he should pray for and expect some personal revelation of God's will. Accordingly we are told that in the ninth year of his residence at Amsterdam, at a time when he did not cease from praying night or day, another vision and revelation came to him similar to the one in his boyhood. As before, God had appeared and filled his being, so now the Holy Spirit poured over him the true love of Jesus Christ as he had promised through his holy prophets, and called him to the service of the holy and reverend Word. He said also to him, "Fear not, I am he who is all in all; I will establish again all things, as I from the beginning have spoken through my prophets, and will re-establish the house of Israel in its glory." The message went on to say further that those things which he had not been able to understand in his youth would be revealed to him so fully, that he would be able to declare them to mankind. "For this purpose have I borne thee on my heart from thy youth as for a house for me to dwell in, chosen and kept until now from all evil. And now is the time of my righteous judgments fulfilled, when the wicked and godless shall inherit eternal death; but the good and obedient eternal life." From this time Henry Nicklaes believed that he was made more and more one with the will and word of God, and that he also received the command to put these revelations in print and publish them.

He believed also that he was commanded to leave Amsterdam and go to Emden in East Friesland. The real reason of his departure from Holland was doubtless his fear of detection and danger, for he does not seem to have thought that he was required to be very much of a martyr. From this time he took the position of a prophet and founder of a sect, and he now first published his writings. In these and on the title-page he is spoken of as H. N., by which letters he is, hereafter, usually referred to. He did not escape suspicion and persecution at Emden, but suffered imprisonment, perhaps torture, though this is not clear. He was further convinced of his mission by a third revelation, and his account of this is written in the same mystical language as the earlier ones. He also gained here his first converts.

From his thirty-ninth to his fifty-ninth year we have no account which gives anything like a full picture of his life. This is particularly to be regretted, as it is the period during which he gathered many adherents.

One curious feature in his character is, that unlike many, if not most, preachers of new religious doctrines, he seems to have applied himself to mercantile business and to have been very successful. During these twenty years he travelled frequently through Holland and Brabant for purposes of trade. This information comes through Coornhert who knew him well and was one of his great enemies.[4] The extent of his property is also shown by his contributions to the expenses of his sect. His wife, whose name is not known, lived through the whole of his residence at Emden, but died soon after his flight from that town. He had three daughters and two sons. Three of these children died before their father; one son appears to have established a printing-office at Cologne, and one daughter was twice married, but none of them seem to have been of any special help to their father in his religious aspirations. He does not appear to have taught openly his doctrines—indeed it would have only resulted in immediate apprehension and imprisonment if not something worse—but to have relied upon his personal intercourse and upon the circulation of his writings. These were printed elsewhere, but conveyed secretly to Emden, where also, during the twenty years of his stay, by far the greater part of his works were written, as many as eighty-seven treatises having been composed, it is said, during these years. Among the printers whom he employed at various times were Christopher Plantin, the celebrated printer of Antwerp, and Dirk van Börne. A certain Augustin van Haffelt he sent to Plantin's to learn the trade and then setting up a printing-office of his own in Kampen, he placed Augustin

---

[4] Spiegelken, Vorrede, quoted by Nippold, Zeitschrift f. die hist. Theologie, 1862, p. 355.

in charge of it. From this was issued a vast number of pamphlets in the Dutch language, which were translated into German, Latin, French, and English. The name of Niklaes however did not appear on the title-pages. He also sent out many pamphlets from another press which he set up at his own expense at Cologne. Not only did he spread his doctrines through the medium of the press, but he was now able to make use of the zeal of his followers. Among the most influential of these was a certain Heinrich Jansen, of the village of Barreveldt, in Guelderland, and hence frequently spoken of as Barreveldt. In the mystical writings of the sect he is called " Hiel." Through him and other followers the doctrines of the " House of Love " were spread over Friesland, Holland, England, and France.

In his fifty-ninth year he was proceeded against by the council of Emden, but receiving intelligence of the action, he had time to escape to a place of safety. When the messenger reached his residence neither Niklaes nor his books were to be found. In consequence of the fright and these extreme measures his wife is said to have died. But previously to her death she sent her son Nicholas, who was acquainted with his father's place of retreat, that her husband might have an opportunity to send a reply to the charges brought against him. Niklaes sent back an answer, addressed " to the honorable, wise, circumspect, benevolent, beloved gentlemen," saying that he never had dared to be a schismatic, nor had he ever composed any misleading or heretical books, nor had he given such to the light. Nippold[5] remarks very severely upon this statement, saying that there scarcely exists an example of equivocation, nay of unmitigated falsehood, such as this " heavenly " prophet considered right and allowable. Niklaes went on to say that his whole former life would disprove these charges; that he had held himself aloof from sectaries; that he felt love to all men; that in this love all religion was founded and that it surpassed all ceremonies; that he had known of these slanders for a year, but had been unable to dis-

[5] Zeitschrift f. hist. Theologie, 1862, p. 367.

cover the author of them. On account of this enmity and because the cares of business were no longer agreeable he had concluded to leave Emden for a while and seek a quiet and safe place, and he hoped that the slander against him would be recognized as such. His letter did not avail much, for his goods were seized, and a warrant issued against him. His children were put out of the house in cold winter weather, without food or money; among them his youngest married daughter with a prematurely born infant. They were sheltered by friends, but suffered much indignity; after six months they gave bond for their good behaviour so they could begin their business anew. Meanwhile H. N. had learned from the experience of his children what he might expect for himself and so remained in concealment, but not without great anxiety lest he might be discovered. "But," he says, " the Lord was with him and enlightened his understanding." He took great comfort in reading the Psalms of David and composed psalms of his own. He did not cease to do his best to spread his doctrines, and as a result of the persecution " The House of Love" gained new adherents. It is not known where H. N. was all this time; the " Acta " and " Cronica," the chief dependence for the facts of his history, are silent. He appears to have gone from Emden to Kampen, possibly to England. He also about this time met personally the great printer, Plantin. He was next at Cologne, where he was seized with a severe illness, in fact, he appears to have gone from place to place, remaining long at no one of them. This seems to be implied by the mystical travels described in his books written during this period, the actual suggesting the spiritual. His adherents kept increasing, particularly in England, which became the central stronghold of his sect.

It was at this time that Holland rebelled against the tyranny of Spain, and the Duke of Alba gained his unenviable notoriety; and when everything was in confusion, H. N., then in his sixty-fifth year, claimed to have a new revelation. " He was commanded," he says, "to travel in a land of rest and peace which was prepared for the chosen, who should follow him so that they might reach the land of peace and become one in heart and soul with God." · The journeyings which he had now to go through with, were to be the preparation for the new birth in Christ, and it was necessary that all future elders should have the like experience. It was also revealed that he should here- after keep silence before his enemies and only reveal to his friends what he heard, and specially to four-and-twenty "Elders" and four "Seraphim"' who should travel with · him in "The House of Love." This similitude of travel was a very favorite one with him and is found all through his writings.

A new and more complete organization of the society was now established (about 1567) and new and improved editions of his writings issued. These had been misunderstood by his enemies and were not fully comprehended, even by the well- disposed. This was an important era in the history of the sect, and not unlike similar epochs in the history of other sects. An effort to elaborate a system of doctrine or practice which ignores to any great degree the rank and file of the adherents, or which is beyond their average intelligence, or comprehen- sion, generally tends to weaken the body if not to sow the seeds of final destruction, and so when the Family of Love to outward appearance was starting upon a new lease of life, it was really on the way to death.

The idea of the spiritual life being a journey was very fully carried out. The twenty-four Elders who were to accompany H. N. in his spiritual travels were concealed under typical names. They were: Abia, the fatherly will of God; Abdiel, his testimony; Banaias, his understanding; Colia, his voice; Daniel, his judgment; Elidad, his love; Foelicitas, his holiness; Gabriel, his strength; Hananias, his pity; Jadaja, his knowl- edge; Joacim, his resurrection; Lazarus, his help; Malaliel, his illumination; Melchiel, his kingdom; Nehemias, his con- solation; Odaja, his creed; Patroba, his fatherliness; Rasias, his secrecy; Salamiel, his peace; Sophia, his wisdom; Tobias, his goodness; Urias, his light; Veritas, his truth; Zacharias, his remembrance.

Likewise the four chief Seraphim who should stand con- tinually before him, covering and hiding him with their great wings, were the four apostolic evangelists in the House of Love, viz.: Fidelitas, God's faithfulness, or the lion of the tribe of Judah and the root of David; Raphael, God's healthfulness, or the lovely human countenance, out of the tribe of Benjamin and the root of Paul; Josue, God's holiness, or the bull out of the tribe of Levi and the root of Aaron; Prudentia, God's foresight, or the eagle of the tribe of Joseph and the root of Peter.

He claimed to have received a further revelation as to the beginning and continuance of this spiritual travel. It was to be entered upon in a spirit of obedience and reliance upon God, and with a complete renunciation of every earthly dependence. The descriptions which follow often suggest the "Pilgrim's Progress." The time of travel was to continue seven times seven days, during which time no food which had any life in it should be eaten, and neither wine nor strong drink be drunk.

During the first week, which would be without any trouble or temptation, the traveller was to reach the land *Contemplatio Justitiæ* or *Speculum Justitiæ*, where, as in a clear mirror, the true righteousness was to be seen. At the end of every six days the pilgrim was to reach an inn, where he was to rest the seventh day, being entertained and instructed by a mystical host and hostess, suitable to the advance made in spiritual knowledge, and to whose direction the pilgrim was to submit himself wholly. At the end of the second week the land, *Doctrina* or *Disciplina*, was reached, and the host and hostess of the inn were, respectively, the Love of doing God's will, and Willing obedience. The third week, during which the traveller had to contend with many lusts of the flesh, brought him to the land *Abstinentia*, where he was to learn, through fasting and prayer, how to conquer these wicked desires. The fourth week brought him to the land *Angustia*, where he learnt that the way to the new life was a narrow one. The fifth week he came into *Perseverantia*. The sixth week again had many temptations and the land reached was *Coena*, where the true supper of the Lord was eaten; here the host was the Life of Jesus Christ, and the hostess the Blood of Jesus Christ, the cup was the Passion of Christ, and during this week the pilgrims were to become full of Christ's spirit. During the seventh week they should be able to conquer all enemies, because of their union with Christ, but they would be greatly slandered, because of their claim of being one with Christ. At the end of the week the land *Consummatio* would be reached, where the completeness of the satisfaction of Christ would be understood, and where it would be learned that those who would triumph with him must also suffer with him. The Scriptures would be opened to them, and afterwards they were to betake themselves to Mount Nebo, where they could see the hereditary land of God and of His living ones. The forty-ninth day was to be one of rest. On this day of rest with Christ in his death and burial the journey to the land of the living was to be completed.

On the fiftieth day a new command was to be given. Those who reached this point were to understand that this was the time of the fulfilment of the word spoken by the prophets. "Now is the time of the judgment of God and of his saints fulfilled," and they shall appear with him to judgment. They have received his spirit and his understanding which is beyond all human knowledge. The wonder-working of God has been revealed to them and they are to declare it to mankind. Especially however are they to obey the last revealed will of God concerning the service of His holiest priesthood. As He had in earlier times spoken through Moses, so now He spoke through H. N. It was His will that all peoples should be obedient to the Love, because only such were His true children, while those who resisted were forever accursed.

As a final duty the pilgrims were to transcribe fairly and distinctly the writings of H. N., but at the same time in such a way that the wicked should remain in ignorance of them. The task should not be laid aside until completed, but during this period meat could be eaten and wine drunk.

One hardly knows whether to call this last command an act of foolishness or of shrewdness. As the completion of a time of spiritual experience it certainly seems to border on the absurd, and yet on the other hand it was undoubtedly a shrewd thing to require a careful reading of the fundamental works of the sect.

Moreover when this " Land of the Living " was reached the organization of the priesthood and of the whole company of the Love was to be made known. " An organization," says Nippold, " perhaps unsurpassed in the number of its precepts and in the fulness of its regulations."

But this fuller revelation was not accepted by some of his followers with that submission which would ensure success. The son-in-law of H. N. and others who had been his early supporters refused to obey the new commands, denying that such blind obedience could be the command of God. It was quite in accord with the previous experience of H. N. to claim to have a new revelation suggested by the new experience. This happened in his sixty-ninth year, the fifth of the " new reign of the majesty of God upon earth." The faithful were to be brought into the desert, *Unitas,* where they were to remain three weeks fasting and praying for the awaking of men; the desert was thus bounded,—on the east was the land *Abstinentia,* on the west *Angustia,* on the north *Maledictio,* and on the south *Purgatio ;* each one of these districts is carefully described, but it is unnecessary to go more fully into the description as the names are enough to indicate what they were intended to symbolize.

The rebellion against the requirement of unquestioned obedience increased; some of H. N.'s earliest friends leaving " the service of the House of Love;" among those were Hubert, a minister of Rotterdam; Cornelius Jansen ; Heinrich Jansen (Hiel); and probably Plantin, the printer. Niklaes did his best to win back these seceders, writing to them, and visiting some of them personally and using entreaty. But though in his presence they were polite and even friendly, when he left them they did not cease their attacks upon him, boldly saying that his revelations were of his own manufacture. It is unnecessary to go into the particulars of this division. Few founders of sects have seen their followers so quickly separated by schisms as H. N. The secession was doubtless due to several causes, the chief being, as pointed out by by Nippold and by Max Rooses,[6] a disbelief in the reality of the revelations

---

[6] Christophe Plantin, M. Rooses, pp. 63–68, Anvers, 1883.

of H. N. The latter also suggests that the times had changed and that several of the sects which had arisen about the time of the Reformation had become less extravagant and hence more attractive. The Anabaptists had calmed their first ardor; the predictions of most of the " prophets " had been unfulfilled; there was a general disillusion; and Menno Simons had arisen, whose teaching was less exalted and took the place of old reveries.

Heinrich Niklaes died, probably, in 1570, but there are no particulars of his death. As has already been said, the chief strength of the sect was in the Netherlands and in England. There were a few members in Paris, but little seems to be known about them there. The principal cities where the sect flourished were Amsterdam, Emden, Antwerp, Kampen, Cologne, Rotterdam and Dordrecht. The sect never was firmly established, owing to the early divisions and differences, and soon its numbers must have become inconsiderable, as the traces of it are scanty. In 1577 we know, through Cornelius Coornhert, one of its most violent enemies, that there were members in Harlem, and it was after the death of H. N. that a certain Cornelis Cornelissen, a corrector of the Latin school in Dordrecht, was brought before the church council, charged with being a follower of Heinrich Niklaes, and with possessing one of his books, the " Glass of Righteousness." He was expelled from the congregation, his position taken away from him, and he exiled from the town. In 1614, also in Dordrecht, Caspar Grevinchoven published perhaps the most systematic attack that was made against the sect. This is the last contemporary notice met with on the continent, and the Familists gradually disappeared from Holland. Their doctrines seem to have taken deeper root in England, though the membership was chiefly confined to London and the eastern counties, particularly the latter. We also find them mentioned as being in New England, and there are frequent references to them in the English theological literature of the sixteenth and seventeenth centuries.

The notices we have are almost exclusively from hostile sources, and as most ecclesiastical writers have been content to accept these statements with little examination, the accounts of the sect, with few exceptions, are erroneous, or must be received with considerable allowance.

Probably few bodies have been as much maligned. Their name was fatally against them, and it was impossible to persuade such men as Rutherford, Baxter, Henry More, and Fuller the historian, that they were not libertines. Even William Penn speaks of some of them as having "brought forth a monstrous birth to the scandal of those that feared God,"[7] though he does give them credit for holding some valuable doctrines.

The first notice of the sect in England which I have been able to find is in a letter of Archbishop Cranmer, September 27, [1552.] "'A letter' was sent from the council 'to the archbishop to examine a new sect newly sprung up in Kent.' 'It may be they were of the Family of Love or David George's sect who made himself sometimes Christ and sometimes the Holy Ghost.'"[8] According to Strype, a certain "Christopher Vittells, a joyner by trade, with his complices, came out of Delph in Holland, to Colchester, in the reign of Queen Mary and joyned himself with the professors of the Gospel there, and taught that the Godly have in themselves Freewill to do good, and could not away with predestination." "About the third year of Queen Mary, 1555," a certain Henry Crinel met with this Vittells who endeavored to convert him to what he found were the teachings of "one Henry Nicolas, a mercer of Delph in Holland."[9] In 1576 a certain Thickpenny, a curate of Brighthelmstone, was suspended by the Bishop of Chichester, on suspicion of his favoring the sect "called the Family of Love."[10] In the "Exposition of the Thirty-nine Articles," by Thomas Rogers, the first part published in 1579, the second part in 1585, and the whole enlarged and revised in 1607, the references to the Family of Love are numerous, occurring on almost every page.[11] In the tenth sermon

---

[7] Pref. Journal George Fox, p. viii, 1694.

[8] Strype's Cranmer ii, p. 410, E. H. Soc. ed., Oxford, 1848.

[9] Annals of Reform. in Eng., ii, book ii, chap. 18, pp. 596, 597, London, 1725.

[10] Grindal's Remains, p. 361, Parker Soc., Cambridge, 1843.

[11] Exposition of the Thirty-nine Articles, Rogers, Parker Soc., Cambridge, 1854.

preached soon after his appointment as Archbishop of York, 1576, Archbishop Sandys speaks of the sect, along with the Donatists, Arians, and Anabaptists, as apparently well-known.[12] In a sermon preached 19th April, 1549, before Edward VI, Bishop Latimer seems to refer to the sect when he says, "There be new spirits start up now of late, that say, after we have received the Spirit, we cannot sin."[13]

Freak, Bishop of Norwich, writing 4th June, 1579, says he "had been diligent in searching after them (members of the Family of Love), endeavoring by punishments as well as gentler methods to reclaim them. Some of them were by his orders imprisoned." Some of those accused were of the clergy and had livings.[14] Thomas Whitaker, Regius Professor of Divinity, Cambridge, in his Disputation on Scripture, first published in 1588, says: "Do you yourself deem him a Christian who denies the whole scripture? Certainly, he replies; for he affirms that some Christians deny the scriptures, such as the Schwenkfeldians, Anabaptists, and in England the Familists and Superilluminati. I answer, our question is about real Christians. These are not Christians truly but equivocally as the papists are equivocal catholics."[15]

In 1575 the Familists laid a confession of their faith, with a number of their books, before the English Parliament and prayed for toleration.[16] In 1578, John Rogers says H. N. then had as many as a thousand followers in England, but he probably underrated the number.[17] The petition of 1575 did not have much effect, for on the 9th of October, 1580, a royal proclamation was issued against them. "It would be difficult

---

[12] Sermons by Archbishop Sandys, p. 91, Parker Soc., Cambridge, 1841.

[13] Sermons of Bishop Latimer, p. 229, Parker Soc., Cambridge, 1844.

[14] Strype Annals of the Reform., ii, chap. 17, p. 584, London, 1725.

[15] Whitaker, Disputation on Scripture, p. 298, Parker Soc., Cambridge, 1849.

[16] Mosheim Eccles. Hist. cent. xvi, chap. iii, 25. Murdock's notes; Rutherford, Survey Spiritual Antichrist, p. 353, London, 1648. Walch, J. G. Religionsstreitigkeiten ausser der Evangel. luther. Kirche, iv, 848, Jena. Boehme, A. W. Reformation der Kirchen in England, Book iv, chap. 5, Altona, 1734.

[17] Keble's Hooker 1, pp. 148, 149, Fifth Ed., Oxford, 1865.

2

to find within so small a compass, in any state paper, so much abuse." [18]

The following "Abjuration," dated October 10, 1580, was also to be tendered to them:

The form of abjuration tendered to those of the Family of Love.

Whosoever teacheth, that the dead, which are fallen asleep in the Lord, rise up in this day of his judgment, and appear unto us in godly glory, which shall henceforth live in us everlastingly with Christ and reign upon the earth, is a detestable heretic. Whosoever teacheth, that to be born of the Virgin Mary out of the seed of David, after the flesh, is to be exponed of the pure doctrine out of the seed of love, is a detestable heretic. Whosoever teacheth, that Jesus Christ is come again unto us, according to his promise, to the end, that they all which love God and his righteousness, and Christ and perfect being, might presently enter into the true rest, which God has prepared from the beginning for his elect, and inherit everlasting life, is a detestable heretic. [19] [1580.]

In September 1592 some of the " Gentry of Suffolk " sent an " Address " to the Royal Council in regard to the state of the Church in their county "which every day grows more sick, and those whom it most concerns have been so careless, that the hope of its recovery is almost desperate;" they complain of the lack of uniformity, and that religion is brought into contempt. They say, they do not allow Papists their treacheries, subtilties and heresies, nor the Family of Love, an egg of the same nest, nor the Anabaptists nor the Brownists, the overthrowers of Church and commonweal, but abhor and punish all these. . . . The Papist is pure and immaculate, and has a store of goodness for himself and plenty for others. The Family of Love cannot sin, but the writers, thank God, cry out in the bitterness of their souls, "*peccavimus cum patribus nostris.*" [20] In 1603 King James I, in the preface to his Basilcon Doron, says: " First then, as to the name of Puritans, I am not ignorant

[18] Marsden. Early Puritans, p. 140, Second Ed. London, 1853. For Proclamation see Cardwell's Documentary Annals, xciv, Oxford, 1844. Stow's Annals, p. 688, London, 1605; Camden's Elizabeth, 1580; Fuller, Church History, Book ix, cent. xvi, 36, 38. Nichol's Ed., 1868.

[19] Cardwell's "Documentary Annals," xcii, Oxford, 1844; Fuller's "Church History," Book iv, Cent. XVI, 39, 40; Rutherford, "Survey of the Spiritual Antichrist," p. 354, London, 1648. Compare Keble's Hooker, as above.

[20] Calendar of State Papers, Domestic, Elizabeth, 1591–1594, vol. ccxliii, pp. 275 277. See also vol. cxxxiii, p. 55.

that the style thereof doth properly belong only to that vile sect amongst the Anabaptists called the Familie of Love, because they think themselves only pure and in a manner without sin, the only true church and only worthy to be participants of the Sacraments, and all the rest of the world to be but abomination in the sight of God. Of this special sect I principally mean when I speak of Puritans." [21]

In 1604 the Family of Love presented a petition [22] to James I. The tone of this document is almost pathetic, but it is especially interesting in its disclaiming any sympathy with Puritans. The petitioners say, "the people of the Family of Love or of God, do utterly disclaim and detest all the said absurd and self conceited opinions and disobedient and erroneous sects of the Anabaptists, Browne, Penry, Puritans, and all other proud minded sects and heresies whatsoever." They go on to protest that they are faithful and loyal subjects. They complain that they have been pursued with malice, especially by the Puritans and others, for upwards of twenty-five years; foul errors and odious crimes have been charged against them; but that they had behaved themselves "in all orderliness and peaceableness of life"; they say if they have swerved from "the established Religion in this land either in service, ceremonies, Sermons, or Sacraments or have publicly spoken or inveighed either by word or writing against our late Sovereigne Princesse government in cases spirituall or temporall, then let us be rejected for Sectaries, and never receive the benefits of Subjects." They acknowledge that they have "read certain bookes brought forth by a Germane Author under the characters of H. N. who affirmeth therein that hee is prepared, chosen and sent of God to minister and set forth the most holy service of the Love of God and Christ or of the Holy Ghost unto the children of men upon the universall earth out of which service or writings we bee taught all dutifull obedience towards God and Magistrates, and to live a godly and honest life." They know of no law against them, the author, nor against his books; that they sup-

---

[21] K. James. Basilicon Doron. Pref. 6th Par., London, 1603.
[22] Rutherford, Survey Spiritual Antichrist, p. 343. London, 1648. Fuller, Ch. Hist., Book x, Cent. XVII, §§ 18-22.

pose, under "his Highnesse correction," that he had never
seen the books nor had been informed of their contents by impartial judges. They go on to say that "the volume" of H.
N.'s writings would equal the whole Bible, but that there is
nothing in them that "takes part" against "any particular party
or company whatsoever as naming them by their names, nor
yet praise nor dispraise any of them by name: but doth only
show…the unpartiall service of love;" "Notwithstanding deare
Sovereigne, yet hath the said Author and his doctrine a long
time, and still is, most shamefully and falsely slandered by our
foresaid adversaries both in this land and in divers others as to
bee replenished with all manner of damnable errors and filthy
liberty of the flesh." After dwelling further on the injustice
with which they have been treated, " much like as it was practiced in the primitive Church," in efforts of all kinds being
made to force them to criminate themselves, they say they have
used this method of a petition "to acquaint [his] highnesse
with the truth and state of their cause, of which they think his
"Majesty is altogether ignorant." They ask with great
humility that he would grant them the favor as soon as the
affairs of importance which he has on hand "be overpast" at
his "fit and convenient time to peruse the books [himself]
with an unpartiall eye, conferring them with the holy Scripture." They will also, if he will appoint the time, "doe their
best endeavours to procure so many of the bookes as they can
out of Germany (where they be printed)." They will also "doe
[their] like endeavours to procure some of the learned men
in that country (if there be any yet remaining alive that were
well acquainted with the Author and his workes in his life
time, and which likewise have exercised his works ever since)
to come over" and explain any difficulties. They agree if after
such examination the works be found " heretical or seditious
and not agreeable to God's holy word and testimonies of all the
Scriptures, to leave them." They pray that all of them who
are then in prison may be released upon such bail or bond as
they are able to give and that they be not further persecuted or
troubled until the decision above referred to be reached. They
say "we are a people but few in number, and yet most of us

very poore in worldly wealth." They beg him to remember that in his "booke of Princely, grave and fatherly advice, to the happy Prince, your royal son [he] doth conclude *Principis est parcere subjectis debellare superbos.*" They finish by repeating the statement of the belief of the Family of Love presented to the Parliament in 1575[23] that he may better understand their innocent intent and profession whatever he may have reported to him.

This supplication Rutherford states[24] was "answered by one of the Universitie."[25]

The extended comments on this petition by Samuel Rutherford are an interesting example of the intolerance and narrowness of that day. He seems completely oblivious of the fact that, by his treatment of the petitioners, he was laying himself open to charges quite as just and as severe as those he was heaping upon his unfortunate countrymen the petitioners. It must seem almost incredible to those who only know Rutherford through his spiritual "Letters" or through the familiar hymn founded upon some of his dying words, "Glory dwelleth in Immanuel's Land," that he could be so unfair and captious in his treatment of those who differed from him on theological points. His was no unusual case, however; certainty in your own belief, in those times, was accompanied by certainty in the belief of the total depravity of all who differed from you ; and it was often the case that the attacker thought he knew better what his opponent believed than the opponent himself. Rutherford's opening note on the Supplication is:—"There is nothing in this Petition that smels of Christs ointments, nothing that looks with any face, like the anointing that teacheth all things, nothing to heighten Christ, much to flatter K. Iames, and to lift that abominable imposter *H. Nicholas* up above

---

[23] See p. 17, *ante.*

[24] Survey etc., p. 169.

[25] A Supplication of the Family of Love said to be presented into the Kings royall hands knowen to be dispersed among his Loyall subjects for grace and fauor examined and found to be Derogatorie in an hie degree Vnto the Glorie of God the honour of our King and the Religion in this Realme both soundly professed and firmly established. Reuel. 2 ver. 14. "I have" etc. Printed for John Legate Printer to the Vniversity of Cambridge, 1606.

Christ, the stile and words full of gall against Puritans, and the truly godly in England; the words base, earthly, low, devilish, hereticall, temporizing, etc. . . . King *Iames* was misinformed . . . . for Familists and the godly, unjustly called *Puritans* are as contrary as light and darknesse." This is almost the only point in which he allows the petitioners to be right. On the paragraph relating to worship and ceremonies he remarks: "To Familists all outward worship and ordinances are traditions, they live upon love within and are swine without, and yet sinn not." In regard to their request that the King should read their books he says:—"They tempt the King to forsake the Protestant religion." Again, speaking of their tenets, he says:—"Not more said than truth can beare, for *H. Nicholas* his doctrine is a *sentina*, a pumpe dunghill, and a sea of many fleshly errors and heresies." Again, "Neither by oath or by any other way could they be brought to make confession of the secrets of unpure Familisme." "The foulest of the bookes of *H. Nicholas* containing the mystery of Familisme and fleshly loosenesse are only to be seen by the wise and experienced Elders who can digest them." On the clauses in which the petitioners refer to King James's probable ignorance on the subject, he remarks: "It is not like but Q. *Elizabeth* heard of these books and saw them, since many of her and K. *Iames* his Court favoured them." "Divers of the court of Queen *Elizabeth* and of K. *Iames* and some nobles were Familists."[27]

We find little public notice of the sect in England after the address to King James, though the many allusions to their belief leads to the opinion that there must have been quite a number of members. Several of H. N.'s books were reprinted in England from 1645 to 1655, and a collection of some of his works, without date of publication, was illustrated with emblematical designs, engraved in 1656. In the examination of the petition "by one of the Vniversitie"[28] the author says in regard to their own statement of being few in number, "it is well-known how twenty-five years ago the number of them was great, and they dispersed in divers parts, as Surrey,

---

[27] Survey, etc., pp. 343, 346, 347, 348, 349.
[28] See p. 28.

Sussex, Middlesex, Barkshire, Hamshire, Essex, Isle of Ely, Cambridgeshire, Suffolk, Norfolk, in the Northeast, and finally in most shires of this realm. In those days they did most abound and were grown to such a number, as the displayer of the Sect delivered how his heart did rue to speak that which one of the same society did avouch to him for truth, not a few ministers of the simple sort have with H. N. his fancies entangled, nor are the chiefest places of the Realm free from these men.[29] Since that they are diminished I hear not, but them to be hugely increased through ruful connivance I have arguments to think ; but that their increase may be hindered I hope authority will take order. They say they are also poor, or the most of them ; but if the book of their names called of them the book of Life could be seen it would then appear, I doubt not, that both the number of them is great, and most of them very rich." It is impossible to get the facts in the case, but as antagonists are always likely to exaggerate the faults of their opponents and to over-estimate their number and resources, never more so than in the seventeenth century, it seems likely that the petitioners were nearer the truth than this critic. The unknown author also says they have books which they use in their services, have "conventicles, verbal traditions, private exercises," etc., though as he gives no evidence, his assertion is probably based upon hearsay or is a mere supposition.[30] The work of propagation seems to have been accomplished, as on the continent, chiefly by means of personal effort with individuals, and by books or pamphlets.

Among the references to the sect is that of Hooker in the preface to his Ecclesiastical Polity, entered for publication in 1593 and probably published the following year; he says: "When they the 'Family of Love' have it once in their heads that Christ doth not signify any one person, but a quality whereof many are partakers; that to be 'raised' is nothing else but to be regenerated or endued with the said quality; and that when separation of them which have it from them that have it not is here made, this is 'judgment' how plainly do they

---

[29] John Rogers. The Displaying of an Horrible Sect, etc. Pref., London, 1579.
[30] The Discovery of the Blasphemous Doctrine of Familism, London, 1645.

imagine that the Scripture everywhere speaketh in favor of that sect." [31]

In the tract, " Persecution for Religion, Judged and Condemned," published in 1615, we find —"The Familists who say that religion standeth not in outward things, and therefore they would submit to any outward service, and they that do not so are justly persecuted." [32]

Robinson, the Pilgrim father, writes in 1624, " A riddle better befitting H. N. than the professors of the truth in simplicity." [33] " All agree in this . . . the frenzy of some Familists and Anabaptists only excepted, who cashier all governments and governors out of churches and commonwealths." [34]

Roger Williams in his " Mr. Cotton's Letter, lately printed, Examined and Answered," printed 1644, speaking of " backsliders," says : " I have known no small numbers of such turn to absolute Familism, and under the pretences of great raptures of love deny all obedience to, or seeking after the pure ordinances and appointments of the Lord Jesus." [35] Rutherford says : " The Familists of our time, Del, Saltmarsh, Bacon, Randel, and others." [36] Alexander Ross in his " View of all Religions," first published in 1653, has a violent attack upon the Familists, but says nothing about the existence of the sect, though it might be inferred from what he says. [37]

Fuller's Church History was first published in 1665, and in it he writes, " Some will say ' where are these Familists now-a-days? Are they utterly extinct or are they lost in the heap of other sects, or are they concealed under a new name ?'. The last is most probable. This Family which shut their doors before,

---

[31] Keble's Hooker. Pref., p. 148, 5th ed., Oxford, 1865.

[32] Tracts on Liberty of Conscience, p. 147, (see also p. 113). Hanserd Knollys Soc., London, 1846.

[33] John Robinson, Works, i. 390. London, 1851.

[34] Hooker and Cotton's Survey of the Sum of Church Discipline. Part ii., chap. ii, London, 1648, quoted in Hanbury's Historical Memorials of the Independents, iii, 299, London, 1839.

[35] The Bloody Tenent of Persecution, etc., p. 428. Hanserd Knollys Soc., London, 1648.

[36] Survey, etc., p. 351, London, 1648.

[37] Alex. Ross, View of all Religions, pp. 364, 365, 4th ed., London, 1664.

keeps open house now. Yea, Family is too narrow a name for them, they are grown so numerous."[38]

Familist books in English were published as late as 1655 and probably in 1656, so it is highly likely that some of the sect were in existence at that date. In 1673 Henry Hallywell, vicar of Cowfold, Sussex, published a little book entitled " An account of Familism as it is revived and propagated by the Quakers," which implies that the sect had nearly become extinct; nor does Leslie seem to speak of the Familists as being still among English "sectaries," though he compares the Friends with them and says the Familists were the precursors of the Quakers.[39] William Penn speaks of them as of the "last age."[40] Henry More, particularly in his "Explanation of the Grand Mystery of Godliness "[41] (1676), and also in "Enthusiasmus Triumphatus"[42] speaks of H. N. and the Familists, in the former treatise quite at length, but he seems to imply that there were few when he wrote.

An interesting reference occurs in John Evelyn's Diary, under date of June 16th, 1687, where he writes: "But this [an Address from the People of Coventry to James II] is not so remarkable as an Addresse of the week, before (as I was assured by one present) of some of the *Family of Love.* His majesty ask'd them what this worship consisted in,. and how many their party might consist of; they told him their custom was to read the Scripture and then to preach, but did not give any further account onely sayd that for the rest they were a sort of refin'd Quakers, but their number very small, not consisting, as they sayd, of above threescore in all, and those chiefly belonging to the Isle of Ely."

One of the last references to their public service is found in Strype, who says: "This Familism could not be rooted out (however absurd it was) but it remained even to the last age; when

---

[38] Fuller, Ch. Hist., Book x, Cent. XVII, 19, 20. London, 1868.

[39] Chas. Leslie's Works, vi, 312, 315. Oxford, 1832.

[40] Journal, George Fox, Pref. p. viii. London, 1694.

[41] Theological Works, Books v, chap. 8 ; Book vi, chaps. 12-18 ; Book vii, chaps. 1-3. Fol., London, 1703.

[42] Philosophical Writings, §§ 21, 40, Fol., London, 1708.

one Randal was a preacher to these sectaries in a house within
the Spittle Yard without Bishopsgate in London in the year
1645 teaching this very doctrine, and many flocking after him. [43]
Again, writing not later than 1725, he says, "I remember a
great admirer of this sect within less than twenty years ago
told me that there was then but one of the Family of Love
alive and he an old man.[44]

Neal, writing in 1720, speaks of them as being "something
akin . . . to the Quakers among ourselves." [45]   The disappearance of the body as a sect may then be fairly placed as
about 1670, though individuals continued to hold the doctrines
longer.   The reason of this disappearance has hardly been
touched upon by the historians, whose views have been based
upon hostile testimony.   For the present it is sufficient to say
that the chief causes are apparently two: first, the lack of a
definite working organization, and secondly, all that was really
valuable in their teaching was now held by other bodies,
notably by the Society of Friends, and held and taught free
from the extreme mistiness and positive error which pervaded
the books of H. N. and the teaching and preaching of his
followers.

Charges against the Familists.

Before attempting to give an epitome of the doctrine of the
Familists it will be well to consider briefly some of the more serious of the charges brought against them.   Coornhert is the only
antagonist, who, meeting Niklaes personally, has left his views
on record.[46]   It appears from reading his account to be quite clear
that he misunderstood the real position of H. N.   He criticized
him mainly on the ground of allegorizing scripture, and claim-
ing to be filled with God, or as he said, to be God.   The charge then

---

[43] Annals, etc., II, Book ii, chap. 17, p. 599.   London, 1725.

[44] Ibid., ii 1, p. 561.

[45] Hist. of the Puritans, i, p. 227.   London, 1754.   Jer. Collier, in his Ecclesiastical History of Great Britain, published 1708–1714, says "His [H. N's] opinions died not with him, but exist at this day in new modifications."   vi, p. 609,
note.   London, 1840.

[46] See G. Brandt, History of the Reformation in the Low Countries.   Translated
i. 105, 106, fol.   London, 1720.

really was blasphemy. Whatever H. N. may have said, there is nothing in his writings to show that he claimed more than to be "godded with God," which, in his view, meant to be filled with the spirit of God, to be regenerate, as is shown by many passages, of which the following are fair examples: "There was much false doctrine through the unregenerated or ungodded men,"[47] "The renewed or godded man."[48]

The most common charge, that of Antinomianism, is found in almost every notice of the sect down to the present day, it therefore merits special notice. Professor Nippold, the most thorough student of the Familists, thinks that the tendency of their whole teaching was clearly Antinomian, and rather infers that they would have carried these opinions into daily life if it had been practicable.[49] He does not however seem to make sufficient allowance for the allegorical and mystical character of H. N.'s writings, and moreover he seems to be biassed in regard to this special point. If passages can be cited to support his view, far more can be cited to support the opposite. There can be no doubt that H. N. accepted the Decalogue, and in his writings dwells often on the duty of leading a life of righteousness, as the following passages chosen almost at random show:

"They also commit not any adultery for they are all honest and chaste of life, and clean and pure of heart. They do not desire nor lust for anything that is against the Law or Ordinance of the Lord, so are they likewise faithful therein."[50] Again in a long list of the sins of the world H. N. mentions "fighting, persecuting, lying, war or battle, vexing or troubling, cursing, swearing, destroying, spoiling, oppressing, killing, murdering, unchastity."[51]

The special charge of immorality, one of the most per-

---

[47] Evangelium Regni, 20 A. 1. London, 1649.

[48] Ibid., xxvi, 2, 3.

[49] Zeits. f. die histor. Theologie, 544, 1862. See also Robert South, Sermon xix, p. 342, Philadelphia, 1844.

[50] Terra Pacis, xxxvi: 10, 11. London, 1649.

[51] A Figure of the True and Spiritual Tabernacle, xix, 145. London, 1655.

sistent contemporary charges, is reiterated again and again by most historians.[52]

Some ignore the sect altogether, while a few have evi-. dently looked into the subject carefully and endeavor to give an impartial judgment.[53]

Marsden says, though he holds that their doctrine was antimonian, "Their lives were pure," and the "grave insinuation [of immorality] is utterly without support. It has often been revived, (and in general by ignorant persons of careless, if not licentious minds) whenever a Christian communion has insisted upon the doctrine of that divine love which God by His Spirit diffuses in the soul, and of that mutual and warm affection which believers owe to one another."[54]

Max Rooses, in his splendid folio on Christopher Plantin, the printer of Antwerp, speaking of the doctrine of H. N. says: "Au point de vue de la morale, elle est d'une grande pureté: *le Miroir de la Justice* prêche à chaque page l'abnégation, la sacrifice volontaire, la pratique du bien pour le bien, et condamne l'égoïsme sous toutes ses formes. On dirait un livre écrit par un disciple de Thomas à Kempis, par un mystique sévère, un ascète dur pour lui-même et pour les autres. Cette religion sans dogmes, cette morale sans préceptes déterminés ni sanction surnaturelle, malgré ses allures mystiques et

---

[52] See Fuller, Church History, Cent. XVII, 18, p. 228, Nichols' edition, London, 1868. Neal, Hist. of the Puritans, i chap. v., p. 227, London, 1754. Jer. Collier, Eccles. Hist. of Great Britain, vi. 609; vii. 311, London, 1840. T. V. Short, Hist. Church of Eng. ii, 619, Oxford, 1832. G. G. Perry, Hist. Church of Eng., ii, 194, London, 1862, Masson Life of Milton, iii, 152, where it is inferred. Blunt, Dict. of Sects, Heresies, etc., under Familists. Benham, Dict. of Religions, London, 1887. Alex. Ross, View of all Religions, p. 365, 4th ed., London, 1664. S. Rutherford, Survey of Spiritual Antichrist, p. 267, London, 1648. Henry More, Philosoph. Writings, Enthusiasmus Triumphatus, § xl, London, 1662. R. Baxter, Life i. Part I, p. 76, 91, London, 1696. Survey, etc., Richard Bancroft, London, 1593.

[53] Mosheim, Eccles. Hist., Book iv, Cent. XVI, § iii, part ii, chap. vi. J. Hunt, Religious Thought in England, i, pp. 234-237, London, 1870. R. Barclay, Inner Life of the Religious Societies of the Commonwealth, pp. 25-35, London, 1876. J. B. Marsden, Hist. of the Early Puritans, chap. v, pp. 138-141. 2d edition, London, 1853.

[54] Hist. Early Puritans, p. 139. 2d edition, London, 1853.

ascétiques, n'est en somme que le culte de l'humanité; c'est la négation de toute religion et de toute église."[55]

The adverse judgments of the sect are in almost every case based upon secondhand testimony or upon inference, and are repetitions of the statements of Rogers, Fuller, Henry More, and Strype, which are plainly one-sided. The extreme rarity of the books put forth by H. N. and his followers is some excuse for modern historians, though copies have always been available in the Libraries of the British Museum and of the Universities of Oxford and Cambridge. While it may be a fact that here and there the charges were true as regarded individuals—charges which would be of equal weight against individuals of any sect—there is no evidence that they were true as regarded members of this sect in general.

A bitter attack is preserved in the Harleian Miscellany,[56] a reprint of a tract first printed in 1641, but this gives the impression of a slander and is unsupported by any evidence.

It is remarkable that the author of the anonymous examination of the Supplication of the Familists to King James[57] slurs over their statement that they were slandered in being charged with "filthy liberty of the flesh." From the whole tenor of the tract the author evidently would have refuted this statement could he have done so.

One of their most vigorous antagonists in later times was Henry More, the Platonist, who devotes several chapters to the examination and refutation of the errors of the Familists, one sentence of which is interesting as showing upon what it is likely the current opinion of the sect was based. After giving a list of the evil practices, etc., to which, he presumes, H. N. was addicted, he goes on—" all which to any man that has but a moderate nasuteness, cannot but import, that in the title of this sect, that call themselves the *Family of Love*, there must be signified no other love than that which is merely *natural* or *animal*."[58]

---

[55] Max Rooses, Christophe Plantin, p. 65, Bruxelles, 1883.

[56] Vol. iv, p. 446, London, 1809.

[57] See p. 21, note, *ante*.

[58] Theological Works, Grand Mystery, etc., viii, 2, p. 258, London, 1708.

The next serious charge is that perjury was allowed in order to escape persecution or punishment. The strongest argument in support of the charge is Niklaes' letter to the council of Emden,[59] which certainly seems to be equivocal in meaning. The "Epistle sent unto two daughters of Warwick from H. N.," etc.,[60] is also open to the charge of encouraging equivocation, but that lying, or perjury was distinctly taugh or generally practiced has not been proved.

The argument usually is something like this: the Familists believe that the outward life does not matter, therefore they lie when it suits them; therefore whatever they say is not to be believed. This conclusion is accepted not only by their opponents, but also by many historians.

Other charges are mostly doctrinal ones, and often similar to many which were frequently brought against the majority of the so-called "sectaries" of the time, and which were pushed with all the virulence and intolerance common at that day.[61]

The Familists also provoked great opposition by holding so strongly to the spiritual interpretation of Scripture, a position which their opponents believed was due to diabolical influence, but which, whatever its origin, was, nevertheless, a standing protest against the prevailing literalism of the day. Their view is shown by the following already quoted: "The Familists, who say that religion standeth not in outward things, and therefore they would submit to any outward service, and they that do not so, but suffer persecution, say they are justly persecuted."[62]

---

[59] See p. 9 *ante*.

[60] H. Ainsworth, An Epistle, etc., London and Amsterdam, 1608.

[61] A long list of charges may be found in the index to Rogers on the XXXIX Articles, pp. 369, 370, Parker Society, Cambridge, 1854; in A Survey of the Spiritual Anti-Christ, etc., S. Rutherford, London, 1648, and in Anti-Familist literature generally.

[62] Persecution for Religion Judged and Condemned, 1615, Tracts on Liberty of Conscience, p. 147; see also pp. 113, 164, Hanserd Knollys Soc., London, 1846; also Robert South, Sermon xix, "Satan transformed into an Angel of Light," p. 339, Philadelphia, 1844.

Vnſe Herte/ is Godes Gemȫt.
Vnſe Weſen lieflick/ alſe de Lelie ſȫt.
Vnſe Trůwe/ Lieſte/ vnde Waerheit/
Is Godes Licht/ Leuen/ vnde Klaerheit.

The Teaching of The Familists.

Henry Niklaes was certainly not a Protestant in the ordinary sense of the term, though until the researches of Professor Nippold, he and his followers were classed as Protestants, and generally as Anabaptists. It is however likely that the English members of the sect were more nearly in general sympathy with the Protestants than were the Continental. The not infrequent charge brought against them of being Catholics in disguise, though a common one against all heretics, is thus seen to have had a foundation in fact.[63]

On the main doctrines of Christianity the Familists seem to have been orthodox. Though they have been charged again and again with denying the divinity of Christ, a careful reading of several of their chief books has failed to substantiate the charge. It is true that there are many passages which appear to have such a meaning, but there are also many which will equally bear a contrary one. The tendency of controversial writing was to dwell upon isolated passages and to neglect the general trend of statements and of doctrine; and in addition to this the misty thought, and the involved sentences of H. N.'s language rendered it peculiarly liable to be misunderstood.

The following are his own words on the subject:

"Even thus verily was this like-being of God, the true Christ and only born son of God from Eternity; born of the seed of David according to the flesh, to be a Saviour to the generation of Israel, for to set up Israel in his righteousnesse. But certain of the wise and scripture-learned ones after the Law, have neither believed nor received the same Jesus Christ according to the flesh, but have withstood him and refused both him and his requiring, & not allowed of him, but have delivered him over unto the Heathen, to the death of the Crosse. ; . . . Seeing now that it was impossible that the death could hold him . . . therefore he is risen again from the death, for a perpetuall conquering of the sinne and death, through his death of the Crosse, and hath made himselfe manifest unto his friends, that loved him, and were his Disciples: and renewing them in the word of his doctrine, he shewed them (through his suffering and death of the Crosse) the victory against the sinne, death, Devill, and Hell.[64] . . . This selfe same

---

[63] Rogers on XXXIX Articles, p. 187; Strype Annals, Vol. ii, Book ii, Chap. 17, pp. 590, 591. See also Evangelium Regni, xxxi, A, 1. London, 1649.

[64] [Four Epistles of H. N.] Third Epistle, 4th chap. 2, 4, pp. 30, 31 [London 1649], title-page lost.

Christ, the true Son and like-beeing of God his Father (although he (from eternity) be the first-born of all creatures, and the only born Son of God) is also (according to his birth of the seed of David after the flesh) named the Son of Man." [65]

Again:

" We do witness also, that he is the true Messiah, or Christ, which was preached in the world in times past, and likewise published of time in his coming, that he should be a King or Prince over the house of Jacob for ever: of whose Kingdom also there shall be no end. He is a Saviour to all people that believe on him and salvation is or cometh only by him, and none other, neither in heaven, nor yet upon the earth. . . . Behold this high Priest is spirit and life, the true King and a faithful Lord, a peaceable prince, and not this or that without us; but he is in us all which believe on him according to the truth. And we all which abide stedfast in the faith have the life through him who is neither unfaithfull nor falling away like a man." [66]

His opinions as to the Bible are expressed in the following:

"The Bible is not the Word of God, but a signification thereof, and the Bible is but ink and paper, but the Word is spirit and life." [67]

"It is neither the Scripture nor yet the knowledge thereof that maketh us righteous, but the life of Jesus Christ, wrought through the belief or faith." [68]

Ceremonies he declares are in their right form and use

"set forth, administered and taught by them that are chosen or raised up thereunto by God, which follow after Christ in his death, because renewed with him in a new life, and in whom the living God with his Christ hath evenso then obtained his dwelling and shape, from whose bodies likewise the words of God and Christ, do then flow forth as living water, which also concordably agree with the testimonies of the Holy Ghost, and with our writings and their requiring; as also with the requiring of the law, of the prophets, and of the Apostles of Christ." [69]

" Alas how great contention and disputation hath there been among many touching the baptism. The one would have the baptism thus, the other so. But whilst that it was yet right with them, so hath no man been able, before this day of love, which is the true light and the glory of God himself to understand nor distinct the baptism of John nor the baptism of Christ.[70] Behold this is the right passover with Christ or the right supper which the upright believers and disciples of Christ, keep with Christ: to wit, that they depart evenso with Christ out of the

---

[65] Ibid, 4th Epistle, 5th chap. 5, p. 55.

[66] The Spiritual Tabernacle, chap. v. 7, 8, 15, London, 1655.

[67] Confutation of certain articles delivered unto the Family of Love, by W. Wilkinson, 1579.

[68] The Spiritual Tabernacle, chap. xvii, 5, London, 1655.

[69] Evangelium Regni, xxxvii, E, 12.

[70] Ibid, xix, 12.

flesh into the eternal life of everlasting immortality, wherethrough the sin and all destruction becometh vanquished." [71]

But the fundamental doctrine of H. N. and that which was the reason of the existence of the sect was that of Love. He held that Love is the fulfilment of God's will and purpose, "the greatest thing in the world." This is "the joyful mission of the Kingdom," "which was promised to be published in the world and unto all people," which "the God of heaven hath brought forth through his holy ones and through his elected minister, H. N."

"The Love is the Light of the world;" "the Love is the gracious word of the Lord, or bread of Life, which is come unto us out of heaven. For the Love is essentially the very true good, the head-sum of the commandment and the bond of perfection. Through which Love the secret Treasures of God the Father and the abundant Riches of his spiritual and heavenly goods be revealed." [73]

"For the end, or perfection of all things, (namely, the chief sum of all good, or all what one can name for rightousnesse and truth) that is the Love: Yea, all what is to be known or understood of the godly things, that is the Love ; and her mistery is the everlasting life." [74]

The revelations were made

"To the end we should now in the last timed, through his Love, and through the Mediator his Christ, become surely saved; live always, and for ever, uprightly lovely, and peaceably in the same Godhead, with each other; and so inhabit the world, according to the promises of God the Father, in righteousness for evermore." [75]

The sum of the teaching so far seems to be that man through grace may attain to such an experience that he will be able to resist temptation and live according to the divine command-

[71] Ibid xxi.

[73] A Figure of the True and Spiritual Tabernacle, etc. To the Reader, 13, 14, 15. London, 1655.

[74] The second Epistle, chap. ii., 13, London, n. d.

[75] Prophecy of the Spirit of Love, chap. viii, 1, London, 1649. South seems to have these views in mind when he says, "The personal indwelling of the Spirit in believers, as they call it. . . . I find has been confidently asserted by some and particularly by those called Familists." R. South, "Enthusiasts not led by the Spirit of God." Sermon xxiii, p. 402, Philadelphia, 1844.

ments,—that is, to use the words of H. N., live "in the Love" or "dwell in the spiritual Land of Peace." All who reject the Love "are rooted out from the Earth and buried in the Hell: where [their] death and the burning of [their] condemnation shall endure for ever and ever."[76]

There is no doubt that H. N. considered himself a prophet of equal value with those of the Bible, and equally inspired, but the charge that he claimed to be equal to Christ and even to God is not supported by his books. Nor do they teach that he demanded the reverence due to the Deity, nor that it was rendered by his followers. It seems likely that he was one of that class of religious teachers who are themselves deceived. That he gained many followers, even among intelligent men, is not surprising, for the essence of the doctrines which he preached was true, and reached the witness in the hearts of many who longed for more spiritual teaching than was afforded at that time by the Roman church, or by the Protestants. When he elaborated a complicated hierarchy, and claimed absolute obedience many were driven off. It is probable that in England these claims were never enforced very strongly, and that the hierarchy was never set up there. It is however impossible to speak with any degree of positive assurance, as there is no documentary evidence known, but, as the adversaries of the sect were active, it is altogether likely that if the hierarchy had existed, they would have discovered positive proof of practices so contrary to their opinions.

It will be interesting to see whether the Familists in England affected other sects. Many of their views closely resembled those of the early Friends. This resemblance has been noted, not only by adversaries, but by the Friends themselves.

George Fox began his preaching in 1647, and the more carefully the history of the sixteenth and seventeenth centuries is examined the more evidence will be found to substantiate his claim that he did not preach any new doctrine. "History shows that the early Friends had been anticipated at one time or another in almost all of their peculiar testimonies, and in

---

[76] Prophecy of the Spirit of Love, chap. ii. 6. London, 1649.

the seventeenth century they held many of these in common with the early Baptists."[77]

In 1673 Henry Hallywell, Vicar of Cowfold, Sussex, published a small book with the title, " Familism as it is revived and propagated by the Quakers, London, 1673." In this he sums up the likeness between "Quakery" and "Familism," mentioning six main points of agreement.

"1. H. N. says . . . the Pelagogy of the Law and Gospel are to be cast aside when men come to the Spirit, and this Dispensation of the Spirit is only in the Familists and their doctrin. And that this is the full sense of the Quakers appears from their own Books which they cunningly spread abroad to infect and poison the minds of weak and ignorant People . . .

"2. The second thing wherein the Familists and Quakers are all one is the Pretence of immediate Revelation . . .

"3. A third Manifestation of the Familists and Quakers being one and the same Sect is their abrogating aud disanulling all outward Ordinances and Institutions of Religion . . .

"4. With a like silly and weak confidence they exclaim against Forms of Prayer.

"5. Now as for Baptism it is no wonder if they throw that by as a useless carnal Ordinance . . . They that refuse and despise the Governour, will not stick to slight his law."

"6. By the same Diabolical Spirit wherewith they are possessed, they lay aside the Sacrament of the Lord's Supper as a thing too carnal for such high flown and conceited Spiritualists as they are."[78]

The author seems incapable of understanding such doctrines as the non-necessity of outward ordinances, and the direct revelation of the will of God to the individual believer. He quotes in support of the above allegations—most of which are true, though they seem to him to be diabolical—various passages from John Crook, Humphry Smith and William Gibson; but in his comments, which are couched in very emphatic language, he evidently misunderstands the real meaning and ignores the context. His conclusion is so much like that which was said of the Familists about a century before that it is worth while to quote it. "And though the Quaker will impudently deny all this [his summary of the errors] and boldly affirm that he holds no such things, yet I have produced nothing as their

---

[77] Jane Budge, Glimpses of George Fox and his Friends, p. 10, London, 1889.
[78] H. Hallywell, Familism, etc. pp. 10-30, London, 1673.

judgment but what I find published by some of them in their printed papers, or has been delivered by them at their own conventicles and meetings, and therefore is sufficiently known to be their own opinion. But it need not startle any man to hear a Quaker out-face his own errors when challenged with them; for he that takes away all distinction between good and evil, will not stick to a lie when it is for his advantage." (*Ibid.*, p. 130, 131).

So striking was the resemblance between some of the doctrines of Quakerism and of Familism that it was made one of the points in the most elaborate attack which has ever been made upon the Society of Friends—that by Charles Leslie, the Non-Juror, who beginning with "The Snake in the Grass," published in 1697, continued his attack through several volumes. Leslie, in his "Answer to the Switch," compares several statements of George Fox and of William Penn with some of H. N.'s, showing their similarity. He also says, "I have now before me the works (or part of them) of Henry Nicholas, before mentioned, the father of *the family of love;* they were given to a friend of mine by a Quaker, with this encomium, that he believed he would not find one word amiss, or one superfluous, in the whole book; and commended it as an excellent piece. It is not unlikely that he took it for a Quaker book; for there is not his name at length, only H. N. to it, and it has quite through the Quaker phiz and mien, that twins are not more alike. And though he directs it *to the family of love,* yet an ignorant Quaker might take that for his own family and apply it to the Quakers."[79]

The language used by all theological writers of the sixteenth and seventeenth centuries was very similar, and too much stress must not be laid upon mere resemblances of expression. Even Leslie tells us[80] that he had "a collection of several Ranter's books in a thick quarto: and though I am

---

[79] An Answer to the Switch, C. Leslie's Theological Works, vi. pp. 298, 301, 304 305. Oxford, 1832.

[80] Ibid., vi, p. 305. Henry More, warns "the honester and better-meaning Quakers how they turn in thither," that is towards Familism. "Grand Mystery of Godliness," Book x, Chap. 13, p. 372. London, 1708.

pretty well versed with the Quaker strain, I took all these authors to be Quakers," and Leslie, it must be remembered, was one of the most learned English theologians of his day.

There seems no doubt that Hallywell, Leslie and others were greatly mistaken in their opinion relative to the influence of the Familists upon the early Friends, and also regarding the connection between them, for it would be difficult to prove any direct connection whatever. At the same time when it is remembered that the Familists were most numerous in the eastern and central counties of England, and that their books were republished between 1645–1656, it is not improbable that George Fox and the early Friends knew of those books, and may have met with some who held their views. Yet, taking all things into consideration, it is altogether likely that Fox arrived at his conclusions independently of the Familists, and that those who represented the old sect were drawn to Fox rather than that Fox was drawn to them.

What influence the Familists had upon other denominations cannot be known, though it seems probable that they must have exercised a leavening influence in many ways. The revival of the sect, about the middle of the seventeenth century, seems to have been but a brief awakening.

FAMILISTS IN AMERICA.

THE chief authorities for the statement relating to Familism in New England are those who were violently opposed to Antinomianism, and as the Familists had been charged with the various errors of Antinomianism a century before, the charges were still preferred. What Dr. Ellis says of the Quakers might be said of all who opposed the Puritans of Massachusetts Bay. " Their opinions and actions identified them with various types of fanatics and enthusiasts, who in their previous appearance had held these heresies in connection with some gross immoralities, some really malignant and defiant outrages and avowals which made them justly amenable to restraints and penalties."[81]

---

[81] George E. Ellis, Puritan Age, p. 420, Boston, 1888.

It will be well however to refer to the statements made and quote some of them. Samuel Rutherford, in his "Survey of the Spiritual Antichrist," 1648, already referred to, has three chapters (xvi, xvii, xviii) almost wholly devoted to " The Familists and Antinomians of New England." His chief authority, he tells us, is the " *Short Story of the Rise, Reigne and Ruine of the Familists and Libertines that infected the Churches of New England,*" etc. *T. Weld, London,* 1644. Rutherford tells us that this book was " penned (as I am informed) by Mr. *Winthrope, Governor,* a faithful witness, and approved by *M. T· Weld* in his preface to the book." [82]

Rutherford gives a catalogue of fifty of those " wicked tenets," " gathered out of the storie," some of which resemble the doctrines of the Familists and some do not.

To show how much Rutherford and Welde or Winthrop really knew about the facts, it is sufficient to say that John Wheelwright and Ann Hutchinson [83] are called Familists, as well as their followers.[84] William Dyer and his wife, Mary Dyer, the Quaker who afterward suffered death upon Boston Common, he characterizes as the grossest and most active Familists,[84] which is clearly proven in his eyes by the fact that she gave birth to a deformed child which died almost immediately. Again he calls Samuel Gorton a Familist.[84] So also Cotton Mather, quoting Welde, says of Gorton " a most prodigous minter of exhorbitant novelties, and the very dregs of Familism." [85]

Hubbard in his " New England " speaks of the Gortonites " who deny the Humanity of Christ, and most blasphemously and proudly profess themselves to be personally Christ; " and the " Familists who depend upon rare revelations, and forsake the sure revealed Word of Christ; " he also distinguishes between

---

[82] Survey, etc., p. 171. Chas. Deane in his Critical Essay, in Narrative and Critical History of America (vol. iii, p. 351) confirms this opinion as to the authorship of the "Short Storie."

[83] So also Shepard, Memoir; Young's Chronicle of Mass., p. 546, Boston, 1846. Morton, New England's Memorial, p. 133, Boston, 1855.

[84] Survey, etc., pp. 180, 181, 183.

[85] Magnalia Christi, Book viii. Chap. 2, p. 11, London, 1702.

them and the Antinomians.[86] Hubbard also speaks of a "small ship" which came to Nantasket July 6, 1631 with a company of Familists, but they not liking the place went to Watertown and then " vanished away and came to nothing."[87] The same story is told by Prince in his Annals.[88]

The care which was taken to prevent the entrance of heresy into the colony is shown by the advice given to the Massachusetts General Court by the Commissioners of the United Colonies, in the course of which they advise that "Anabaptism, Familism, Antinomianism and generally all errors of like nature . . . may be reasonably and duly supprest."[89]

Writing concerning the year 1642 Hubbard says:

> "About these times a door of liberty being opened by the Parliament in London, Familistical opinions began to swarm in many of the Plantations of the English abroad in other parts, to the disturbance of the civil governments where they came. In the year 1643 the Governor of Massachusetts received letters from Philip Bell, Esq., Governor of the Barbadoes, complaining of the distracted condition of that island in regard of divers sects of Familists sprung up there and their turbulent practices which had forced him to proceed against some of them by banishment, and others of mean quality, by whipping etc., earnestly desiring him to send them some godly minister and other good people that the island might be planted with men of better principles."[90]

These quotations only show that those who opposed the Puritans were branded with the most opprobrious names which they could find, particularly those which had been applied to the so-called sectaries in England. There is little or no ground for thinking that those who troubled the New England Colonists had any acquaintance with the true Familists or their books. They were branded with the name, partly because of a real or fancied resemblance of some of their doctrines to those of the hated sect, but chiefly because Familist represented to a Puritan pretty nearly all that was bad, and suited those who rebelled against the rigidness of the Puritan rule

---

[86] Mass. Hist. Soc. Coll. 2 ser., ii, p. 51.

[87] Ibid., v. 141.

[88] Ibid., vii. p. 31 (at end of volume).

[89] Acts of Commissioners of United Colonies, Records of Colony of New Plymouth, Vol. i, p. 81, Boston, 1859.

[90] Mass. Hist. Soc. Col. 2d Ser., vi, 346.

better than any other name, except perhaps that of Antinomian. The present writer has been unable to find satisfactory evidence that any real Familists were ever in America, or that any of H. N.'s books were circulated in this country.

WRITINGS OF HENRY NIKLAES.

So far as appears the writings of H. N. were all originally written and published in Dutch, though it is likely some were very soon issued in German, Latin, French, and English.

Of the Familist writings three still exist in manuscript which do not appear to have been printed. They are preserved in the Library of the *Maatschappy van Nederlandsche Letterkunde* at Leyden. They are described as being "masterpieces of calligraphy, and are in general easily to be understood." They are divided into chapters, and these again into numbered paragraphs. They are,

1. *Chronika* (or Cronica) *des Hüsgesinnes der Lieften.* (Chronicles of the House of Love): this consists of 53 chapters and 160 pages.

2. *Acta H. N.* A detailed account of H. N., and the "wonderful things which befel him;" this consists of 25 chapters, and 70 pages.

3. *Ordo Sacerdotis.* "The arrangement of the priestly orders in the House of Love."

These manuscripts are of the greatest importance for gaining a knowledge of the inner life of Henry Niklaes and the sect, and they are the main authority for the history; this statement is particularly true of the first two. The third is the description of the organization of the body as Niklaes wished it to be, but it does not appear that the plan was carried fully into execution. These are all the manuscripts known. Of the printed works Nippold enumerates 29 in Dutch or "Base-Almain," and 15 in German. Of this list most are in prose, but he names five in verse. It will be interesting to give a specimen. If the translations are anything like the original, as they probably are, the so-called poems are the veriest doggerel.

"Men sal hyr spelen ein Spel van Sinnen:
Willet wol bekinnen, dat ick dy hyr vortone:

Seet, hyr machstu seen des Minschen Krone,
Die he, sündigende, heft vorlaten,
Ingaende den errenden Wech, up frembde Straten.
Wilt dit doch vaten, dat dy hyr wert vorklaert.
Went seet, spelende, wert dy geopenbaert,
Idt inwendige Ryck Godes, ane smerte,
Dat gefonden wert in des Minschen Herte,
Van Godt gebouwet, vohr des Werlts Anfangk." [91]

The following translation of these lines was published about 1574.

" Here shall be played a play of minds as shall appear therein,
Therefore mark then well, what 1 show here to thee :
Behold the man's crown, here mayst thou plainly see,
Which he through his sinning hath left or forsaken,
And hath in strange paths the way of error taken.
Comprehend this well in mind, that is declared here,
For lo, in manner of Enterlude, to thee shall plain appear
The inward Kingdom of God, void of grief and smart,
The which is found to be, within the man his heart,
By God himself builded ere the world began to be." [92]

The emblematical pictures, and mottoes which adorn most of the Familist tracts, must not be passed by unnoticed. Nippold describes seven.[93]

There are at least seven more which he does not appear to mention. ·All these illustrations are not only curious in themselves, but they also throw considerable light upon the teachings of H. N. In one of them appear the well-known Masonic ·symbols—the pendulum, the balance, circle, and square.

Three of these emblematic pictures have been reproduced for this ·article. They are of the same size as the original. Plate I (p. 1) is a reproduction from the frontispiece of H. N.'s *Revelatio Dei*, published in London, 1649; it also appears in other of his writings, as " Epistolæ," etc., 1577, Prophetie des Geistes der Lieften, 1573. The plate does not need much ex-

---

[91] Comœdia D. Prolog., 119, quoted by Nippold, Zeits. f. d. histor. Theologie, 1862, p. 528.

[92] " Comœdia, | A Work in Ryme | contayning an Enter | lude of Myndes witnessing | the Mans Fall from God | and *Christ* | set forth by H. N. and by him newly | perused and amended. | Translated out of the Base-almayne | *into English*." No date, but probably 1574, and evidently printed abroad, 8vo, 32 leaves. Bodleian Library, Oxford, M. 257.)

[93] Zelts. f. d. histor. Theologie, 1862, pp. 336, 337, 530–535.

planation, the design evidently being taken from Revelation xii, particularly the tenth and fifteenth verses. The Lamb bearing a banner, with a cross and the word VICTORIA upon it, stands upon a skeleton (Death), and this rests upon a dragon, or monster, out of whose mouth streams of water are pouring over the world; beneath this is the Devil with his darts broken and he himself on his back. The conventional horns and tail are present but his feet are claws.

Plate II (p. 42) is a reproduction of one of five curious plates in H. N's *The True and Spiritual Tabernacle*, published in London, 1655. It bears in the Dutch edition the title "*Abbildung der Zwierley Wege,*" (The Picture of The Two Ways). A nude young man is represented standing on a small globe; he bears the inscription, "The inward man." Above him is a sun with the Hebrew word Jehovah; from it extend two streamers, the one having the word "Blessing," the other "Cursing;" above the latter word is a drawn sword, the blade of which has the appearance of a holly branch, while over the former is a lily-stem. The entrance to the two ways is pointed out by two streamers; the right bearing the words, "The forthgoeing in the heathenish impurity bringeth the man to ye sin of Death;" the left bearing the words, "The forthgoeing in the feare of God and ye obedience to ye ordinanc of ye Lord bringeth ye man to the "Righteousness of the Life." The right streamer is fastened to a skull, from which issue seven dragon necks with horrible heads; these necks bear the words, "Sloth," "Wrath," etc. To this skull another streamer is fastened, the other end of which issues from the open jaws of a monster; this streamer bears the words, "The sin of death bringeth ye man into all Ignorance, hypocrisy and falsehood," etc. Opposite to the skull are the two tables of stone with the words "Love God," and "Love thy neighbor." Above these tables, on a white field, are the words, "Through ye righteousness of the life," etc.[94]

Plate III (p. 43) is frequently placed at the end of H. N's. books; in the English editions the words are translated. The

---

[94] Description adapted from Nippold, p. 532.

four lines under the picture are thus given at the end of the "Fourth Epistle," probably published at London, 1649:

> "Our heart is the mind of God most High,
> Our beeing amiable, as the sweet Lilly,
> Our faithfulness, love, and truth upright,
> Is Gods light life, and cleerness bright."

The heart represents the spiritual part of man, and on it are the two words Liefte (Love), and Waerheit (Truth), clasped hands, indicating faithfulness, and a lily indicating purity.

The Appendix to Alexander Ross's "View of all Religions"[95] is the "Apocalypsis,"[96] which contains the "Effigies" of certain "notorious Advancers of Heresie;" among these is a portrait of "Henry Nicholas," "who excelled the rest in rashnesse, impudence, and lying done." There is however no evidence of its genuineness, and it also bears a striking resemblance to others in the same collection which suggests grave suspicions that the portrait is altogether imaginary.

In addition to the emblematical plates, with one or more of which his books were generally illustrated, Niklaes continually used certain expressions, almost always ending his prefaces and his books with them. These are in the Dutch editions "Nemet idt tor herten," "Charitas extorsit per H. N." which in the English editions appear as "Take it to heart," or "Take all this effectually to heart, H. N." "Charitas extorsit."

The style and character of the writings of H. N. and the Familists is sufficiently indicated by the extracts which have been given. It is altogether likely that many adherents of the sect did not know exactly what the doctrines professed by them meant in their fulness, so misty are the statements of the books which they took as their guides; but men were attracted by the emphasis laid upon the spiritual side of religion, by the

---

[95] View of all Religions, etc., Alex. Ross, 4th ed. London, 1664. This is the book referred to in Hudibras, Canto ii, ll., 12:
> "There was an ancient sage philosopher
> That had read Alexander Ross over."

[96] In the 6th ed., 1683, this is paged continuously with the main book. The tract is said to be "translated out of the Latine" by J [o] D [avies].

doctrine that in this life there was a possibility of a continual victory over sin, and that love was "The greatest thing in the world."

NOTE 1.—The influence of David Joris (or George) upon the views of Henry Niklaes appears to have been greatly overrated; indeed, it is questionable if he had any. The discussion of this subject has been purposely omitted.

NOTE 2.—It would be unfitting if the author did not express his appreciation of the kindness shown him by the Librarians of the Cambridge University Library, and of the Bodleian Library, Oxford, while making researches in those noble collections. To the Librarian of the former, the late Henry Bradshaw, he is particularly indebted for special help given, and he is pleased to say that he is the "American professor" mentioned on p. 381, of G. W. Prothero's "Life of Henry Bradshaw."

AUTHORITIES AND REFERENCES.

1. Arnold, G. Kirchen und Ketzer-Historie, Part II, Book xvi, Cap. xxi, 36. Folio. Frankfort-am-Main, 1700.
2. Bancroft, Richard. A Survey of the Pretended Holy Discipline, etc. 4to. London, 1593.
3. Barclay, Robert. The Inner Life of the Religious Societies of the Commonwealth. Second Edition pp. 25-35. Royal 8vo. London, 1877. Best and fairest account in English.
4. Böhme A. W. Acht Bücher von der Reformation in England. B. iv, Cap. v, pp. 536-573. 12mo. Altona, 1734. Fullest account of the Familists in England.
5. Bloudy Tenent of Persecution. Hanserd Knollys Society. 8vo. London, 1848.
6. Brandt, Gerard. History of the Reformation in the Low Countries. Translated from the Dutch. 2 vols., folio. London, 1720.
7. Camden, William. Annals of the Reign of Elizabeth. Fourth Edition in English. Folio. London, 1688.
8. Cardwell, Edward. Documentary Annals of the Reformed Church of England, 1546-1716. 2 vols., 8vo. Oxford, 1844.
9. Denison, Stephen. The White Wolfe, or a Sermon preached at Paul's Crosse, February 11th, 1627. 4to. London, 1627.
10. Domestic State Papers, Calendar of. Elizabeth, 1547-80. Vol. cxxxiii, 55; 1591-94, vol. ccxliii. (1592 ccxliii § 25). 4to.
11. Edwards, Thomas. Gangræna. A Catalogue and Discovery of many of the Heresies, etc. Third Edition. 4to. London, 1646.
12. Fuller, Thomas. The Church History of Britain. Book ix, Cent xvi, § 36-40; Book x, Cent. xvii, §§ 18-22. Nichols' Edition. 12mo. London, 1868.
13. Grégoire, M. Histoire des Sectes Religieuses. V. 8vo. Paris, 1829.
14. Grindal's Remains. 8vo. Parker Society. Cambridge, 1843.
15. Hallywell, Henry. An Account of Familism as it is revived and propagated by the Quakers. 24mo. London, 1673.

16. Hanbury, Benjamin. Historical Memorials of the Independents. 3 vols., 8vo.. London, 1839.

17. Harleian Miscellany. Vol. iv. 8vo. London, 1809.

18. Hooker, Richard. Works. Keble's Edition. Fifth Edition and Notes. 3 vols., 8vo. Oxford, 1865.

19. Hornbeck, Johannis. Summa Controversiarum Religionis, etc. 8vo. Second Edition. Waesberge, 1658.

20. Hubbard, William. New England. 8vo. Massachusetts Historical Society Collections. Second Series, ii.

20. James I, King. Basilikon Doron. 4to, Edinburgh, 1623.

21. Jessop, Edmund. A Discovery of the Errors of the English Anabaptists, etc. 4to. London, 1623.

22. Kortholtus, Christianus. Historia Ecclesiastica. 4to. Hamburg, 1708.

23. Leslie, Charles. Works, vol. vi. 8vo. Oxford, 1832.

24. Marsden, J. B. History of the Early Puritans. Second Edition. 8vo. London, 1853. History of the Later Puritans. Second Edition. 8vo. London, 1854.

25. Masson, David. Life of Millon. Vol. iii, p. 152. 8vo. London, 1873.

26. Mather, Cotton. Magnalia Christi. Folio. London, 1702.

27. More, Henry. An Explanation of the Grand Mystery of Godliness. Book . v, Cap. 8; Book vi, Caps. 3, 12-18; Book viii, Cap. 2, etc. Theological Works. Folio. London, 1708.

> The most elaborate of the later attacks upon the Familists.

Enthusiasmus Triumphatus, §§ 21, 40. Philosophical Works. Folio. London, 1712.

28. Mosheim, J. L. von. Ecclesiastical History, Murdock's Translation. Book iv, Cent. xvi. § iit, Part ii. London, 1848.

29. Neal, Daniel. History of the Puritans. Vol. i, Chap. v, 8vo. London, 1754.

30. Nippold, Fr. Heinrich Niclaes und das Haus der Liebe. Zeitschrift für die historische Theologie. 36 Band. Gotha, 1862.

> This monograph, written with German thoroughness, is the fullest and most accurate study of the Familists which has yet appeared. It is indispensable for the study of Henry Nicklaes and his sect. The writer of the preceding article is under obligation to it on almost every page.

31. Notes and Queries. Fourth Series. Vol. iv, 1869.

> A Bibliography by J. H. Hessels, which is the most complete one yet issued. It is expected to publish, in another number of the *Studies*, a new Bibliography of Familist and Anti-Familist literature.

32. P[agitt], E[pbraim]. The Mystical Wolfe set forth in a sermon, etc. London, 1645.

P[agitt], E[phraim]. Heresiography or a Description of the Heretics and Sectarians sprung up in these latter times. London, 1649.

33. Rogers, Thomas. Exposition of the XXXIX Articles. 8vo. Parker Society. Cambridge, 1854.

34. Rooses, Max. Christophe Plantin, Imprimeur Anversois. Folio, Anvers, 1883.

> This magnificent folio, issued in honor of the great Antwerp printer, describes at length the connection of Plantin with Henry Niklaes, and gives incidentally much information relative to the sect.

35. Ross, Alexander. Pansebeia. A View of all Religions in the World, etc. 16mo. Fourth Edition. London, 1664. Apocalypsis, or the Revelation of certain notorious advancers of Heresie, etc., with portrait of Henry Nicholas. Third Edition. London, 1764. An Appendix to Ross's work. No author given, "said to be translated out of the Latine by J. D. [Jo Davies?]"

36. Rutherford, Samuel. A Survey of the Spiritual Antichrist, etc. 4to. London, 1648.

37. Sandys, Archbishop. Sermons. 8vo. Parker Society. Cambridge, 1841.

38. Schröckh, J. M. Kirchen-Geschichte seit der Reformation. Band V, B. ii, Cap. vi. 8vo. Leipzig, 1806.

39. Stowe, John. Annals. Folio. London, 1605.

40. Strype, John. Annals of the Reformation in England. vols. ii, iii. Folio. London, 1725.
   Strype, John. Life and Acts of John Whitgift. 8vo. Oxford, 1832.
   Strype, John. Edmund Grindal. 8vo. 1821.

41. Tracts on Liberty of Conscience, 1614-1661. Hanserd Knollys Society. 8vo. London, 1846.

42. Walch, J. G. Historische und theologische Einleitung in die Religionsstreitigkeiten ausser der evang. lutherischen Kirche. Band iv, 840-853. 8vo. Jena, 1736.

43. Weingarten, H. Die Revolutionskirchen Englands. 8vo. Leipzig, 1868.

44. Welde, Thomas. A short story of the Reigne and Ruine of the Familists and Libertines. London, 1644.

45. Whitaker, Thomas. Disputation on Scripture. Parker Society. 8vo. Cambridge, 1849.

46. Wilkinson, William. A Confutation of certaine Articles delivered unto the Family of Love, etc. 4to. London, 1579.

Numerous other historians have been consulted, as well as many contemporary treatises, but the above list covers most of the valuable authorities. Some few works, as " Baillie's Dissuasive," were inaccessible to the writer.

ALLEN C. THOMAS.

Haverford, Pennsylvania, 1893.

ON THE READING "τὸ πάσχα" IN JOHN VI, 4.

In Westcott and Hort's Greek Testament, the words τὸ πάσχα are marked "⌈ ⌉," the notation by which these careful editors designate suspected readings. The attention of the student of the chronology of the life of Christ is at once arrested by this fact, as it suggests most interesting possibilities. The length of the ministry of our Lord is indicated by the number of passovers which occurred during the period of that ministry. It is well known that the Synoptists record but one passover. They give the general impression, however, that the ministry continued at least a year. In John there are possibly four passovers; one in Chapter ii, 13, 23, another in Chapter v, 1, a third in vi, 4, and a fourth in Chapter xi, 55. As is well known, however, it is very doubtful whether the nameless feast of Chapter v, 1, is a passover. The MSS. are divided between the readings "The feast of the Jews" and "A feast of the Jews," even the two most ancient, the Sinaitic and the Vatican, ranging themselves on different sides, If the reading "A feast" be adopted, scholars are agreed that it would probably not be a passover. If the reading "The feast" be preferred, many would regard this feast as a passover, though others, as Westcott and Hort, would then regard it as the feast of tabernacles. The critical editors (except Tischendorf, who assigned undue authority to the Sinaitic MS.) read "A feast," and a number of careful interpreters as *e. g.* Meyer, regard the feast of this passage as the feast of purim.

If, therefore, with the character of the feast in Chapter v, 1, doubtful, we should find strong reason for suspecting the reading "The passover" in Chapter vi, 4, it would leave but two passovers in the Gospel of John, and that Gospel, like the Synoptists, would make Christ's ministry a little more than a year in duration. This would remove one of the strong grounds for attack upon the historical character of the Fourth Gospel. One of its chief points of difference from the Synop-

(47)

tists—the length of the ministry of Christ—would be removed, and the reconciliation of John's chronology with that of the other evangelists would become a much easier matter. It is because of these important results that we are so deeply interested in knowing the grounds upon which Westcott and Hort suspect the reading "τὸ πάσχα" in Chapter VI, 4.

The late Professor Hort's letter to Professor Sanday* warns us not to suspect them of having been influenced by harmonistic motives. A reference to their "Notes on Select Readings" enables us to see that their suspicion is based on the apparent absence of these words from the MSS. used by some Fathers and other writers, though they are present in all extant versions and MSS.

The main points of their argument are as follows:—1. Epiphanius in his *Haer.*, 444, tells us that the *Alogi* found fault with St. John's Gospel as assigning *two* passovers to the ministry, while the other Gospels spoke of only one. 2. Irenæus maintains three passovers, the second being the "feast" of Chapter v, 1, while he is silent as to vi, 4, though he goes on to refer to particulars furnished by neighboring verses. 3. Origen, whose commentary on John is defective for the whole of Chapters v–vii, in contending that the saying of iv, 35, was uttered at an earlier time than the winter following the passover of Chapter ii, urges that the unnamed feast of v, 1, was not likely to be a passover, giving as a reason that "shortly afterwards the statement occurs 'Now the feast of the Jews, the feast of tabernacles, was near at hand.'" As these words now stand only in Chapter vii, 2, either he must have treated vi, 4, as referring to the feast of tabernacles, or his text lacked it altogether. 4. Cyril of Alexandria, in his comment on Chapter vi, 4, has two indirect quotations of the words, "The passover of the Jews was near," but he shortly afterwards mentions twice what is evidently the same feast as the feast of tabernacles. This is either a blunder, or a free use of the language of a predecessor (probably Origen) without noting its disagreement with his own. 5. Besides these several writers are shown indirectly to have known nothing of a

* See Expositor for March, 1892, p. 182.

passover here, by their reckoning the interval between the baptism and crucifixion as a year, or but a little more. It is thought that this idea never could have been maintained without strange carelessness by anyone who read "τὸ πάσχα," in John vi, 4, since John distinctly speaks twice of an earlier passover (Chapter ii, 13, 23) as well as the final passover. The principal writers who assume a single year are: Ptolemy, Irenæus, Clement of Alexandria, Origen, Rufinus, Jerome, Hippolytus, Augustine, and apparently Justin Martyr. Tatian's harmony, so far as Ephrem's commentary enabled Westcott and Hort in 1881 to determine, placed Tatian in the same ·list. 6. There is a series of writers who directly or indirectly identify the year of the passion with the fifteenth or sixteenth of Tiberius, and who would thus be manifestly contradicting the notice of the fifteenth of Tiberius, in Luke iii, 1, f., if a passover intervened at this place. These are such writers as Clement of Alexandria, Julius Africanus, Julius Hilarianus, Tertullian, etc.

Such is an outline of the grounds on which these acute and careful scholars base their suspicions of this reading. Surely, when we look at this array of patristic evidence it produces a strong impression. If the arguments outlined above are valid, there was a text known in regions as widely separated as Alexandria, Carthage and Gaul which knew no reading " τὸ πάσχα " in John vi, 4.

We are now, however, in a better position than in 1881 to interpret these patristic phenomena. Since that time Tatian's Diatessaron has come to light, and affords us the key to the method by which the Fathers harmonized the Gospels, so as to make the ministry of Christ about a year in length. In 1883, as is well known, Ciasca discovered an Arabic version of this Diatessaron in the Vatican library, which he published in 1888. From a study of this version it appears that the reading " The passover " in this place was known to Tatian, and that his scheme of feasts was as follows: 1. The Passover of John vi, 4. (See Tatian, Chapter xviii.) 2. The "feast" of John v, 1, which he apparently regarded as Pentecost. (See Tatian, Chapter xxii.) 3. The Feast of Tabernacles of John vii, 2.

(See Tatian, Chapter xxvii.) 4. The Passover of ii, 23, which he identifies with that in Matt. xxi, and hence with that in John xi, 55. (See Tatian, Chapters xxxii, xxxviii.)

This scheme may have been suggested, as Dr. Hort supposes, by the "Acceptable year of the Lord" in Luke iv, 19. However that may be, the Diatessaron reveals to us the means by which the necessary harmonizing of the accounts was accomplished, and proves that it does not rest upon the basis which, reasoning from our modern standpoint, Westcott and Hort so naturally supposed it to do. The method of reasoning among the Fathers was not modern. On the ground of the similarity between the account of the cleansing of the temple in John ii and Matt. xxi, they identified what the modern scholar regards as the first and last passovers. Having done this, the rest was easy. The passover of our passage then became the first passover of the ministry, and the nameless feast of Chapter v, 1, was not necessarily a passover, so that the only remaining paschal feast, that of ii, 23, and xi, 55, became the last passover in this "Acceptable year." The method of Tatian is presumably the method of the men of his time. As he reasoned, so, probably, did other Fathers, and not as a modern scholar would reason. It therefore follows that the grounds upon which Westcott and Hort suspect the text τὸ πάσχα in John vi, 4, entirely break down. If the *Alogi* found fault with John's Gospel for assigning *two* passovers to the ministry, while the other Gospels spoke of only one, they probably reduced the number to two by identifying ii, 13, 23 with xi, 55, as Tatian does, and were not ignorant of a passover in Chapter vi, 4. In the same way, if Irenæus maintains three passovers, the second being the feast of Chapter v, 1, his first was presumably that of vi, 4.

Origen's method of harmonizing was probably similar, so that we may presume that in referring to the feast of tabernacles he had in mind Chapter vii, 2. In the same way it is fair to suppose that all those Fathers who make the length of the ministry about a year reached their result as Tatian reached his, and not in consequence of their ignorance of our present reading in John vi, 4.

Attractive, therefore, as was the suggestion that the words "τὸ πάσχα" did not belong in our passage, and considerable as the evidence seemed in support of that suggestion, the resuscitation of the Diatessaron practically dispels that evidence and leaves us with the authority of the Gospel of John to assure us that there were at least three-passovers in the ministry of our Lord, and that the unparalleled results of His ministry are the results of at least two years of labor. We may hope with Prof. Sanday* that the historical character of the fourth Gospel will soon be acknowledged by all critics, but it will not be in consequence of the reduction of the number of its passovers.

GEORGE A. BARTON.

Haverford, 4 *mo.*, 1893.

---

* See the recent series of articles on " *The Present Position of the Johannean Question* " in the Expositor.

OUR LORD'S QUOTATION FROM THE FIRST BOOK OF MACCABEES.

ONE sees it so frequently stated that Jesus never quoted the Apocrypha, that it will not be amiss to point out an actual use of the First of Maccabees by Him.

In the first place, let us note that His phrase, "[the] Kingdom of God," first appears in Wisdom x, 10; "day of judgment" first appears in Judith xvi, 17; "the law and the prophets" first occurs in 2 Macc. xv, 9; "a treasure that faileth not" (ἀνεκλιπὴς θησαυρός), Wisdom vii, 14 (Luke xii, 33); while certain passages in Ecclesiasticus (e. g., Ecclus. iii, 4; vii, 14; xxviii. 2; xxix. 11) recall the Sermon on the Mount. But these passages are well known to scholars, and moreover nothing determinate can be built upon proverbialisms which cannot be said to begin with any author.

The passages to which I wish to draw attention have been noticed by Grinfield in his *Scholia Hellenistica in Novum Testamentum*, but not connectedly. They are these:

1 Macc. i, 54. "Now on the fifteenth day of [the month] Chasleu, in the hundred forty and fifth year, they builded an *abomination of desolation* upon the altar, and builded altars in the cities of Judah on every side." ·

II, 27, 28. "And Mattathias cried throughout the city with a loud voice, saying, Whosoever is zealous of the law, and maintaineth the covenant, let him come after me.

"So he and his sons *fled unto the mountains*, and left whatever they had in the city."

(52)

The Gospel parallels are:

Matt. xxiv, 15–17.	Mark xiii, 14, 15.	Luke xxi, 20, 21, and xvii, 31.
"When therefore ye see the *abomination of desolation*, which was spoken of by Daniel, the prophet, standing in the holy place (let him that readeth understand),	"But when ye see the *abomination of desolation* standing where he ought not (let him that readeth understand), then let them that are in Judea *flee unto the mountains*.	"But when ye see Jerusalem compassed with armies, then know that her *desolation* is at hand.
"Then let them that are in Judea *flee unto the mountains*,	"And let him that is on the housetop not go down, nor enter in, to take anything out of his house."	"Then let them that are in Judea *flee unto the mountains;* and let them that are in the midst of her depart out, and let not them that are in the country enter therein.
"Let him that is on the housetop not go down to take out the things that are in his house."		XVII, 31. "In that day he which shall be on the housetop and his goods in the house, let him not go down to take them away."

Westcott and Hort rightly refer to Daniel as the author of the phrase, " abomination of desolation," which they uncialize accordingly.

But the quotation of Matthew and Mark has the " abomination of desolation " in direct association with " fleeing unto the mountains." Grinfield has recognized this, and under Mark xiii, 14, he refers to 1 Macc. i, 54. He ought to have added 1 Macc. ii, 28, in the same place, but he has it only under Luke xxi, 21, thereby not only breaking up the association between the two passages, but putting the more important one under just that Gospel which cannot be said to quote it. And here is our point. Luke is peculiar and alone in leaving out all reference to the abomination of desolation and substituting the remarkable words about Jerusalem being compassed with armies, which recall the language of Josephus (Bell. Jud. VI, v, 3): " Phalanxes in arms were seen . . . . . encompassing the cities." Under Matt. xxiv, 16, Grinfield gives two passages from Josephus (Bell. Jud. II, xx, 1; IV, viii, 2), about the people fleeing from Jerusalem into the hill country. He also refers to 1 Macc. ix, 15 (*sic*); Jer. iv, 15; 1 Sam. xiii, 6, and Judges vi, 2, all of which are irrelevant, compared to our verses from Maccabees. Under Matt. **xxiv**, 15, the reference to Jos. Bell. Jud. VI, vi, 1 refers to the Romans bringing their ensigns to the temple; while Prov. **xxiii**, 1, and Ignat. Rom. 6, are merely for the injunction to "understand." Dan. **xi**, 31, accompanies the other citations from Daniel. Under Mark **xiii**, 14, besides referring to Dan. **xii**, 11, and **ix**, 25, Grinfield has Jos. Ant. XII, vii, 6, where that historian quotes the prophecy of Daniel as fulfilled by Antiochus Epiphanes. Grinfield's reference to Clement of Rome (i, 6) is merely for the phrase, τὸ ῥηθὲν ὑπὸ. Of like irrelevance are his references to the same Father, Chapters 31 and 55 under the parallel in Luke. Under Luke **xxi**, 21, he also quotes Gen. **xix**, 17 (Lot escaping to the mountain);* Jer. **iv**, 29; 1 Macc. **iv**, 5; **ix**, 15; 1 Sam. **ii**, 10.

I have set down these references from Grinfield thus fully that the reader may be satisfied that nothing has been over-looked which might serve to fix our Lord's quotation else-where than in the Apocrypha, not even neglecting the early Fathers, though their works are later documents; because they sometimes ascribe a Gospel passage to some other source. If Daniel had, in addition to the "abomination of desolation," some account of men fleeing into the mountains and leaving their goods in the city, we could fairly ascribe the quotation to him. But, as the case stands, we are driven to admit that Jesus quoted the Apocrypha. The very injunction not to take the goods out of the house is a further clinching of the associa-tion of the whole utterance with Mattathias and his sons leav-ing their things behind them and fleeing unto the mountains as soon as the abomination was set up.

But let us return to Luke. First we must note that he places the verse about the housetop in a different though sim-ilar discourse (Luke **xvii**, 20–37), and in that same discourse he refers to Lot, as we have pointed out in our note. This is one weakening of the association with Maccabees. But the great point is that he omits the mystic symbol of Daniel, and puts in its place a definite reference to the siege of Jerusalem. The weird prophetic mystery of Matthew and Mark may be

---

*Cf. Luke **xvii**, 28–32.

applied in a purely spiritual way, and the hint that the reader must "understand" the innuendo, emphasizes yet further the mystical sense intended. Neither Mark nor Matthew uses language which could be definitely applied to a siege of the external Jerusalem. It is Luke alone who does so both here and elsewhere. The following language is quite peculiar to him :

"There shall be great distress upon the land, and wrath unto this people. And they shall fall by the edge of the sword, and shall be led captive into all the nations : and Jerusalem shall be trodden down of the Gentiles, until the times of the Gentiles be fulfilled." (Luke xxi, 23, 24).

In place of this, Matthew and Mark have the following. As their words are almost identical, I give Matthew alone :

" And pray ye that your flight be not in the winter, neither on a sabbath : For then shall be great tribulation, such as hath not been from the beginning of the world until now, no, nor ever shall be. And except those days had been shortened no flesh would have been saved : but for the elect's sake those days shall be shortened." (Matt. xxiv, 20–22 ; Mark xiii, 18–20).

This last utterance can only refer to something spiritual. I do not deny that the Lord, even in Mark and Matthew, was building His prophecy upon the material basis of the literal siege,—the assertion that that generation should see it all fulfilled (Mark xiii, 31 ; Matt. xxiv, 35 ; Luke xxi, 33) is enough to prove that he was. But what I do say is, that, while Mark and Matthew leave the literal siege obscure, Luke makes it vividly described. Luke plainly means to divide the spiritual prophecy from the historic prediction, and hence he has the duplicate in his seventeenth chapter above noted. The way in which he closes that discourse proves our point. For the disciples wish for a definite historic prophecy, and ask, 'Where, Lord ? And he said unto them, Where the body is, thither will the vultures also be gathered together." (Luke xvii, 37.)

Now let us transcribe two more prophecies from Luke, which have no parallel in the other Gospels :

"The days shall come upon thee, when thine enemies shall cast up a bank about thee, and compass thee round, and keep thee in on every side, and shall dash thee to the ground, and thy children within thee; and they shall not leave in thee one stone upon another; because thou knewest not the time of thy visitation." (Luke xix, 43, 44.)

This passage is in Luke's account of the Lord weeping over Jerusalem, which is peculiar to the Third Gospel, though the idea of one stone not being left upon another is common to all the Synoptists in the Eschatological Discourse, and hence is repeated by Luke.

Again: "Daughters of Jerusalem, weep not for me, but weep for yourselves, and for your children. For behold, the days are coming, in which they shall say, Blessed are the barren, and the wombs that never bare, and the breasts that never gave suck. Then shall they begin to say to the mountains, Fall on us, and to the hills, Cover us." (Luke xxiii, 28–30.)

This also is peculiar to Luke.

All this appears to me to point to the probability that Luke's Gospel either was written or at least put into its present form after the siege of Jerusalem, while those of Matthew and Mark had already been in circulation too long to be re-edited with such material additions. (The exigency of the Mark Appendix arose from a different cause.) Which is the more likely to be the real *logion*? The citation of the example of well-known Jewish heroes (1 Macc. i, ii) applied in mystic phrase to a spiritual cataclysm, or a detailed prediction of the destruction of Jerusalem from the lips of Him who refused to answer the question, "Where?" But we might object to this hypothesis that the mystical utterance belongs to the first discourse, represented in Luke xvii; while the external prophecy belongs to the second. This, however, can hardly be so, because Luke's echo of the word "desolation" (xxi, 20) is a hint that he knew of the Maccabean quotation, and would therefore have put it in his seventeenth chapter if he had thought it had been uttered in the earlier discourse. As it is, however, this strange echo of the single word, ἐρήμωσις, is very suspicious; for it means (1) that Luke knew of the Maccabean quotation; (2) that he knew it occurred in the second and great discourse; and (3) that in his conscientious wish to keep it in its right place, according to his literary promise in Chapter i, 3, he preserved as much of it as he could, consistently with substituting the definite prediction. Mark and Matthew preserve the original saying.

That we are not charging Luke with doing anything out of keeping with his usual methods is plain from the case of his alteration of the Synoptic tradition in xxiv, 6. For the parallels in Matthew xxviii, 7, and Mark xvi, 7, are a distinct charge by the angels to the women to go into Galilee, as the Lord had told them. But Luke reduces this to the echo, " Remember how he spake unto you when he was yet in Galilee," etc., so as to leave out all allusion to the post-resurrection appearances in Galilee. He reinforces his position by the command, peculiar to him (Luke xxiv, 49; Acts i, 4), to tarry in Jerusalem, and not to depart from it. Matthew, on the other hand, enforces his account by the appearance on the Galilean mountain (Matt. xxviii, 16); while, to crown all, both he and Mark record that the Lord actually charged the disciples, at the Last Supper, to go into Galilee after His Resurrection (Matt. xxvi, 32 ; Mark xiv, 28). *Luke suppresses this charge* altogether in his account of the Last Supper, and makes the Ascension take place at Bethany on the very day of the Resurrection.* (Luke xxiv, 13, 33, 36, 44, 50.)

If Luke's literary canons allowed such free treatment in other cases, it is reasonable to expect the same in the case before us. Dr. Salmon, in his " Introduction to the New Testament," Lecture ix, remarks that the three accounts of Paul's conversion contained in the Acts of the Apostles, all in substantial agreement amid differences of detail, furnish us with a good standard of comparison for Luke's idea of historical accuracy. (Compare, for example, Acts ix, 7, with xxii, 9.) The present writer has, therefore, done no more than apply Dr. Salmon's admitted principle to a particular case.

---

* Luke's " Forty Days " in Acts i, 3, is very probably symbolic. In any case, the Ascension as a Vision or an external act may have been repeated. And Luke's account in Acts is a re-writing of that in his Gospel.

The aim of this essay has been to establish two things:

(1) That the Lord Jesus quoted the First Book of Macca-bees; and

(2) That Luke altered the quotation in favor of a definite prediction of the siege of Jerusalem.

ALBERT J. EDMUNDS.

Historical Society of Pennsylvania, March 20, 1893.

PARALLAX OF O. ARG. 14320.

THIS star and a neighboring star five minutes south of it have a common proper motion of $3''.75$. On this account, although they are of the ninth magnitude, it seems probable that they are among those stars which are nearest to the sun. For the purpose of determining whether this be true, the following observations were made with the 10-inch equatorial of the Haverford College Observatory.

The comparison star used was a ninth magnitude star, about $66''$ away. The observations consisted of measures of position angle, distance, difference of right ascension and declination. The measures were made in this way in order to detect personal error. The measures of position angle and distance were made in the usual manner.

The measures of difference of right ascension and declination were made with the driving clock running, and were measures of double distance. The first was, therefore, measure of $\Delta a \cos \delta$. As the micrometer wires were not exactly parallel the values of Δa and $\Delta \delta$ should be in error by a small constant amount. But this should have no effect on the measure of parallax. The weights are on the scale of 10.

Date.	S. T.		p. a.	Dist.	$\triangle a$	$\triangle \delta$	Wt.	Ther.
1892.	h	m	°	//	//	//		°
March 3 . .	15	20	337.60	65.33	25.44	. . .	4	24
" 6 . .	16	44	337.60	65.61	25.50	60.33	3	30
" 11 . .	14	27	337.70	65.33	25.33	60.36	4	22
" 20 . .	15	30	338.10	65.55	25.37	. . .	4	22
" 28 . .	15	30	338.10	65.66	25.51	60.51	4	35
April 12 . .	15	50	337.90	65.78	24.99	60.76	4	34
" 18 . .	15	8	338.32	65.87	. . .	60.90	3	38
May 4 . .	15	30	338.02	66.01	25.41	60.93	4	70
" 16 . .	16	0	338.20	66.16	25.33	61.16	4	58
June 1 . .	15	45	. . .	. . .	25.23	61.19	4	71
". 10 . .	15	50	338.30	66.30	25.32	61.41	4	58
" 22 . .	15	20	338.18	66.46	25.12	61.43	4	84
" 25 . .	15	25	338.10	66.64	25.20	61.39	4	72
July 6 . .	16	0	338.36	66.63	24.91	61.12	4	67
" 12 . .	16	43	. . .	. . .	24.82	61.69	6	78

These measures were corrected for proper motion, refraction and temperature. The yearly proper motion, taken from Porter's " Catalogue of Proper Motion Stars," is

$$da \cos \delta \quad - 0''.95 \quad d\delta \quad - 3''.63$$

From these the proper motion in position, angle and distance was computed to be for 1892.4.

$$d \text{ p. a.} \quad + 1°.93 \quad d \text{ dist.} \quad + 3''.01.$$

They were practically constant during the four months of observation. The correction for temperature and refraction is very small and has been combined with the proper motion.

Cor. to Angle.	Cor. to Distance.	Cor. to Δa	Cor. to $\Delta \delta$	Angle.	Distance.	Δa	$\Delta \delta$
°	ʺ	ʺ	ʺ	°	ʺ	ʺ	ʺ
+0.46	+0.723	—0.226	. . .	338.06	66.053	25.214	. . .
+0.48	+0.692	—0.189	+0.845	338.08	66.302	25.311	61.175
+0.40	+0.660	—0.222	+0.784	338.10	65.990	25.108	61.144
+0.36	+0.576	—0.181	. . .	338.46	66.126	25.189	. . .
+0.33	+0.517	—0.152	+0.621	338.43	66.177	25.358	61.131
+0.24	+0.392	—0.109	+0.471	338.14	66.172	24.881	61.231
+0.20	+0.351	—0.105	+0.416	338.52	66.221	. . .	61.316
+0.13	+0.238	—0.046	+0.273	338.15	66.248	25.364	61.203
+0.07	+0.130	—0.021	+0.146	338.27	66.290	ʹ25.309	61.306
. . .	. . .	+0.031	—0.006	. . .	. . .	25.261	61.184
—0.07	—0.071	+0.051	—0.098	338.23	66.229	25.371	61.312
—0.14	—0.142	+0.080	—0.192	338.04	66.318	25.200	61.238
—0.15	—0.192	+0.089	—0.247	337.95	66.448	25.289	61.143
—0.19	—0.287	+0.127	. . .	338.17	66.343	25.037	. . .
. . .	. . .	+0.160	—0.400	. . .	. . .	24.980	61.290

In forming the equations of condition the correction to the proper motion employed was neglected, because the value used is probably very near the truth, and because the observations were continued over so short a period of time.

The assumed values for 1892.4 are:

for angle 338°.20, for dist. 66ʺ.224.
for Δa 25ʺ.205, for $\Delta \delta$ 61ʺ.223.

The equations of condition contain only two unknown quantities x the correction to the assumed values of the quantity measured, and π the parallax.

Angle.	Residual.	Distance.	Residual.
$x - 0.710\,\pi + 0.159 = 0$	$+ 0.225$	$x + 0.540\,\pi + 0.171 = 0$	$+ 0.064$
$x - 0.691\,\pi + 0.138 = 0$	$+ 0.204$	$x + 0.525\,\pi - 0.078 = 0$	$- 0.181$
$x - 0.658\,\pi + 0.114 = 0$	$+ 0.174$	$x + 0.496\,\pi + 0.234 = 0$	$+ 0.135$
$x - 0.585\,\pi - 0.296 = 0$	$- 0.244$	$x + 0.436\,\pi + 0.098 = 0$	$+ 0.015$
$x - 0.508\,\pi - 0.262 = 0$	$- 0.219$	$x + 0.373\,\pi + 0.047 = 0$	$- 0.022$
$x - 0.340\,\pi + 0.068 = 0$	$+ 0.093$	$x + 0.237\,\pi + 0.052 = 0$	$+ 0.014$
$x - 0.266\,\pi - 0.366 = 0$	$- 0.349$	$x + 0.178\,\pi + 0.003 = 0$	$- 0.022$
$x - 0.056\,\pi + 0.057 = 0$	$+ 0.050$	$x + 0.012\,\pi - 0.024 = 0$	$- 0.027$
$x + 0.105\,\pi - 0.081 = 0$	$- 0.105$	$x - 0.116\,\pi - 0.066 = 0$	$- 0.024$
$x + 0.418\,\pi - 0.035 = 0$	$- 0.094$	$x - 0.354\,\pi - 0.005 = 0$	$+ 0.089$
$x + 0.546\,\pi + 0.186 = 0$	$+ 0.112$	$x - 0.450\,\pi - 0.094 = 0$	$+ 0.024$
$x + 0.575\,\pi + 0.290 = 0$	$+ 0.213$	$x - 0.471\,\pi - 0.224 = 0$	$- 0.101$
$x + 0.667\,\pi + 0.035 = 0$	$+ 0.052$	$x - 0.539\,\pi - 0.119 = 0$	$+ 0.020$

$\triangle a$	Residual.	$\triangle \delta$	
$x + 0.894\,\pi - 0.009 = 0$	$+ 0.011$	$x - 0.139\,\pi + 0.048 = 0$	
$x + 0.871\,\pi - 0.106 = 0$	$- 0.087$	$x - 0.155\,\pi + 0.079 = 0$	
$x + 0.827\,\pi + 0.097 = 0$	$+ 0.115$	$x - 0.219\,\pi + 0.092 = 0$	
$x + 0.734\,\pi + 0.016 = 0$	$+ 0.032$	$x - 0.256\,\pi - 0.008 = 0$	
$x + 0.635\,\pi - 0.153 = 0$	$- 0.139$	$x - 0.267\,\pi - 0.093 = 0$	
$x + 0.420\,\pi + 0.324 = 0$	$+ 0.333$	$x - 0.280\,\pi + 0.020 = 0$	
$x + 0.059\,\pi - 0.159 = 0$	$- 0.158$	$x - 0.278\,\pi - 0.083 = 0$	
$x - 0.145\,\pi - 0.104 = 0$	$- 0.107$	$x - 0.255\,\pi + 0.039 = 0$	
$x - 0.406\,\pi - 0.056 = 0$	$- 0.065$	$x - 0.234\,\pi - 0.089 = 0$	
$x - 0.540\,\pi - 0.166 = 0$	$- 0.178$	$x - 0.198\,\pi - 0.015 = 0$	
$x - 0.701\,\pi + 0.005 = 0$	$- 0.010$	$x - 0.187\,\pi + 0.078 = 0$	
$x - 0.737\,\pi - 0.084 = 0$	$- 0.100$	$x - 0.122\,\pi - 0.067 = 0$	
$x - 0.852\,\pi + 0.168 = 0$	$+ 0.147$		
$x - 0.903\,\pi + 0.225 = 0$	$+ 0.205$		

From these were obtained the following normal equations, all observations having the same weight:

Angle.

$$+ 13.000\ x - 1.503\ \pi + 0''.007 = 0$$
$$- 1.503\ x + 3.462\ \pi + 0''.364 = 0$$

Distance.

$$+ 13.000\ x + 0.867\ \pi - 0''.005 = 0$$
$$+ 0.867\ x + 2.084\ \pi + 0''.462 = 0$$

Δa

$$+ 14.000\ x + 0.156\ \pi - 0''.002 = 0$$
$$+ 0.156\ x + 6.416\ \pi - 0''.140 = 0$$

$\Delta \delta$

$$+ 12.000\ x - 2.588\ \pi + 0''.001 = 0$$
$$- 2.588\ x + 0.591\ \pi + 0''.014 = 0$$

The solutions of the above equations give:

	Angle.		Distance.		Δa		$\Delta \delta$
x	$''$ $- 0.013$	$''$ ± 0.038	$''$ $+ 0.016$	$''$ ± 0.016	$''$ 0.000	$''$ ± 0.028	No solution.
π	$- 0.111$	± 0.075	$- 0.228$	± 0.039	$+ 0.022$	± 0.042	
r		± 0.135		± 0.055		± 0.106	
Weight π		3.288		2.026		6.414	0.033

Combining these values of π the general mean becomes
$$\pi = - 0''.114 \pm 0''.027$$

The position of this star from Porter's "Catalogue of Proper Motion Stars" is for 1900:
$$a\ 15^h\ 4^m\ 45^s\quad \delta\ -15°\ 54'\ 4''.$$

F. P. LEAVENWORTH.

University of Minnesota, February, 1893.

ON THE PROPER MOTION AND PARALLAX OF
δ EQUULEI.*

δ EQUULEI is a close binary star, with a period of about twelve years. It is of the fourth magnitude, and has a proper motion of three-tenths of a second of arc. Near it, but not sharing its proper motion, is a third star of the tenth magnitude. On these accounts it seemed an interesting pair to measure for difference of parallax.

In order to satisfy myself that the change appearing in the measures was due to proper motion of the principal star, I have made a new computation of this motion. All measures that could be procured were used. The earlier measures, with the exception of Struve's, and all measures of a single night, were given less weight. These observations, reduced to 1875.0 and corrected for differential refraction, are given in the following table. The formulæ that best represent them are:

$$s \sin p = + 15''.053 - 0''.0482 (T - 1875.0)$$
$$s \cos p = + 33''.664 + 0''.2995 (T - 1875.0)$$

The proper motion of this star from meridian observations is given by Oscar Stumpe in the *Astr. Nachr.*, No. 3,000:

$$\Delta a = + 0^s.0012 \quad \Delta \delta = - 0.''286,$$

and the proper motion from the above formulæ is:

$$\Delta a = + 0^s.0027 \quad \Delta \delta = - 0''.300.$$

The companion, therefore, has little or no proper motion.

---

* Copied from the *Astronomical Journal*.

Observer.	Date.	p	s	O − C		Wt.
				$s \sin p$	$s \cos p$	
		°	″	″	″	
W. Herschel . . .	1781.80	78.75	19.54	−0.33	−1.94	⅕
South	1825.26	42.08	25.82	−0.15	+0.40	⅓
Struve	1828.80	41.56	26.65	+0.40	+0.11	1
J. Herschel	1830.35	39.66	27.84	+0.57	+1.14	⅓
Smyth	1830.67	38.96	27.11	−0.14	+0.70	⅓
Struve	1832.10	39.85	27.49	+0.19	−0.20	1
Struve	1834.90	37.95	27.57	−0.03	+0.09	1
Struve	1835.64	37.94	27.64	+0.03	−0.08	1
Struve	1836.65	37.54	28.08	+0.21	+0.09	1
Smyth	1836.78	37.75	27.91	+0.20	−0.14	½
Struve	1837.77	36.83	28.27	+0.08	+0.27	1
Smyth	1838.59	36.94	28.21	+0.14	−0.21	½
O. Struve	1841.65	34.92	28.84	−0.15	−0.03	½
Kaiser	1842.64	34.13	28.52	−0.61	−0.37	½
Mädler	1843.63	35.02	29.90	+0.60	+0.22	⅓
Kaiser	1844.17	34.02	29.22	+0.19	−0.22	½
O. Struve	1847.82	32.29	30.50	0.00	+0.26	½
O. Struve	1852.23	30.98	31.24	−0.07	−0.06	1
O. Struve	1854.30	29.67	31.63	−0.40	+0.04	1
O. Struve	1857.12	29.06	32.50	−0.11	+0.08	1
O. Struve	1859.12	28.35	32.88	−0.20	+0.02	1
Dembowski	1862.71	27.35	33.55	−0.26	−0.07	1
Dembowski	1863.64	26.95	33.91	−0.24	−0.02	1
Dembowski	1864.90	26.94	34.31	+0.03	−0.05	1
Knott	1865.72	27.54	34.48	+0.44	−0.46	½
O. Struve	1865.91	26.12	34.72	−0.20	+0.38	½
Dunér	1869.67	25.51	35.82	+0.12	+0.26	1
Seabroke	1876.81	24.21	37.68	+0.48	+0.17	½
Flammarion	1877.82	23.99	37.59	+0.36	−0.17	½
Burnham	1880.60	22.58	37.99	−0.23	−0.24	1
Burnham	1881.46	22.28	38.60	−0.09	+0.13	1
Perrotin	1883.65	21.97	39.26	+0.08	+0.14	1
Leavenworth . . .	1889.68	20.55	40.38	−0.18	−0.24	1
Leavenworth . .	1890.88	20.74	41.03	+0.22	−0.04	1
Leavenworth . . .	1891.66	20.54	41.02	+0.17	−0.26	1

The observations for parallax are measures of distance alone. The principal star in all cases appeared single. The sum of the corrections for aberration and refraction, amounting in no instance to more than a few hundredths of a second, together with the assumed proper motion, have been applied. The corrected distances, with the data of observation, are given in the following table:

Date.	Hour Angle.	Ther.	Distance.	Distance, 1891.0.
	h. m.	°	″	″
1889.512	—2 39	69	40.445	40.854
9.515	—2 20	68	40.423	40.830
9.529	+1 33	72	40.263	40.667
9.540	+1 41	59	40.306	40.708
9.731	+2 03	60	40.531	40.884
9.756	+2 27	51	40.505	40 849
9.761	+2 19	52	40.193	40.534
9.772	+0 33	45	40.263	40.597
9.800	+2 14	56	40.454	40.783
9.852	+1 58	39	40.356	40.661
9.923	+2 41	46	40.546	40.845
9.975	+3 51	42	40.283	40.579
90.851	+1 26	62	41.043	41.095
0.873	+2 25	60	41.038	41.087
0.900	+4 31	38	41.001	41.060
91.516	—0 51	49	40.914	40.797
1.524	—2 12	62	40.846	40.728
1.530	—2 12	64	40.953	40.833
1.536	—1 31	70	41.099	40 977
1.560	—0 29	66	41.092	40.962
1.864	+2 35	50	40.938	40.720

From these were formed equations of condition, the distance for 1891.0 being assumed to be 40″.819.

Equation.	Residual.
	″
$x - 1.488y - 0.660\pi - 0.035 = 0$	$- 0.119$
$- 1.485 \quad - 0.655 \quad - 0.011 = 0$	$- 0.095$
$- 1.471 \quad - 0.626 \quad + 0.152 = 0$	$+ 0.069$
$- 1.460 \quad - 0.601 \quad + 0.111 = 0$	$+ 0.030$
$- 1.269 \quad + 0.143 \quad - 0.065 = 0$	$- 0.121$
$- 1.244 \quad + 0.248 \quad - 0.030 = 0$	$- 0.082$
$- 1.239 \quad + 0.271 \quad + 0.285 = 0$	$+ 0.234$
$- 1.228 \quad + 0.315 \quad + 0.222 = 0$	$+ 0.172$
$- 1.200 \quad + 0.419 \quad + 0.036 = 0$	$- 0.010$
$- 1.148 \quad + 0.580 \quad + 0.158 = 0$	$+ 0.119$
$- 1.077 \quad + 0.694 \quad - 0.026 = 0$	$- 0.059$
$- 1.025 \quad + 0.688 \quad + 0.240 = 0$	$+ 0.211$
$- 0.149 \quad + 0.575 \quad - 0.276 = 0$	$- 0.245$
$- 0.127 \quad + 0.625 \quad - 0.268 = 0$	$- 0.235$
$- 0.100 \quad + 0.671 \quad - 0.241 = 0$	$- 0.203$
$+ 0.516 \quad - 0.720 \quad + 0.022 = 0$	$+ 0.077$
$+ 0.524 \quad - 0.721 \quad + 0.091 = 0$	$+ 0.147$
$+ 0.530 \quad - 0.720 \quad - 0.014 = 0$	$+ 0.042$
$+ 0.536 \quad - 0.720 \quad - 0.158 = 0$	$- 0.102$
$+ 0.560 \quad - 0.705 \quad - 0.143 = 0$	$- 0.084$
$+ 0.864 \quad + 0.604 \quad + 0.099 = 0$	$+ 0.201$
$+ 0.883 \quad + 0.643 \quad - 0.149 = 0$	$- 0.045$
$x + 0.889y + 0.652\pi - 0.006 = 0$	$+ 0.099$

From these were derived the normal equations:

$$+ 23.000x - 10.408y + 1.000\pi - 0''.006 = 0$$
$$- 10.408x + 23.672y - 0.553\pi - 1.330 = 0$$
$$+ 1.000x = 0.553y + 8.285\pi - 0.132 = 0$$

The solution of which gives:

$$x = + 0''.031 \pm 0''.024$$
$$y = + 0.070 \pm 0.023$$
$$\pi = + 0.017 \pm 0.035$$
$$r = \pm 0.102$$

Weight π 8.241

$[nn\ 3]$ $0''.453$

$[vv]$ 0.452

Gore's hypothetical parallax for this star is $0''.08$.

June 10, 1892.   F. P. LEAVENWORTH.

DOUBLE STAR OBSERVATIONS.

THE double-star observations given below are a continuation of the work published in "Haverford College Studies," No. 11.

The telescope was the ten-inch Clark Equatorial, with the micrometer and magnifying power of 375, as before.

The approximate places are for 1880.

The following is a list of abbreviations:

β. denotes Burnham.
D'. " Dawes.
F.P.L. " F. P. Leavenworth.
h. " Sir John Herschel.
H.C. " Harvard College Zones.
H.A.H. " H. A. Howe.
H.C.W. " H. C. Wilson.
O.S. " Ormond Stone.
So. " South.
Sh. " South and Herschel.
Σ. " Struve.
OΣ. " Otto Struve.
G.L.J. " Geo. L. Jones.

The observations are divided into two parts—those made previous to the withdrawal of Professor Leavenworth from Haverford College, and those made since.

In Part I four measures of angle were usually made; in Part II, six. In each part two double distances were measured.

WM. H. COLLINS.

Double Star Measures—Part I.*

The measurement of the stars contained in this list was undertaken at the suggestion of Mr. Burnham, who furnished us a list of his double stars which needed re-measuring, and which were not too difficult for our telescope. To these were added a few of the more important binary stars, and several others. The observations were made with the ten-inch Clark Equatorial of the Haverford College Observatory, during the first part of the year 1892. The observers were Wm. H. Collins, assistant in the Observatory, J. H. Dennis, E. H. Gifford and Geo. L. Jones, students of Practical Astronomy, and F. P. Leavenworth.

Σ 23 0^h 11^m : $- 0°$ 21'.

	°	"	wt	m	m	h	
1891.872	343.8	6.66	3	7.5	10.0	23.7	C
.886	342.4	6.59	2	7.5	10.0	0.0	C
.965	343.9	6.66	3	7.5	10.0	0.8	C
2.023	345.3	6.53	3	7.5	10.0	2.6	C
.045	346.5	6.83	3	7.5	10.5	2.6	C
1891.958	344.4	6.65		7.5	10.1		

Σ 262 2^h 19^m : $+ 66°$ 52'.

A : B.

1892.069	256.9	. . .	2	. . .	. . .	5.5	C

A : C.

1892.069	111.0	6.99	2	. . .	. . .	5.5	C

$O\Sigma$ 93 4^h 54^m : $+ 4°$ 55'.

1892.058	49.0	. . .	4	8.5	8.5	5.2	C
.135	47.7	0.98	4	8.0	8.0	5.2	C
1892.087	48.4	0.98		8.2	8.2		

β 885 5^h 5^m : $- 1°$ 55'.

1892.135	186.5	0.72	4	8.0	9.0	5.5	C

O. S. 5^h 18^m : $- 10°$ 32'.

1892.126	124.7	1.08	3	8.0	8.0	5.7	C
.135	122.5	1.16	3	8.3	8.3	6.0	C
1892.131	123.6	1.12		8.2	8.2		

* Copied from the *Astronomical Journal*, with the exception of Σ 23.

D 4   5ʰ 29ᵐ : — 4° 55′.

	°	″	wt	ra	m	h	
1892.126	214.4	1.82	3	4.0	8.0	6.5	C
.135	214.1	1.26	3	4.0	8.0	6.3	C
1892.131	214.2	1.54		4.0	8.0		

β 1021   6ʰ 24ᵐ : + 28° 28′.

1892.148	86.9	0.68	3	8.0	9.2	4.9	L
.184	85.0	0.68	2	8.2	9.5	9.2	L
1892.166	86.0	0.68		8.1	9.4		

β 754   6ʰ 30ᵐ : — 33° 55′.

| 1892.146 | 22.8 | . . . | 2 | . . . | . . . | 6.5 | L |

Very difficult.

OΣ 152   6ʰ 33ᵐ : + 28° 22′.

1892.146	34.5	0.88	2	7.5	8.5	8.4	L
.148	35.9	0.87	3	6.0	8.0	5.1	L
1892.147	35.2	0.88		6.8	8.2		

β 195   6ʰ 37ᵐ : — 23° 7′.

A : B.

1892.146	214.2	5.63	2	7.0	11.5	5.5	L
.148	215.0	5.91	2	7.0	11.0	5.6	L
.189	214.4	5 64	2	7.5	11.0	6.4	L
.242	217.2	5.65	2	7.0	11.0	8.2	C
1892.182	215.2	5.71		7.1	11.1		

A : C.

| 1892.149 | 178.4 | 35.04 | 2 | 7.0 | 12.0 | 5.8 | L |

Companions very faint.

β 100   6ʰ 54ᵐ : + 12° 34′.

| 1892.127 | 256.0 | 2.92 | 3 | 7.5 | 11.0 | 7.0 | C |

H. A. H 64   7ʰ 10ᵐ : — 0° 25′.

1892.102	314.5	2.58	. . .	9.0	9.0	8.1	L
.126	314.9	2.98	3	9.0	9.0	7.7	C
1892.115	314.7	2.78		9.0	9.0		

β 199   7ʰ 20ᵐ : — 20° 56′.

| 1892.102 | 23.2 | 1.63 | 2 | . . . | . . . | 7.7 | L |

Σ 1110   7ʰ 28ᵐ : + 32° 9′.

1892.376	230.3	5.25	. . .	. . .	. . .	8.0	J
.376	228.9	5.41	3	. . .	. . .	9.0	L
.379	230.2	5.30	. . .	. . .	. . .	. . .	J
1892.377	229.8	5.32					

β 902   7ʰ 52ᵐ : — 10° 34′.

	°	″	wt	m	m	h	
1892.189	240.4	. . .	2	8.0	11.0	. . .	L
.203	245.8	1.17	2	8.0	11.5	7.7	L
.223	245.0	. . .	2	8.0	11.5	8.1	L
1892.205	243.7	1.17		8.0	11.3		

β 202   7ʰ 57ᵐ : — 26° 53′.

1892.160	159.9	7.61	2	7.5	10.3	8.7	L
.204	161.2	7.58	2	7.0	10.0	8.0	L
.204	159.9	7.66	2	7.5	11.0	8.6	C
1892.189	160.3	7.62		7.3	10.4		

β 581   7ʰ 58ᵐ : + 12° 38′.

½ (A + B) : C. ·

1892.132	190.5	. . .	3	8.0	11.0	8.5	C

β 904   8ʰ 8ᵐ : — 5° 23′.

1892.146	79.2	3.68	2	8.0	11.5	7.7	L
.149	79.8	3.29	2	8.0	11.2	6.8	L
.204	81.1	3.00	2	8.0	10.5	9.4	C
.242	80.7	2.77	2	8.0	11.0	9.5	C
1892.185	80.2	3.18		8.0	11.0		

Companion very faint.

β 454   8ʰ 10ᵐ : — 30° 29′.

1892.231	15.8	2.34	2	8.0	9.5	8.2	L
.286	17.4	2.64	2	7.5	10.0	9.0	L
1892.258	16.6	2.49		7.8	9.8		

β 24   8ʰ 48ᵐ : — 8° 18′.

1892.132	174.7	1.02	3	7.5	8.0	9.0	C

β 410   9ʰ 4ᵐ : —25° 19′.

1892.209	161.3	1.86	2	7.0	9.0	9.2	L
.231	161.3	1.61	2	8.0	9.5	8.5	L
.294	160.0	1.43	2	7.0	9.0	9.6	C
1892.245	160.9	1.63		7.3	9.2		

β 337   9ʰ 17ᵐ : — 17° 23′.

1892.146	327.2	7.93	2	7.0	10.0	9.5	C
.160	326.4	7.85	2	7.0	10.0	9.1	L
.275	326.8	7.72	2	7.0	10.5	10.3	L
1892.194	326.8	7.83		7.0	10.2		

Σ 1356　9ʰ　22ᵐ : + 9°　35′.

	°	″	wt	m	m	h	
1892.132	103.4	0.86	2	6.5	7.5	9.8	C
.146	103.5	1.11	1	6.5	7.5	11.0	C
.351	106.1	0.69	3	5.5	6.5	11.7	L
.357	104.0	0.76	3	6.0	6.8	11.0	L
.376	105.6	0.94	2	6.5	7.0	12.0	C
1892.273	104.5	0.87		6.3	7.1		

OΣ 215　10ʰ　10ᵐ : + 18°　20′.

1892.379	212.2	0.58	3	. . .	. . .	11.4	L
.401	212.4	0.75	3	7.0	7.4	12.4	L
1892.390	212.3	0.66		7.0	7.4		

Σ 1424　10ʰ　14ᵐ : + 20°　24′.

1892.340	114.6	3.41	2	. . .	. . .	9.8	L
.376	116.4	3.35	. . .	. . .	. . .	8.1	J
.376	113.2	3.49	3	. . .	. . .	8.2	L
.379	112.6	3.46	. . .	. . .	. . .	9.0	J
.464	114.6	3.62	. . .	. . .	. . .	10.4	G
1892.383	114.3	3.47					

β 219　10ʰ　16ᵐ : — 21°　55′.

1892.146	187.2	2.13	2	7.0	9.0	10.0	C
.195	187.8	2.47	2	7.0	9.5	11.2	L
.209	192.5	2.14	2	7.0	9.0	9.5	L
.294	185.0	1.80	1	7.0	9.0	9.6	C
1892.211	188.1	2.14		7.0	9.1		

β 411　10ʰ　30ᵐ : — 26°　3′.

1892.286	290.4	1.17	1	7.0	8.5	. . .	L
.294	291.8	1.63	1	6.5	8.5	10.1	C
.313	289.3	1.03	2	. . .	. . .	10.5	L
.330	291.1	1.34	1	. . .	. . .	10.5	C
1892.306	290.6	1.29		6.8	8.5		

Σ 1457　10ʰ　32ᵐ : + 6°　21′

1892.132	320.3	1.39	2	7.5	8.0	10.5	C
.146	319.8	1.14	2	7.0	8.0	11.5	C
1892.138	320.0	1.26		7.2	8.0		

β 915 10ʰ 43ᵐ: + 24° 55′.

	°	″	wt	m	m	−	
1892.286	239.1	0.8E	1	9.0	9.0	. . .	L
.294	234.7	0.6E	1	. . .	. . .	11.0	L
.302	230.1	0.6E	2	. . .	. . .	. . .	L
.313	226.0	0.8E	2	. . .	. . .	11.0	L
1892.299	232.5	0.7		9.0	9.0		

E estimated. Faint and difficult.

Σ 1523 11ʰ 12ᵐ: + 32° 13′.

1892.447	197.0	1.71	3	4.5	5.5	13.2	L
.453	196.1	1.49	3	5.0	5.5	13.3	L
1892.450	196.6	1.60		4.8	5.5		

OΣ 234 11ʰ 24ᵐ: + 41° 57′.

1892.453	136.5	0.4E	1	. . .	. . .	. . . .	L

E estimated. Very difficult.

OΣ 235 11ʰ 26ᵐ: + 61° 45′.

1892.447	84.2	0.82	2	5.0	7.0	13.5	L
.453	86.6	0.78	3	5.5	7.0	13.7	L
1892.450	85.4	0.80		5.2	7.0		

β 917 11ʰ 37ᵐ: + 11° 22′.

1892.146	173.6	2.98	2	7.5	11.0	10.3	C
.204	175.5	3.02	2	8.0	11.0	10.3	C
.242	174.4	3.39	. . .	. . .	. .	10.5	D
.294	178.3	3.38	2	8.0	11.0	11.9	L
1892.241	175.4	3.19		7.8	11.0		

Σ 1620 12ʰ 10ᵐ: + 9° 46′.

1892.330	81.5	1.93	2	8.5	10.0	12.4	L

β 920 12ʰ 10ᵐ: − 22° 41′.

1892.313	254.1	0.77	3	6.5	7.5	12.5	L
.313	252.6	. . .	. . .	. . .	. . .	12.8	J
.351	248.7	0.8E	1	. . .	. . .	12.7	L
.357	246.2	0.86	2	7.0	8.0	11.7	L
.398	251.0	0.80	2	6.0	8.0	12.1	L
1892.346	250.5	0.81		6.5	7.8		

E estimated.

β 921   12ʰ   12ᵐ : — 23°   21′.

	°	″	wt	m	m	n	
1892.321	221.1	. . .	1	7.2	12.0	. . .	L
.330	218.5	3.05	2	7.0	12.0	12.8	L
.351	217.0	2.93	2	7.0	12.0	12.2	L
.357	217.4	2.86	2	7.0	12.0	12.0	L
1892.340	218.5	2.95		7.0	12.0	·	

Companion very faint and difficult.

Σ 1670   12ʰ   36ᵐ : — 0°   47′.

1892.417	152.6	5.72	3	. . . ′	. . .	12.6	L
.436	151.9	5.62	2	. . .	. . .	11.0	D
1892.427	152.2	5.67					

β 926   12ʰ   52ᵐ : — 5°   24′.

1892.302	268.1	2.34	2	8.0	12.0	13.0	L
3.30	267.8	2.13	2	8.0	11.5	13.2	L
.376	273.7	2.23	1	8.5	11.5	12.6	C
1892.336	269.9	2.23		8.2	11.7		

β 112   12ʰ   55ᵐ : + 19°   1′.

B : C.

1892.302	293.3	1.95	2	9.3	9.8	12.6	L
.313	287.9	1.91	2	9.0	10.0	13.8	L
.351	292.0	1.83	2	9.0	9.5	13.2	L
1892.322	291.1	1.90		9.1	9.8		

β 927   12ʰ   57ᵐ : — 5°   53′.

1892.294	289.2	4.52	2	8.0	10.0	12.5	L
.302	292.2	4.38	2	8.0	10.0	13.5	L
.351	290.2	4.35	2	8.5	10.0	13.6	L
1892.316	290.5	4.42		8.2	10.0		

β 928   12ʰ   57ᵐ : — 5°   57′.

1892.376	305.8	. . .	1	8.0	9.0	. . .	C

Σ 1728   13ʰ   4ᵐ : + 18°   10′.

1892.357	11.9	0.47	2	5.8	6.2	14.2	L
.379	11.5	0.5 E	2	. . .	. . .	13.1	L
1892.368	11.7	0.48		5.8	6.2		

E estimated.

β 610   13^h 17^m : — 20° 19′.

	o	″	wt	m	m	h	
1892.357	17.6	3.81	2	7.0	11.8	13.0	L
.379	˙3.9	4.04	1	7.0	12.0	12.9	L
.398	19.4	3·61	2	7.2	11.5	13.0	L
1892.378	18.5	3.82		7.1	11.8		

β 460   13^h 19^m : — 15° 0′.

1892.357	37.4	2.37	2	8.0	10.5	14.5	L
.379	32.0	2.04	1	8.0	10.3	13.2	L
.398	35.0	2.37	2	8.0	10.5	12.7	L
1892.378	34.8	2.26		8.0	10.4		

β 30   13^h 52^m : + 20° 2′.

1892.173	197.9	. . .	1	8.0	11.5	13.5	L
.302	199.8	8.40	2	8.0	11.0	14.3	L
.321	200.9	8.07	2	7.7	10.5	13.0	L
.357	199.9	8.40	2	8.4	10.8	13.4	L
1892.288	199.6	8.29		8.0	11.0		

β 938   13^h 59^m : — 26° 0′.

1892.409	304.0	0.6E	1	. . .	. . .	14.6	L
.414	299.9	0.60	3	7.5	7.7	14.0	L
.417	294.7	0.65	3	. . .	. . .	14.2	L
.420	297.8	. . .	2	. . .	. . .	14.4	L
1892.415	299.1	0.62		7.5	7.7		

E estimated.

β 615   14^h 18^m : + 49° 4′.

1892.321	236.0	1.97	2	8.2	9.5	13.5	L
.362	235.7	2.76	2	8.5	9.8	14.9	L
.420	233.2	2.82	2	8.5	10.0	13.4	L
1892.368	235.0	2.52		8.4	9.8		

Σ 1888   14^h 46^m : + 19° 38′.

1892.242	240.7	3.16	3	. . .	. . .	13.9	L
.330	242.1	3.14	3	. . .	. . .	17.7	L
.401	237.2	2.94	2	. . .	. . .	17.0	L
1892.324	240.0	3.08					

β 942   14ʰ   47ᵐ : + 0°   2′.

	°	″	wt	m	m	
1892.343	189.8	1.0E	1	. . .	. . .	. . .
.357	190.7	1.17	2	9.0	9.3	14.7
.398	197.1	1.13	2	9.0	9.0	15.0
.409	182.3	0.83	2	9.2	9.2	14.8
.414	189.2	0.99	3	9.2	9.2	14.7
1892.384	189.8	1.02		9.1	9.2	

E estimated; difficult.

β 119   14ʰ   59ᵐ : — 6°   33′.

1892.343	306.8	1.49	3	8.0	8.5	14.8
.351	308.2	1.43	3	8.0	8.4	15.0
.362	306.5	1.50	2	8.0	8.5	15.4
1892.352	307.1	1.47		8.0	8.5	

Σ 1909   15ʰ   0ᵐ : + 48°   5′.

1892.362	241.2	4.53	2	5.0	6.3	14.4
.458	241.9	4.56	4	5.0	5.5	13.2
1892.410	241.6	4.54		5.0	5.9	

β 349   15ʰ   3ᵐ : + 2°   9′.

1892.395	35.1	3.75	2	8.0	11.8	15.2
.398	37.3	3.86	2	8.0	12.0	15 2
1892.396	36.2	3.80		8.0	11.9	

Companion very difficult.

β 809   15ʰ   3ᵐ : — 22°   16′.

1892.395	119.7	1.60	2	8.2	10.2	15.5
.409	118.7	1.67	2	8.0	10.1	15.1
1892.402	119.2	1.64		8.1	10.1	

β 350   15ʰ   8ᵐ : — 27°   9′.

1892.409	160.5	1.13	2	7.0	8.3	15.5
.414	160.0	1.17	3	7.4	8.6	15.1
1892.412	160.2	1.15		7.2	8.4	

β 352   15ʰ   11ᵐ : — 26°   33′.

1892.401	68.4	13.96	2	8.0	9.3	15.0
.414	68.2	13.94	3	8.2	9.0	15.4
1892.407	68.3	13.95.		8 1	9 2	

F. P. L. 15^h 13^m : — 26° 35′.

	°	″	wt	m	m	h	
1892.357	29.3	17.18	2	8.4	9.5	15.2	L
.401	30.0	16.14	3	7.8	9.5	15.3	L
1892.379	29.6	17.01		8.1	9.5		

Observed for β 352.

β 228 15^h 13^m : — 23° 50′.

1892.395	328.1	0.93	2	7.2	8.0	15.8	L
.414	327.0	1.04	3	7.3	8.3	15.7	L
1892.405	327.6	0.98		7.2	8.1		

β 353 15^h 14^m : + 85° 57′.

1892.417	295.5	3.62	2	9 4	9.8	18.7	L
.423	295.7	3.74	2	9.5	10.0	14.3	C
1892.420	295.6	3.68		9.4	9.9		

Σ 1937 15^h 18^m : + 30° 43′.

1892.422	231.7	0.79	2	. . .	. . .	13.0	C
.477	228.5	0.66	2	. . .	. . .	14.4	L
1892.450	230.1	0.72					

Σ 1938 15^h 20^m : + 37° 46′.

1892.422	92.6	0.82	3	. . .	. . .	13.4	C

β 33 15^h 25^m : — 12° 35′.

1892.401	41.8	3.17	2	7.8	10.5	15.7	L
.409	42.4	2.98	2	7.8	10.0	15.8	L
1892.405	42.1	3.08		7.8	10.2		

OΣ 298 15^h 32^m : + 40° 13′.

1892.422	169.9	0.82	2	. . .	. . .	13.7	C

β 620 15^h 39^m : — 27° 41′.

A : B.

1892.414	165.5	0.65	2	7.0	7.6	16.0	L

A : C.

1892.414	215.4	50.53	8	7.0	10.0	16.1	L

β 240 15^h 39^m : + 4° 24′.

A : B.

1892.354	135.4	2.29	2	8.5	9.8	16.2	L
.376	136.6	2.22	2	8.3	9.6	17.4	L
.379	133.1	2.30	2	8.5	10.0	15.7	L
1892.370	135.0	2.27		8.4	9.8		

A : C.

	°	″	wt	m	m	h
1892.354	39.7	28.44	2	. . .	12.0	16.5
.379	40.8	28.22	2	. . .	12.0	15.0
1892.366	40.2	28.33			12.0 ·	

β 415   15^h 45^m : + 65° 57′.
A : B.

1892.417	334.6	12.82	3	8.5	11.0	17.8
.422	336.1	12.72	3	8.0	10.0	14.8
1892.420	335.4	12.77		8.2	10.5	

A : C.

1892.417	358.5	29.12	3	. : .	11.0	17.9
.422	358.1	29.33	3	. . .	10.2	14.8
1892.420	358.3	29.22			10.6	

β 36   15^h 46^m : — 24° 58′.

1892.376	277.3	2.88	2	6.0	7.7	17.2
.395	278.2	2.84	2	5.6	7.6	16.1
1892.386	277.8	2.86		5.8	7.6	

β 37   15^h 55^m : — 24° 15′.

1892.409	43.3	3.30	2	8.8	9.4	10.2
.414	44.0	2.81	3	8.4	10.0	16.5
.434	42.9	3.16	2	8.6	9.6	16.1
1892.416	43.4	3.09		8.6	9.7	

β 948   15^h 59^m : — 5° 58′.
A : B.·

1892.376	151.4	. . .	3	. . .	. . .	17.7
.395	149.3	1.43	2	6.8	9.5	16.4
.409	148.7	1.51	3	7.4	9.2	16.5
.417	147.8	1.68	3	. . .	. . .	17.1
1892.399	149.3	1.54		7.1	9.4	

A : C.

1892.409	234.9	29.15	2	. . .	10.4	16.7
.417	234.6	28.95	3	. . .	. . .	17.1
1892.413	234.8	29.05			10.4	

A : D.

1892.409	194.8	52.66	2	. . .	10.8	16.8
.417	195.0	52.78	3	. . .	. . .	17.1
1892.413	194.9	52.72			10.8 ·	

β 123 16^h 48^m : — 21° 51′.

	°	″	wt	m	m		
1892.444	206.6	1.57	2	8.4	8.8	16.6	L
.477	201.7	1.55	2	8.2	9.0	17.1	L
.518	203.3	1.60	2	8.5	8.5	17.6	L
1892.480	203.9	1.57		8.4	8.8		

β 44 17^h 9^m : + 28° 58′.

1892.453	20.2	5.65	3	8.0	9.5	19.2	C
.477	18.1	. . .	2	. . .	. . .	18.2	L
.516	19.3	5.44	2	8.8	9.5	20.0	L
1892.482	19.2	5.54		8.4	9.5		

β 242 17^h 17^m : — 11° 35′.

A : B.

1892.453	67.7	1.04	3	8.0 · ·	8.0	16.5	C
.477	72.8	1.00	3	8.2	8.2	17.4	L
.516	72.1	0.92	3	8.3	9.3	19.0	L
1892.482	70.9	0.99		8.2	8.7		

½ (A + B) : C.

1892.477	62.0	9.04	3	. . .	11.0	17.6	L

½ (A + B) : D.

1892.477	64.8	47.83	3	. . .	10.0	17.8	L

β 46 17^h 18^m : + 13° 30′.

1892.453	201.4	1.74	3	7.5 ᵣ	10.5	16.7	C
.477	200.9	. . .	2	8.0	12.0	18.0	L
.518	203.9	2.15	2	8.0	10.5	17.8	L
.532	204.0	1.84	3	8.0	11.0	17.3	L
1892.495	202.6	1.91		7.9	11.2		

Σ 2274 17^h 59^m : + 2° 33′.

1892.414	320.5	2.36	2	. . .	. . .	16.2	C

β 244 18^h 1^m : — 27° 53′.

1892.532	257.6	2.11	2	8.0	10.2	17.6	L
.548	258.2	1.98	2	8.0	10.4	17.4	L
1892.540	257.9	2.04		8.0	10.3		

β 245 18^h 2^m : — 30° 45′.

1892.518	353.8	3.99	2	6.2	8.8	18.3	L
.524	352.8	3.97	1	6.5	9.0	19.1	L
1892.521	353.3	3.98		6.4	8.9		

β 132   18ʰ 4ᵐ : — 19° 52′.

	°	″	wt	m	m	h
1892.518	226.4	0.83	2	7.2	7.3	18.1
.524	229.3	· 0.95	2	7.3	7.3	18.9
1892.521	227.8	0.89		7.2	7.3	

F. P. L.   18ʰ 5ᵐ : — 15° 42′.

1892.548	27.2	3.61	2	8.0	11.3	18.1
.568	25.6	3.54	2	8.2	11.2	18.2
1892.558	26.4	3.58		8.1	11.2	

F. P. L.   18ʰ 6ᵐ : — 15° 24′.

1892.518	276.7	3.66	2	8.4	11.0	19.5
.524	276.3	. . .	1	8.0	12.0	. . .
.548	281.0	3.95	2	8.0	12.0	17.6
1892.530	278.0	3.80		8.1	11.7	

β 292   18ʰ 7ᵐ : — 21° 5′.

A : B.

1892.554	258.0	17.18	1	4.0	11.0	17.7
.562	259.2	17.06	3	5.0	11.5	17.6
1892.558	258.6	17.12		4.5	11.2	

A : D.

1892.562	312.8	48.63	2	. . .	9.5	17.8

A : E.

1892.562	116.0	49.96	2	. . .	9.7	17.9

β 131   18ʰ 7ᵐ : — 15° 38′.

1892.518	279.9	2.76	2	8.0	9.5	19.8
.548	280.4	2.77	2	8.0	9.5	17.9
1892.533	280.2	2.76		8.0	9.5	

β 48   18ʰ 14ᵐ : — 19° 43′.

1892.562	0.2	2.17	2	8.2	10.2	18.2

β 49   18ʰ 17ᵐ : — 19° 37′.

1892.532	46.1	8.63	2	8.0	10.8	18.5
.548	45.3	8.30	2	8.4	11.0	18.5
.562	46.7	8.25	3	8.5	10.3	19.1
1892.548	46.0	8.39		8.3	10.7	

6

$$\beta\ 1128\quad 18^h\quad 23^m : -33°\quad 4'.$$

	°	''	wt	m	m	h
1892.562	201.0	. . .	2	6.0	11.0	19.4

$$\beta\ 135\quad 18^h\quad 31^m : -14°\quad 6'.$$

1892.532	187.1	. . .	1	8.0	12.0	18.8

$$\beta\ 136\quad 18^h\quad 37^m : +5°\quad 37'.$$

1892.532	8.0	4.64	2	9.0	9.2	19.0
.554	7.4	4.72	2	9.0	9.1	18.2
1892.543	7.7	4.68		9.0	9.2	

$$\beta\ 969\quad 18^h\quad 44^m : -8°\quad 3'.$$

1892.553	238.4	. . .	1	7.5	12.0	18.7
.562	237.7	14.82	2	7.2	11.5	19.6
.568	238.8	14.76	2	7.8 '	11.5	18.5
1892.561	238.3	14.79		7.5	11.6	

$$\beta\ 467\quad 19^h\quad 39^m : -21°\quad 49'.$$

1892.518	134.2	3.13	2	8.0	11.0	20.0

$$\beta\ 829\quad 19^h\quad 43^m : +5°\quad 27'.$$

1892.516	307.8	0.83	2	8.0	8.8	20.7
.518	310.1	0.76	2	8.0	8.4	20.2
1892.517	309.0	0.80		8.0	8.6	

$$\beta\ 361\quad 19^h\quad 45^m : +22°\quad 22'.$$

1892.516	349.2	3.83	2	9.0	9.2	20.9
.518	350.8	4.09	3	9.0	9.0	20.5
1892.517	350.0	3.96		9.0	9.1	

$$\beta\ 266\quad 19^h\quad 52^m : +11°\quad 5'.$$

1892.568	167.0	15.94	2	8.0	11.0	19.8

$$\beta\ 428\quad 20^h\quad 1^m : +12°\quad 36'.$$

1892.568	351.4	0.61	2	7.5	8.8	20.0

$$\text{F. P. L.}\quad 20^h\quad 48^m : -11°\quad 20'.$$

1892.562	298.0	. . .	2	8.5	9.8	20.3

Double Star Measures—Part II.

Nearly all these measures were made by Mr. Geo. L. Jones, a student of Practical Astronomy.

Σ 3060 0ʰ 0ᵐ : + 17° 25′.

	°	″	wt	m	m	h	
1892.746	117.8	3.51	. . .	. . .	. . .	0.5	J
.773	116.6	3.49	2	9.0	9.0	20.7	J
.828	117.1	3.62	2	8.0	8.3	22.5	J
1892.784	117.2	3.54		8.5	8.6		

Σ 3061 0ʰ 0ᵐ : + 17° 10′.

1892.748	146.3	7.63	. . .	. . .	. . .	2.0	J
.768	147.6	7.70	3	. . .	. . .	21.0	J
.778	147.4	7.74	2	7.8	8.0	1.0	J
1892.765	147.1	7.69		7.8	8.0		

Σ 3062 0ʰ 0ᵐ : + 57° 46′.

1892.778	326.6	1.58	. . .	7.0	8.0	4.3	C
.934	324.7	1.46	3	8.0	8.5	1.6	C
1892.856	325.6	1.52		7.5	8.2		
1892.936	323.7	1.62	3	6.5	7.5	1.5	J

Σ 12 0ʰ 9ᵐ : + 8° 9′.

1892.828	149.6	12.31	2	5.2	7.0	23.0	J
.880	151.0	11.68	2	5.2	7.2	1.8	J
.921	149.5	11.46	2	5.2	7.2	2.6	J
1892.876	150.0	11.82		5.2	7.1		

Σ 19 0ʰ 11ᵐ : + 35° 58′.

1892.936	135.1	2.29	2	7.0	9.5	2.2	J
3.058	135.0	2.34	3	7.4	10.0	3.3	J
1892.997	135.0	2.32		7.2	9.8		

Σ 22 0ʰ 11ᵐ : + 8° 12′.

1892.828	235.9	4.55	2	7.1	7.7	23.2	J
.830	236.3	4.44	3	6.7	7.5	1.0	J
.880	235.1	4.71	1	7.0	7.5	1.6	J
1892.846	235.8	4.57		7.0	7.6		

H. C. 30   0ʰ   32ᵐ : + 2°   21′.

	°	″	wt	m	m	h	
1892.787	43.4	5.79	3	8.8	9.3	23.3	J
.822	42.6	5.87	3	8.5	9.3	23.3	J
1892.804	43.0	5.83		8.6	9.3		

Σ 51   0ʰ   37ᵐ : + 16°   42′.

1892.748	127.1	3.86	. . .	. . .	. . .	23.3	J
.787	127.2	3.89	2	8.0	9.2	22.0	J
.828	129.1	4.23	2	8.0	9.2	23.5	J
.847	130.1	4.08	2	8.0	9.0	3.1	J
1892.802	128.9	4.02		8.0	9.1		

Σ 60   0ʰ   42ᵐ : + 57°   11′.

1892.778	195.0	4.88	. . .	4.0	7.5	4.7	C
.924	199.6	4.92	3	4.0	8.0	1.8	C
1892.851	197.3	4.90		4.0	7.8		
1892.946	197.4	4.75	2	4.0	8.0	3.7	J

β 1   0ʰ   46 ᵐ : + 55°   58′.

A : B.

1892.866	83.7	1.46	2	8.2	10.0	2.7	J
3.049	84.0	1.49	2	8.0	10.2	4.2	J
1892.958	83.8	1.48		8.1	10.1		

A : C.

1892.866	132.2	3.66	3	8.2	8.4	2.8	J
.926	133.3	3.55	2	8.2	8.7	2.9	J
1892.896	132.8	3.60		8.2	8.6		

A : D.

1892.866	193.2	8.60	2	8.2	9.1	2.9	J
.926	193.3	9.06	2	8.2	9.2	3.0	J
1892.896	193.2	8.83		8.2	9.2		

Σ 73   0ʰ   48ᵐ : + 22°   58′.

1892.852	11.8	1.30	1	6.0	6.8	4.2	J
.880	12.5	1.11	2	6.2	6.7	2.0	J
1892.866	12.2	1.20		6.1	6.8		

OΣ 20   0ʰ   48ᵐ : + 18°   32′.

1892.926	348.0	. . .	2	6.5	. . .	2.5	J
.932	344.6	0.74	2	6.5	7.0	1.9	J
1892.929	346.3	0.74		6.5	7.0		

So. 390 0ʰ 52ᵐ : — 16° 20′.

	°	″	wt	m	m	h
1892.921	214.6	5.98	2	7.2	7.8	2.3
.926	213.4	6.34	2	6.8	7.6	0.5
1892.924	214.0	6.16		7.0	7.7	

Σ 87 0ʰ 59ᵐ : + 14° 44′.

1892.787	193.6	6.98	3	8.0	9.0	22.8
.789	194.4	6.86	3	8.0	8.8	23.1
1892.788	194.0	6.92		8.0	8.9	

Σ 91 1ʰ 1ᵐ : — 2° 24′.

1892.748	322.1	4.30	. . .	. . .	. . .	1.3
.778	321.3	4.15	3	7.0	8.0	1.8
.817	322.3	3.79	2	7.0	8.0	23.8
.822	322.2	3.90	3	7.5	8.2	23.8
.921	320.6	4.09	2	7.1	8.1	3.1
1892.817	321.7	4.05		7.2	8.1	

β 303 1ʰ 3ᵐ : + 23° 9′.

1892.847	283.6	0.92	. 2	7.0	7.0	2.7
.850	285.4	0.94	3	7.0	7.2	21.8
1892.848	284.5	0.93		7.0	7.1	

β 235 1ʰ 3ᵐ : + 50° 22′.

1892.850	86.5	0.81	3	7.0	7.4	22.1
.866	. . .	0.92	2	6.8	7.2	2.3
.926	81.6	0.87	3	7.6	7.6	3.0
1892.884	84.0	0.87		7.1	7.4	

OΣ 24 1ʰ 4ᵐ : + 50° 22′.

1892.926	47.9	. . .	2	9.0	10.2	3.3
3.049	47.9	6.34	2	9.6	10.6	3.9
1892.988	47.9	6.34	↿	9.3	10.4	

Companion very faint.

H. C. W. 1ʰ 12ᵐ : — 23° 20′.

1892.882	242.9	9.08	1	8.5	9.5	1.4
.932	240.7	9.27	1	8.1	9.3	2.2
1892.907	241.8	9.18		8.3	9.4	

Σ 113 1ʰ 14ᵐ : — 1° 8′.

	°	″	wt	m	m	h
1892.830	348.0	1.33	4	6.5	7.2	1.2.
.847	350.7	1.38	2	6.6	7.1	3.3
1892.838	349.4	1.36		6.6	7.2	

h. 2036 1ʰ 14ᵐ : — 16° 25′.

1892.882	17.4	1.16	3	9.2	10.2	1.0
.902	18.2	1.17	2	9.5	10.5	1.6
1892.892	17.8	1.16		9.4	10.4	

G. L. J. 1ʰ 16ᵐ : + 16° 14′.

1892.894	16.2	2.69	1	9.2	10.2	1.3
.899	15.9	3.02	2	9.5	10.5	0.2
1892.896	16.0	2.86		9.4	10.4	

Σ 122 1ʰ 21ᵐ : + 2° 55′.

1892.784	325.8	7.06	2	7.0	9.2	0.3
.787	325.3	7.05	3	. . .	. . .	22.3
1892.786	325.6	7.06		7.0	9.2	

Σ 138 1ʰ 30ᵐ : + 7° 0′.

1892.946	214.1	1.19	3	7.5	7.5	1.8
3.019	213.2	1.33	1	8.2	8.2	2.9
1892.982	213.6	1.26		7.8	7.8	

Σ 147 1ʰ 36ᵐ : — 11° 55′.

1892.784	90.0	4.10	2	6.5	7.3	0.8
.787	89.9	4.08	3	6.3	7.0	23.7
.817	87.8	3.53	3	6.0	7.2	0.3
.822	86.9	3.51	3	6.0	7.5	0.1
1892.802	88.6	3.80		6.2	7.2	

Σ 155 1ʰ 38ᵐ : + 8° 51′.

1892.882	331.5	4.62	3	7.0	7.2	1.7
.902	330.3	4.48	2	• 7.2	7.6	1.7
1892.892	330.9	4.55		7.1	7.4	

Σ 174 1ʰ 44ᵐ : + 21° 41′.

1892.828	174.1	2.92	1	6.5	6.9	23.9
.847	168.2	2.96	3	6.0	7.3	3.8
1892.838	171.2	2.94		6.2	· 7.1	

Σ 178 1ʰ 46ᵐ : + 10° 13′.

	o	″	wt	m	m	h
1892.817	196.7	3.28	3	7.5	7.5	1.0
.822	197.5	2.96	3	7.5	7.5	0.4
1892.820	197.1	3.12		7.5	7.5	

Σ 180 1ʰ 47ᵐ : + 18° 42′.

1892.899	178.9	8.53	3	4.5	4.5	23.8
.918	180.2	8.25	3	4.7	4.7	1.8
· 1892.908	179.6	8.39		4.6	4.6	

β 260 1ʰ 47ᵐ : + 14° 51′.

1892.866	232.7	0.70	2	8.0	8.0	0.9

Σ 202 1ʰ 56ᵐ : + 2° 11′.

1892.946	320.5	2.94	3	3.5	4.5	1.6
3.019	320.9	3.11	1	4.0	5.0	3.1
1892.982	320.7	3.02		3.8	4.8	

Σ 218 2ʰ 2ᵐ : − 1° 0′.

1892.882	250.6	4.57	3	7.2	8.0	1.9
.921	247.6	4.78	2	7.2	8.2	2.3
1892.902	249.1	4.68		7.2	8.1	

Σ 227 2ʰ 5ᵐ : + 29° 44′.

1892.789	76.7	3.89	3	5.3	6.3	23.4
3.036	77.4	3.67	2	5.0	6.2	0.7
1892.912	77.0	3.78		5.2	6.2	

Σ 232 2ʰ 8ᵐ : + 29° 50′.

1892.789	247.3	6.21	3	8.0	8.0	23.8
.828	248.4	6.15	2	7.5	7.5	0.2
1892.808	247.8	6.18		7.8	7.8	

Σ 262 2ʰ 19ᵐ : + 66° 52′.
A : B.

1892.885	255.5	2.04	2	4.5	8.0	0.8
3.049	255.6	2.06	3	4.5	7.5	6.2
1892.967	255.6	2.05		4.5	7.8	
1992.924	254.5	2.05	3	5.0	8.0	1.0

A : C.

	°	″	wt	m	m	h	
1892.885	111.6	7.02	2	4.5	8.4	0.9	J
3.049	111.9	7.14	3	4.5	8.2	6.2	J
1892.967	111.8	7.08		4.5	8.3		
1892.924	111.9	7.29	3	5.0	8.5	1.2	C

Σ 280   2ʰ 28ᵐ : — 6° 10′.

1892.828	345.9	3.38	2	7.5	7.5	0.4	J
.830	345.6	3.23	3	7.5	7.7	1.4	J
1892.829	345.8	3.30		7.5	7.6		

Σ 291   2ʰ 34ᵐ : + 18° 17′.

1892.822	119.2	3.36	3	7.2	7.5	0.8	J
.830	118.2	3.32	3	7.5	7.7	1.8	J
1892.826	118.7	3.34		7.4	7.6		

Σ 299   2ʰ 37ᵐ : + 2° 45′.

1892.784	294.7	2.97	3	4.0	6.2	1.3	J
.789	293.8	3.37	3	4.0	6.2	0.1	J
.817	293.0	3.49	. . .	. . .	. . .	0.7	J
1892.797	293.8	3.28		4.0	6.2		

Σ 300   2ʰ 38ᵐ : + 28ᵘ 57′.

1892.946	304.6	3.01	2	7.8	8.0	0.6	J
.959	302.0	2.90	1	8.0	8.2	5.7	J
1892.952	303.3	2.96		7.9	8.1		

β 83   2ʰ 40ᵐ : — 5ᵘ 28′.

1892.880	112.6	0.86	2	8.0	8.8	2.3	J

Σ 305   2ʰ 41ᵐ : + 18° 52′.

1892.830	319.3	2.86	3	7.5	7.9	1.7	J
.847	319.9	2.75	2	7.0	7.8	4.1	J
.946	316.9	3.02	3	7.0	7.8	1.4	J
1892.874	318.7	2.88		7.2	7.8		

Σ 313   2ʰ 43ᵐ : + 8° 27′..

1892.828	192.9	5.32	2	8.8	9.0	0.7	J
.880	192.8	5.23	3	9.0	9.2	2.6	J
1892.854	192.8	5.28		8.9	9.1		

Σ 315 2^h 44^m : $- 11°$ $2'$.

	°	″	wt	m	m	h
1892.830	156.9	2.43	3	7.5	8.2	2.1
.847	156.8	2.50	2	7.5	8.5	3.6
1892.838	156.8	2.46		7.5	8.4	

Σ 323 2^h 46^m : $+ 5°$ $59'$.

1892.828	283.0	2.95	2	8.0	8.2	0.9
.830	282.6	2.59	3	7.8	7.8	2.4
1892.829	282.8	2.77		· 7.9	8.0	

Σ 334 2^h 53^m : $+ 6°$ $10'$.

1892.822	318.7	1.63	3	7.9	8.2	2.5
.830	318.9	1.67	3	7.5	7.9	2.5
1892.826	·318.8	1.65		7.7	8.0	

Σ 355 3^h 1^m : $+ 7°$ $56'$.

1892.784	146.8	.2.62	3	8.9	9.3	1.5
.789	144.5	2.56	3	9.0	9.2	0.4
.817	139.7	2.52	2	9.0	9.2	1.1
.946	144.5	. . .	1	9.0	9.2	1.0
1892.834	143.9	2.57		9.0	9.2	

OΣ 50 3^h 1^m : $+ 71°$ $6'$.

1892.852	201.3	1.08	2	7.2	7.2	4.5
.885	204.8	1.20	2	7.0	7.0	1.4
1892.868	203.0	1.14		7.1	7.1	

OΣ 52 3^h 7^m : $+ 65°$ $13'$.

1892.852	129 6	0.75	3	6.0	6.8	5.8
.932	133.3	0.87	2	6.5	7.0	1.7
1892.892	131.4	0.81		6.2	6.9	

Σ 394 3^h 21^m : $+ 20°$ $3'$.

1892.789	161.3	7.52	3	6.0	7.5	1.6
.817	161.0	7.23	2	6.0	7.2	1.6
1892.803	161.2	7.38		6.0	7.4	

Σ 403 3^h 24^m : $+ 19°$ $22'$.

1892.789	176.5	3.30	2	8.2	8.2	1.3
.817	176.7	3.22	2	8.0	8.0	1.3
1892.803	176.6	3.26		8.1	8.1	

Σ 422 3^h 30^m : + 0° 12'.

	°	''	wt	m	m	h	
1892.789	247.2	6.74	3	6.0	8.3	0.7	J
.817	247.2	6.37	3	6.0	8.2	2.2	J
1892.803	247.2	6.56		6.0	8.2		

Σ 425 3^h 32 : + 33° 44'.

1892.748	99.0	2.29	. . .	. . .	. .	0.5	J
.828	97.8	2.58	1	8.0	8.0	1.2	J
1892.788	98.4	• 2.44		8.0	8.0		

Σ 460 3^h 50^m : + 80° 22'.

1892.885	41.3	1.00	2	5.0	6.0	1.7	J
.918	38.8	1.03	2	5.6	- 6.5	1.3	J
1892.902	40.0	1.02		5.3	6.2		
1892.924	38.2	0.98	3	. . .	. . .	2.2	C

Σ 491 3^h 59^m : + 10° 39'.

1892.822	109.7	2.85	2	8.2	9.0	2.8	J
.932	108.2	· 2.82	3	8.0	9.0	3.3	J
1892.877	108.0	2.84		8.1	9.0		

OΣ 531 3^h 59^m : + 37° 46'.

1892.890	132.3	2.18	3	9.6	9.5	6.5	J
3.047	131.0	2.19	2	7.6	9.9	6.2	J
1892.968	131.6	2.18		7.6	9.7		

Σ 494 4^h 1^m : + 22° 47'.

1892.789	185.7	5.23	3	8.0	8.0	1.0	J
.822	188.7	5.31	2	7.8	7.8	1.4	J
1892.806	187.2	5.27		7.9	7.9		

Σ 495 4^h 1^m : + 14° 50'.

1892.828	222.5	3.70	2	6.2	8.5	2.8	J
.946	220.3	3.70	2	6.0	8.2	2.4	J
1892.887	221.4	3.70		6.1	8.4		

Σ 536 4^h 16^m : — 4° 58'.

1892.926	163.5	1.72	2	7.8	8.6	3.9	J
3.036	165.4	1.60	1	8.0	8.8	5.6	J
1892.981	164.4	1.66		7.9	8.7		

Σ 535   4^h 17^m : + 11° 5′.

	o	″	wt	m	m	h
1892.882	331.7	0.98	2	7.2	8.2	2.2
.932	331.9	1.52	3	7.0	8.2	3.8
1892.907	331.8	1.25		7.1	8.2	

Σ 565   4^h 30^m : + 41° 52′.

						.
1892.847	173.5	1.92	2	7.2	8.4	1.9
.932	173.6	1.46	2	7.0	8.0	6.6
.946	172.6	1.73	2	7.3	8.5	1.1
1892.908	173.2	1.70		7.2	8.3	

Σ 577   4^h 34^m : + 37° 15′.

1892.891	73.1	1.43	2	7.7	7.9	6.8
.946	73.3	1.24	2	8.0	8.0	2.3
1892.918	73.2	1.34	•	7.8	8.0	

Σ 589   4^h 38^m : + 5° 4′.

1892.784	301.8	4.85	2	8.0	8.0	2.3
.789	299.4	4.61	2	8.0	8.0	1.9
1892.786	300.6	4.73		8.0	8.0	

Σ 622   4^h 51^m : + 1° 29′.

1892.789	169.7	2.33	2	8.0	8.5	2.4
.918	173.4	2.46	3	8.2	8.7	4.3
1892.854	171.6	2.40		8.1	8.6	

Σ 630   4^h 56^m : + 1° 26′.

1892.918	49.6	14.40	2	6.6	7.8	4.5
3.019	49.2	14.27	2	7.0	8.0	3.8
1892.968	49.4	14.34		6.8	7.9	

OΣ 98   5^h 1^m : + 8° 20′.

1892.852	189.3	1.02	3	6.0	6.5	3.9
.891	187.9	0.96	3	6.0	7.0	7.2
1892.872	188.6	0.99		6.0	6.8	

Σ 644   5^h 2^m : + 37° 9′.

1892.847	224.3	1.74	2	7.0	7.0	2.2
.932	223.0	1.38	4	7.0	7.0	3.4
1892.890	223.6	1.56		7.0	7.0	

h 3752   5ʰ   17ᵐ : — 24° 53′.

	°	″		m	m	h
1892.932	103.2	3.37		5.6	6.8	5.6
.946	104.9	3.22	⚥	6.0	7.2	5.4
1892.939	104.0	3.30		5.8	7.0	

O. S.   5ʰ   18ᵐ : — 10° 32′.

1892.932	126.2	1.17	2	8.2	8.2	5.8
3.049	127.5	1.13	1	8.0	8.0	5.3
1892.990	126.8	1.15		8.1	8.1	

Σ 716   5ʰ   22ᵐ : + 15° 3′.

1892.926	200.2	4.45	2	6.0	6.5	4.1
.929	200.9	4.74	3	6.0	6.5	6.8
1892.928	200.6	4.60		6.0	6.5	

Σ 734   5ʰ   27ᵐ : — 1° 48′.

1892.918	356.2	1.60	2	7.5	8.5	4.1
.932	352.2	1.68	3	7.0	8.5	4.2
1892.925	354.2	1.64		7.2	8.5	

Σ 742   5ʰ   29ᵐ : + 21° 55′.

1892.926	259.1	3.38	3	7.2	7.7	4.2
.929	258.0	3.31	4	7.2	7.7	7.0
1892.928	258.6	3.34		7.2	7.7	

D 4   5ʰ   29ᵐ : — 4° 55′.

1892.929	217.6	1.80	2	4.5	8.0	6.0
3.047	218.1	1.80	2	5.0	8.0	6.6
1892.988	217.8	1.80		4.8	8.0	

β 94   5ʰ   44ᵐ : — 14° 31′.

1892.932	178.3	2.43	3	6.0	8.4	5.4
3.049	179.0	2.52	2	5.9	8.3	5.6
1892.990	178.6	2.48		6.0	8.4	

So. 503   5ʰ   49ᵐ : + 13° 56′.

1892.891	348.2	5.13	2	7.4	8.5	7.0
.918	345.5	5.37	2	7.2	8.5	4.7
.926	343.4	5.68	2	6.8	8.0	4.4
.932	344.3	5.27	4	6.8	8.0	4.3
1892.917	345.4	5.36		7.0	8.2	

β 18 6^h 11^m : — 12° 0'.

	o	"	wt	m	m	h
1892.932	273.5	1.21	2	8.0	9.0	5.9

β 568 6^h 18^m : — 19° 43'.

| 1892.932 | 156.1 | 1.07 | 1 | 7.0 | 8.0 | 6.1 |

Σ 941 6^h 30^m : + 41° 41'.

1892.929	81.0	1.78	2	7.0	7.8	8.3
.932	81.1	1.78	4	7.0	8.0	3.6
1892.930	81.0	1.78		7.0	7.9	

Σ 948. 6^h 36^m : + 59° 34'.

A : B.

1892.902	119.9	. . .	. . .	5.5	6.0	2.5
.918	119.3	1.32	2	5.5	6.0	3.7
.929	122.0	1.56	4	5.7	6.0	8.6
1892.916	120.4	1.44		5.6	6.0	

A : C.

1892.918	307.9	8.40	2	5.5	7.2	3.8
.929	305.0	8.58	4	5.7	7.2	8.6
1892.924	306.4	8.49		5.6	7.2	

β 324 6^h 45^m : — 23° 56'.

| 1892.932 | 199.0 | 1.74 | 2 | 7.0 | 8.2 | 6.3 |

Σ 1110 7^h 27^m : + 32° 9'.

1892.932	227.7	5.62	3	. . .	. . .	4.8
3.044	229.7	5.51	2	3.0	4.0	10.8
1892.988	228.7	5.57		3.0	4.0	

Σ 1157 7^h 49^m : — 2° 29'.

1892.929	245.4	1.01	3	8.0	8.0	7.5
3.047	245.9	1.00	3	8.C	8.0	7.8
1892.988	245.6	1.00		8.0	8.0	

Σ 1196 8^h 5^m : + 18° 1'.

A : B.

1892.852	30.5	1.06	3	5.0	5.8	6.3
.880	30.0	0.99	4	5.2	5.7	9.7
.929	25.6	0.91	3	. . .	. . .	7.8
1892.887	28.7	0.99		5.1	5.8	

A : C.

	°	″	wt	m	m	h	
1892.852	117.6	4.80	2	5.0	5.8	6.5	J
.880	117.7	5.29	4	5.2	5.8	9.5	J
.929	118.4	5.49	3	. . .	. . .	7.7	J
1892.887	117.9	5.19		5.1	5.8		

β 1244 8ʰ 8ᵐ : + 2° 21′.

1892.880	51.1	0.70	2	8.0	8.0	9.8	J

β 24 8ʰ 48ᵐ : — 8° 18′.

1892.929	172.2	0.95	2	7.5	8.0	8.8	J

Σ 1670 12ʰ 36ᵐ : — 0° 47′.

1892.880	152.0	5.80	4	. . .	. . .	10.1	J
3.044	152.2 ·	5.86	3	. . .	. . .	12.6	J
1892.962	152.1	5.83					

Σ 2130 17ʰ 3ᵐ : + 54° 37′.

1892.704	155.2	2.60	2	5.0	5.0	20.2	C

Σ 2481 19ʰ 7ᵐ : + 38° 36′

1892.746	224.0	3.67	. . .	. . .	. . .	23.5	J
.762	225.5	4.05	. . .	. . .	. . .	0.0	J
.765	226.7	3.76	. . .	. . .	. . .	23.8	J
1892.758	225.4	3.83					

Σ 2579 19ʰ 41ᵐ : + 44° 50′.

1892.724	307.7	1.57	2	3.0	8.0	21.6	C

Σ 2576 19ʰ 41ᵐ : + 33° 20′

1892.762	114.7	3.01	. . .	8.0	8.0	23.5	J
.778	114.3	3.01	3	8.0	8.0	23.5	J
1892.770	114.5	3.01		8.0	8.0		

Σ 2583 19ʰ 43ᵐ : + 11° 31′.

1892.850	118.0	1.25	2	6.0	6.5	20 3	J
.866	118.2	1.43	2	6.0	6.4	21.4	J
1892.858	118.1	1.34		6.0	6.4		

Σ 2596 19ʰ 48ᵐ : + 14° 59′. ·

1892.748	327.9	1.99	. . .	. . .	. . .	22.0	J
.822	330.9	2.04	2	7.0	9.0	22.7	J
1892.785	329.4	2.02		7.0	9.0		

Σ 2644   20ʰ   6ᵐ : + 0°   31′.

	°	″	wt	m	m	h
1892.809	216.4	3.44	. . .	6.5	7.0	21.1
.817	212.2	3.41	2	6.8	7.0	22.0
1892.813	214.3	3.42		6.6	7.0	

Σ 2725   20ʰ   40ᵐ : + 15°   28′.

1892.748	0.6	4.47	. . .	. . .	. . .	21.5
.778	1.7	4.55	3	7.5	8.0	23.0
1892.763	1.2	4.51		7.5	8.0	

Σ 2742   20ʰ   56ᵐ : + 6°   42′.

1892.817	223.5´	2.51	1	7.0	7.0	22.3
.828	223.9	2.55	1	7.3	7.3	21.3
1892.822	223.7	2.53		7.2	7.2	

h 5252   21ʰ   6ᵐ : — 15°   29′.

1892.748	321.3	3.04	. . .	. . .	. . .	22.3
.768	319.9	3.01	1	. . .	. . .	0.5
.781	320.7	3.04	3 .	8.0	8.0	20.8
1892.766	320.6	3.03		8.0	8.0	

Σ 2804   21ʰ   27ᵐ : + 20°   11′.

1892.746	330.4	2.80	. . .	. . .	. . .	0.0
.765	331.8	2.94	. . .	. . .	. .	0.3
1892.756	331.1	2.87				

Σ 2826   21ʰ   41ᵐ : — 13°   41′.

1892.828	84.6	3.64	2	8.0	8.5	22.3
.882	82.6	3.88	1	8.0	8.3	23.2
1892.855	83.6	3.76		8.0	8.4	

Σ 2843   21ʰ   49ᵐ : + 65°   11′.

1892.847	138.0	2.12	3	7.4	7.7	0.3
.885	138.0	1.83	3	7.2	7.5	23.0
1892.866	138.0	1.98		7.3	. 7.6	

Σ 2854   21ʰ   58ᵐ : + 13°   4′.

1892.850	82.4	2.76	2	7.5	8.0	22.8
.882	81.5	2.78	2	7.5	7.7	23.3
1892.866	82.0	2.77		7.5	7.8	

Σ 2863 22ʰ 0ᵐ : + 64° 2′.

	°	″	wt	m	m	h	
1892.768	283.3	6.75	3	. . .	. . .	1.8	J
.778	282.7	6.80	3	5.0	7.0	0.7	J
1892.773	283.0	6.78		5.0	7.0		

Σ 2903 22ʰ 18ᵐ : + 66° 6′.

1892.885	96.6	4.44	2	7.0	8.0	23.7	J
.918	96.9	4.00	2	7.0	8.0	1.1	J
1892.902	96.8	4.22		7.0	8.0		

Sh 345 22ʰ 20ᵐ : — 17° 21′.

1892.789	306.5	7.46	3	6.8	6.8	21.8	J
.822	308.1	7.66	3	6.6	6.6	22.9	J
.921	306.6	. . .	1	6.0	6.5	23 7	J
.932	306.8	7.07	2	6.0	6.5	0.6	J
1892.866	307.0	7.40		6.4	6.6		

Σ 2905 22ʰ 21ᵐ : + 14° 32′.

1892.850	283.1	3.37	2	8.0	8.3	22 5	J
.882	283 5	3.23	1	8.0	8.5	23.7	J
1892.866	283.3	3.30		8.0	8.4		

h 3114 22ʰ 21ᵐ : — 17° 53′.

1892.921	93.7	6.57	1	7.8	8.6	23.9	J
.932	94.7	7.11	2	8.0	9.0	0.3	J
1892.926	94.2	6.84		7.9	8.8		

β 1218 22ʰ 23ᵐ : + 29° 5′.

1892.926	58.4	1.07	2	8.0	8.5	0.7	J
.932	55.9	1.14	2	8.0	8.5	1.4	J
1892.929	57.2	1.10		8.0	8.5		

Σ 2909 22ʰ 23ᵐ : — 0° 38′.

1892.740	323.8	3.27	. . .	. . .	. . .	0.0	J
.743	325.7	3.11	. . .	. . .	. . .	19.5	J
.765	323.9	3.04	. . .	. . .	. . .	23.0	J
1892.749	324.5	3.14					

Σ 2913 22ʰ 24ᵐ : — 8° 44′.

	°	″	wt	m	m	h	
1892.830	331.4	8.66	3	6.5	7.5	21.8	J
.847	330.5	8.19	1	6.6	7.5	21.7	J
1892.838	· 331.0	8.42		6.6	7.5		

Σ 2915 22ʰ 27ᵐ : + 6° 48′.

1892.743	152.3	11.40	. . .	. . .	. . .	23.0	J
.778	152.5	12.30	3	8.5	·	8.5	22.5	J
1892.760	152.4	11.85		8 5	8.5		

Σ 2928 22ʰ 23ᵐ : — 13° 14′.

1892.748	312.9	.4.04	. . .	. . .	. . .	22.7	J
.778	312.4	4.00	3	. .	. . .	0.0	J
.817	318.0	4.42	2	8.0	8.0	22.8	J
.828	319.8	4.22	1	7.8	8.0	21.5	J
.932	315.7	4.16	2	8.0	8.2	0.8	· J
1892.821	315.8	4.17		7.9	8.1		

Σ 2935 22ʰ 37 : — 8° 56′.

1892.828 ·	311.9	2.70	1	7.5	8.0	22.0	J
.830	311.1	2.76	2	7.0	8.0	22.4	J
1892.829	311.5	2.73		7.2	8.0		

Σ 2944 22ʰ 42ᵐ : — 4° 51′.

1892.746	255.7	3.67	. . .	. . .	. . .	1.5	J
.765	255.4	3.86	. . .	. . .	. . .	0.8	J
.828	256.8	3.63	1	7.0	7.2	21.8	J
.830	251.2	3.54	2	6.8	7.0	21.5	J
.926	257.1	3.28	3	7.0	7.5	23.8	J
1892.819	255.2	3.59		6.9	7.2		

Σ 2947 22ʰ 45ᵐ : + 67° 56′.

1892.768	68.6	3.55	3	. . .	. . .	1.5	J
.778	68.6	3.31	3	7.0	7.0	1.5	J
.847	65.7	3.39	3	6.8	7.0	0.6	J
1892.798	67.6	8.42		6.9	7.0		

Σ 2948 22ʰ 45ᵐ : + 65° 55′.

1892.847	3.7	2.76	3	6.5	8.0	1.8	J
.885	2.4	2.65	3	6.5	8.2	0.2	J
1892 866	3.0	2.70		6.5	8.1		

Σ 2950 22ʰ 47ᵐ : + 61° 4′.

	°	″	wt	m	m	h	
1892.847	312.7	2.28	3	5.8	7.0	1.1	J
.885	307.6	2.26	2	5.6	6.8	1.1	J
.926	312.9	2.37	3	6.2	7.4	0.4	J
1892.886	311.1	2.30		5.9	7.1		

OΣ 483 22ʰ 53ᵐ : + 11° 5′.

1892.926	221.3	0.73	2	6.5	8.0	0.1	J
.932	223.3	0.98	2	6.5	7.6	. 1.3	J
1892.929	222.3	0.86		6.5	7.8		

OΣ 489 23ʰ 4ᵐ : + 74° 44′.

1892.778	43.0	1.23	2	5.0	8.0	3.3	C
1892.885	31.9	1.40	1	5.0	8.0	3.3	J

Σ 2988 23ʰ 6ᵐ : — 12° 35′

1892.817	280.6	3.74	2	7.5	7.5	23.0	J
.828	280.0	3.61	2	7.6	7.6	22.8	J
1892.822	280.3	3.68		7.6	7.6		

Σ 3001 23ʰ 14ᵐ : + 67° 27′.

1892.847	195.1	2.73	2	5.0	7.3	1.3	J
.866	193.0	2.77	4	5.0	7.0	2.2	J
.926	197.2	2.93	3	5.0	7.0	1.2	J
1892.880	195.1	2.81		5.0	7.1		

Σ 30υ8 23ʰ 18ᵐ : — 9° 7′.

1892.926	246.9	4.03	3	5.2	7.2	1.3	J
.932	246.3	4.39	3	5.5	6.8	1.0	J
1892.929	246.6	4.21		5.4	7.0		

So. 356 23ʰ 40ᵐ : — 19° 21′.

1892.789	140.1	. 6.20	3	6.2	8.0	22.2	J
.817	138.9	6.38	2	6.0	8.0	2.25	J
.882	140.3	5.97	3	5.5	6.5	0.0	J
.902	137.4	6.17	3	6.0	7.0	23.9	J
1892.848	139.2	6.18		5.9	7.4		

Σ 3050 23ʰ 53ᵐ : + 33° 4′.

1892.926	209.0	2.70	4	6.0	6.0	1.8	J
.973	211.0	2.51	2	6.2	6.2	1.8	J
1892.950	210.0	2.60		6.1	6.1		

			β 1154	23^h	55^m : + 74°	10′.		
	°	″	wt	m	m	h		
1892.866	129.6	0.96	2	8.0	8.0	1.9	J
.885	129.8	0.86	1	8.0	8.4	23.5	J
1892.876	129.7	0.91		8.0	8.2		

			Σ 3057	23^h	59^m : + 57°	52′.	
1892.778	295.4	3.56	2	7.0	9.0	3.8	C

OBSERVATIONS OF VARIABLE STARS.

The method pursued in the following observations is similar to Argelander's except that two stars were always chosen, the one brighter than the variable, the other fainter, and the difference in magnitude between these two was called ten steps.

As the values of these steps varied for the different pairs of comparison stars, it was considered impracticable to reduce them all to one standard. Hence no light series has been made. Care was taken that the difference in magnitude between the comparison stars be not too great, more than 0.8 of a degree being considered unreliable. "Harvard Photometry Observations" were used as authority for magnitudes.

The observations between July 4th and September 18th were made at Union Springs, N. Y., the remainder at Haverford College.

β Lyræ R. A. 18ʰ 46ᵐ: Dec. + 33° 14′.

	mag.			mag.			mag.
July 4,	3.71		Aug. 3,	3.72		Sept. 2,	3.40
" 5,	3.60		" 10,	3.75		" 3,	3.43
" 6,	3.40		" 15,	3.46		" 6,	3.52
" 9,	4.29		" 16,	3.64		" 7,	3.58
" 11,	3.83		" 17,	3.92		" 8,	3.46
" 12,	3.72		" 18,	4.16		" 10,	3.40
" 14,	3.72		" 19,	4.40		" 11,	3.42
" 16,	3.95		" 20,	4.00		" 12,	3.88
" 18,	3.52		" 21,	3.72		" 15,	3.43
" 19,	3.46		" 23,	3.72		" 16,	3.40
" 20,	3.74		" 27,	3.52		" 17,	3.32
" 21,	3.95		" 28,	3.52		" 18,	3.40
" 22,	4.22		" 29,	3.69		" 20,	3.40
" 23,	4.44		" 30,	3.86		" 22,	3.30
" 25,	3.72		" 31,	4.11		" 23,	3.40
" 26,	3.66					" 24,	3.43
" 28,	3.77					" 25,	3.94
" 30,	3.83					" 26,	3.88
" 31,	3.52					" 27,	3.61
						" 28,	3.40

η Aquilæ R. A. 19ʰ 47ᵐ : Dec. + 0° 44′.

	mag.			mag.			mag.			mag.
Aug. 18,	3.62 ·	Sept.	2,	4.15	Oct.	1,	3.93	Nov. 4,	4.18
" 19,	3.71	"	3,	4.15	"	2,	4.04	" 5,	3.69
" 20,	3.88	"	4,	3.93	"	7,	3.88	" 6,	3.83
" 21,	3.92	"	6,	4.20	"	9,	3.85	" 8,	4.04
" 23,	4.10	"	7,	4.30	"	11,	4.21		
" 27,	3.93	"	8,	3.93	"	12,	4.48		
" 28,	3.93	"	9,	3.69	"	13,	4.35		
" 29,	4.10 ·	"	10,	3.81	"	14,	3.93		
" 30,	4.25	"	11,	3.88	"	16,	3.88		
" 31,	4.35	"	12,	3.93	"	18,	4.00		
		"	15,	3.94	"	20,	4.85		
		"	16,	3.82	"	21,	4.23		
		"	17,	3.91	"	26,	4.42		
		"	18,	3.97	"	28,	4.18		
		"	20,	4.00	"	29,	3.86		
		"	22,	4.10	"	30,	3.93		
		"	23,	3.69					
		"	24,	3.62					
		"	25,	3.83					
		"	26,	3.85					
		"	27,	4.47					
		"	28,	4.52					
		"	29,	4.35					
		"	30,	4.15					

There seems to have been a period of special brightness in β Lyræ from September 2d till September 28th, the maximum having occurred September 22d, when the magnitude was estimated at 3.30. β Lyræ and η Aquilæ are both so well known that it is unnecessary to estimate their periods from the observations. But from a magnitude curve which has been drawn it is evident that the observed periods and those already established are sufficiently accordant.

R Lyræ R. A. 18ʰ 52ᵐ : + 43° 48′.

	mag.			mag.			mag.
Oct. 18,	4.49	Nov. 5,	4.44	Dec. 1,	4.43
" 19,	4.49	" 6,	4.25	" 2,	4.47
" 20,	4.53	" 8,	4.35	" 3,	4.47
" 21,	4.49	" 13,	4.34	' 5,	4.46
" 26,	4.76	" 17,	4.36	" 9,	4.45
" 28,	4.52	" 18,	4.35	" 10,	4.51
" 29,	4.52	" 20,	4.35	" 12,	4.47
" 30,	4.47	" 21,	4.34	" 20,	4.45
		" 22,	4.40		

Fifteen observations were made between September 26th and October 18th, but as the curve is nearly regular, the magnitude varying less than 0.2 of a degree, it is not thought necessary to record them.

The following were taken as maximum and minima:

	mag.			mag.
Max. Nov. 6,	4.25	Min. Oct. 26,	4.76
		" Dec. 10,	4.51

These would give a period of 45 + days.

104 Aquarii R. A. 23ʰ 37ᵐ: Dec. — 18°42'.

	mag.			mag.			mag.			mag.
Sept. 26,	5.05	Oct. 1,	4.81	Nov. 6,	4.73	Dec. 5,	4.95
" 27,	4.85	" 2,	4.76	" 8,	4.85	" 12,	4.75
" 28,	4.80	" 7,	5.04	" 13,	4.76	" 18,	4.75
" 30,	4.69	" 9,	5.04	" 16,	4.91	" 20,	4.91
		" 11,	4.97	" 17,	4.96		
		" 12,	4.93	" 18,	4.98		
		" 16,	4.86	" 20,	4.94		
		" 18,	4.76	" 21,	4.91		
		" 19,	4.88	" 22,	4.94.		
		" 21,	4.85				
		" 26,	4.84				
		" 28,	4.96				
		" 29,	5.05				
		" 30,	4.95				

From the magnitude curves drawn, the following were estimated as maxima and minima:

	mag.			mag.
Max. Oct. 1.0	4.66	Min. Oct. 9.5	5.08
19.4	4.76	30.3	5.05
Nov. 7.4	4.73	Nov. 19.0	5.00
. . . . . ,		Dec. 9.4	5.04
Dec. 16.5	4.67		

These give a mean period of 19.6 days.

GEORGE L. JONES.

January, 1893.

OBSERVATIONS OF COMETS.

Wolf's Periodic Comet (b 1891).

Swift's comet (a 1892).

Haverford M. T. 1892	*	No. Comp.	Comet—* Δα	Δδ	Comet's apparent α	δ	log pΔ for α	for δ	Obs.
2 17 9 23 55	1	9, 5	−0 16.52	+ 7 29.8	4 45 5.75	− 6 59 35.3	9.434	0.798	C
3 20 16 54 46	2	8, 5	−0 30.66	− 5 35.0	20 2 57.46	−18 45 25.4	n9.548	0.834	L
3 28 17 7 32	3	1, 3	−3 21.28	+ 5 15.8	20 36 27.27	−10 25 40.4	n9.518	0.808	L
3 29 16 36 38	4	4, 3	−6 25.29	+ 0 5.7	20 40 23.79	− 9 23 22.7	n9.556	0.797	J
4 6 16 25 57	5	7, 5	−0 5.52		21 10 55.19		n9.632		D
4 11 16 7 8	6	7, 5	+1 26.84	− 1 507	21 29 11.57	+ 4 3 1.2	n9.592	0.712	C
4 16 15 30 50	7	3, .	+5 31.28		21 46 31.42		n9.628		C
4 16 15 30 50	8	3, .	+5 17.30		21 46 31.25		n9.628		C
4 16 15 50 10	9	. 2	−4 17.44	− 1 58.0	22 9 50.77	+ 8 45 51.4	n9.534	0.710	L
4 23 1. 18 46	10	5, 3	+3 21.46	+ 0 34.4	22 19 20.05	+15 0 39.6	n9.619	0.649	G
4 26 15 51 26	11	6, 4	+0 48.50	+ 0 5.2	22 19 20.14	+17 25 31.6	n9.619	0.645	G
4 26 15 51 26	12	6, .	−0 7.24	− 2 19.1	22 43 36.50	+23 16 57.9	n9.660	0.623	C
5 4 15 17 10	13	10, 6	−6 53.40	+ 3 47.2	23 3 35.83	+27 43 4.7	n9.632	0.517	C
5 11 15 53 12	14	4, 1	−7 11.09	+ 5 1.1	23 3 36.04	+27 43 7.2	n9.632	0.517	C
5 11 15 53 12	15	4, 1	+2 53.40		23 19 31.46		n9.708		C
5 17 14 32 29	16	10, 5		− 8 52.9		+31 1 5.5		0.594	C
5 17 15 41 15	17	. 5	−1 40.72	+ 7 53.8	23 19 31.62	+31 1 6.3	n9.708	0.594	C
5 17 14 32 29	18	10, 5	−1 54.32	+ 3 10.7	23 34 39.47	+33 58 48.3	n9.708	0.594	C
5 23 14 48 39	19	10, 3	−7 30.48	+ 3 45.9	23 34 38.94	+33 58 50.6	n9.708	0.897	C
5 23 14 51 24	20	12, 6	+1 39.97	+ 0 52.2	23 50 59.26	+37 0 18.2	n9.730	0.897	C
5 30 14 25 6		12, 5	+0 40.77	− 5 41.1	23 50 59.65	+37 0 18.0	n9.730	0.914	C

Haverford M. T. (1892) mo d h m s	*	No. Comp.	Comet—* Δα (m s)	Δδ (' ")	Comet's apparent α (h m s)	δ (° ' ")	log pΔ for α (s)	for δ (")	Obs.
6 10 15 3 28	21	3, 3	−1 15.71	+4 15.7	0 12 51.16	+41 2 6.2	n9.703	0.753	C
7 18 12 2 23	22	6, 6	+0 29.31	+3 39.2	1 1 8.66	+50 4 5.0	n9.835	0.379	C
7 18 12 10 46	23	5, 5	−1 46.92	−4 10.3	1 1 8.42	+50 4 0.3	n9.835	0.379	C
9 24 9 7 58	24	6, 6	+0 16.80	−11 23.2	0 11 31.58	+48 40 35.8	n9.659	9.533	C
10 14 15 15 51	25	3, 3	+2 25.44	+2 28.2	23 51 30.07	+43 35 2.9	9.781	0.463	C
10 19 15 5 57	26	5, 5	−2 39.84	+1 48.3	23 49 7.89	+42 5 37.4	9.776	0.517	C
10 26 15 7 36	27	5, 5	−0 34.63	−8 47.8	23 45 57.62	+40 0 18.7	9.770	0.612	C
Winnecke's Periodic Comet (b 1892).									
5 16 11 11 11	28	5, 5	+0 58.14	−6 3.9	11 10 55.85	+44 30 6.0	9.719	0.131	C
5 31 11 6 34	29	5, 5	−1 40.83	+3 28.5	10 52 54.06	+43 23 19.8	9.776	0.447	C
Brooks' Comet (d 1892.)									
9 2 14 19 16	30	5, 6	−0 23.01	+5 25.6	6 11 41.52	+31 29 47.2	n9.708	0.588	C
9 15 14 46 59	31	5, 5	−2 28.56	−8 26.8	6 45 27.20	+29 49 15.2	n9.670	0.534	C
10 16 15 28 27	32	3, 3	−6 58.44	−12 18.8	8 19 31.26	+20 36 8.2	n9.545	0.462	C
11 13 17 30 41	33	2, 1	+0 51.73	−7 20.2	10 9 21.60	+0 52 52.3	n9.656	0.745	J
11 16 14 58 9	34	5, 5	+1 52.34	+1 0.9	10 22 51.22	−1 45 9.3	n9.565	0.762	C
11 20 16 22 49	35	3, 4	+4 12.94	+2 31.7	10 42 29.69	−5 59 7.2	n9.423	0.792	J
12 1 16 44 47	36	5, 5	−0 10.97	+6 59.6	11 35 32.62	−17 13 20.9	n9.388	0.850	J
12 4 17 52 51	37	3, 3	−4 57.60	−0 25.1	11 51 3.44	−20 12 52.5	n9.088	0.878	J
12 5 17 51 28	38	5, 5	+1 43.00	+4 23.8	11 56 55.54	−21 9 50.7	n9.119	0.883	C
12 11 18 0 36	39	5, 5	−2 18.67	−0 21.0	12 29 41.42	−26 32 54.5	n9.150	0.915	J

Holmes Comet (f 1892).

11 13 14 15 36	40	6, 3	—6 54.42	— 2 36.4	0 43 54.04	+37 52 38.9	9.746	0.546	C
11 13 14 15 36	41	6, 3	—3 5.53	— 5 32.0	0 43 5.88	+37 52 38.7	9.746	0.546	C
11 16 11 45 57	42	8, 5	—2 21.14	+ 0 59.8	0 42 58.13	+37 34 46.8	9.586	0.155	J
11 16 11 45 57	43	8, 5	—0 42.34	— 2 49.5	0 42 58.18	+37 34 46.6	9.586	0.155	J
11 18 12 15 32	42	4, 5	—2 48.03	— 5 56.9	0 42 31.24	+37 21 50.4	9.652	0.290	C
11 21 11 31 9	44	10, 5	+0 20.74	— 0 3.1	0 42 11.20	+37 2 52.0	9.594	0.195	J
11 23 12 4 21	45	2, 3	—5 34.19	— 0 52.3	0 42 1.00	+36 49 35.4	9.642	0.292	J

Brooks' Comet (g 1892).

12 11 16 37 39	46	4, 4	—2 20.10	+ 3 20.9	13 38 34.71	+27 48 58.0	n9.615	0.495	J

L = Prof. Leavenworth.   C = W. H. Collins.   D = J. H. Dennis.   G = E. H. Gifford.   J = Geo. L. Jones.

MEAN PLACES FOR 1892.0 OF COMPARISON STARS.

*	α	Red. to app. place	δ	Red. to app. place	Authority.
	h m s	s	o ′ ″	″	
1	4 45 22.27	−0.02	− 7 7 0.9	− 4.2	Schjellerup 1556.
2	20 3 28.82	−0.70	−18 39 42.0	− 8.4	Yarnall (F) 8915.
3	20 39 49.21	−0.65	−10 30 46.3	−10.2	Yarnall (F) 9271.
4	20 46 49.73	−0.65	− 9 23 18.1	−10.3	Mean Ephemeris, 1892.
5	21 11 1.26	−0.57	+ 4 5 4.6	−12.6	Seeliger, Vol. I, 27830.
6	21 27 45.30	−0.58	+ 8 50 36.9	−13.0	Ast. Ges. (Albany) 7535.
7	21 41 0.70	−0.55	+ 8 48 2.3	−13.0	$\frac{1}{2}$(Seeliger, Vol. I, 29471 + Lamont 6137).
8	21 41 14.50	−0.55	+15 0 18.5	−13.1	$\frac{1}{2}$(Seeliger, Vol. I, 29482 + Lamont 6139).
9	22 14 8.75	−0.54	+17 25 39.8	−13.4	Schjellerup 9123.
10	22 15 59.13	−0.54			Seeliger, Vol. I, 30772.
11	22 18 32.18	−0.54			Seeliger, Vol. I, 366.
12	22 44 3.25	−0.52	+23 19 29.0	−13.0	W. B.: XIII, $\frac{1}{2}$ (986 + 987).
13	23 10 29.77	−0.50	+27 39 30.8	−12.8	Yarnall (F), 10533.
14	23 10 47.67	−0.50	+27 38 19.3	−12.8	B. A. C. 8099.
15	23 16 38.48	−0.42	+31 13 14.6	−12.4	$\frac{1}{3}$(W. B.: XXIII, $\frac{1}{2}$ [306 + 307]) + $\frac{2}{3}$ [Leiden, Vol. V.]
16	23 21 12.79	−0.42	+31 9 12.2	−12.4	$\frac{1}{3}$(W. B.: XXIII, $\frac{1}{2}$ [395 + 396]) + $\frac{2}{3}$ [Leiden, Vol. V.]
17	23 36 34.20	−0.41	+33 55 48.3	−11.7	Leiden, Vol. V.
18	23 42 9.86	−0.41	+33 55 16.1	−11.7	Leiden, Vol. V.
19	23 49 19.55	−0.27	+36 59 37.0	−11.0	W. B.: XXIII, 994.
20	23 50 19.16	−0.27	+37 6 10.2	−11.0	W. B.: XXIII, $\frac{1}{2}$ (1012 + 1013.)
21	0 14 7.05	−0.18	+40 58 0.5	− 9.8	W. B.: XXIII, 344.
22	1 0 38.33	+1.02	+50 8 30.5	− 4.7	O. Arg., 1096.
23	1 2 54.32	+1.02	+50 8 15.3	− 4.7	O. Arg., 1138.
24	0 11 11.85	+2.93	+48 51 43.0	+16.0	Paris, 221.
25	23 49 1.85	+2.78	+43 32 12.4	+22.3	W. B.: XXIII, 990.
26	23 51 45.01	+2.72	+42 3 25.9	+23.2	W. B.: XXIII, 1032.
27	23 46 29.60	+2.65	+40 8 41.0	+25.5	W. B.: XXIII, 943.
28	11 9 56.35	+1.36	+44 36 0.6	+ 9.2	W. B.: XI, $\frac{1}{2}$ (138 + 139.)

29	10 54 33.92	+0.97	+19 40.8	+10.5	Paris 13466.
30	6 12 3.21	+1.24	+31 24 15.9	+ 4.4	W. B: VI, 258.
31	6 47 54.25	+1.51	+29 57 38.6	+ 3.4	W. B: VI, 1377.
32	8 26 27.85	1.83	−20 48 27.4	− 0.4	American Ephemeries, 1892.
33	10 8 28.05	+1.83	+ 1 0 15.8	− 3.4	Schjellerup 3745.
34	10 20 57.09	+1.79	− 1 46 6.6	− 3.6	Seelilger, Vol. I, 5294.
35	10 38 14.97	1.70	− 6 1 35.1	− 3.8	Seeliger, Vol. I, 5686.
36	11 35 41.69	1.67	−17 6 16.5	− 4.8	Seeliger, Vol. II, 4033.
37	11 56 31 07	1.70	−20 12 21.8	− 5.3	Cinn. Zone Cat. 2138.
38	11 55 10.84	1.70	−21 14 9.3	− 5.2	Yarnall (F) 5112.
39	12 31 58.39	+2.98	−26 32 27.6	− 5.9	Yarnall (F) 5365.
40	0 50 45.48	2.98	+37 54 48.7	+26.4	American Ephemeris, 1892.
41	0 46 56.43	+2.95	+37 57 44.4	+26.4	Yarnall (F) 450.
42	0 45 16.32	+2.95	+37 27 20.4	+26.6	W. B: O, Id.
43	0 43 37.57	2.86	+37 36 58.9	+26.6	Lalande 1323.
44	0 41 47.60	+2.90	+37 2 28.2	+26.9	W. B: O, 1029.
45	0 47 32.29	+2.90	+36 50 0.4	+27.3	W. B: O, 1172.
46	13 40 53.38	1.43	+27 45 59.7	−23.3	W. B: XIII, 822.

OBSERVATIONS OF THE PARTIAL ECLIPSE OF THE SUN, OCTOBER 20, 1892.

THE following observations were made by students of Practical Astronomy.

George L. Jones, with the 10-inch equatorial, reduced to about 4.5 inches, and with a magnifying power of 75, the record being made upon the chronograph:

First contact, 0^h 5^m 32.7^s, standard time.

Last contact, 3^h 6^m 23.1^s, standard time.

William S. Vaux, Jr., with the 8-inch reflector, reduced to 4 inches, and with a comet eye-piece of very low power:

First contact, 0^h 5^m 31.3^s, standard time.

Last contact, 3^h 6^m 18.3^s, standard time.

Edward Rhoads, with the 8-inch equatorial, with helioscope and power of about 75.

Last contact, 3^h 6^m 16.5^s, standard time.

SUN-SPOT OBSERVATIONS.

Made with the 8-inch Equatorial.

By W. H. Collins.

1892.	Time	Grs.	Spots	Fac Grs.	Def. and size.	1892.	Time	Grs.	Spots	Fac Grs.	Def. and size.
Jan. 1	2	5	42	0	bad	Feb. 8	10	4	72	1	fair; 2 lar
2	1	5	49	0	poor	9	9	3	94	3	good; 3 lar
3	2	7	71	1	good; 2 lar	10	10	2	80	0	fair; 3 lar
4	9	6	56	1	fair; 3 lar	11	2	5	171	2	good; 2 lar
5	11	5	46	1	poor; 2 lar	12	5	4	59	0	bad
7	9	3	26	0	poor; 1 lar	13	10	4	89	2	bad; 3 lar
8	10	3	40	1	good; 2 lar	14	10	5	145	1	good; 2 lar
9	12	3	20	0	poor	15	10	7	169	0	good; 2 lar
16	10	6	45	0	fair	16	11	7	121	0	poor; 2 lar
17	10	8	34	1	bad	17	10	7	97	0	poor; 2 lar
20	3	7	48	1	fair; 1 lar	18	10	9	95	1	fair; 1 lar
21	9	7	43	1	bad; 1 lar	19	11	9	56	1	poor
22	11	9	97	2	very g'd; 21	22	11	5	21	0	bad
23	9	8	81	1	fair; 2 lar	23	2	4	14	0	poor
25	10	5	26	1	bad; 2 lar	27	9	2	8	1	poor
26	1	5	19	1	bad; 2 lar	Mar. 3	10	3	18	2	fair
27	10	4	17	0	poor; 2 lar	4	10	4	17	1	fair
28	12	4	19	2	bad; 1 lar	6	10	3	22	1	fair
31	10	6	49	1	fair; 1 lar	7	12	1	12	1	fair
Feb. 1	11	6	44	1	fair; 1 lar	9	10	2	32	0	fair
2	3	5	12	0	bad	11	10	3	32	1	poor
4	9	6	27	0	poor	12	10	4	37	1	fair
5	8	6	32	0	bad	14	11	4	32	0	poor
6	10	5	49	2	poor	15	10	3	10	0	poor

SUN-SPOT OBSERVATIONS.

Made with the 8-inch Equatorial.

By W. H. COLLINS.

1892.	Time	Grs.	Spots	Fac Grs.	Def. and size.	1892.	Time	Grs.	Spots	Fac Grs.	Def. and size.
Mar. 16	1	2	8	0	bad	Apr. 23	10	10	193	3	fine
19	10	4	35	2	good	24	9	8	194	1	fine; 4 lar
20	9	5	52	2	good; 1 lar	28	10	5	37	0	bad
21	9	7	49	3	fair; 1 lar	29	6	6	36	1	good; 2 lar
22	9	6	49	1	poor; 1 lar	30	9	7	36	3	good; 2 lar
24	9	7	78	1	fair; 2 lar	May 1	9	5	32	2	fair; 3 lar
25	9	6	65	0	fair; 2 lar	2	9	7	46	1	poor; 4 lar
28	10	8	61	2	fair	3	9	6	79	1	fair; 4 lar
29	11	6	55	1	fair	4	10	7	35	1	bad; 5 lar
30	10	6	25	2	poor	5	10	8	35	1	poor; 4 lar
April 1	10	5	14	3	poor; 1 lar	6	10	6	24	0	bad; 3 lar
3	10	5	22	1	poor; 1 lar	7	9	6	31	1	poor; 3 lar
4	10	2	2	2	bad; 1 lar	8	9	5	21	2	fair; 1 lar
6	10	5	15	5	poor	9	9	5	16	3	fair; 3 lar
8	9	6	27	2	fair; 3 lar	10	8	7	20	1	good; 3 lar
9	9	5	18	2	fair; 3 lar	11	1	4	28	2	fair; 2 lar
10	9	5	20	1	poor; 1 lar	12	3	5	28	2	fair; 1 lar
11	9	6	35	2	fair; 2 lar	13	1	5	23	0	poor; 2 lar
12	10	7	60	1	poor; 1 lar'	16	11	3	34	3	poor; 1 lar
13	10	5	42	1	poor; 1 lar	17	9	2	43	2	fair; 1 lar
15	3	4	16	1	bad; 1 lar	18	9	3	58	2	fair; 2 lar
16	9	4	27	3	poor; 1 lar	20	9	3	18	0	poor
19	9	5	46	2	poor; 1 lar	23	9	7	48	2	poor; 2 lar
20	10	4	60	1	fair; 1 lar	24	10	7	57	3	fair; 3 lar

SUN-SPOT OBSERVATIONS.

Made with the 8-inch Equatorial.

By W. H. COLLINS.

1892.	Time	Grs.	Spots	Fac Grs.	Def. and size.	1892.	Time	Grs.	Spots	Fac. Grs.	Def. and size.
May 25	10	7	65	3	fair; 4 lar	June 25	11	5	46	0	bad; 1 lar
26	9	6	73	4	good; 2 lar	26	10	6	34	3	fair; 1 lar
27	9	7	88	2	good; 4 lar	27	11	4	18	0	poor
28	9	8	100	1	poor; 3 lar	July 2	2	3	20	0	poor
29	10	7	125	1	fair	3	10	5	30	2	fair
30	11	6	135	1	good; 2 lar	4	9	4	53	3	good; 2 lar
June 1	9	8	106	1	fair, 3 lar	5	9	3	77	1	fair; 4 lar
2	10	7	78	1	poor; 3 lar	6	8	3	63	0	poor; 5 lar
3	10	5	19	1	bad; 3 lar	7	9	5	92	2	fair; 4 lar
9	3	5	23	2	poor	8	9	7	169	2	good; 4 lar
11	10	5	31	1	poor	9	9	5	127	0	good; 7 lar
12	9	5	32	2	poor; 2 lar	10	10	5	134	2	good; 2 lar
13	10	7	55	2	fair; 2 lar	11	9	5	83	1	poor; 3 lar
14	10	6	45	1	fair; 2 lar	12	8	5	91	2	fair; 3 lar
15	10	6	35	1	poor; 2 lar	13	9	4	95	2	fair; 4 lar
16	2	5	65	1	fair; 1 lar	14	2	5	80	1	fair; 3 lar
17	10	6	·92	1	good; 3 lar	15	8	4	59	2	fair; 2 lar
18	9	6	68	0	fair; 6 lar	16	9	5	43	1	fair; 3 lar
19	1	4	56	1	fair; 2 lar	17	9	5	33	1	poor; 2 lar
20	10	7	105	4	fair; 5 lar	18	9	6	90	2	poor; 1 lar
21	9	7	161	2	good; 5 lar	20	9	5	43	0	poor; 1 lar
22	9	7	115	1	fair; 8 lar	21	10	3	14	2	fair; 1 lar
23	1	5	31	1	bad	22	9	5	22	3	fair; 1 lar
24	9	6	50	1	poor; 2 lar	23	9	4	18	3	poor

SUN-SPOT OBSERVATIONS.

Made with the 8-inch Equatorial.

By W. H. Collins.

1892.	Time	Grs.	Spots	Fac Grs.	Def. and size.	1892.	Time	Grs.	Spots	Fac Grs.	Def. and size.
July 24	9	5	38	1	good	Sept. 14	9	4	40	2	bad
25	8	7	56	1	fair	15	8	6	41	1	fair; 1 lar
26	9	6	58	2	poor; 3 lar	16	9	5	41	0	poor; 1 lar
27	8	5	49	2	fair; 2 lar	17	8	5	2S	1	poor; 1 lar
28	9	6	37	0	poor; 4 lar	18	9	6	29	2	poor; 1 lar
29	8	6	79	0	poor; 2 lar	19	8	4	43	1	fair
30	9	6	70	0	poor; 2 lar	20	8	3	42	2	poo.
Aug. 3	9	5	79	0	fair; 3 lar	21	10	3	49	1	poor
4	9	4	71	1	fair; 3 lar	23	12	4	60	1	fair
5	9	6	66	3	fair; 2 lar	24	11	5	59	1	po ··
30	9	5	52	3	fair; 2 lar	25	9	5	47	2	poor
31	2	5	30	3	fair; 3 lar	26	10	8	51	3	fair
Sept. 1	9	6	40	2	good; 2 lar	27	10	7	106	3	good, 2 lar
2	9	5	30	2	poor; 2 lar	28	9	7	86	2	fair
3	8	5	29	1	poor; 2 lar	29	11	6	60	1	fair
4	2	4	21	1	bad; 2 lar	30	11	7	97	2	fair; 4 lar.
5	9	4	15	2	poor; 1 lar	Oct. 1	10	7	94	0	fine; 1 lar
6	9	4	10	2	fair	2	9	6	60	0	poor; 2 lar
7	9	7	38	2	poor	3	9	7	100	2	fair; 1 lar
9	11	5	54	2	poor	5	9	7	109	1	poor; 2 lar
10	9	6	107	2	fair	6	9	5	77	2	fair; 1 lar
11	9	5	85	2	poor	7	10	5	11S	2	fine; 1 lar
12	8	6	95	2	poor	8	9	5	94	2	good; 2 lar
13	11	4	57	2	bad	9	2	6	64	1	fair; 2 lar

SUN-SPOT OBSERVATIONS.

Made with the 8-inch Equatorial.

By W. H. COLLINS.

1892.	Time	Grs.	Spots	Fac Grs.	Def. and size.	1892.	Time	Grs.	Spots	Fac Grs.	Def. and size.
Oct. 10	9	6	63	3	fair	Nov. 6	9	4	46	3	poor; 2 lar
11	10	2	40	1	good ; 1 lar	8	3	3	42	2	good
12	9	1	24	0	fair	11	9	4	13	1	poor
13	2	3	72	0	fine	13	9	4	23	1	poor
14	10	5	89	2	fine	14	10	3	37	1	fair
15	10	6	59	1	fair; 1 lar	16	12	4	93	1	fair
16	9	4	44	0	fair	17	9	3	87	1	good
17	9	7	35	2	fair	19	12	3	33	0	poor; 2 lar
18	10	2	21	0	fair	20	9	3	51	2	fair; 2 lar
19	9	4	22	2	bad	21	4	5	69	2	good; 2 lar
20	10	5	43	1	poor; 1 lar	22	11	3	62	1	fair; 5 lar
21	9	6	46	2	fair	23	9	5	59	0	poor; 5 lar
22	9	7	51	2	fair	26	10	3	55	0	poor; 1 lar
23	9	6	33	2	fair	27	10	4	53	0	bad; 1 lar
24	8	7	28	1	poor	30	10	8	65	1	bad; 1 lar
25	10	5	19	2	fair	Dec. 1	9	10	64	1	fair; 1 lar
26	11	3	28	1	good	2	11	9	99	3	poor; 1 lar
27	10	3	33	3	good	3	11	7	60	1	good; 1 lar
30	10	5	79	1	fair; 2 lar	4	9	10	106	2	good; 1 lar
31	12	7	115	1	good; 2 lar	5	10	11	102	3	fair
Nov. 1	10	7	89	2	good; 2 lar	6	9	9	63	1	fair
2	11	7	80	3	fair; 2 lar	7	4	11	89	1	fair; 4 lar
3	10	6	73	2	poor; 2 lar	9	10	9	80		fair; 3 lar
5	10	3	40	1	poor; 5 lar	10	3	11	88	5	good; 5 lar

SUN-SPOT OBSERVATIONS.

Made with the 8-inch Equatorial.

. By W. H. COLLINS.

1892.	Time	Grs.	Spots	Fac Grs.	Def. and size.	1892,	Time	Grs.	Spots	Fac Grs.	Def. and size.
Dec. 11	9	8	71.	3	fair; Liar	Dec. 21	3	3	27.	1	fair
12	.10.	8	107	6	fair; l'lar	22	10.	3	41.	2.	fair .
18	9.	2	20	1	bad	23	12	3	14.	0.	bad
20	12.	2	10.	2.	poor						

The observer was absent from August 5th to 30th, and from December 23d to 1893, January 1.

Lightning Source UK Ltd.
Milton Keynes UK
UKHW011250070119
335137UK00015B/901/P